sports

sports
A REFERENCE GUIDE

Robert J. Higgs

American Popular Culture

GREENWOOD PRESS

WESTPORT, CONNECTICUT • LONDON, ENGLAND

Library of Congress Cataloging in Publication Data

Higgs, Robert J., 1932-
  Sports.

  (American popular culture, ISSN 0193-6859)
  Bibliography: p.
  Includes index.
  1. Sports.   2. Sports—United States.   I. Title.
  II. Series.
  GV704.H53   796   81-20320
  ISBN 0-313-21361-5 (lib. bdg.)   AACR2

36,930

Library of Congress Catalog Card Number: 81-20320
ISBN: 0-313-21361-5
ISSN: 0193-6859

First published in 1982

Greenwood Press
A division of Congressional Information Service, Inc.
88 Post Road West, Westport, Connecticut 06881

Printed in the United States of America

10 9 8 7 6 5 4 3 2 1

Copyright Acknowledgment

I am grateful to the author, Robert W. Hamblin, and to Robert A. Burns, editor of *The
Cape Rock*, Southeast Missouri State University, Cape Girardeau, Missouri, for permission to
use the poem "On the Death of the Evansville University Basketball Team in a Plane Crash,
December 13, 1977." The poem originally appeared in *The Cape Rock* 14 (Winter 1978).

I am grateful also for permission to reprint from Arthur Ashe, "Send Your Child to the
Library," *New York Times*, 6 February 1977. Copyright © 1977 by The New York Times
Company. Reprinted by permission.

To Mary Lee Higgs
(1902-1980)
and
Robert Lee Higgs

Contents

Preface

Any book bearing a title as broad as *Sports: A Reference Guide* requires a few words in explanation of its scope and limitations. First, this book is more a guide to reference sources than a reference book itself. Its purpose is to introduce the researcher to the issues surrounding modern sports and to lead him or her to some of the most important thoughts and comments on these issues. The approach is general; perhaps a better term is humanistic. I make no claim to special knowledge in the various disciplines and topics discussed in the book, except perhaps in the literature of sports, which I have been reading for nearly two decades.

I believe that the topics discussed in the following chapters are those that a layman would recognize as pertinent, or soon would recognize as pertinent with some reading in the field. For this reason the book may be of more value to the generalist, or the beginning student of sports, than to the specialist or professional educator, although all of us could learn more about various aspects of sports outside our own areas of interest. I hope that this book will be of value to librarians in identifying basic reference and critical works essential for the study of sports, which continues to grow in importance throughout the academic world. I have tried to offer in the following chapters some perspective on the flood of books and articles that have poured forth from the presses in recent years.

The principal focus of the book is on American sports, although I have tried to show relevant influences from abroad and in some cases comparisons and contrasts with conditions in the ancient world. Though sports (competitive games) and sport (hunting and fishing) both properly belong to the world of play, I have concentrated on sports rather than sport or play. I have made less effort to distinguish between sports and physical education because of the overlap that exists between them. In discussing the theories and controversies about sports, I have not tried to hide my own beliefs, but I have attempted to present opposing views so that the reader will be able to make his or her own judgments and find those sources with which I might disagree. Believing that objective consciousness is a myth, I have made no attempt to achieve it. However, I have not registered any opinion without also identifying other sources, both pro and con, that have a bearing on the topic.

While I take full responsibility for the views presented herein as well as for any shortcomings, any success this book may achieve must be widely shared. So many people have helped me in so many ways on this project that I cannot acknowledge all of them, except to express a general thank you to those colleagues, friends, and students who have brought some book or article to my attention or offered other assistance. In particular, I should like to thank Dr. Jack Berryman, editor of the *Journal of Sport History*, for preparing the chronology of important events and for responding to my requests for information on numerous occasions. Dr. Don Johnson of Bridgewater State College has been a constant source of knowledge on sporting material and so has my friend and neighbor, Professor Charles Gunter of the Geography Department at East Tennessee State University. My friend and colleague in the Department of English, Dr. Styron Harris, has been another very helpful bibliographic source. I am grateful to Professor Judith Johnston, chairman of the Physical Education Department at ETSU, for sharing her personal library with me and to others on the staff, especially Professors John Anderson, Ralph Hensley, and former chairman Dr. Sid Rice for many stimulating conversations on sports. Professor Jan Shelton, assistant director of athletics at ETSU, was kind enough to share her bibliography on sports and aggression with me and to provide helpful insights on that topic and others. Professor Jack Schrader, chairman of the Art Department at ETSU, provided information on sports art and so did Harvey Dean, director of the Reece Museum at ETSU. Professor Wendell Hester of the Department of Sociology sent me valuable material relating to sports and sociology. I wish to thank the Research Development Council at ETSU for the assistance of Kent Garland and Judith Easley. Bill Schroeder of Citizens Savings Athletic Foundation greatly facilitated my search for halls of fame, especially those recently founded. I am grateful to my colleagues in ETSU's English Department, Dr. John Tallent, former chairman, and Dr. Ted Tucker, present chairman, for providing the ambience wherein research on a topic once considered nonacademic could proceed without engendering on my part a feeling of sedition. Their sporting spirit is genuinely appreciated.

I would especially like to thank the staff of the Charles Sherrod Library, ETSU, without whose assistance this work could not have been completed. A work of this nature cannot be written in a garret; it can only be written in a library with the daily assistance of a trained and dedicated staff. The aid of Edith Keys, reference librarian, and her staff has been absolutely indispensable as has been the aid of David Parsley, the acquisitions librarian, and his staff. I also am appreciative of the assistance of Dr. Ed Walters, head librarian, and Don Hurst, systems librarian, for instructing me in the basic principles of computer search. I am grateful to Jean Culp Flannigan, librarian for the Instructional Materials Center, for sharing with me her knowledge of films and other reference works relating to sports and education. Pollyanna Creekmore, bibliographer for special collections, generously assisted me on several topics of research. Professor Ben Shearer, documents librarian, brought to my attention information on collections, while Rolly Harwell of the Periodicals Department offered me information on bibliographies. A note of appreciation also goes to Dorothy Jones (circulation), Rita Scher (cataloging) and Hal Smith (microforms). I am grateful, too, to Haynes Phillips, a professional statistician of Kingsport, Tennessee, for sharing with me information on round robin 'rithmetic and for enlightening me on the subject of sports statistics.

On matters of typing I wish to thank Janice Barnett, Judy Dougherty, Janice Loudy Lyles, Robin Mayes, Lisa Triplett, and especially Laura Higgs who also helped with proofreading. My thanks go to other members of my family, Reny and Julia, for help in various ways. I wish to acknowledge the contribution of Dr. M. Thomas Inge, general editor of this reference series, Marilyn Brownstein of Greenwood Press for guidance and advice on numerous matters, and Patricia Carda for her extensive and indispensable work as copy editor and Louise Hatem, production editor, for seeing this through to completion. Finally I wish to express my gratitude to the some one hundred and twenty-five scholars, librarians, and curators in the United States and Canada who responded to my requests for information. If this book in any way helps to draw attention to their work, it will have succeeded in one of its major goals.

sports

Introduction

A reference guide on any subject should begin with definitions, and in the case of this guide, the definition is perhaps the most difficult part of all. The truth is that no one has successfully defined sport or sports and the challenge to define them, or at least to describe their characteristics, has engaged the attention of some of the best scholars of our time. Their efforts always produce beneficial results but never answers that completely satisfy us, for as Johan Huizinga states in *Homo Ludens: A Study of the Play Element in Culture*, the *sine qua non* on the subject of sports, "In our heart of hearts we know that none of our pronouncements is absolutely conclusive."[1] While we know that sport *is*, we don't know with certainty what it is. Nevertheless, anything that so engages the interest of mankind compels us to seek an understanding of it. Play has become so important that it can no longer be left exclusively to the players. The influence of games on societies from the bloody Roman spectacles to the staged demonstrations of the modern Olympiad and the Super Bowl staggers the mind. Indeed, sport has become as ubiquitous as the weather and is understood just about as well.

Drawing upon earlier works, Paul Weiss grappled with the problem of definitions in *Sport: A Philosophic Inquiry* and provided worthwhile distinctions between "sport," "play," and "game," but he does not, and indeed cannot, remove the overlap that exists in the common understanding of the terms. According to Weiss, " 'Sport,' 'athletics,' 'games,' and 'play,' have in common the idea of being cut off from the workaday world."[2] Here he is in agreement not only with Huizinga but also with Roger Caillois, who in *Man, Play, and Games* claims that play is free, separate, uncertain, unproductive, and governed by both rules and make believe.[3] "Sport," Weiss reminds us, "means" to disport, "that is, to divert and amuse."[4] Hence, in this guide I will regard sports as that aspect of culture by which men divert themselves from labor as opposed to work. I should note, too, that the major emphasis is upon sports and competitive games as opposed to sport in the sense of hunting and fishing.

The important distinction between labor and work is well made by Hannah Arendt in *The Human Condition* in her discussion of the difference between *animal laborens*, laboring animal, and *homo faber*, man the maker or artist, which is so succinctly implied in the phrase "the work of our hands and the labor of our body."[5] It is essential to realize that today in professional sports the athlete is quite often player, laborer, and artist all: that is, one who laboriously sculpts a life of meaning out of his physical nature. Though the lines between different activities frequently become blurred, I shall regard sports in this book as a diversion from labor. Sports may be a form of art—and usually are—but they can also be purposeless or even chaotic. I am considering them as "unnecessary" actions in that they are not required for survival. I must also add that I regard sports as activities that require the expenditure of substantial amounts of physical energy, more than that needed to play a game of bridge or checkers, although these are certainly forms of play and diversions from labor.[6]

Even though the books and articles dealing with definitions of sports would fill a long shelf in a library, there still is no uniform agreement on terms. Probably the best book on the subject is Roger Caillois's *Man, Play, and Games*; reading this, one soon discovers just how complex the matter really is. Caillois has pointed a way toward definition in his brilliant classification of games. The four main rubrics he identifies are *agôn* (competition), *alea* (chance), *mimicry* (simulation), and *ilinx* (vertigo), all forms of play. Running through these quadrants of play are two principles that he calls *paidia* and *ludus*. Paidia is a type of "uncontrolled fantasy," frolicsome, impulsive, or capricious; ludus represents the tendency toward "effort, patience, skill, ingenuity."[7] In this study I deal principally with games that fall under the classification of *agôn* (competition). Although in the view of Caillois sports are part of "the universe of play," not all play is sports. Both Caillois and Huizinga state that play must have rules, but some of the activities that Caillois lists under *mimicry* and *ilinx* do not require rules. Competitive sports require rules almost by definition.

Are all sports make believe? The answer here appears to depend upon what one considers reality to be. Is reality the Platonic world of pure forms, the opposite world of blind nature, or the commonplace aspect of culture? Whatever definition one chooses, play is an *extra*-ordinary activity, an activity different from labor, commerce, resting, eating, or sleeping. Sports are idealized activities but not make believe. Ellen Gerber has challenged this "nonreal," "nonserious" aspect of Huizinga's thesis in a short article entitled "Arguments on the Reality of Sport" in *Sport and Body: A Philosophical Symposium*, of which she is also the editor.[8] In so doing, however, she has raised other questions that are dealt with in an essay by William J. Morgan entitled "On the Path Towards an Ontology of Sport," which appeared in the September 1976 *Journal of the Philosophy of Sport*. After carefully examining the terms used by both Huizinga and Gerber, Morgan argues that Huizinga, in saying sport is nonreal, intends to convey "the point that the fundamental disposition of play differs, in a significant measure, from the instrumental demeanor of ordinary (real) life." Morgan goes on to say that the modifier "non" signifies "different from" in contradistinction to "non-existence."[9] Sports, then, are not make believe as some other forms of play may be. Unlike *mimicry*, they are real (perhaps *sur*-real) but different from other forms of human endeavor. Strictly speaking, the only games of make believe in sports are the diagrams of plays made during chalk talks and sketches of play action drawn on clip boards by basketball coaches during the time-outs. This same distinction exists between war, the thing, and *Kriegspiel*, the representative thing.

Perhaps it will help some in determining what sports are if they are considered as a form of leisure. The word "leisure" comes from the Latin word *licere*, which means "to be permitted." Hence leisure is closely related to opportunity. As can be seen in Table 1, in contrast to labor, the forms of leisure are many.

Table 1

LABOR (tax paid to nature)			LEISURE (freedom to do)	
Animal Laborens (Laboring Animal)	*Homo Ludens* (Man the player)	*Homo Faber* (Man the Maker)	*Homo Sapiens* (Man the Thinker)	*Homo Agonistes* (Man the Aggressor)
Farming	Play	Arts	Philosophy	War
Business	Sports	Sports	Literature	Sport (hunting
Bureaucracy		Crafts	Science	and fishing)
Housework		Manufacture	Law	
Industry (assembly line)		Architecture		

Depending upon the element of drudgery involved and the imagination of the participant, most of these activities can appear under other classifications. Fishing when done commercially, for example, would be a business and a form of labor; to some farming may be an art or a type of play. Even war may be regarded as an art and occasionally as a game. However, such a correlation strains the accepted meaning of both art and game.

Sports, while commonly conceived of as forms of play, the activities of *homo ludens*, may also be considered as the endeavors of *homo faber*, man the maker or artist. In fact, I prefer to regard sports as art forms. While generally the goal of play is pleasure, the goal of sports is both pleasure *and* meaning. Sports represent a middle way between the mindlessness of play and the chaos of war. By the same token they offer alternatives to labor and war, two of the several curses of mankind. War is hell, Sherman said, and so is labor, or Sisyphian drudgery. Men would rather go to war and frequently have done so in history than remain in a state of slavery, or unrelieved labor. Recognizing what war now can do to the only known life in the universe, it behooves us to explore other possibilities for relief from aggression.

I shall, then, regard sports as competitive games that are bound by rules in space and time, thus differing from other forms of play in this regard, and requiring strain or agony, both mental and physical, on the part of contestants. While a bridge game or chess game requires mental agony, it does not demand physical suffering; boxing, for example, requires both. I shall regard sports as real but a different form of reality from the routine world associated with labor, or getting and spending.

Whatever sports are, Americans have shown a fondness for them even from the early days of the colonies. The idea of America as a new Eden suggested in itself a continent at play rather than burdened by labor. The fabulous forests and rivers fired the imagination of the early settlers and provided not only many of the necessities of life but also a stage for sporting adventure. It can be inferred from several injunctions against them that games, too, were popular from the start. In Massachusetts Bay in 1647, for instance, a court order was issued prohibiting shuffleboard, and in 1650 it was extended to include "bowling or any other play or game in or about houses of common entertainment." The Puritan detestation of idleness was by no means confined to New England. In 1619 the Virginia Assembly prohibited play at dice and cards, and in 1659 a fast day was proclaimed in New Amsterdam in which all sports and games were prohibited. It is probably safe to say that the early Puritan hostility toward fun and games remained the single greatest obstacle to sports in America until the twentieth century, but even this restraining force was destined to fail.

Throughout American history, even in the face of puritanical disapproval, there has been a steady rise in the popularity of sports. In the twentieth century advances in technology have allowed the popularity of sports to flourish even more. Technology has not only provided exemptions from the backbreaking labor essential for the prosperity of sports but also transformed both the manner in which sports are played and viewed. The fiberglass rod in pole vaulting and the "live" ball in baseball, for example, have had a significant impact upon the quality of play of the participants. Rapid transportation has made it possible for mass crowds to attend sporting events, while radio and television have created even larger audiences at a distance. Mass audiences in turn have created such heroes as Dizzy Dean, Arnold Palmer, Joe Namath, and Muhummad Ali, as well as thousands of lesser lights. The most striking aspects of sports in America today have been the demise of the Puritan antipathy toward games, the appropriation of technology in the promotion of sports, and the rise of superstars. From their humble beginnings in the early seventeenth century, sports in America have evolved into a major American industry, and some would say a religion as well, a religion as far from the vision of the Puritan fathers as one can imagine. They looked forward to a "new Jerusalem," but in that city there were no plans for a super dome and certainly not a Super Sunday. America in the twentieth century, like ancient Greece and Victorian England, has achieved those conditions that, according to E. Norman Gardiner in *Athletics of the Ancient World*, allow sports to flourish:

> The athletic spirit cannot exist where conditions of life are too soft and luxurious; it cannot exist where conditions are too hard and where all the physical energies are exhausted in a constant struggle with the forces of man or nature. It is found only in physically vigorous and virile nations that put a high value on physical excellence; it arises naturally in those societies where the power is in the hands of an aristocracy which depends on military skill and physical strength to maintain itself.[10]

America may not have a genuine aristocracy and may consist of a plutocracy and a mob as H. L. Mencken argued, but it is a plutocracy and mob that dearly love sports.

The influence of sports upon our lives in America is both subtle and profound. Our tastes, our language, our educational standards, and indeed our values are affected not only by thousands of annual athletic events but the unending flow of sports language and information. Sports, like the weather, get equal time on the evening news at every local television station across the country. They command an entire section in every major daily newspaper and usually in small-town weeklies as well. Whereas labor has only one day a year set aside in its honor and work (or art) none at all, every day is sporting day with Sunday, traditionally a day of rest, the busiest of all. Indeed, if Americans ever took seriously the Socratic dictum, "know theyself," sports would be an essential area of study. It is, in fact, possible that sports have become the opiate of the masses, freely administered in the modern world.

Beyond serving the goals of healthy bodies and simple pleasures, sports have become industries and, in the view of many, ends in themselves, thus leaving their values increasingly open to question. According to Robert Lipsyte in his book *Sports World: An American Dreamland*, these values "tend to create a dangerous and grotesque web of ethics and attitudes, an amorphous infrastructure that acts to contain our energies, divert our passions, and socialize us for work or depression."[11] It is this infrastructure that Lipsyte has called "sports world" and Neil Isaacs, in a similar vein, has named "jock culture, U.S.A." In *Jock Culture, U.S.A.*, Isaacs puts forth his claim that we have become plainly and simply a "jococracy" with all the implications that such a term suggests.[12]

If support for these theses is needed, one need only to turn to the popular heroes, among whom are scores of athletes and coaches. Some, like Muhummad Ali, Pelé, and Vince Lombardi, have reached the status of demigods at some point in their careers. The old Latin proverb, *qualis rex, talis grex* [like king, like people] is as true today as it was in ancient Rome, and today's kings are frequently the reigning gods of sport. This point is well made by Dixon Wector in *The Hero in America*:

> No doctor has ever become a first-class hero to the American people. Walter Reed and William Gorgas as victors over yellow fever, Osler as a brilliant adopted son, Harvey Cushing as the pioneer of brain surgery, and among the older generations even Oliver Wendell Holmes as the innovator of asepsis to check puerperal fever—these men have received less personal adoration than Lindbergh or Jack Dempsey or Babe Ruth.[13]

While the lament for a public taste that exalts physical prowess over intellectual achievement—a common complaint from ancient times to the present—continues, the masses, rightly or wrongly, do not seem in the least concerned. According to the figures of A. C. Neilson and CBS Inc., 86 million people watched Super Bowl XII on January 15, 1978. It was the largest televised sporting event in history, surpassing by 4 million the record of Super Bowl XI. For Super Bowl XIII the estimated TV audience was 95 million. Each year brings a new record.

At the same time, criticism of the American sporting scene has also increased. Though voices opposed to the commercialization of sports have often been raised in America, it was not until the 1960s that dissent, in part as a reaction against the Vietnam War and the military-industrial complex, took on the fervor of a cause. Although Thorstein Veblen in *Theory of the Leisure Class*, Lewis Mumford in *Technics and Civilization*, the Carnegie Commission in its condemnatory report of intercollegiate athletics in the late 1920s, and scores of novelists and playwrights pointed out the negative aspects of modern sports and indicated clearly the direction sports were taking, the authors of the plethora of books in the late 1960s and the 1970s pointed out abuses in the sporting establishment as if original sin itself had just been discovered or rediscovered, not so much on the playing field and in the locker room as in the front offices of professional organizations.

The authors of these books emphasize and reemphasize the exploitation of athletes and discrimination in sports based on sex and race. Though the problems of discrimination had not been dealt with to any great extent previously, they grew out of the larger problem of the industrialization of sports, a problem that a number of writers had been warning of for years. Some of the books almost took the forms of exposés, the purpose of which was to spread the alarm on the dehumanization of sports throughout the camp of the counterculture, the sporting establishment, and all of American society. The fact that athletes like Dave Meggysey joined the ranks of dissidents provided impetus to the cause of reform as well as a sense of urgency and authority.

Jack Scott called the whole movement "the athletic revolution" in a book by the same name published in 1971.[14] To what extent the revolution has succeeded in transforming attitudes and public policies in sports is open to some question, but there is no denying that the spate of books and articles has raised public consciousness on vital questions about sports. Among these questions, basically the same questions asked by writers in ancient Greece and Victorian England, are the following: What values, if any, are inherent in sports? What purposes do sports serve or what purpose can they serve? Are spectator sports merely forms of entertainment or are sports dramatic by nature or even religious? What role should sports play in the schools? What is the connection between sports and art? What should be the role of the state in promoting and sponsoring athletic events? Do sports promote violence or sublimate it? Are athletes, especially highly paid athletes, desirable role models for the young? The list is long.

If these questions are not apt to be asked frequently in athletic departments, there is every indication that they will continue to be raised in the halls of academe. Courses in humanistic sports are springing up all over the country, and increasingly scholars are devoting their time and energies to the subject. The topic is now a familiar one at professional meetings. In 1971 the American Historical Association devoted a session to sports, and at the 1982 meeting of the Popular Culture Association of America there were ten separate panels on various aspects of sports and popular culture. Both the popularity of sports and the complex social questions they raise should insure a secure place for sports in academic curricula for years to come. In the long run this could be the single most important result of the so-called athletic revolution. Perhaps a study of these issues will bring about understanding, and through understanding, changes that will bring sports more in line with the humanistic goals of society.

NOTES

1. Johan Huizinga, *Homo Ludens: A Study of the Play Element in Culture*, trans. R. F. C. Hull (Boston: Beacon Press, 1960), p. 212.

2. Paul Weiss, *Sport: A Philosophic Inquiry* (Carbondale: Southern Illinois University Press, 1969), p. 134.

3. Roger Caillois, *Man, Play, and Games*, trans. Meyer Barash (New York: Free Press, 1961), pp. 9-10.

4. Weiss, p. 133.
5. Hannah Arendt, *The Human Condition* (Chicago: University of Chicago Press, 1958), p. 85.
6. The demands of physical *and* mental energy are criteria of sports in the view of Allen Guttman in his impressive book *From Ritual to Record: The Nature of Modern Sports* (New York: Columbia University Press, 1978), sports being " 'playful' contests, that is, . . . non-utilitarian contests which include an important measure of physical as well as intellectual skill." Guttman points out similarities between his definitions and those of John Loy in "The Nature of Sport: A Definitional Effort," *Quest*, no. 10 (May 1968), 1-15. Anyone pursuing work on the troublesome but important problem of definition must read Bernard Suits's thoroughly delightful *The Grasshopper: Games, Life, and Utopia* (Toronto: University of Toronto Press, 1978) for a full appreciation not only of the difficulties involved but ironies as well. Instructive distinctions between the activities of mankind can also be found in Sebastian de Grazia, *Of Time, Work, and Leisure* (Garden City, N.Y.: Anchor Books, 1964).
7. Caillois, p. 13.
8. Ellen W. Gerber, "Arguments on the Reality of Sport," in *Sport and Body: A Philosophical Symposium*, ed. Ellen Gerber (Philadelphia: Lea and Febiger, 1972), pp. 68-69.
9. William J. Morgan, "On the Path Towards an Ontology of Sport," *Journal of the Philosophy of Sport* 3 (September 1976), 27.
10. E. Norman Gardiner, *Athletics of the Ancient World* (London: Oxford University Press, 1930), p. 2.
11. Robert Lipsyte, *Sports World* (New York: Quadrangle, New York Times Book Co., 1975), p. ix.
12. Neil D. Isaacs, *Jock Culture, U.S.A.* (New York: W. W. Norton, 1978), p. 17.
13. Dixon Wector, *The Hero in America* (Ann Arbor: University of Michigan Press, 1963), p. 480.
14. Jack Scott, *The Athletic Revolution* (New York: Free Press, 1971).

BIBLIOGRAPHY

Arendt, Hannah. *The Human Condition*. Chicago: University of Chicago Press, 1958.
Caillois, Roger. *Man, Play, and Games*. Translated by Meyer Barash. New York: Free Press, 1961.
de Grazia, Sebastian. *Of Time, Work, and Leisure*. Garden City, N.Y.: Anchor Books, 1964.
Gardiner, E. Norman. *Athletics of the Ancient World*. London: Oxford University Press, 1930.
Gerber, Ellen. "Arguments on the Reality of Sport." In *Sport and the Body: A Philosophical Symposium*, edited by Ellen Gerber. Philadelphia: Lea and Febiger, 1972.
Guttman, Allen. *From Ritual to Record: The Nature of Modern Sports*. New York: Columbia University Press, 1978.
Huizinga, Johan. *Homo Ludens: A Study of the Play Element in Culture*. Translated by R. F. C. Hull. Boston: Beacon Press, 1960.

Isaacs, Neil D. *Jock Culture, U.S.A.* New York: W. W. Norton, 1978.

Lipsyte, Robert. *Sports World: An American Dreamland.* New York: Quadrangle, New York Times Book Co., 1975.

Loy, John. "The Nature of Sport: A Definitional Effort." *Quest,* no. 10 (May 1968), 1-15.

Morgan, William J. "On the Path Towards an Ontology of Sport." *Journal of the Philosophy of Sport* 3 (September 1976), 25-34.

Mumford, Lewis. *Technics and Civilization.* 1934. Reprint. New York: Harcourt, Brace and World, 1963.

Scott, Jack. *The Athletic Revolution.* New York: Free Press, 1971.

Suits, Bernard. *The Grasshopper: Games, Life, and Utopia.* Toronto: University of Toronto Press, 1978.

Veblen, Thorstein. *Theory of the Leisure Class.* 1899. Reprint. New York: Macmillan Co., 1953.

Wector, Dixon. *The Hero in America.* Ann Arbor: University of Michigan Press, 1963.

Weiss, Paul. *Sport: A Philosophic Inquiry.* Carbondale: Southern Illinois University Press, 1969.

CHAPTER I

History of Sports:
A Survey

Although sports actually precede recorded history, the first Olympics in 776 B.C. may be taken as a starting point. While there are a number of explanations for the origin of the Olympic Games, there seems little doubt that religion, regardless of any other factor involved, played a prominent role in the creation and perpetuation of the games. According to M. I. Finley and H. W. Pleket in *The Olympic Games: The First Thousand Years*, "The Olympic Games were founded in 776 B.C. because Olympia was already an established sacred rite, not the other way around. In consequence, religious ceremonies occupied a substantial part of the five-day period of Games, the normal duration once the Games had achieved their classical organization early in the fifth century B.C."[1] When the religious emphasis of the ancient games is remembered, the role of religion in the current sporting scene should be less surprising.

The Greeks, Edith Hamilton remarked in *The Greek Way*, were the first people to engage in games.

> All over Greece there were games, all sorts of games; athletic contests of every description: races—horse-, boat-, foot-, torch-races; contests in music, where one side outsung the other; in dancing—on greased skins sometimes to display a nice skill of foot and balance of body; games where men leaped in and out of flying chariots; games so many one grows weary with the list of them. They are embodied in the statues familiar to all, the disc thrower, the charioteer, the wrestling boys, the dancing flute players. The great games—there were four that came at stated seasons—were so important, when one was held, a truce of God was proclaimed so that all Greece might come in safety without fear.[2]

The Greek love of play was unique. It was lost upon their Roman conquerors, who turned play into spectacle, an unmistakable sign of decadence. According to Hamilton in *The Roman Way*,

How savage the Roman nature was which the Roman law controlled is seen written large in Rome's favorite amusements, too familiar to need more than a cursory mention: wild beast hunts—so called, the hunting place was the arena; naval battles for which the circus was flooded by means of hidden canals; and, most usual and best loved by the people, the gladiators, when the great amphitheatre was packed close tier upon tier, all Rome there to see human beings by the tens and hundreds killing each other, to give the victor in a contest the signal for death and eagerly watch the upraised dagger plunge into the helpless body and the blood spurt forth.[3]

Roman decadence was one factor in the demise of the Greek spirit of play; another was Christian piety. After 1,200 years the Olympic Games were disbanded by the Christian emperor Theodosius I, who regarded the events as forms of "pagan idolatry." Thus, as Rudolph Brasch states in *How Did Sports Begin? A Look at the Origins of Man at Play*, "while one religion had given birth to the Olympic Games, in the name of another they were destroyed."[4]

Just as Greeks were the first to play, so too, in the view of many, they were the last, at least for a long time. In Edith Hamilton's view, "Play died when Greece died and many and many a century passed before it was resurrected."[5]

In fact, it was not until the nineteenth century that sports again enjoyed anything approaching their popularity in ancient Greece. While they were by no means dead during the Middle Ages as Joseph Strutt's *The Sports and Pastimes of the People of England* clearly reveals, it was not until the Victorian period that there was a sudden, perhaps unmatched in history even, proliferation of sports.

According to Bruce Haley in "Sports and the Victorian World":

The middle decades of the nineteenth century witnessed the introduction in England of such novelties as golf, athletics (track and field), mountaineering (as a sport), badminton, tennis, and croquet. Meanwhile, many of the traditional sports—rowing, football and cricket, for example—enjoyed an awesome increase in their following.

The first organized athletics competition was held in 1849. During the next ten years the public schools and the two major universities began to hold annual meets, and by 1860 athletics had become an important part of the British school life. Mountaineering prospered as rapidly. The Alpine Club, founded in 1857 with twenty-eight members, grew tenfold in two decades. Soon this and other climbing groups had a total membership of several thousand.[6]

In 1896 in Athens Baron Pierre de Coubertin, inspired by the idealism of the ancient motto Faster, Higher, Stronger, successfully revived the Olympic

Games. In contrast to the attitude of the Greeks for whom winning was everything, the spirit of the modern games focused upon participation rather than victory. As the bishop of Pennsylvania noted in a London sermon on the occasion of the 1908 Olympics, "The important thing in the Olympic games, is not the winning but taking part, for the essential thing in life is not so much conquering as fighting well."[7] In lines that *Time* magazine has called "classic corn," Grantland Rice extended the same philosophy to all sporting endeavors with the belief that the most important thing is "how you played the game."[8]

The zeal and interest of the British did not abate in the twentieth century as Supreme Court Justice Byron R. White observed in an address, entitled "Athletics: . . . 'Unquenchably the Same'" delivered in 1965.

> The British . . . have an old and solid commitment to athletics. Indeed, among their most valuable exports in the eighteenth and nineteenth centuries were their athletic games and all that the idea of sports implied. This tradition is very much alive today. On July 17, 1956, at the Guildhall in London in the presence of Her Majesty the Queen, the Lord Mayor interrupted the city's reception for King Faisal of Iraq to announce the score in the cricket match with Australia. And in January, 1957, there was widespread surprise, disappointment and anger that the famous football player, Stanley Matthews, had not been knighted. The *New Statesman* went so far as to say that Sir Anthony Eden would lose more votes over this than over the Suez Canal or petrol rationing.[9]

What has been true in England has been true in America, but here the impact of professionalism upon amateur sports has been much greater and a subject of ongoing debate. It was the English, in fact, who influenced American sports far more than any other nation, as Jennie Holliman has pointed out in *American Sports (1785-1835)*.

Like their British relatives, many early Americans displayed a passion for games, but a number of them, usually of Calvinistic persuasion, were unalterably opposed to play of any kind. In Virginia in 1619 "the assembly decreed that any person found idle should be bound over to compulsory work; it prohibited gaming at dice or cards, strictly regulated drinking, provided penalties for excess in apparel and rigidly enforced Sabbath observance."[10] Interdictions against racing within the city limits of New Amsterdam were issued in 1657, and two years later governor Peter Stuyvesant proclaimed a day of fast on which would be forbidden "all exercise and games of tennis, ball-playing, hunting, fishing, plowing, and sowing, and moreover all unlawful practices such as dice [and] drunkenness. . . ."[11] These injunctions against sports are perhaps the clearest signs of their growing popularity.

On May 29, 1618, James I of England issued *The King's Book of Sports*, a work that engendered much controversy over the years because of its restrictions on the games that were permissible on "the Sabbath." The document, according to Robert W. Henderson in "The King's Book of Sports in England and America," set in motion a chain of events that contributed, at least in part, to the beheading of Archbishop Laud and King Charles I and later played a small part in the struggle for American independence. Restrictions on Sunday activities in some form could be found wherever the new American civilization was extended, and thus lend some credence to H. L. Mencken's definition of Puritanism as "the haunting fear that somewhere, somebody might be happy."[12]

In the long run the narrow sanctions of Calvin's followers had little chance. The human propensity to play could not be stilled, and sports grew not only in New England but all along the frontier. Hunting and fishing flourished not only as the means for gaining food but also as forms of diversion. Forests and rivers seemed to contain an endless supply of game and fish. As Foster Rhea Dulles noted in *America Learns to Play: A History of Popular Recreation, 1607-1940,* "Even Cotton Mather fished. Samuel Sewall tells of the time when the stern old puritan went out with line and tackle and fell into the water at Spy Pond, 'the boat being ticklish.' "[13] For those who have read Mather's prose, this is a pleasing image indeed.

The growth of recreation even during the latter part of the seventeenth century can be inferred from the journal of Sarah Kemble Knight who, as quoted in Dulles, wrote of her travels through Connecticut in 1704:

> Their diversions in this part of the country are on Lecture days and Training days mostly: on the former there is Riding from town to town ... and on Training days the Youth divert themselves by Shooting at the Target, as they call it (but it very much resembles a pillory). When hee that hitts neerest the white has some yards of Red Ribbin presented him, which being tied to his hattband, ... he is led away in Triumph, with great applause as the winners of the Olympiack Games.[14]

Judging from the accounts of American observers at the time, the first quarter of the nineteenth century marked a transformation in habits of leisure from sport (hunting and fishing) to sports (games, contests, and amusements). Henry David Thoreau, born in 1817, noted the changes in his own lifetime in a passage from "Higher Laws" in *Walden* that would be music to the ears of any good NRA (National Rifle Association) member:

> Almost every New England boy among my contemporaries shouldered a fowling piece between the ages of ten and fourteen; and his

hunting and fishing grounds were not limited like the preserves of an English nobleman, but were more boundless even than those of a savage. No wonder, then, that he did not oftener stay to play on the common. But already a change is taking place, owing, not to an increased humanity, but to an increased scarcity of game, for perhaps the hunter is the greatest friend of the animals hunted, not excepting the Humane Society.[15]

The wildness that Thoreau loved in all its myriad forms was disappearing to be replaced by civilization in all its equally myriad forms. According to Timothy Dwight, the president of Yale, a tremendous diversion of play already existed at the beginning of the nineteenth century. Henry Adams quoted Dwight in his *History of the United States during the Administration of Jefferson* when he wrote:

The principal amusement of the inhabitants are visiting, dancing, music, conversation, walking, riding, sailing, shooting at a mark, draughts, chess, and, unhappily, in some of the larger towns, cards, and dramatic exhibitions....Our countrymen also fish and hunt. Journeys taken for pleasure are very numerous, and are a very favorite object. Boys and young men play at foot-ball, cricket, quoits, and at many other sports of an athletic cast, and in the winter are peculiarly fond of skating. Riding in a sleigh, or sledge, is also a favorite diversion in New England."[16]

"Nine pins, skittles, and bowls were common at inns in the North for convenience of the guests," says Jennie Holliman in *American Sports (1785-1835)*,[17] while in the South shooting matches, especially "beef shooting," in which targets were shot at and a beef or steer was won by the best shot, were preferred.[18]

The sports that seemed to attract the most attention in the South at that time, however, were cockfighting and horse racing. According to Hugh Jones whom Herbert Manchester quotes in *Four Centuries of American Sport, 1490-1890*, "the common planters [in 1724] don't much admire labour or any other manly exercise except Horse racing, nor diversion, except Cock-fighting, in which some greatly delight." In tones suggestive of William Byrd in his portraits of North Carolinians, Jones adds, "The Way of Living and the Heat of the Summer make some very lazy, who are then said to be Climate-struck."[19]

While Henry Adams noted that foreign travelers, especially the English, "charged the Virginians with fondness for horse-racing and cock-fighting, betting and drinking, . . . the popular habit which most shocked them, and with which books of travel filled pages of description was the so-called rough and tumble fight. The practice was not one on which authors seemed likely to dwell; yet foreigners like Weld, and Americans like Judge Long-street in 'Georgia Scenes' united to give it a sort of grotesque dignity like that of the bull-fight, and under their treatment it became interesting as a popular habit.''[20]

Rough and tumble, Adams argued, did not originate in Virginia but came to America from England, like, according to Jennie Holliman, most American sports, except for those learned from the Indians. While methods of hunting and trapping deer and bear, the use of bows and arrows, fishing at night with lights, lacrosse, and even rolling hoops were adapted from the Indians, the European influence remained predominant.[21] The gun itself is a good example. ''Up to 1830,'' says Holliman in *American Sports (1785-1835)*, ''a few fine guns had been made in America, but they did not sell to an advantage simply because they were not imported.'' Fishing equipment, such as twine, tackles, hooks, flies, and rods, imported from Holland and England, also sold better than their American counterparts. Sleighs were imported from Holland while bridles, harnesses, and saddles came from England.[22]

Today cockfighting is more popular in the South and other parts of the nation than ever before. As Charles McCaghy and Arthur G. Neal point out in ''The Fraternity of Cockfighters: Ethical Embellishments of an Illegal Sport,'' there are now three magazines with a total circulation of 6,000 each, dealing with cockfighting. Horse racing, perhaps because it is legal and less cruel to the creatures involved, has grown into both a major sport and a major industry. Popular interest in the Triple Crown now equals that of the World Series and the Super Bowl. Betting for the 1977 Kentucky Derby exceeded 3.5 million dollars and broke all previous records.

The history of horse racing to a large extent has been the history of selective breeding of which two horses provide excellent examples. Diomed was brought to Virginia in 1798 and came to be held in such esteem that his death in 1808 caused, according to Holliman, almost as much mourning as that for Washington in 1799. Messenger, bred by the Earl of Grosvenor on his Yorkshire farm, was brought to America a few years after the American Revolution by Thomas Berger of Pennsylvania. Prized as a stud, Messenger was the sire of a long line of racing immortals, including American Eclipse who defeated Sir Henry of Virginia at the Union Course on Long Island in 1823, the first intersectional race. This race illustrated once and for all the popular appeal of the sport. Another offspring of Messenger was Hamble-tonian, the horse that turned harness racing into a national mania. ''In the 1850's,'' writes Wells Twombly in *200 Years of Sport in America,* ''the nation worshipped Hambletonian. It brought commemorative plates on which his likeness was inscribed. Children talked about him as if he were human.''[23] Spurred on by the creation of jockey clubs, the establishment of race courses, and the support of the aristocracy, horse racing became America's first organized sport and unquestionably has remained one of its most popular.

By the middle of the nineteenth century sports had gained wide acceptance by the American public. Growing numbers of organizations and associations fostered and encouraged them. As John R. Betts points out in *America's Sporting Heritage, 1850-1950*:

> Social historians are able to record a strong array of boating, racing, cricket, and similar clubs in the years prior to mid-century. It was only in the 1850's, however, that sport was transformed, to any significant degree, in the direction of organization. The prize ring, patronized surreptitiously, gained increasing popularity in a few metropolitan areas with the arrival of numerous English and Irish pugilists. Thoroughbred, trotting and pacing horses were introduced at the county and state fair. Baseball enthusiasts formed a National Association; yachting clubs appeared on inland waters; cricket and shooting clubs were organized for social purposes; intercollegiate athletics appeared on the sporting horizon. Turnvereins cropped up in German communities; and professional rowing acquired a wider following.[24]

The wide interest in racing helped to bring about the rise of sports literature in the three decades before the Civil War. The *American Turf Register*, published in Baltimore in 1829 by John Stuart Skinner, was the first sports magazine in America. Ten years later Skinner sold the *Register* to William Trotter Porter, who had already begun his own weekly sporting publication called *Spirit of the Times*, one of the most famous of all American publications. Porter's publication is a reservoir of the history of American popular culture from 1830 to 1861. Prominent among contributors to this magazine were Thomas B. Thorpe, who inaugurated the "Big Bear School of Humor," and Henry William Herbert, an Englishman, who wrote under the pen name of "Frank Forester." Herbert in his contributions to the magazine introduced "something of the English point of view of sport for sport's sake."[25]

Baseball, like horse racing, has its roots in the nineteenth century and owes more to the English than we are inclined to admit. The belief that Abner Doubleday invented baseball is totally without foundation. According to Robert W. Henderson in *Ball, Bat, and Bishop: The Origin of Ball Games*, Doubleday made no contribution whatever to baseball. He did not invent the name, the game, or the diamond. Henderson claims that the name "of baseball existed as early as 1700 in England and was in popular use in the United States before 1830."[26] Rules for baseball, which is derived from the English "rounders," were in print, according to Henderson, by

1834. Herbert Manchester points out in *Four Centuries of American Sport* that both the game and the name spread quickly in America, and by the 1850s the *Spirit of the Times* was calling it "the national game."[27] By the 1880s daily attendance at games was some sixty thousand. It had become, says Foster Rhea Dulles, "far and away the leading spectator sport."[28]

It is interesting to note the emergence of references to this national pastime in literature. The evolution of the game and its name can be traced through the works of major nineteenth-century American writers. In 1838 James Fenimore Cooper made what well may be the first reference to baseball in American literature in chapter 11 of *Home as Found*, though the game described is not named. In 1846 Walt Whitman, writing in the Brooklyn *Daily Eagle*, speaks of the game of "base": "In our sun-down perambulations of late, through outer parts of Brooklyn, we have observed several parties of youngsters playing 'base,' a certain game of ball. We wish such sights were more common among us. . . ."[29] In section 33 of the 1855 edition of *Leaves of Grass* the word is hyphenated (base-ball), but by the following year Thoreau used it as one word (baseball) in his journal entry for April 10, 1856.[30] Thus in a period of less than twenty years the game and its name evolved into baseball.

Baseball is a pastoral game, even if played in town. Basketball is a city game, as Pete Axthelm has so aptly named it, even when Labove of William Faulkner's *Hamlet* played in Frenchman's Bend. By "city," Neil D. Isaacs writes in *All the Moves: A History of U.S. College Basketball*, "Axthelm means 'an urban society that breeds invisibility,' a place where basketball can be a major part of the fabric of life."[31] Basketball, unlike other major sports, has a purely American origin. It was invented by James A. Naismith, who in 1890 enrolled at the YMCA school in Springfield, Massachusetts under Dr. Luther Gulick. Naismith, a Presbyterian minister and a good athlete himself, was asked by Gulick to devise a game for aspiring young athletes during the winter months between football and baseball. Naismith's solution was basketball, which derived its name from the peach baskets that served as goals for the first game, which was played on December 21, 1891. The class of eighteen was divided into teams of nine. The peach baskets soon gave way to metal hoops, and after a good deal of experimentation the five-man squad was accepted as standard. Interest in the game spread rapidly, and by the turn of the century games were being played by universities in various parts of America. In 1900 Yale University first initiated intersectional play with a western tour. The consequences of such a relatively minor innovation never could have been foreseen and even in retrospect are difficult to assimilate. It is probably safe to say that as much interest is aroused each year in the NCAA (National Collegiate Athlete Association) playoffs as in the World Series, and when the top college teams compete in tournament or regular play there are never enough seats for all those who would like to attend. One example among many will suffice: In March 1982, 61,612 watched Georgetown and North Carolina in the NCAA playoff at the New Orleans Superdome, and millions more were watching in their homes. The game appears to have become as important to a significant portion of the American population as it was to the young men at the YMCA school in Springfield.

Basketball is not only a major spectator sport but also one of the most widely played games. "With a single electronic exception," it is, according to Isaacs:

[the] most popular sport in the United States. Basketball has the highest level of participation of any sport: there are many more players playing more games on more teams in more leagues at all levels of play than in any other sport; and the organized games themselves are outnumbered by the informal play in driveways, schoolyards, playgrounds, and gyms. As for attendance, more people go to watch live basketball games than go to see any other sport, and no sport turns away as many would-be spectators as basketball because of limited seating facilities. Early in the fifth decade of its existence, that is by the mid-thirties, basketball had become the number one participant/spectator sport in the country, and it has widened its lead ever since. Basketball has at least as good a claim to the title of American pastime as any other.[32]

Yet, as Foster Rhea Dulles has observed, in the decades after the Civil War colleges did not play leading roles in the rise of sports. The only sport that undergraduates developed during this period was football, and again the English influence is incontrovertible. In *War Without Weapons* Philip Goodhart and Christopher Chataway show just how widespread this influence was:

As the scene of the first industrial revolution, Britain had, in the nineteenth century, a prosperous middle class and good communications. These basic conditions allowed seven schools and two universities—Rugby, Eton, Harrow, Charterhouse, Westminster, Winchester, Shrewsbury, Oxford, and Cambridge—to exercise a considerable influence in Britain, on the continent of Europe, and throughout an expanding empire. In these schools and universities international sport was born. Most of the games that are now played across the world and which command such earnest attention from kings and presidents, were invented by a few hundred wealthy young Victorian Englishmen. Football, which, in its various forms, was far and away the world's most popular game, was their greatest innovation.[33]

American football evolved from soccer to Rugby to "American Rugby" and finally to the game we know today. While the basic forms were derived from England, Americans had long demonstrated a fondness for games of mayhem. "Harvard," says Ivan N. Kaye in *Good Clean Violence: A History of College Football*, "had a festival in the early 1800's which qualified vaguely as football. It was called Bloody Monday, but the upperclassmen mostly kicked the freshmen and only occasionally the ball."[34]

Although it was essentially soccer instead of Rugby, what is called the first intercollegiate football game took place in 1869 between Princeton University and Rutgers in New Brunswick, New Jersey. Rutgers won, no thanks to the player who, becoming confused and endearing himself to all future generations, kicked the ball through Princeton's goal. The first contest was played before a small crowd, but approximately twenty years later Princeton played Yale before a crowd of almost forty thousand. Thus, long before the turn of the century football was well established as a mass spectator sport. The development of other rivalries, Harvard-Yale, Army-Navy, Army-Notre Dame, Michigan-Minnesota, Tennessee-Alabama, USC-UCLA, the rise of network broadcasting, the creation of bowls, and the establishment of professional teams have all combined to give football a sacrosanct position in American life that is as secure as that of baseball.

Because of the violence inherent in football, the game has been subjected to a great deal of criticism over the years, but it has been praised just as frequently for its supposedly character-building features of teamwork and discipline. In 1905 Teddy Roosevelt, one of a long line of avid apologists for football, called a conference in order to deal with the question of violence, which then seemed to endanger the continued existence of the game. Two decades later, the game was so well entrenched in colleges that in the opinion of the Carnegie Commission's *American College Athletics*, the villain had become commercialism rather than violence and had spread to other sports as well. "The workings of commercialism," the commission concluded, "have almost obliterated the non-material aspects of athletics."[35] Three decades later, some disenchanted players themselves, including Dave Meggysey, Chip Oliver, Bernie Parrish, Pete Gent, and Gary Shaw reached the same conclusions with the same negligible results. Football, especially in the larger colleges, is now a bigger business than ever, and the only thing bad for business is a losing season.

Any survey of the history of football must make mention of a book that has become a classic, Dr. L. H. Baker's *Football: Facts and Figures*. Those students of popular culture born before the publication of this work in 1945 will be swept by a flood of nostalgia when they see the photographs of All-Americans and legendary coaches and peruse the records of favorite teams and the fascinating lists for each: Best Seasons, Worst Seasons, Highest Game Scores, Lowest Game Scores, and the like. Baker's book reveals a fascinating facet of popular culture that is so taken for granted that few have remarked on the phenomenon—our passion for statistics, averages, and forecasts. In his 1950 article "Touchdown by Slide Rule" in *Nation's Business*, John Lardner called Baker and others "football scientists."[36] They came onto the scene after the stock market crash in 1929 and prospered until the early 1950s, or as Haynes Phillips, a statistician in Kingsport, Tennessee, calls it, "the start of the computer era." In an unpublished article entitled "Dr. Baker and the 'Football Scientists': The Early Era of Football Ratings and Forecasts," Phillips writes:

> So in those years between 1929 and 1952 are at least these names: Baker (Dr. Football), Paul Williamson, E. E. Litkenhous, Richard Poling, Harry DeVold, Dean Houlgate, Dick Dunkel, Bill Boand, Joe Harris, Pitts Smith, and Norman Sper.
> The influence of these football scientists cannot be measured but can be imagined. They have brought a great amount of enjoyment to the sport of football through remarkable researches into the game; and with ingenious formats presenting an overview. Their work has become part of the sport.[37]

Today, Phillips points out, there are over 200 football information services operating across the country. "The football scientists" had no idea what their passion for the game would lead to.

Another major professional sport today is ice hockey. Although field hockey is perhaps the oldest stick and ball game and is played in many parts of the world, it has never been particularly popular in the United States, especially when compared to ice hockey. The origins of ice hockey have been the subject of controversy for a number of years. By general consent, Canada is thought to have the chief claim to fame. A three-man investigating team has traced the game back to 1855 when, in Kingston, Ontario, it was played in some form by a unit of Her Majesty's Royal Canadian Rifles. Some Montreal inhabitants claim that, regardless of whatever was played elsewhere, the first game of true ice hockey was played in Montreal by teams of McGill University students in 1875. The student responsible for introducing the sport to McGill, however, came from Halifax, which complicates the question of origins even more. The word "hockey" is believed to be an Anglicization of *hoquet*, the Middle French term for a shepherd's crook, which resembles a hockey stick. As interesting as this explanation may be, it does not explain what Henry David Thoreau meant when he wrote in his journal entry for April 24, 1854, that "hawkie," like the game of ball, was played all over the state of Massachusetts. Finally, it might be interesting to Americans to hear the Canadian explanation for the allusion to hockey found in Varning Lansing Collins' *Princeton* in which the diary reveals that hockey was played on Stony Brook in the winter of 1786, almost three quarters of a century before that "first" game in Canada in 1855.[38] The reference to Collins' work is found in Robert W. Henderson's invaluable *Ball, Bat, and Bishop.*

The first ice hockey league was established in Kingston, Ontario, in 1885. Professional hockey began in the early 1900s, and the National Hockey League was formed in 1917 after the disbanding of an earlier association. Since 1967 there has been a virtual explosion of professional hockey teams, which resulted in the organization of the WHA (World Hockey Association) in 1972. Not only is hockey fun to play, as evidenced by the large number of amateur leagues, but it is also fun to watch, as indicated by the success of the professional leagues. As Arthur Daley, who is quoted in Brian McFarlane's *The Lively World of Hockey*, has observed, it is "the most productive moneymaker in the entire history of athletics."[39]

Another big "moneymaker" in sports is auto racing. Almost 300,000 fans turn out annually for the Indianapolis 500 on Memorial Day, while millions more watch it on TV. Defenders of auto racing attribute their avid interest to the love of excitement and drama, but some critics, such as Lewis Mumford in "Sport and the 'Bitch-Goddess' " in *Technics and Civilization*, see a deeper and different motive:

> The cry of horror that escapes from the crowd when the motor car overturns or the airplane crashes is not one of surprise but of fulfilled expectation: is it not fundamentally for the sake of exciting just such blood-lust that the competition itself is held and widely attended? By means of the talking picture that spectacle and that thrill are repeated in a thousand theatres throughout the world as a mere incident in the presentation of the week's news: so that a steady habituation to blood-letting and exhibitionistic murder and suicide accompanies the spread of the machine and, becoming stale by repetition in its mild forms, encourages the demand for more massive and desperate exhibitions of brutality.[41]

While the Indianapolis 500 is the biggest of the races, thousands more are held throughout the country on a weekly or twice weekly basis. The crowds are always large and enthusiastic and the purses fat. The various categories —stock car, midget car, sports car, and dragster—allow for wide participation. The Sports Car Club of America, for example, has over 8,000 members.

The origins of auto racing, like the origins of ice hockey, are the subject of much controversy. To a large extent, the problem centers around the question of who built the first automobile. Although the controversy is much too complex to summarize in a short space, the first automobile race in history was arranged in France for June 22, 1894. The route was from Paris to Rouen, and the race was to determine which manufacturer was building the most durable car in France. When other factors, such as "reliability," became considerations, other races were run in Paris and abroad. The first race in the United States was for the purpose of testing both the speed and stamina of American-made cars. It was sponsored by the Chicago *Times Herald* on November 28, 1895. The route was from the heart of Chicago to the suburbs and return, a distance of 54.36 miles, and the race was won by Frank Duryea in a Duryea car running at a rate of 7.5 miles per hour. For a description with pictures, see *American Automobile Racing: An Illustrated History*, by Albert R. Bochroch. Other "runs" and races followed, such as the Vanderbilt Cup races on Long Island, which were held from 1904 to 1917, and beginning in 1911, the Indianapolis 500, one of the great sports spectacles of the world.

The one overriding fact concerning sports in America is their phenomenal growth. From William Bradford's admonition against games on December 25, 1621 to Super Sunday, 1982, there has been a complete reversal of attitudes. How did such occur? No one seems to be able to offer any conclusive answers except for the human love of sports and the need for heroes. It is undeniable, however, that the widespread acceptance of sports was brought about in part by the revolution in technology in the decades after the Civil War. According to John R. Betts, "Ante-bellum sport had capitalized on the development of the steamboat, the railroad, the telegraph, and the penny press, and in succeeding decades the role of technology in the rise of sport proved even more significant."[41]

Of major importance in the promotion of sports has been the press, a key product of technology. Following the lead of the *Spirit of the Times*, new periodicals drawing attention to sport began to appear after the Civil War. Among these were *Baseball Magazine*, *Golfer's Magazine*, *Yachting*, and *Saturday Evening Post*. Newspapers from coast to coast began to devote more and more space to sports until finally they had a section of their own. "Frank Luther Mott," Betts states, "designated the years 1898-1914 as a period in newspaper history when sporting news underwent remarkable development, being segregated on special pages, with special makeup pictures, and news writing style."[42] Books, too, continued to arouse interest, especially among the younger generation. Among the many writers bringing dreams of fair play and heroism to millions of American youth was Burt R. Standish, who under the pseudonym of Gilbert Patten wrote a Frank Merriwell story once a week for nearly twenty years. Estimates of the sales of Merriwell novels, at least by the author, run as high as 500 million copies.[43]

The press helped to bring together heroes and hero-worshippers, but other developments also played crucial roles in the expansion of sports. It would be hard, for example, to overestimate the importance of the railroad and the telegraph in the spread of games, as Betts has shown. Because of the growing rail network, the Cincinnati Red Stockings could travel from Maine to California, and John L. Sullivan could go on a grand tour of athletic clubs, opera houses, and theaters. Revolutions in mass transit meant mass audiences, and for those who couldn't come to the games the telegraph provided instant news. The Atlantic cable, electrification, radio, and television all influenced sports in profound ways that are still only vaguely understood. Because of technology, in 1974 the city of New Orleans could build a bronzed-topped stadium with a gigantic screen for instant replays at a total cost of over $285 million. As Wells Twombly asks, "Was this only the beginning. . . . or was it the end?"[44]

One might also ask, "For whom is all this being done?" The answer, according to William Johnson in "TV Made it All a New Game," is for a new being—the "Super Spectator," a composite creature made from those millions who watched Super Bowl III.

> They gazed, as one, entranced by the miniature facsimile of the game on their screens. For them the Super Bowl was played by electric Lilliputians: Joe Namath was no taller than a highball glass and, on occasion, the entire Baltimore team could have walked on the palm of a child. No matter. Many times the game faltered to a halt, the teams faded from view, the screen filled with cheerful pictures calculated to convince at least a few that they must soon purchase Gillette razor blades or Schlitz beer or a sedan made by Chrysler. No matter. The 60 million did not take open offense at the spiel of salesmen in their parlors. To be sure, it had cost up to $135,000 a minute to advertise that day on TV, but most of the 60 million watchers did not find that significant. Indeed, they took advantage of the lull in the athletic action to go do other things. As nearly always happens during commercials on major telecasts, the running of water all over America sent pressure dropping.[45]

The 60 million viewers of Super Bowl III grew by 35 million for Super Bowl XIII, and future Super Bowls undoubtedly can count on even larger audiences. Just where the marriage between super star and super spectator will end is anyone's guess. We can only attempt to understand the path that sports have taken through the ages through those who have written most cogently about them.

NOTES

1. M. I. Finley and H. W. Pleket, *The Olympic Games: The First Thousand Years* (New York: Viking Press, 1976), p. 15.

2. Edith Hamilton, *The Greek Way* (New York: W. W. Norton, 1958), p. 22.

3. Edith Hamilton, *The Roman Way* (New York: W. W. Norton, 1970), p. 130.

4. Rudolph Brasch, *How Did Sports Begin? A Look at the Origins of Man at Play* (New York: David McKay Co., 1970), p. 414.

5. Hamilton, *The Greek Way*, p. 23.

6. Bruce E. Haley, "Sports and the Victorian World," *Western Humanities Review* 22 (1968), 116. For more detail on the history of sports in nineteenth-century England, see Haley's book, *The Healthy Body and Victorian Culture* (Cambridge, Mass.: Harvard University Press, 1978).

7. Quoted in Brasch, p. 416.

8. The famous quatrain of Rice is actually the last *two* of a poem entitled "Alumnus Football," which, says Rice in *The Tumult and the Shouting*, he wrote "back in the gloaming." The complete poem appears in *Only the Brave* (New York: A. S. Barnes, 1954) and like all of Rice's verse contains humor, insight, and sympathy. Rice was certainly no John Keats whom he admired, but it should be said that some disservice has been done to him as a poet by extracting the two lines from the longer poem and regarding them as a jingle. By such emendation much of the "spunk" of the poem is lost. The two final lines appear on a plaque in the ticket office of the Athletic Department at Vanderbilt University, Rice's alma mater, where he was a fine first baseman and member of Phi Beta Kappa.

9. Byron R. White, "Athletics:...'Unquenchably the Same'?" An address presented at the opening session of National Federation of State High School Athletic Associations, Forty-sixth Annual Meeting, Williamsburg, Virginia, June 27, 1965. Reprinted in *The Sporting Spirit: Athletes in Literature and Life*, ed. Robert J. Higgs and Neil D. Isaacs (New York: Harcourt, Brace, Jovanovich, 1977), p. 154.

10. Foster Rhea Dulles, *America Learns to Play: A History of Popular Recreation, 1607-1940* (New York: Peter Smith, 1952), p. 5.

11. Herbert Manchester, *Four Centuries of American Sport, 1490-1890* (1931; reprint ed., New York: Benjamin Bloom, 1968), p. 19.

12. H. L. Mencken, *The Vintage Mencken*, ed. Alistair Cooke (New York: Alfred A. Knopf and Random House, Inc., Vintage Books, 1955), p. 233. The Puritans may not have been as totally opposed to sport as many of us have commonly believed. See, for example, Nancy Struna, "Puritans and Sport: The Irretrievable Tide of Change," *Journal of Sport History* 4 (Spring 1977), 1-21.

13. Dulles, p. 25.

14. Sarah Kemble Knight, *Private Journal of a Journey from Boston to New York in the Year 1704* (Albany, N.Y., 1825), pp. 52-53. Quoted in Dulles, p. 29.

15. Henry David Thoreau, *Walden and Other Writings*, ed. Joseph Wood Krutch (New York: Bantam Books, 1962), p. 261. For a good treatment of Thoreau's attitude toward the physically active life, see Roberta J. Park, "Attitudes of Leading New England Transcendentalists Toward Healthful Exercise, Active Recreations and Proper Care of the Body: 1830-1860," *Journal of Sport History* 4 (Spring 1977, 42-44.

16. Quoted in Henry Adams, "The United States in 1800," *Henry Adams: The Education of Henry Adams and Other Selected Writings*, ed. Edward N. Saveth (New York: Washington Square Press, 1963), pp. 72-73.

17. Jennie Holliman, *American Sports (1785-1835)* (1931; reprint ed., Philadelphia: Porcupine Press, 1975), p. 81.

18. Ibid., p. 23.

19. Quoted in Dulles, p. 35.

20. Adams, p. 74.

21. For an appreciation of the almost incredible variety of Indian sports and games see Robert Stewart Culin, *Games of the North American Indians*, Twenty-Fourth Annual Report of the Bureau of American Ethnology (1907; reprint ed., New York: AMS Press, 1973). Still other information on the subject can be found in the journal surveys under "Sports and Games of the North American Indians" in *Journal of Sport History* 8 (Spring 1981): 66-67.

22. Holliman, pp. 6-7.

23. Wells Twombly, *200 Years of Sport in America* (New York: McGraw-Hill, 1976), p. 30.

24. John R. Betts, *America's Sporting Heritage, 1850-1950* (Reading, Mass.: Addison-Wesley Publishing Co., 1974), p. 91.

25. Manchester, p. 77.

26. Robert W. Henderson, *Ball, Bat, and Bishop: The Origin of Ball Games* (New York: Rockport Press, 1947), p. 189.

27. Manchester, p. 127.

28. Dulles, pp. 223-24.

29. Walt Whitman, "Brooklyn Young Men.—Athletic Exercises," *The Gathering of the Forces*, 2 vols. (New York: Putnam, 1920), 1: 207-209.

30. See, for example, Walt Whitman, *Complete Poetry and Selected Prose*, ed. James E. Miller (Boston: Houghton Mifflin Co., 1959), p. 49 and Henry David Thoreau, *Journal*, vols. 7-10, ed. Bradford Torrey (1906; reprint ed., New York: AMS Press, 1968), 8: 270.

31. Neil D. Isaacs, *All the Moves: A History of U.S. College Basketball* (Philadelphia: J. B. Lippincott, 1975), p. 67.

32. Ibid., p. 15.

33. Philip Goodhart and Christopher Chataway, *War Without Weapons* (London: W. H. Allen, 1968), p. 22.

34. Ivan N. Kaye, *Good Clean Violence: A History of College Football* (Philadelphia: J. B. Lippincott, 1973), p. 17.

35. Howard S. Savage, John T. McGovern, Howard W. Bently, and Dean F. Smiley, *The Carnegie Foundation for the Advancement of Teaching American College Athletics*, Bulletin no. 23 (New York: Carnegie Foundation, 1929), p. 310.

36. John Lardner, "Touchdown by Slide Rule," *Nation's Business* 38 (October 1950), 52.

37. Haynes Phillips, "Dr. Baker and the 'Football Scientists': The Early Era of Football Ratings and Forecasts" (Unpublished article, n.d.), p. 1. With the exception of Richard Poling of Mansfield, Ohio, most of the "football scientists" are either dead or no longer practicing their particular skills. The scientific study of prediction and football statistics, however, may be just beginning. For a pioneering effort, see Haynes Phillips, *The Round Robin Tournament in High School Football* (Kingsport, Tenn.: by author, 1981).

38. See Henderson, p. 136.

39. See Brian McFarlane, *The Lively World of Hockey* (New York: New American Library, 1968), p. 9.

40. Lewis Mumford, *Technics and Civilization* (New York: Harcourt, Brace and World, 1963), pp. 304-305.

41. Betts, p. 69.
42. Ibid., p. 68.
43. Gilbert Patten [Burt L. Standish], *Frank Merriwell's "Father": An Autobiography* (Norman, Okla.: University of Oklahoma Press, 1964), p. 181.
44. Twombly, p. 287.
45. William Johnson, "TV Made it All a New Game," in *Sport and Society: An Anthology*, ed. John T. Talamini and Charles H. Page (Boston: Little, Brown, and Co., 1973), p. 455.

BIBLIOGRAPHY

Note: Bibliography for Chapter 1 is subsumed under bibliography for Chapter 2.

CHAPTER 2

Sources on the History of Sports

The student of American sports will find it both desirable and necessary to learn something about sports in other times and places, especially ancient Greece and Rome. It is almost impossible to evaluate today's sports without some comparisons and contrasts, and for this reason it is essential to have some knowledge of the role of sports in other cultures. While there is probably no conclusive answer to the question of whose way of play is better or worse, there can be no clues at all without some understanding of how and for what purposes others have used their leisure time. If the true meaning of Greek sports is lost forever, as some have argued, then something can be gained from a study of the forms of play and attitudes expressed toward it by poets, artists, and philosophers.

In the study of the history of sports in the Western world all roads lead to Rome and through Rome to Athens and Sparta. Although a study of the history of sports can go beyond Greece to Egypt, for example, for the purposes of most students of sports the action began in Greece with the Olympics in 776 B.C. Fortunately, the obvious book to begin with is a very good one, *The Olympic Games: The First Thousand Years* by M. I. Finley and H. W. Pleket. This highly praised work not only provides a comprehensive, in-depth look at fascinating phases of human history but cautions against facile comparisons between ancient and modern games. "What we choose to think about sport in the modern world," they argue, "has to be worked out and defended from modern values and modern conditions."[1] Finley and Pleket also warn against the acceptance of platitudes that are really without support, for example, the belief that the rise of professional athletics was linked with the decline in the aristocratic monopoly of sports. Allen Guttman's *From Ritual to Record: The Nature of Modern Sports* bravely attempts comparisons and contrasts between Greek sports and modern sports. Says Guttman in a passage that reflects his thesis, "Once the gods have vanished from Mount Olympus or from Dante's paradise, we can no longer run to appease them or to save our souls, but we can set a new record. It is a uniquely modern form of immortality.''² Guttman's book contains excellent notes on sources, especially German sources on various aspects of sports.

Earlier scholars such as E. Norman Gardiner are not as cautionary as Finley and Pleket in their examinations of Greek beliefs and attitudes. Whereas Finley and Pleket are hesitant to make sweeping statements, in Gardiner's *Athletics of the Ancient World* such statements appear in the form of theses, for example, "Excess begets Nemesis: The Nemesis of excess in athletics of professionalism, which is the death of all true sport.''³ While such pronouncements may not be true in all times and in all places, Gardiner provides sufficient examples to give us pause if not to convince us. In any event, Gardiner remains a fundamental figure in the scholarship of ancient athletics, and H. A. Harris in his *Greek Athletes and Athletics*, although he adds to the findings of Gardiner in light of recent scholarship, does right to pay tribute to him. It is worth noting that Finley and Pleket acknowledge the work of both men in their book. Rachel Sargent Robinson's *Sources for the History of Greek Athletics* is an invaluable book in identifying numerous literary and historical references to sports in Greek and Roman writing through the fourth century A.D.

Most of the books published on ancient sports deal with athletics, but if one wished to learn something of hunting and fishing in the Greco-Roman world, the work to refer to is *Sport in Classic Times* by Alfred Joshua Butler, which was recently reprinted by William Kaufman, Inc. Just as E. Norman Gardiner believes that because of the British there is more good sportsmanship during and after athletic contests today than in ancient Greece, so Dr. Butler feels that today's philosophies in field sports are an improvement upon earlier philosophies.

For lofty as was Plato's conception of sport, and great as was the value he set upon it in his scheme of morals and politics, it was perhaps a somewhat hard conception. Tried by his standard, much of what is called sport today would be condemned, and scathingly condemned, as spurious. But we do not find in Plato's theory of hunting, for example, any trace of that feeling of compassion for victims of the chase which distinguishes Arrian, yet was unknown to the Romans, by whom the noblest animals were butchered to make a holiday. Nevertheless that feeling lies at the heart of every true sportsman today, whatever may be said to the contrary. One other contrast may be drawn. In Plato's theory of sport the elements of strenuousness and self-discipline dominate all others. But in these unquiet days what is most valued—at least by the angler—is a certain refinement of mood in escape from the noise of the world, in the peace and restfulness of the riverside.⁴

While the literature of Greece is an excellent primary source for knowledge about the athletics of the time, some modern literature is equally good, especially if the writer is Mary Renault. This is the thesis of a dissertation by Mary Roby, which was completed in 1971 at the University of Southern California under Eleanor Metheny, a pioneer not only in women's physical education but also in the study of the meaning of sport. Roby's dissertation, "The Significance of Sport in Ancient Greece as Depicted Through the Historic Novels of Mary Renault," concentrates on Renault's *The King Must Die, The Last of the Wine*, and *The Mask of Apollo*. For those who have been awed by these novels, the identification, classification, and discussion of athletic themes is a delight. A panorama of ancient life and the role of sports in that society can be found also in *The Greek Way* and *The Roman Way* by Edith Hamilton. For a general introduction to the ancient world, the Hamilton books are probably without equal. *The Arena: The Story of the Colosseum* by John Pearson is an engrossing work on the gaudy and brutal spectacle that some feel we are again approaching. It is also helpful for its references to other notable works about the Colosseum and sports in Rome by Edward Gibbon, Lewis Mumford, and Arthur Koestler.

For a deeper and more philosophical treatment of the Greek mind, Werner Jaeger's *Paideia: The Ideals of Greek Culture* is a definitive work. Jaeger's *Paideia* is essential to any in-depth understanding of those concepts that are related to the athletics of Greece, such as *aidos* (sense of duty to an ideal) and *aretê* (excellence). Johan Huizinga's *Homo Ludens: A Study of the Play Element in Culture*, the virtual bible of the humanistic study of sport, is another work attempting to explain the meaning of the Greek concepts of play, as well as those of other nations.

On the origins of sports, the basic source to start with is the sixth edition of Frank G. Menke's *Encyclopedia of Sport*. Rudolph Brasch's *How Did Sports Begin? A Look at the Origins of Man at Play* is a good reference book, but its stature is weakened by the author's failure to include references or even a bibliography. *Supermen, Heroes and Gods: The Study of Sport Through the Ages* by Walter Umminger is a better book and valuable guide to the evolution of sports, especially in terms of various sports heroes. It has an extensive bibliography of sources, including many German studies that American scholars might not otherwise know. The definitive work on the origins of ball games is Robert H. Henderson's *Ball, Bat, and Bishop: The Origin of Ball Games*. Among the ball games Henderson mentions are polo, tennis, stoolball, football, golf, billiards, baseball, and lacrosse. It is an impressive work of scholarship containing 167 references on the origins and development of ball games.

Marvin H. Eyler's "Origins of Some Modern Sports" is another contribution to history of games. Using the documentary evidence available at the University of Illinois, the Library of Congress, and the New York Public Library, Eyler attempts to determine the date, place, personnel, and significant circumstances associated with the origins of seventy-five sports extant in the English-speaking world. He has published some of his conclusions in an essay entitled "Origins of Contemporary Sports."

The standard survey of sports in the medieval period is Joseph Strutt's *Sports and Pastimes of the People of England*. It provides history and commentary on English games from Roman and Saxon times to the nineteenth century. In the 1903 edition, enlarged and edited by J. Charles Cox, the history is extended to the twentieth century. Sports in the Middle Ages, as in Rome, were spectacle and principally for the leisure class. Roger Sherman Loomis's article, "Arthurian Influence on Sport and Spectacle" in *Arthurian Literature in the Middle Ages* well illustrates the alliance between royalty and sport, but it should not be assumed that only the aristocracy engaged in play. According to Johan Huizinga in *Homo Ludens*: "Mediaeval life was brimful of play: The joyous and unbuttoned play of the people, full of pagan elements that had lost their sacred significance and been transformed into jesting and buffoonery, or the solemn and pompous play of chivalry."[5] Since play is inextricably bound up with chivalry and the idealism of the Renaissance, anyone wishing to pursue the subject in any depth should read Huizinga's *Waning of the Middle Ages*. A primary work stemming from the late Middle Ages is Baldassare Castiglione's *The Book of The Courtier*, which has been influential in determining the games a gentleman of court engaged in and how he was expected to behave generally. The courtier was the Renaissance's answer to the all-round man of the Greeks who formulated such concepts as "music and gymnastic" and "strength and beauty."

Essentially the same ideal emerged during the Victorian period (1837-1900) in the Latin platitude *mens sana in corpore sano*, which was originally attributed to the Latin poet Juvenal. According to Bruce E. Haley's article, "Sports and the Victorian World," "in 1830...one seldom comes upon the notion [*mens sana*] in novels or periodicals: by 1860 it is everywhere, developing into a major controversy."[6] Haley's article is the best general introduction to the rise of sports in England in the nineteenth century, and his book, *The Healthy Body and Victorian Culture*, provides a detailed account of the controversy. Another excellent study dealing with British sports in a period of transition is Robert W. Malcolmson's *Popular Recreations in English Society, 1700-1850*. Malcolmson's study will be of special interest to students of popular culture. For a comprehensive survey of the preceding periods of English history there is Dennis Brailsford's *Sport and Society: Elizabeth to Anne*. John Arlott and Arthur Daley provide a good general survey of English and American sports from the twelfth to the nineteenth centuries in *Pageantry of Sport*, which also has full-color prints and illustrations.

Sports in the Western World, by William J. Baker, presents an even broader perspective from the historian's point of view. This is a real contribution, since the big picture of modern sports and their antecedents tends to get out of focus when too much emphasis is placed upon individual periods and cultures. Baker's book contains an extensive bibliography that is especially strong on British sources.

The Victorian controversy that Bruce E. Haley examines centers, as always, on the matter of emphasis, which was also the focus of criticism in ancient times. Rightly or wrongly, parallels between trends in ancient and modern sports are frequently drawn. The most notable of these parallels is perhaps that drawn by the British historian Arnold Toynbee in *The Breakdowns of Civilizations*, the fourth volume of his *A Study of History*. Toynbee finds in the rise of stadia and the adoration of the athlete, the same symptoms that characterized the decline of Greek civilization. A counterview can be found in Paul Weiss's *Sport: A Philosophic Inquiry* in which the author argues that the widespread practice of sports is a reflection of the human desire for excellence and not an indication of idolatrous decline.

In tracing the history of American sports, it would be wise to begin with John A. Krout's *Annals of American Sport*, the first full-length study of the subject. Krout's influence is acknowledged in one way or another by the authors of other important histories, including Jennie Holliman in *American Sports (1785-1835)*, Foster Rhea Dulles in *America Learns to Play: A History of Popular Recreation, 1607-1940*, and John R. Betts in his invaluable *America's Sporting Heritage, 1850-1950*. Betts's work grew out of his 1951 dissertation at Columbia University, and it is without question the most comprehensive work yet done on the history of American sport. It is especially strong on the discussion of the impact of technology upon sports, and its extensive references probably are the most exhaustive ever published on the popular aspects of sport. An excellent bibliography of sources up through the 1850s is Robert W. Henderson's *Early American Sport: A Checklist of Books by American and Foreign Authors Published in America Prior to 1860 including Sporting Songs*, and a good, general bibliography can be found in the appendix to Robert W. Boyle's *Sport: Mirror of American Life*. A book similar in scope and purpose to Strutt's *Sports and Pastimes* is Herbert Manchester's *Four Centuries of American Sport, 1490-1890*. Manchester's work contains nearly one hundred illustrations and a listing of invaluable sources on early American sports. *200 Years of Sport in America* by Wells Twombly is a later, general pictorial and narrative history that overlaps Manchester's work to some extent but also complements it. A more scholarly book than Twombly's but just as readable is the *Saga of American Sport* (also illustrated) by John A. Lucas and Ronald A. Smith.

One oversight in almost all bibliographies is Henry Adams' *History of the United States during the Jefferson and Madison Administrations*, especially chapters one through six, which is included in *The Education of Henry Adams and Other Selected Writings*. Not only does Adams offer humorous and penetrating insights of his own, but he also effectively summarizes the opinions of a number of foreign travelers commenting upon American culture during the formative years of the country. Robert B. Weaver's *Amusements and Sports in American Life* is another work dealing with sports and the history of popular taste. It also contains brief histories of seventeen sports. Some important connections between sports and society can be found in Dixon Wector's *The Saga of American Society: A Record of Social Aspirations, 1607-1937*. The same can be said of *The Rise of Sports in New Orleans: 1850-1900* by Dale A. Somers. Somers's book is a model of local history that transcends local boundaries in its comprehensive treatment of subject. These are at least two articles that provide good surveys of the evolution of American sport: "The Rise of Sport" by Frederic Paxson and "The Bizarre History of American Sport" by Robert H. Boyle.

If one believes that the study of sports is the study of the great men who have played them, then the American book to begin with is Paul Gallico's *Farewell to Sport*. Gallico's book focuses upon the heroes of the 1920s and early 1930s. This was the period of America's first athlete demigods, Jack Dempsey, Babe Ruth, Gene Tunney, Bill Tilden, Bobby Jones, Johnny Weissmuller and others. Gallico's portraits, drawn from his firsthand knowledge as a sportswriter, are realistic and sentimental at the same time. For some reason there is something about the period that warms the heart, and Gallico himself was unable to bid it farewell. In 1964 he wrote *The Golden People*, also about that era and those who made it the golden age of sport, or as Westbrook Pegler called it, "The Era of Wonderful Nonsense." Although there is some overlap between *Farewell* and *The Golden People*, the latter is not merely a rerun. With the aid of some remarkable photographs it provides in some ways a better feel for the times than the earlier, more famous work. Because the sportswriter's perspective is important in the history of modern sport, *Sports' Golden Age: A Closeup of the Fabulous Twenties*, edited by Allison Danzig and Peter Brandwein, is worth noting. It contains several memorable accounts of heroic deeds by men who observed them, and it is especially valuable for its articles on the development of football in various parts of the country.

"The Golden Age" with its hype and hoke was followed by *The Gilded Age*, the title of Herbert Warren Wind's book about sports in the years after World War II. The subtitle *A Loving, Critical Look at the Dramatic if not-so-Golden Years* well describes the book. The look is indeed "loving," almost as if Wind were reviewing the 1930s, but it is not "critical." It is instead a gracefully written tribute to some of the heroes of those years, Yogi Berra, Ben Hogan, Rocky Marciano, Bob Cousy, Pee Wee Reece, Maurice Richard, Ted Williams, Sam Snead, and Herb Elliott. Wind touches upon the drama of Jackie Robinson in his chapter on Reece but otherwise hardly mentions the racial prejudice that existed during this gilded age. Furthermore, it is almost inconceivable that a book professing to be as wide-ranging as this one would have nothing on Joe Louis. The problem with this work is one common to sportswriters in general: a tendency to overlook troublesome aspects of sports and to moralize with heartwarming episodes. Grantland Rice, "the dean of American sportswriters" during his career, is guilty of the same sentimentalism in *The Tumult and The Shouting: My Life in Sports*, which, like *The Gilded Age*, is otherwise admirable. Not even Paul Gallico, who considered himself a tough and seasoned writer, is free from what was apparently the occupational hazard of the time. Gallico is to be commended, however, not only for his own attempts to integrate sports but for his honest depiction of racism in the 1930s, long before it was fashionable or even safe to decry obvious prejudices. Gallico also indignantly denounced the decadence in college sport, pointing out abuses and hypocrisies that have, if anything, become worse in the intervening years. With one major exception, Gallico was prophetic on most issues and articulated a broad, humanized view similar to those prevailing in the 1960s. On the subject of women in sports, however, Gallico's opinion was a mixture of the attitudes of Juvenal, H. L. Mencken, and Bobby Riggs. Concluding his chapter on "Farewell to Muscle Molls, Too," in *Farewell to Sport*, he writes:

> It is a pity, with all the effort, the publicity and the acclaim, that actually, none of the girls can be taken seriously at their games, because, always excepting the amazing Miss Joyce Wethered, the English golf star, who could keep pace with the men and was the only woman I ever knew who could, they are at best second-rate imitations of all the gentlemen. Miss Didrikson was unquestionably a great all-around girl athlete, the best in the world in her day, but any first-class high-school track man could easily have beaten her in any of her events. Mrs. Moody would be lucky to take two games from a player like Ellsworth Vines or Tilden. A man has swum a hundred yards in fifty-two seconds. A girl takes one minute and three seconds for the same distance, and so it goes. No matter how good they are, they can never be good enough, quite, to matter.[7]

As perceptive as he is in other matters, Gallico seems to have missed the point on women in sport. Such macho statements are the other side of the romantic mind and as sentimental as the stories of Babe Ruth hitting the homer for the handsome kid from a "pleasant, middle class suburban family" who had had an operation and would have died except for Ruth's certifiable "genuine grade-A special number one miracle."[8] It is a miracle, Gallico seems to imply, almost on a scale with that of Joan of Arc.

There are numerous histories of the major sports. The principal work to begin with in baseball is the previously mentioned *Ball, Bat, and Bishop* by Robert W. Henderson. Among many other assets, Henderson's book contains a detailed analysis of the explosion of the Abner Doubleday-Cooperstown myth. Baseball, however, is only one of the ball games that Henderson discusses. A comprehensive treatment of issues surrounding the game, as opposed to its origins and growth, can be found in David Q. Voigt's *America Through Baseball*. Voigt examines the symbiotic relationship between baseball and America in a discussion of nationalism, heroism, and commercialism. He more than adequately proves the thesis of Jacques Barzun whom he quotes in the first chapter, "He who would know the heart and mind of America had better learn baseball." Essentially the same point is made in two other fine books on the subject, *The American Dream and the National Game* by Leverett T. Smith, Jr. and *Baseball: America's Diamond Mind* by Richard Crepeau. For general information and sheer enjoyment the book to read is Roger Angell's *The Summer Game*. Still other excellent books are *Baseball, I Gave You All the Best Years of My Life* by Kevin Kerrane and Richard Grossinger, and *The Glory of Their Times: The Story of the Early Days of Baseball Told by the Men Who Played It* by Lawrence S. Ritter. Ritter's work is a superb primary source, as it is the firsthand accounts of the players themselves who played during the first three decades of the twentieth century.

Basketball's answer to Angell's book is Pete Axthelm's *The City Game*. The author in explaining the appeal of the game to city youth and its inherent adaptiveness to a city milieu gives the history of the game as well. The evolution of college basketball can be traced in Neil D. Isaacs's *All the Moves: A History of U.S. College Basketball*, which, as the name implies, discusses moves off the court as well as on. It is in part an inquiry into values of the game as well as a history. Some of the material, such as the discussion of UCLA's all-time winner John Wooden in a section entitled "Plastic Man, Wooden Soldiers," has led to some controversy.

Good Clean Violence: A History of US College Football by Ivan N. Kaye is in the same Lippincott series as *All the Moves*. Since football, like basketball, has grown and prospered under the aegis of American colleges, it is reasonable to start with the history of the game in colleges through a good, thorough, highly readable book like Kaye's. Another enjoyable survey of the college scene and its heroes is *Oh, How They Played The Game* by Allison Danzig. Those wishing information on the development of professional leagues should read *The History of Professional Football* by Harold (Spike) Classen. On the history of English football, an unlikely but excellent source is *History of Football from the Beginnings to 1871* by Frances Peabody Magoun, Jr., a noted scholar of Old English and a former professor of comparative literature at Harvard University. This is a delightful book of special interest to literary students as well as sport enthusiasts.

Reading Magoun, one comes to the inescapable conclusion that football has been a popular metaphor for men of piety for hundreds of years. John Wyclif, for example, in 1384 complained, "In these days Christian men are kicked around now by popes and now by bishops, now by the popes' cardinals, now by the prelates under the bishops; and the latter clout their shoes with censures as if they were playing football."[9] Chaucer's young friend and disciple Thomas Occleve was also fond of the football metaphor, which he used in describing his lady Money-Bag:

> Her mouth—with grey lips—is nowise small
> Her chin can scarce be seen at all;
> Her comely body is shaped liked a football
> And she sings just like a parrot.[10]

Although the football was shaped differently in the fourteenth century than it is today, it is reasonable to assume that Money-Bag would not have won a Miss England contest.

Stan Fischler is a name to keep in mind in looking for popular books on hockey. His collaborative effort, *Hockey! The Story of the World's Fastest Sport*, with Richard Beddoes and Ira Gitler, is an excellent introduction. Since hockey almost has come to mean the NHL (National Hockey League), the researcher should examine the background of that organization, and two books that serve this purpose admirably are *The Lively World of Hockey* by Brian McFarlane and, more recently, *Checking Back: A History of the National Hockey League* by Neil D. Isaacs. Much of the drama of the game is captured in the photography of *The Stanley Cup: A Complete Pictorial History* by John Devaney and Burt Goldblatt. In a totally different field, superb photos and illustrations as well as detailed narrative make up *American Automobile Racing: An Illustrated History* by Albert R. Bochroch. The book is a good starting point for anyone researching this popular American sport.

A satisfactory history of American boxing can be found in Nathaniel S. Fleischer's *Fifty Years at Ringside*, but the best general book on boxing remains A. J. Liebling's classic *The Sweet Science*. In his introductory chapter Liebling pays tribute to the nineteenth-century pugilist Pierce Egan whom he calls "the greatest writer about the ring who ever lived." A listing of Egan's works published in America appears in Henderson's *Early American Sport*. Another important writer on boxing is Paul Magriel, the author of *Bibliography of Boxing: A Chronological Checklist of Books in English Published Before 1900*. The Magriel papers are housed in the Butler Library of Columbia University (see Appendix 2). In addition to the factual information available through encyclopedias and halls of fame (see Appendix 2), some basic, reliable works to draw on for the histories of golf and tennis are Will Grimsley's *Golf: Its History, People, and Events* and Parke

Cummings's *American Tennis. A World History of Track and Field Athletics* by R. L. Quercetani is an authoritative work for track and field.

Much of the history of sports is found in magazines, journals, and periodicals. *Poole's Index to Periodical Literature* by William Frederick Poole lists several articles on sports in the nineteenth century, and *Ulrich's International Periodicals Directory* offers a listing of contemporary publications. A brief discussion of major nineteenth-century sporting journals can be found in Frank Luther Mott's five-volume work, *A History of American Magazines*. A number of nineteenth-century and early twentieth-century periodicals are available on microfilm from Greenwood Press.[11] Further information on periodicals can be found under the heading of periodicals in the following bibliographies: *Sports* by Marshall E. Nunn, and *Guide to Baseball Literature* and *Guide to Football Literature* by Anton Grobani. Early periodicals on sport that have been printed on microfilm by University Microfilm International are listed in *American Periodicals—1741-1900: An Index to Microfilm Collections*. For a listing of other bibliographies see Theodore Besterman's *A World Bibliography of Bibliographies* under headings of "Games" and "Sports." There is also a listing under "sports" in the indexes of *America: History and Life*. The entries in this index are perhaps not as extensive as those found in other bibliographies, but they do represent some of the best scholarship done in the field. Since hundreds of periodicals are surveyed for the *Five-Year Index*, it is a valuable research aid. Still another source for historical bibliography is *Sporting Books in the Huntington Library* by Lyle H. Wright. Published in 1937, this work is a listing of approximately 1,400 rare books and other materials on some twenty-five sports and games as well as a number of related topics dating from the sixteenth century to the present. In addition, there are a few old bibliographies mentioned at the beginning section on a particular sport. A listing of twenty-three bibliographies appears in the front of Robert W. Henderson's indispensable work, *Early American Sport*. The study of sports has become so popular in the last few years that some periodicals have devoted issues, or large parts of issues, to the topic. Two of the most recent are *National Forum: The Phi Kappa Phi Journal* and *The Wilson Quarterly: A National Review of Ideas and Information*. Both contain bibliographic information.

The computer serves the modern researcher as another handy bibliographic aid. For reasonable fees, topics can be scanned in a matter of minutes by such systems as Lockheed-Dialog, Systems Development Corporation, and AGRICOLA, which are available to many libraries. An Information Retrieval System for the Sociology of Leisure and Sport (SIRLS) has been operating for a number of years at the University of Waterloo in Waterloo, Ontario, and offers retrieval services for a fee on a wide range of topics. For further information, see Appendix 2. Just recently a data base known as Sport Information Resource Center (SIRC) has been added by the Systems Development Corporation of Ottawa, Ontario. As of July 1979 there were 45,000 entries on file (see Appendix 2).

There are two periodicals devoted entirely to the history of sport. One is *Journal of Sport History* published by the North American Society for Sport History. Their "Journal Surveys," or abstracts of articles, are essential for any serious historian of sports. The section entitled "Booknotes" is also valuable. Compiled by Lawrence W. Fielding, the section is a periodic listing of published works in various sports as well as categories such as "Sport and Law," "Popular Culture," "Social History," "Women," and "Y.M.C.A." The second publication is the *Canadian Journal of History of Sport and Physical Education*, which is published by the faculty of human kinetics at the University of Windsor and cosponsored by the Canadian Association of Health, Physical Education, and Recreation. Articles on history as well as on scores of other topics are listed in the *Physical Education Index* and abstracted in the *Completed Research in Health, Physical Education and Recreation*, which is published annually by the American Alliance for Health, Physical Education and Recreation (AAHPER). This kingpin of bibliographies in the field of sports consists of three parts: an index of cross references for the listings; a bibliography of published research; and a bibliography of master's and doctoral theses from institutions offering graduate programs. Among the many periodicals abstracted is *Research Quarterly*, which frequently contains articles on sports history. It too is published by AAHPER. Another valuable publication of the North American Society for Sport History is *A Directory of Scholars Identifying with The History of Sport*, which is edited by Angela Lumpkin and John Findling. The University of Oregon Microform Publications provides access to many in-depth studies, especially master's theses and papers presented at professional meetings. The selection of these materials is accomplished through the cooperation of the research council of AAHPER.[12]

Sports history is a recent field, and an excellent survey of its emergence and the problems encountered can be found in an article by Jack W. Berryman entitled "Sport History as Social History?" There is at least one dissertation devoted to the status of the history of sports in academe, "The History of Sport in Physical Education as a Field of Study in Higher Education" by Raymond Clyde Thurman. The study contains two bibliographies, one of over 1,500 master's theses and doctoral dissertations on sports and physical education from 1927 to 1975 and another of over 1,000 articles from eight professional physical education journals covering the period from 1894 to 1975. Thurmond states that the type of history most frequently published was cultural history and the most frequent subject was biography.

While the history of sports is not by any means the history of great athletes, students of sports should consider sporting biographies as valuable sources of information. The basic reference work to consult in this area is *Biography Index*, a ten-volume cumulative index of biographical material in books and magazines dating from 1946 to the present. In the area of sports almost one hundred categories and associated fields are listed, and a further distinction is made between adult and juvenile items. Literally hundreds, perhaps thousands, of biographies and autobiographies have been written on American sports figures. Most of the autobiographies are coauthored and seem to follow the same general pattern of describing the hero's childhood, early promises and disappointments, and the subsequent rise to fame. Joseph Campbell's theory of the monomyth is confirmed in every issue. (See chapter 7 for a discussion of the monomyth.) Because sports biographies usually are slanted toward a youthful audience, the style is generally simplistic, but the student of popular culture should not overlook biographical items relating to the subject of his research. Furthermore, many of these biographies make excellent reading. Some of the best of these can be found in the bibliography of Michael Novak's *The Joy of Sports: End Zones, Bases, Baskets, Balls, and the Consecration of the American Spirit* under the telling title of "Hagiography." To this list should be added *Second Wind: The Memoirs of an Opinionated Man* by Bill Russell and Taylor Branch. This is not only a good book on sports but on other subjects as well. *Who Was Who in American Sports* by Ralph Hickok provides data on the heroes of over forty sports as well as a listing of fundamental sources in various sports.

The need for basic information in any research is unending. In sport the best source is Frank G. Menke's *The Encyclopedia of Sport*. The sixth edition of this work is over 1,000 pages long and contains in addition to historical summaries a listing of records in both amateur and professional sports as well as attendance figures, all-American teams, money won on horse and dog racing, and other data. The thirteenth edition of the *Encyclopedia of Associations* lists 475 athletic and sports organizations, and most of these, if not at all, maintain records. There are many encyclopedias on sports that contain facts and data, the most well-known perhaps being *The Baseball Encyclopedia: The Complete and Official Record of Major League Baseball.*[13] A source not to be overlooked for facts and figures is *The World Almanac and Book of Facts*, which has a large section on sporting records in each annual issue. Another handy repository of information is *Facts on File: Weekly World News Digest with Cumulative Index*, which has been published at five-year intervals since 1940. *Webster's Sports Dictionary* is well designed to offer a quick explanation of the many games that saturate the world of sports. Other helpful features of the dictionary are diagrams of courts and fields with measurements, action illustrations, as well as illustrations of referee signals and methods of keeping score. *The Oxford Companion to World Sports and Games*, edited by John Arlott, also contains this information in even more detail. Both are extremely useful.

Government documents, which are listed in a number of indexes, can be a great aid in historical research. Two of the most basic are the *Cumulative Index to the Monthly Catalog of United States Government Publications, 1900-1971* and *CIS (Congressional Information Service) Annual Index to Congressional Publications and Public Laws*. There is also a *CIS Annual Abstracts of Congressional Publications and Legislative Histories*. The CIS publications are especially valuable for obtaining information on matters relating to litigation, regulation of sports monopolies, and gambling. Some imagination is needed in using government indexes, or any other for that matter. The researcher should look under several related topics even when these topics are not suggested in the index. Voluminous statistical information can be found in government documents on a wide range of subjects. In fact, whatever the topic, there is a good chance that someone has done a statistical study of it. A good place to begin searching is the 1974 *American Statistics Index Annual and Retrospective Edition*. The index is accompanied by an abstract, and there are yearly supplements to both. The 1974 annual is not too retrospective but the annuals since then are quite comprehensive. The list of government studies in itself serves as an index of the interest and involvement of the government in sports. CIS is a private organization that began in 1980 to compile indexes of the statistical studies done by private groups. The title of that work is *Statistical Reference Index*.

Another important source of facts and figures that is not limited to facts and figures only is *A Geography of American Sport: From Cabin Creek to Anaheim* by John F. Rooney, Jr. This third publication in the Addison-Wesley series, The Social Significance of Sport, is a fascinating work in a field that attempts to answer the question, Where are people involved in sport? Rooney not only tells where but how many. Such information can form the basis of social evaluations. An excellent bibliography is appended. Rooney is also the author of *A Social and Cultural Atlas of the United States*, which contains a section on American attitudes, tastes, and preferences with considerable emphasis on sports and games. In his *The Recruiting Game: Toward a New System of Intercollegiate Sports*, Rooney draws upon geographical statistics to fashion a recommendation for a regional draft for high-school players. In addition to his other work, Rooney is the executive director of The Society for the North American Cultural Survey, which devotes a great deal of attention to sport. (See Appendix 2.)

Facts and figures are important but they are only a part of the picture of sports. The rest of the story lies in the continuing drama of heroism and the relationship between sports and the other endeavors of man.

NOTES

1. M. I. Finley and H. W. Pleket, *The Olympic Games: The First Thousand Years* (New York: Viking Press, 1976), p. 132.

2. Allen Guttman, *From Ritual to Record: The Nature of Modern Sports* (New York: Columbia University Press, 1978), p. 55.

3. E. Norman Gardiner, *Athletics of the Ancient World* (London: Oxford University Press, 1930), p. 99.

4. Alfred Joshua Butler, *Sport in Classic Times* (1930; reprint ed., Los Angeles: William Kaufmann, 1975), p. 208.

5. Johan Huizinga, *Homo Ludens: A Study of the Play Element in Culture*, trans. R. F. C. Hull (Boston: Beacon Press, 1950), p. 179.

6. Bruce E. Haley, "Sports and the Victorian World," *Western Humanities Review* 22 (1968): 115.

7. Paul Gallico, *Farewell to Sport* (New York: Alfred A. Knopf, 1941), p. 244.

8. Ibid., p. 37.

9. Francis Peabody Magoun, Jr., *History of Football from the Beginnings to 1871* (1938; reprint ed., New York: Johnson Reprint Company, 1966), p. 8.

10. Occleve quoted in Magoun, p. 11.

11. These, edited by Donald J. Mrozek and Arne H. Richards, include the following: *All Outdoors*, vols. 1-9; *American Athlete and Cycle Trade Review*, vols. 1-15; *American Gymnasia and Athletic Record*, vols. 1-4; *Annals of Sporting and Fancy Gazette*, vols. 1-13; *Chicago Field*, vols. 1-15; *Illustrated Outdoor News*, vols. 1-7; and *Western Field*, vols. 1-23. Inquire with publisher for further information.

12. For latest information on the collection, see *Health, Physical Education and Recreation Microform Publications Supplement*, vol. 4, no. 4 (Eugene: University of Oregon Press, 1979).

13. I am not listing other encyclopedias of individual sports, but the beginning researcher should keep in mind the library classification number of sports so that he or she can readily locate materials on the shelves. Sports are listed as 796 in the Dewey Decimal System and GV in the Library of Congress. The Library Shelf List of books arranged by subject also provides a handy reference.

BIBLIOGRAPHY

Adams, Henry. *Henry Adams: The Education of Henry Adams and Other Selected Writings*. Edited by Edward N. Saveth. New York: Washington Square Press, 1963.

America: History and Life. Santa Barbara, Calif.: American Bibliographical Center, Clio Press, 1964-.

American Periodicals, 1741-1900: An Index to the Microfilm Collections, eds. Jean Hoornstra and Trudy Heath. Ann Arbor: University Microfilms International, 1979.

Angell, Roger. *The Summer Game*. New York: Popular Library, 1973.

American Statistics Index Annual and Retrospective Edition. Washington, D.C.: Congressional Information Service, 1973-.

Arlott, John, ed. *Oxford Companion to World Sports and Games*. London: Oxford University Press, 1975.

Arlott, John, and Arthur Daley. *Pageantry of Sport*. New York: Hawthorne Books, 1968.

Axthelm, Pete. *The City Game: Basketball in New York from the World Champion Knicks to the World of the Playgrounds*. New York: Harper's Magazine Press, 1970.

Baseball Encyclopedia: The Complete and Official Record of Major League Baseball. Bicentennial ed. New York: Macmillan Co., 1976.

Baker, Louis Henry. *Football: Facts and Figures*. New York: Farrar and Rinehart, 1945.

Baker, William J. *Sports in the Western World*. Totowa, N.J.: Rowman and Littlefield, 1982.

Beddoes, Richard, Stan Fischler, and Ira Gitler. *Hockey! The Story of the World's Fastest Sport*. New York: Macmillan Co., 1971.

Berryman, Jack. "Sport History as Social History?" *Quest* 20 (June 1973), 65-73.

Besterman, Theodore. *A World Bibliography of Bibliographies*. 4th ed. Totowa, N.J.: Rowman and Littlefield, 1971.

Betts, John R. *America's Sporting Heritage, 1850-1950*. Reading, Mass.: Addison-Wesley Publishing Co., 1974.

Biography Index. New York: H. W. Wilson, 1946-1976.

Bochroch, Albert R. *American Automobile Racing: An Illustrated History*. New York: Viking Press, 1974.

Boyle, Robert H. *Sport: Mirror of American Life*. Boston: Little, Brown & Co., 1963.

_____. "The Bizarre History of American Sport." *Sports Illustrated*, 8 January 1962, 54-63.

Brailsford, Dennis. *Sport and Society: Elizabeth to Anne*. Toronto: University of Toronto Press, 1969.

Brasch, Rudolph. *How Did Sports Begin? A Look at the Origins of Man at Play*. (New York: David Mckay Co., 1970).

Butler, Alfred Joshua. *Sport in Classic Times*. 1930. Reprint. Los Altos, Calif.: William Kaufman, 1975.

Canadian Journal of History of Sport and Physical Education. Windsor, Ontario: Faculty of Human Kinetics, 1970-.

Castiglione, Baldassare. *The Book of the Courtier*. Translated by George Bull. Baltimore: Penguin Books, 1967.

CIS Annual Abstracts of Congressional Publications and Legislative Histories. Washington, D.C.: Congressional Information Service, 1970-.

CIS Annual Index to Congressional Publications and Public Laws. Washington, D.C.: Congressional Information Service, 1970-.

CIS Statistical Reference Index. Washington, D.C.: Congressional Information Service, 1970-.

Classen, Harold (Spike). *The History of Professional Football*. Englewood Cliffs, N.J.: Prentice-Hall, 1963.

Completed Research in Health, Physical Education and Recreation. Washington, D.C.: American Alliance for Health, Physical Education and Recreation, 1959-.

Crepeau, Richard. *Baseball: America's Diamond Mind*. Gainesville: University Presses of Florida, 1980.

Culin, Robert Stewart. *Games of the North American Indians.* Twenty-fourth Annual Report of the Bureau of American Ethnology, 1907. Reprint. New York: AMS Press, 1973.

Cummings, Parke. *American Tennis: The Story of a Game and Its People.* Boston: Little Brown, 1957.

Danzig, Allison. *Oh, How They Played the Game.* New York: Macmillan, 1971.

Danzig, Allison, and Peter Brandwein, eds., *Sports' Golden Age: A Closeup of the Fabulous Twenties.* Freeport, N.Y.: Books for Libraries Press, 1969.

Devaney, John, and Burt Goldblatt. *The Stanley Cup: A Complete Pictorial History.* New York: Rand McNally, 1975.

Dulles, Foster Rhea. *America Learns to Play: A History of Popular Recreation, 1607-1940.* New York: Appleton-Century, 1940.

Eyler, Marvin H. "Origins of Contemporary Sports." *Research Quarterly* 32 (1961), 480-89.

————. "Origins of Some Modern Sports." Ph.D. dissertation, University of Illinois, 1956.

Encyclopedia of Associations. 16th ed. Detroit: Gale Research Co., 1981.

Facts on File: Weekly World News Digest with Cumulative Index. New York: Facts on File, 1940-.

Finley, M. I., and H. W. Plecket. *The Olympic Games: The First Thousand Years.* New York: Viking Press, 1976.

Fleischer, Nathaniel S. *Fifty Years at Ringside.* 1958. Reprint. Westport, Conn.: Greenwood Press, 1977.

Gallico, Paul. *Farewell to Sport.* New York: Alfred A. Knopf, 1941.

————. *The Golden People.* New York: Doubleday, 1965.

Gardiner, E. Norman. *Athletics of the Ancient World.* London: Oxford University Press, 1930.

Grimsley, Will. *Golf: Its History, People, and Events.* Englewood Cliffs, N.J.: Prentice-Hall, 1966.

Grobani, Anton. *Guide to Baseball Literature.* Detroit: Gale Research Company, 1975.

————. *Guide to Football Literature.* Detroit: Gale Research Company, 1975.

Guttman, Allen. *From Ritual to Record: The Nature of Modern Sports.* New York: Columbia University Press, 1978.

Haley, Bruce E. *The Healthy Body and Victorian Culture.* Cambridge, Mass.: Harvard University Press, 1978.

————. "Sports and the Victorian World." *Western Humanities Review* 22 (1968), 115-25.

Hamilton, Edith. *The Greek Way.* 1930. Reprint. New York: Avon, 1973.

————. *The Roman Way.* 1932. Reprint. New York: Avon, 1973.

Harris, H. A. *Greek Athletes and Athletics.* Bloomington: Indiana University Press, 1966.

Henderson, Robert W. *Ball, Bat, and Bishop: The Origin of Ballgames.* New York: Rockport Press, 1947.

————. *Early American Sport: A Checklist of Books by American and Foreign Authors Published in America Prior to 1860 including Sporting Songs.* 3d. ed. Cranbury, N.J.: Fairleigh Dickinson University Press, 1977.

————. "The King's Book of Sports in England and America." *Bulletin of the*

New York Public Library 52 (November 1948), 539-53.

Hickok, Ralph. *Who Was Who in American Sports*. New York: Hawthorne Books, 1971.

Holliman, Jennie. *American Sports (1785-1835)*. 1931. Reprint. Philadelphia: Porcupine Press, 1975.

Huizinga, Johan. *Homo Ludens: A Study of the Play Element in Culture*. Translated by R. F. C. Hull. Boston: Beacon Press, 1960.

_____. *Waning of the Middle Ages*. Translated by F. Hopman. London: E. Arnold, 1924.

Isaacs, Neil D. *All the Moves: A History of U.S. College Basketball*. Philadelphia: J. B. Lippincott, 1975.

_____. *Checking Back: A History of the National Hockey League*. New York: W. W. Norton, 1977.

Jaeger, Werner. *Paideia: The Ideals of Greek Culture*. Translated by Gilbert Highet. New York: Oxford University Press, 1945.

Johnson, William. "TV Made It All a New Game." In *Sport and Society: An Anthology*, edited by John T. Talamini and Charles H. Page. Boston: Little, Brown & Co., 1973.

Journal of Sport History. Penn State University, University Park, Pa.: North American Society for Sport, 1974-.

Kaye, Ivan. *Good Clean Violence: A History of US College Football*. Philadelphia: J. B. Lippincott, 1973.

Kerrane, Kevin, and Richard Grossinger, eds. *Baseball, I Gave You All the Best Years of My Life*. Oakland, Calif.: IO Publishers, 1977.

Krout, John A. *Annals of American Sport*. Pageant of America Series, vol. 15. New Haven: Yale University Press, 1929.

Lardner, John. "Touchdown by Slide Rule." *Nation's Business* 38 (October 1950), 52-54, 86.

Liebling, A. J. *The Sweet Science*. 1956. Reprint. Westport, Conn.: Greenwood Press, 1973.

Loomis, Roger Sherman. "Arthurian Influence on Sport and Spectacle." In *Arthurian Literature in the Middle Ages*. Edited by R. S. Loomis. Oxford: Clarendon Press, 1959.

Lucas, John A., and Ronald A. Smith. *Saga of American Sport*. Philadelphia: Lea and Febiger, 1978.

Lumpkin, Angela, and John Findling. *A Directory of Scholars Identifying with the History of Sport*. 2d ed. University Park, Pa.: Pennsylvania State University Press, 1975.

McCaghy, Charles, and Arthur G. Neal, "The Fraternity of Cockfighters: Ethical Embellishments of an Illegal Sport." *Journal of Popular Culture* 8 (Winter 1974), 557-69.

McFarlane, Brian. *The Lively World of Hockey*. New York: New American Library 1968.

Magoun, Francis Peabody, Jr. *History of Football from the Beginnings to 1871*. 1873. Reprint. New York: Johnson Reprint Company, 1979.

Magriel, Paul. *Bibliography of Boxing: A Chronological Checklist of Books in English Published before 1900*. New York: The New York Public Library, 1948.

Malcolmson, Robert W. *Popular Recreations in English Society, 1700-1850.* Cambridge: Cambridge University Press, 1973.

Manchester, Herbert. *Four Centuries of American Sports (1490-1890).* 1931. Reprint. New York: Benjamin Bloom, 1968.

Menke, Frank G. *Encyclopedia of Sport.* 6th ed. Cranbury, N.J.: A. S. Barnes, 1978.

Microform Publications. College of Health, Physical Education and Recreation, University of Oregon, Eugene, Oregon 97403.

Mirozek, Donald J., and Arne H. Richards, eds. *Sports Periodicals.* Microfilm Collection. Westport, Conn.: Greenwood Press.

Mott, Frank Luther. *A History of American Magazines.* 5 vols. Cambridge, Mass.: Harvard University Press, 1966-1968.

Mumford, Lewis. *Technics and Civilization.* New York: Harcourt Brace and World, 1963.

Novak, Michael. *The Joy of Sports: End Zones, Bases, Baskets, Balls, and the Consecration of the American Spirit.* New York: Basic Books, 1976.

Nunn, Marshall E. *Sports.* Spare Time Guides: Information Sources for Hobbies and Recreation no. 10. Littleton, Calif.: Libraries Unlimited, 1976.

Park, Roberta J. "The Attitudes of Leading New England Transcendentalists Toward Healthful Exercise, Active Recreations and Proper Care of the Body: 1830-1860." *Journal of Sport History* 4 (Spring 1977), 34-50.

Patten, Gilbert ("Burt L. Standish"). *Frank Merriwell's "Father": An Autobiography.* Norman: University of Oklahoma Press, 1964.

Paxson, Frederic, "The Rise of Sport." *Mississippi Valley Historical Review* 4 (September 1917), 143-68.

Pearson, John. *Arena: The Story of the Colosseum.* New York: McGraw-Hill, 1973.

Phillips, Haynes. "Dr. Baker and the 'Football Scientists': The Early Era of Football Ratings and Forecasts." Unpublished article, n.d. Copy available from the author, P. O. Box 3202, Kingsport, Tenn. 37664.

———. *The Round Robin Tournament in High School Football.* Kingsport, Tenn.: By author, 1981.

Physical Education Index. Cape Girardeau, Mo.: Ben Oak Publishing, 1978-.

Poole, William Frederick. *Poole's Index to Periodical Literature.* 6 vols. Gloucester, Mass.: Peter Smith, 1963.

Quercetani, R. L. *A World History of Track and Field Athletics: 1864-1964.* London: Oxford University Press, 1964.

Renault, Mary. *The King Must Die.* New York: Pantheon Books, 1958.

———. *The Last of the Wine.* New York: Pantheon Books, 1956.

———. *The Mask of Apollo.* New York: Pantheon Books, 1966.

Research Quarterly. Washington, D.C.: American Alliance for Health, Physical Education and Recreation, 1930-.

Rice, Grantland. *The Tumult and the Shouting: My Life in Sport.* New York: A. S. Barnes, 1954.

Ritter, Laurence S. *The Glory of Their Times: The Story of the Early Days of Baseball Told by the Men Who Played It.* New York: Macmillan Co., 1966.

Robinson, Rachel Sargent. *Sources for the History of Greek Athletics.* 1955. Reprint. Chicago: Ares, 1980.

Roby, Mary P. "The Significance of Sport in Ancient Greece as Depicted Through the Historic Novels of Mary Renault." Ph.D. dissertation, University of Southern California, 1971.

Rooney, John F. Jr. *A Geography of American Sport: From Cabin Creek to Anaheim.* Reading, Mass.: Addison-Wesley Publishing Co., 1974.

_____. *The Recruiting Game: Toward a New System of Intercollegiate Athletics.* Lincoln: University of Nebraska Press, 1981.

_____. *A Social and Cultural Atlas of the United States.* Chicago: Denoyer Geppert, 1979.

Russell, Bill, and Taylor Branch. *Second Wind: The Memoirs of an Opinionated Man.* New York: Random House, 1979.

Savage, Howard S., John T. McGovern, Howard W. Bently, and Dean F. Smiley. *The Carnegie Foundation for the Advancement of Teaching American College Athletics.* Bulletin #23. New York: The Carnegie Foundation, 1929.

Smith, Leverett T., Jr. *The American Dream and the National Game.* Bowling Green, Ohio: Popular Culture Press, 1978.

Somers, Dale A. *The Rise of Sports in New Orleans: 1850-1900.* Baton Rouge: Louisiana State University Press, 1972.

Southern Exposure 7 (Fall 1979).

"Sports and Games of the North American Indians." In "Journal Surveys." *Journal of Sport History* (Spring 1981), 66-67.

"Sports in America." *National Forum: The Phi Kappa Phi Journal* 62 (Winter 1982).

Struna, Nancy. "Puritans and Sport: The Irretrievable Tide of Change." *Journal of Sport History* 4 (Spring 1977), 1-21.

Strutt, Joseph. *Sports and Pastimes of the People of England.* Enlarged and edited by J. Charles Cox. 1903. Reprint. New York: A. M. Kelley, 1970.

Thurmond, Raymond Clyde. "The History of Sport and Physical Education as a Field of Study in Higher Education." Ph.D. dissertation, University of Oklahoma, 1976.

Toynbee, Arnold. *A Study of History.* Vol. 4: *The Breakdowns of Civilizations.* New York: Oxford University Press, 1939.

Twombly, Wells. *200 Years of Sport in America: A Pageant of a Nation at Play.* New York: McGraw-Hill, 1976.

Ulrich's International Periodical Dictionary. 17th ed. New York: R. R. Bowker, 1977.

Umminger, Walter. *Supermen, Heroes and Gods: The Study of Sport Through the Ages.* Translated by James Clark. London: Thames and Hudson, 1963.

Voigt, David Q. *America Through Baseball.* Chicago: Nelson-Hall, 1976.

Weiss, Paul. *Sport: A Philosophic Inquiry.* Carbondale: Southern Illinois University Press, 1969.

Wilson Quarterly: A National Review of Ideas and Information 3 (Summer 1979), 57-87.

Wind, Herbert Warren. *The Gilded Age of Sport, A Loving, Critical Look at the Dramatic if not-so-Golden Years.* New York: Simon and Schuster, 1961.

Weaver, Robert B. *Amusements and Sports in American Life.* Chicago: University of Chicago Press, 1939.

Webster's Sports Dictionary. Springfield, Mass.: G. C. Merriam, 1976.

Wector, Dixon. *The Sage of American Society: A Record of Social Aspirations, 1607-1937.* New York: Scribner, 1937.

White, Byron R. "Athletics:... Unquenchably the Same?" In *The Sporting Spirit: Athletics in Literature and Life,* edited by Robert J. Higgs and Neil D. Isaacs. New York: Harcourt, Brace, Jovanovich, 1977.

The World Almanac and Book of Facts. New York: Newspaper Enterprise Association, 1979.

Wright, Lyle H. *Sporting Books in the Huntington Library.* San Marino, Calif.: Huntington Library, 1937.

CHAPTER 3

Sports and Traditional Arts: Sculpture, Painting, Literature

The relationship between sports and other arts has been symbiotic in theory and antagonistic in practice. The Greeks, great lovers of form, sought a balance between mind and body and therefore established sculpture and poetry. There is, of course, a vast gulf between what the Greeks espoused and what they practiced, but we should thank them for their recognition that sports do not exist *in vacuo*. Sports for the Greeks lay at the heart of the cultural process and not alongside it, as Johan Huizinga claimed in *Homo Ludens: A Study of the Play Element in Culture*, or as Thorstein Veblen argued in *Theory of the Leisure Class*: "football had no more relationship to physical culture than the bullfight to agriculture."[1] It is slightly ironic that both Veblen and Huizinga, two great minds who have dealt extensively with sports, have viewed them as existing outside the mainstream of modern culture. Their arguments in this regard are questionable, especially as they themselves present evidence to the contrary. Sports, in fact, never have existed as things sui generis, and do not do so now; for good or for ill, sports always have had a profound influence upon other arts and the overall quality of life.

For purposes of this volume I shall rely on the definition of art given by Emerson in *Nature*: "Thus is art a nature passed through the alembic of man."[2] By man, Emerson meant conscious man, discerning man, and creative man. The statement can be read without loss of meaning as, "Art is nature passed through the alembic of mind." In the creative process there is a constant interaction between mind and matter, and the result of that involvement is art. Thus, art is that which is artificial as opposed to natural. Whether the art is high, low, irrelevant, utilitarian, inspirational, or pornographic depends upon point of view. For purposes of this chapter, I shall regard art as an activity of *homo faber*, a mysterious activity that helps to define a culture but is not absolutely necessary for physical survival. Sports, too, are not absolutely necessary for survival, but they constitute an activity that artists interpret and record by hammer and chisel, brush, pen, and camera. In the words of Wallace Stevens, art "is never the thing but the version of the thing."[3] In this case, sports are the things and related arts the version, the rendering of physical acts in words, music, canvas, film, or stone.

The alliance between sports and art is immediately evident in the Greek athletic ideal of strength and beauty, matter and mind. The evolution of this intriguing concept occurred in part because of the Greek contempt for specialization, which is why Aristotle admired the all-round athlete, or pentathlete, more than the participant in a single event. This disdain for the specialist was also derived from something unknowable in the Greek mind, or in any mind, that mysterious aesthetic sense, which is ultimately a sense of balance. The Greeks loved form no less than energy. According to E. Norman Gardiner in the chapter "Athletics and Art" in *Athletics of the Ancient World*:

> Though we have no means of comparing their athletic performances with those of our own time, it may be safely asserted that no nation ever attained so high a level of physical fitness as the Greeks did at the close of the sixth and the beginning of the fifth century. But the Greeks were also a nation of artists, and in the beauty of the athlete the Greek artist found an inspiration no less strong than that of religion and indeed closely related to it. Thus there arose an athletic art which in its turn refined athletics and helped to produce the athletic ideal which found its highest expression in the sculpture of the fifth century.[4]

In the same chapter Gardiner goes on to say, "It has been well said that without athletics Greek sculpture cannot be conceived." The reverse also appears to be true. Indeed much of what is known about ancient sports is derived from the surviving art, sculpture, amphorae, reliefs, and poetry of the times. While two of Gardiner's books, *Athletics of the Ancient World* and *Greek Athletic Sports and Festivals*, contain reproductions and sketches of classic art, the most comprehensive reference source is E. A. Gardner's *Handbook of Greek Sculpture*, which Gardiner himself acknowledged. Another excellent work is the carefully researched and abundantly illustrated *Olympia: Gods, Artists, and Athletes* by Ludwig Drees.

A more lavishly illustrated book of the same nature is *The Eternal Olympics: The Art and History of Sport*, which was edited by Nicolaos Yalouris. It contains a large number of full-color photographs of athletic art and some reconstructions of the games. The true temper of the games can never be recaptured, but through the art of the period it is possible to gain at least a glimpse of the original.

In their analysis of ancient sports and sculpture, scholars point out that each not only reflects the other, but together they reflect the age. Gardiner's *Athletics of the Ancient World*, for example, states, "The union of strength and beauty belongs especially to the time of full-grown youth and opening manhood. And it is the ideal of youthful strength and beauty that dominates the art of the Periclean Age."[5] Thus, art and sports are indices of cultural taste. In Gardiner's view, striking evidence of this theory exists when a comparison is made between the strong but graceful statuary of the fifth century, typified in the work of Myron and Polyclitus, with that of later periods, for example, Glycon's almost muscle-bound *Farnese Hercules*, which, according to Gardiner, is "in accordance with the degraded taste of the time [about A.D. 200]."[6] Sir Kenneth Clark's *The Nude: A Study in Ideal Form* also traces the sweeping variations of the male form in art not just during ancient periods but throughout the history of the nude, including a discussion of the work of Henry Moore. *The Nude* is especially instructive in its treatment of the athletic figures of the Renaissance, especially those of Michelangelo. It is a work that anyone at all interested in athletic art should not overlook. Clark is not as prone to draw cultural conclusions from statuary as Gardiner is, but he too laments the loss of the ennobling and inspiring in art, for example, strength and beauty, the athletic ideal:

> The Hermes of Praxiteles represents the last triumph of the Greek idea of wholeness; physical beauty is one with strength, grace, gentleness, and benevolence. For the rest of its course we witness, in antique art, the fragmentation of the perfect man, and the human body becomes either very graceful or very muscular or merely animal.[7]

In the view of Gardiner, R. Tait McKenzie is the modern artist who has best perpetuated the ancient approach to athletic sculpture. A medical doctor, professor of physical education at the University of Pennsylvania, and artist, McKenzie embodied the classical ideal of the complete man in himself. Like his ancient precursors, he possessed a meticulous eye for detail and constructed his remarkable statuettes on average measurements of several picked American athletes. His "delightful bronzes," says Gardiner, "are the nearest parallel that the modern world has produced to the athletic art of the Greeks."[8] McKenzie was also noted for his medallions, some of which are still used by various athletic organizations. The catalogue of McKenzie's sports sculpture is contained in *R. Tait McKenzie: The Sculptor of Athletes* by Andrew J. Kozar, who was himself an all-American football player at the University of Tennessee during the 1950s. The quality of the plates and the author's scholarship in this work are very impressive. The footnotes themselves are an invaluable source of information on the history of sports and art in America. Kozar is also responsible for assembling the striking collection of McKenzie's pieces now on permanent display at the new physical education building at the University of Tennessee, Knoxville campus (see appendix 2).

According to Kozar, McKenzie did not, with the notable exception of Joe Brown who is currently a sculptor in residence at Princeton University, succeed in convincing other artists to use sports as their constant theme. "If any sculptor has carried on in the McKenzie tradition," says Kozar, "it is Brown. The theme of his work overlaps, and in some ways surpasses McKenzie's, and his boxing pieces are excellent."[9] An impression of the artist's style can be gained from his catalogue, entitled *Joe Brown: Retrospective Catalog, 1932-1966* and from the *Sports Illustrated* article by Joe Marshall, "Heroes with Feet of Clay," which appeared in the November 5, 1973 issue. Whether Brown's works surpass McKenzie's in some respects or whether McKenzie's closely parallel those of Polyclitus in proportion is a matter of opinion. I feel that Brown's work tends to be more Roman and realistic than that of McKenzie, whose pieces are highly stylized in the manner of the Greeks. Brown leans more toward strength; McKenzie toward beauty though both characteristics are clearly evident in the art of both men. There is one notable piece by Joe Brown that also could be classified as Christian, and this is his *Pieta, 1944 A.D.* This completely captivating piece of sculpture in which both figures are the same, depicts a referee lifting a battered boxer to his feet and captures the essence of both the Hellenic and Christian worlds. Sir Kenneth Clark has said in *The Nude* that "the Christian acceptance of the unfortunate body has permitted the Christian privilege of a soul. The conventional nudes based on classic originals could bear no burden of thought or inner life without losing their formal completeness."[10] This is true, but Brown's *Pieta* is an exception. It reflects both the strength of the classical world and the compassion of the Christian, a rare achievement indeed.

The most striking fact, and the most reassuring one, about modern athletic sculpture is the realization that a glorious tradition is alive and well. Like all great artists, these modern sculptors are men of wide interests who appreciate excellence wherever it occurs. It is interesting to note that the literary artists McKenzie and Brown sculpted were men who were also interested in sports. McKenzie did a commemorative medallion of Walt Whitman who called himself "the teacher of athletes" in poetry and sang the glories of the sporting life in prose. McKenzie was also the creator of the huge statue on the campus of the University of Pennsylvania of Benjamin Franklin, famous for many things but also known to be an avid swimmer. In the manner of his mentor, Joe Brown has used some of the noted literary figures of this century for his works, namely Robert Frost, John Steinbeck, and Thomas Wolfe, all by coincidence baseball fans. It would seem that a devotion to athletic art is not a sign of narrow interests but on the contrary an indication of rare versatility.

What certainly must be the definitive work on sports and art is Benjamin Lowe's *The Beauty of Sport: A Cross-disciplinary Inquiry.* A carefully done book, it should become an indispensable reference as sports become more and more humanized, that is, as they move in the direction that Jack Scott has advocated in *Athletics for Athletes*:

> The athlete would be viewed as an artist and he would be taught how to express himself through the use of the body. . . . For some this self-expression would come from primarily esthetic activities such as dance and gymnastics, while for others it might come from long-distance running, weight-lifting, or some other physically exhausting activity. . . . Athletes would be more concerned with expressing themselves as well as possible rather than with proving themselves superior to their opponents.[11]

Concentrating on painting and sculpture, Lowe classifies artists as "athlete-artists" or "non-athlete artists." Among the "athlete-artists," in addition to Joe Brown, are Thomas Eakins and George Bellows;[12] among the "non-athlete artists" are McKenzie, Winslow Homer, and Fletcher Martin. While Lowe's work may be lacking somewhat in interpretation, it is strong in the philosophy and theory of art, and the bibliography of over 360 items is in itself a justification for the book's existence, even if there were not several other reasons. Because it presents discussion questions after each chapter, the book is valuable as a text as well as a reference.

Of the artists in either the "athlete-artist" or "non-athlete-artist" groups Thomas Eakins is the most famous for sporting scenes. According to Eakins's biographer, L. Goodrich, whom Lowe quotes, "When we think in terms of art in athletics, and athletes in art in America, there is certainly no one single personality that more surely symbolizes both phases than that of Thomas Eakins."[13] Something of Eakins's accomplishments can be gathered from Goodrich's book, *Thomas Eakins: His Life and Work* and from a later publication with an almost identical title, *The Life and Work of Thomas Eakins* by Gordon Hendricks. Of the two books, Hendricks's is more profusely illustrated. Lowe's bibliography is a mine of information for books on other artists. A new work on George Bellows that should be mentioned in addition to Emma Bellows's *The Paintings of George Bellows* is *Drawings of George Bellows*, edited by Charles Morgan. To discover which works of these artists have been the most widely reproduced, a researcher should consult the category "Games and Sports" in the *Index to Reproductions of American Paintings* (1948) by Isabel Stevenson Monro and Kate M. Monro and its 1964 supplement. From this reference book and its supplement, it is evident that sports art has not been neglected entirely by artists, critics, or the public. The criteria for entry in the 1948 main volume was reproductions in over 800 books and over 400 for its 1964 supplement. *Currier and Ives Prints: An Illustrated Check List* by Frederic A. Conningham also mentions hundreds of prints of sporting scenes.

An essential reference for research on sports and art is *Art Index*, an annual publication that contains such relevant headings as "Sports," "Sports in Art," and "Olympics." Considering the recent growth in interest in this area, which can be seen, for example, in the formation of the Sports Art Academy in the Alliance of Health, Physical Education, and Recreation, and in the collecting efforts of such individuals as Dr. Merle Rousey, founder of the Sports Art Center in Cortland, New York (See Appendix 2) and Bill Goff, director of Spectrum Fine Art (See Appendix 1), there is every indication that reading and research in sports art will be abundant in the years ahead. The growing number of sports art exhibitions in recent years is further evidence of the ballooning interest in it.[14]

The kinship between sport and literature, like that between sport and sculpture, dates back to early times. The epics of Homer contain several accounts of contests of strength and skill. By the fifth century B.C. athletic verse had developed into a genre known as *epinicion*, the most noted creator of which was Pindar. The book to consult on Pindar's athletic ideal is again Gardiner's *Athletics of the Ancient World*, which covers most aspects of sport in ancient times. Among several translations of Pindar's odes Richard Lattimore's is highly regarded. For other references to athletic themes in classical literature and philosophy, Rachel S. Robinson's *Sources for the History of Greek Athletics* is a fine guide. While references to athletic themes can be found in the literature of subsequent eras, the impact of sports on literature is best reflected in literature of Victorian England as described by Bruce E. Haley in *The Healthy Body and Victorian Culture*.

Nineteenth-century American literature, excluding the juvenile fiction in the last two decades of the century, has few references to team sports. In fact it primarily described episodes of hunting, fishing, and horse racing, sport as opposed to sports. William T. Porter's periodical, *Spirit of the Times*, which appeared from 1830 until 1861, is the greatest reservoir of material for that period. Sports, that is athletics, did not really become prominent in adult fiction until the second decade of this century, and the writer who best introduced the subject to the American public was Ring Lardner. The first Busher Keefe story appeared in 1914, the year that Frank Merriwell disappeared from the pages of *Tip Top Weekly* after a run of nearly twenty years. Some idea of the picture of the times and the impact the busher had upon baseball can be gained from Gilbert Seldes's *The 7 Lively Arts*.

56

Those were the days when the manager of a baseball team was rewarded as a combination of captain of finance . . . a Freud and an unborn Einstein. A fine body of college graduates, clean-living, sport-loving, well-read boys were the players; and a sport-loving, game-for-the-game's sake body of men the enthusiasts. Hughie Fullerton and Paul Elmer More might be seen any day in the same column, and John J. McGraw, who allowed himself to be called Muggsy to show what a good democrat he was, lunched daily at the President's table. Into this pretentious parade Mr. Lardner injected the busher—and baseball has never recovered.[15]

Seldes's work is a penetrating look at Lardner and the popular arts as well, but the most comprehensive treatment of Lardner is found in Donald J. Elder's biography, *Ring Lardner: A Biography.* "Ring," the title of F. Scott Fitzgerald's essay in the *Crack-up*, is an honest and sympathetic treatment of his friend. Also noteworthy are Virginia Woolf's comments on Lardner and games in *The Moment and Other Essays.*

Just as the forest and frontier were predominant themes for the major authors of the nineteenth century, so team sports and athletes have been the favorite subjects for authors of the twentieth century. The list of American authors who have focused on sports and the athlete to one degree or another reads like a hall-of-fame roster. In addition to Lardner, these are Frank Norris, Jack London, Sherwood Anderson, F. Scott Fitzgerald, Ernest Hemingway, James T. Farrell, Sinclair Lewis, William Faulkner, Damon Runyon, Thomas Wolfe, Robert Penn Warren, Irwin Shaw, Mark Harris, Bernard Malamud, Budd Schulberg, Wright Morris, John Updike, Norman Mailer, Eugene O'Neill, Clifford Odets, Robert Sherwood, Arthur Miller, William Inge, and Tennessee Williams. And there are many more, including such poets as W. H. Auden, Marianne Moore, Randall Jarrell, James Dickey, and James Wright. *Sprints and Distances: Sports in Poetry and the Poetry of Sports* edited by Lillian Morrison well illustrates the appeal that sports have had for American poets as well as poets of other times and places. *Sports Poems*, edited by P. R. Knudson and P. K. Ebert is another collection that attests to the natural kinship between sports and verse. Most poems on sports are short but *Ko; or, A Season on Earth* by Kenneth Koch uses a narrative form to describe a Japanese baseball star finding his way in a surrealistic world. The short lyric, however, seems to be the most suitable form for the subject of sports, for example, the ode "Baseball and Writing" by Marianne Moore, and Randall Jarrell's elegy "Say Good-bye to Big Daddy," which are included in a number of sports literature anthologies mentioned in chapter 5. Poets try to stir the heart by freezing a scene from the world of movement. The poet is a photographer with words who transforms the ordinariness of life into significance through the magic of a created image. As sports are a part of the ordinariness of our lives, it is not surprising that poets draw upon them for themes illustrating the human predicament, for example, Michael Culross's *The Lost Heroes*. While Grantland Rice's *Only the Brave and Other Poems* is more sentimental than ironic, it too is enjoyable. Rice's nostalgia often exasperates, but there is an appeal about his view that refuses to die, and if one isn't careful it grows stronger as the years roll on.

There are numerous collections of sports short stories, but three of the best are *The Roar of the Sneakers*, edited by Robert S. Gold, *Roller Ball Murder* by William Harrison, and *Winners and Losers*, edited by L. M. Schulman. The title of Harrison's book comes from one of the stories that formed the basis for the excellent film by the same name.

In spite of the abundance of sporting literature in all literary genres, there exists surprisingly little criticism of this literature. The first to be published on the subject is Wiley Lee Umphlett's *The Sporting Myth and the American Experience*. Umphlett's thesis is that "much serious American fiction, from the pure romance of James Fenimore Cooper to the neo-romanticism of recent years, makes use of figures with a sporting background to give form and meaning to American experience."[16] He goes on to discuss the "encounter" in which the hero through "his relationship with either nature or society is confronted with the moral decision of choosing between a self-effacing code of behavior or his own private self-interests."[17] The sporting hero, Umphlett believes, through confrontation with experience must "either face or flee self." There are three "encounters" for the individual, those with nature, those with society, and neo-romantic encounters. To illustrate his thesis, he draws upon a wide range of authors, including Franklin, Washington Irving, James Fenimore Cooper, Ring Lardner, Caroline Gordon, William Faulkner, Ernest Hemingway, Irwin Shaw, James Jones, John Cheever, Bernard Malamud, John Updike, Robert Coover, Jay Neugeboren, Jeremy Larner, and Frederick Exley. Umphlett has been selective in his choice of authors, but he has chosen a sufficient number to prove his thesis.

Umphlett's study, like the fictional works he examines, is an inquiry into the eternal conflict between idealism and materialism, the self and the world. Another book, *Laurel and Thorn: The Athlete in American Literature* by Robert J. Higgs, examines the types of athletes in American literature as representatives of the balance or imbalance between body and mind in American life. In Higgs' view there are three basic types of athletes in American literature, the Apollonian, or conformist, the Dionysian, or hedonist, and the Adonic, the rebel with a cause. Within each category are several athletic models who either illustrate the fragmentation of the traditional athletic ideal of strength and beauty or embody or approximate that ideal. Almost inevitably the praise heaped upon the athlete (the laurel) is followed by some form of disappointment (the thorn). Neil D. Berman's *Playful Fiction and Fictional Players: Games, Sport, and Survival in Contemporary American Fiction* is a work devoted to more recent sports fiction. Berman deals with only five books, *Fat City*, *North Dallas Forty*, *End Zone*, *One on One*, and *The Universal Baseball Association*, but he does an excellent job in arriving at his truly disturbing conclusion. Berman comes to believe through the protagonists in the novels he examines, most notably perhaps J. Henry Waugh in Robert Coover's *The Universal Baseball Association, Inc. J. Henry Waugh, prop.* that in order to become a transforming reality in the modern world, play must be internalized.

Neil D. Isaacs also arrives at an alarming conclusion in his section on literature, entitled "The Laurel and the Ivy," in his book *Jock Culture U.S.A.* In this chapter Isaacs concludes that America has lost its mind over its body. Literature, according to him, reveals just how far the distortion has gone and how long the process has been underway. To illustrate both the pervasiveness of sport in literature and the reflecting power of literature as a mirror of society, Isaacs draws upon a range of modern writers from Fitzgerald through Don Delillo.

There are scores of articles dealing with sporting themes by individual authors, but there are fewer that attempt to look at relatively new sports genres as mirrors of society. Among those that do and do so well are "The Sports Novel: Mythic Heroes and Natural Men" by Melvin D. Palmer in *Quest*, monograph 19, and two articles that can be found in *Sports: A Social Scoreboard*, edited by Eldon E. Snyder: "Reality 35, Illusion 3: Notes on the Football Imagination in Contemporary Fiction" by Kevin Kerrane and "Sunday Heroes: The Emergence of the Professional Football Novel" by Max Webb. A valuable dissertation on sports literature is Stewart Rondon's "Sports, Sporting Codes, and Sportsmanship in the works of Ring Lardner, James T. Farrell, Ernest Hemingway, and William Faulkner," which deals extensively with the two leading American novelists of this century, Hemingway and Faulkner. So too does *Sport and the Spirit of Play in American Fiction: Hawthorne to Faulkner*, a new book by Christian K. Messenger. Both Hemingway and Faulkner wrote about sport (fishing and hunting) as well as about sports (athletics). Faulkner, however, seems to have emerged the champion, especially in Messenger's view. "Faulkner's work with play images is the most complete for he could create in all the play modes (*agôn, alea, mimicry, ilinx*). He could convey a sense of great contest while retaining the low humor of the grotesque or an exalted sense of play's majesty before ultimate realities."[18] Messenger also traces the development of the popular sports hero and the school sports hero in American literature and culture. So too does Michael Oriard in chapter 2 of *Dreaming of Heroes: American Sports Fiction, 1868-1980.* Other themes Oriard treats in sports fiction are country and city, youth and age, sex roles, and history and myth, all of which figure prominently in Bernard Malamud's *The Natural* which Oriard examines at some length, relating events in the novel to events in American life as well as to ancient myths. Although criticism of sports literature is only in its infancy, there is every indication that it will become a fruitful field of study.

The literature of the old Southwest formed the first substantial body of sporting writing in American letters, and the man most responsible for initiating the genre was William T. Porter. In addition to serving as editor of the influential *Spirit of the Times*, which published numerous sporting pieces from various parts of the country in the three decades prior to the Civil War, Porter edited two of the most famous collections of humorous and sporting writing of the century, *The Big Bear of Arkansas* (1845) and *A Quarter Race in Kentucky* (1846). Norris W. Yates's *William T. Porter and the Spirit of the Times: A Study of the "Big Bear" School of Humor* is the most comprehensive work yet done on the subject of Porter and his magazine. *Gyascutus: Studies in Antebellum Southern Humorous and Sporting Writing*, edited by James L. W. West III, contains additional material worthy of note. In this collection Leland H. Cox, Jr., discusses in detail Porter's edition of *Instructions to Young Sportsmen*. Porter's edition was the American edition of the ninth London edition of Peter Hawker's *Instructions to Young Sportsmen*, which was well known on both sides of the Atlantic throughout the nineteenth century. In fact Hawker's book went through eleven editions in all, from 1814 to 1893. Cox shows Porter's insight in recognizing the value of the English material and his ingenuity in modifying it for American readers. In the source material of *Gyascutus* one will find for the first time mention of the Far West letters of T. B. Thorpe, who was without question one of the greatest humorists and authors of sporting stories America has produced. It is truly surprising that these letters have never been published before. Much of their success, as Cox observes, is derived from the spoofing of the romantic idea that travel and sport (in the sense of fun) "were synonymous terms." For a picture of Thorpe's view of real sport one should see his *Mysteries of the Backwoods or Sketches of the Southwest: Character, Scenery, and Rural Sport.* In this work Thorpe provides sketches of piscatory archery, alligator killing, and the hunts for bear, wildcat, and even bee. Thorpe's "The Big Bear of Arkansas" was not included in this volume but does appear in many anthologies of American and southern literature.

Another great humorist of the antebellum South was George Washington Harris, who began his career by writing sporting epistles. Harris is the author of *High Times and Hard Times* as well as the uproarious *Sut Lovingood Yarns*, which more and more frequently is considered a major work in nineteenth-century American literature. (See, for example, the lead essay by Noel Polk in *Gyascutus*). Unfortunately the Civil War practically annihilated Gyascutus, the patron beast of the tall tale and sporting story, who was, says James L. West in the preface, "a near relative of the Whang Doodle and distinct cousin of the Snipe." With the interest in American humor, popular culture, and the literature of sports, there is a chance that Gyascutus can be removed from the list of endangered species.

Well before sports had become a popular topic for so-called serious writers, they had been a favorite theme for writers of juvenile fiction. According to Robert Cantwell's article, "A Sneering Laugh with the Bases Loaded," "from 1885 until the mid nineteen-twenties there were countless books for boys." Though the first newspaper account of a baseball game appeared in 1859, "it wasn't until 1882 that a piece of baseball fiction got into print."[19] The book was entitled *The Captain of the Orient Baseball Nine*, and the author, then a junior at Brown University, was Charles M. Sheldon, author of *In His Steps*. Sheldon's book apparently opened the floodgates, for there followed in the next decades a deluge of boys' books on sports by such writers as Ralph Henry Barbour, William Heyliger, Albertus True Dudley, Christy Mathewson, Zane Grey, Gilbert Patten, and Edward Stratemeyer. The best of these books, those of Barbour and Heyliger, provided not only a lot of action for youthful readers but also a real sense of the contest, the feeling of time and place and how the weather was. Cantwell quotes Heyliger's *The Captain of the Nine* as an example:

> They shrieked their joy and pounded their fists on each other's backs. The wide, free field, the smell of early grass, the ripple of soft breeze over the flushed faces, the damp give of the spring turf. . . .[20]

"This," says Cantwell, "was Magic."

In Cantwell's view it is sad that the genre is dead. Where once there were hundreds of authors of these stories, today there are only a handful "trying —but failing—to keep alive a vanished art form that everyone once appreciated." Says Cantwell, "Millions of future little leaguers are going to play ball without a deep source of solace and inspiration, the romance of the diamond, in which the young star walloped a bully, was disgraced by a false accusation, usually a theft (something was planted in his locker) but was cleared in time to play in the big game and often wound up saving the town from destruction by fire and flood as well."[21] The heroes of juvenile novels were all-round men, as heroes usually are.

Of all the stars of all the juveniles, no one was more "all-round" or heroic than Frank Merriwell, the creation of Gilbert Patten (Burt L. Standish). Robert Boyle states in his superb essay "The Unreal Ideal: Frank Merriwell" in *Sport: Mirror of American Life*:

> He was the unreal ideal, and even today his very name is synonymous with the spectacular in sport. From 1896 to 1914, he performed

unmatchable feats of derring-do in *Tip Top Weekly*, the most widely read nickel novel ever published. He was a whiz at boxing, baseball (his "double shoot," which curved in both directions, was always good in the clutch), football, hockey, lacrosse, crew, track, shooting, bicycle racing, billiards, golf—in fact, any sport he deigned to play. No matter what plots the villains hatched, Frank always emerged triumphant, swaggering Herbert Hammerwell, the son of "a pompous vain, conceited, narrow minded, back-number politician," and the rest of their ilk—routed.[22]

Barbour and Heyliger may have been the best of the writers of boys' baseball fiction, but Patten probably was the most prolific and apparently the most widely read. Though Street and Smith, publishers of *Tip Top Weekly*, kept the exact circulation secret, it was estimated to have reached at one time 300,000. Patten claims in *Frank Merriwell's Father: An Autobiography* that total sales reached 5 million and many of these passed through a number of hands. Even though Patten's claim seems excessive, he could be off by several million and still be the most productive of all the breed.

Incidentally, Patten suggests that he was the inventor of boys' baseball fiction, or at least one of the pioneers. In discussing his decision to turn to another subject for his novels in autobiography. Patten explained his choice:

> Believing the old-fashioned dime novel was on its way out, I decided to set a new style with my stories and make them different and more in step with the times. As the first issues were to be stories of American school life, I saw in them the opportunity to feature all kinds of athletic sports, with baseball, about which I was best informed, predominating.
>
> Such stories would give me the opportunity to preach—by example —the doctrine of a clean mind in a clean and healthy body.[23]

To quote statistics of the sales of juvenile fiction is not to imply that Patten and the others were concerned merely with churning out books. Indeed the novels, Patten's novels especially, had an impact. They not only influenced a significant part of one generation, as Boyle contends, but also many of that generation's notables as well. Among Patten's admirers were Stanley Ketchel, Franklin P. Adams, Jess Willard, Floyd Gibbons, Jack Dempsey, Jerry Geisler, Frederick March, Christy Mathewson, Woodrow Wilson, Babe Ruth, Al Smith, Wendell Willkie, George Jean Nathan, and Westbrook Pegler, who, says Boyle, "lamented that Patten had never received the Pulitzer Prize."[24]

Though not nearly so popular as he once was, Frank Merriwell is still around and may be enjoying a minor comeback. The current edition of *Books in Print* lists ten titles. Also Frank's son shows up in a novel laid in California (*Frank Merriwell Returns* by Mike Frederick) in the mid-sixties, but the chances of his ever matching the exploits of his father are slim indeed.

We do not allow the heroes of yesteryear to rest, and it is good that we don't. In 1969 Collier Books reissued a novel about another Yale hero who, although perhaps not as famous as Frank, may be even more significant as an interpreter of American values. With the reappearance of *Stover at Yale* by Owen Johnson, author of the Lawrenceville stories also featuring Stover, Dink Stover returned to the American scene. The review by Michael J. Halberstam entitled "Stover at the Barricades" in *The American Scholar* makes it clear that *Stover at Yale* is a book quite different from the other college-hero fiction of the turn of the century. It is, says Halberstam, not only a classic but a subversive book that "starts us thinking about our own condition." Frank Merriwell is kind, modest, and intelligent, but Dink Stover is conscious. At least he is capable of consciousness. He is, as Halberstam points out, "radicalized by his companions." He is drawn to Regan, a gruff, older freshman who is working his way through Yale in order to go into reform politics back west. He comes to respect Gimbel, a classmate who is politicking to overthrow the sophomore societies. Johnson even hints that Gimbel may be Jewish—despite being an Andover athlete he has no chance of making society—but never uses the word. When Stover makes a condescending visit to a couple of grinds from a small New England town, he discovers a respect for learning unknown among his own carefree friends. The decent, well-meaning Stover is caught between the old ideal and the new awareness of democracy and the meaning of America. It is not, however, just Stover who is at the barricades, says Halberstam, but Yale and America itself:

> But Stover is so genuinely decent, so manly in a long-lost way, that even today we focus on him and not the institutions around him. The messages of Stover—and they are real ones—continue to be obscured by the charm of its main character. But if we in the academic world are up against the wall these days, we should look over our shoulders and note that the handwriting has been there a good long time.[25]

Thus, there is good reason for reading and studying the juvenile fiction of yesteryear not only for its charm and mindlessness but also in those rare instances, such as *Stover at Yale*, for its consciousness of revolt.

Edward Stratemeyer is another important name in juvenile sports fiction. Arthur Prager, author of "Edward Stratemeyer and his Book Machine" points out that Stratemeyer, using sixty-five pseudonyms, wrote more than 800 books that were translated into a dozen languages. Certainly not all of the Stratemeyer heroes were athletes, but they were, like most young protagonists, athletic, and many were "Saturday Heroes," the title of the chapter on the boy athlete hero in Prager's excellent book, *Rascals at Large; or the Clue to the Old Nostalgia*. Not only did Stratemeyer author the fourteen books in the Baseball Joe Series under the name "Lester Chadwick," he also wrote the College Sports series, according to Prager. In addition, he "came up with 'Graham B. Forbes' and the eight-volume series about the Boys of Columbia High, one of whom (Frank Allen) was graduated into a series of three volumes of his own."[26] If this weren't enough, "he drafted 'Elmer A. Dawson' and 'John R. Cooper' who produced, respectively the Gary Grayson football stories and the Mel Martin Stories."[27] Prager also has a brief but good discussion of the Merriwell boys and provides a short Patten bibliography that updates and supplements Boyle's. Mentioned in Prager's bibliography is Russel B. Nye's *The Unembarrassed Muse: The Popular Arts in America*, which contains a brief but excellent portrait of Patten and Frank.

There are two other works that must be mentioned in any discussion of juvenile literature. These are the two-volume work, *The House of Beadle and Adams* by Albert Johannsen and *The Fiction Factory, or from Pulp Row to Quality Street* by Quentin Reynolds. The former is a superb reference work that is of inestimable worth in the study of American popular culture. It deals with almost every aspect of the publishing ventures of Beadle and Adams. It lists and abstracts hundreds of publications, provides capsule biographies of such authors as Patten and Stratemeyer (including an incredible number of pseudonyms), and offers samples of writing styles, as well as scores of engaging illustrations. There are, for example, illustrations of *Beadle's Dime Base Ball Player* by Henry Chadwick, the first "continuous" series of baseball booklets ever issued, and ample descriptions of the annual issues from 1860 to 1881. *The Fiction Factory* describes the one hundred-year operation of the rival firm, Street and Smith, who also employed Patten and Stratemeyer. A shorter but still excellent survey of the subject of juvenile sports fiction is "Sport in the Dime Novel" by Christian Karl Messenger in *Journal of American Culture*.

NOTES

1. Thorstein Veblen, *Theory of the Leisure Class* (1899; reprint ed., New York: New American Library, 1953), pp. 173-74. Elbert Hubbard had used the same metaphor earlier and may have been the unnamed source Veblen had in mind.
2. Ralph Waldo Emerson, *Selections from Ralph Waldo Emerson*, ed. Stephen E. Whicher (Boston: Houghton Mifflin, 1957), p. 31.
3. Wallace Stevens, "The Pure Good of Theory," *The Collected Poems of Wallace Stevens* (New York: Alfred A. Knopf, 1961), p. 332.

4. E. Norman Gardiner, *Athletics of the Ancient World* (London: Oxford University Press, 1930), p. 53.

5. Ibid., p. 66.

6. Ibid., p. 108.

7. Kenneth Clark, *The Nude: A Study in Ideal Form* (New York: Doubleday, 1956), p. 77.

8. Gardiner, *Athletics of the Ancient World*, p. 65.

9. Andrew J. Kozar, *R. Tait McKenzie: The Sculptor of Athletes* (Knoxville: University of Tennessee Press, 1975), p. 35.

10. Clark, p. 441.

11. Quoted in Benjamin Lowe, *The Beauty of Sport: A Cross Disciplinary Inquiry* (Englewood Cliffs, N.J.: Prentice-Hall, 1977), p. 113.

12. Although he discusses some of the athletic art of Frederic Remington, Lowe for some reason does not refer to him as an athlete-artist. That he was a very good athlete is inarguable. According to Peter H. Hassrick, "Remington loved football. He was a natural athlete, displaying strength and skill which enabled him to excel in all sports, including boxing and horsemanship. As a rusher he knocked heads on the line, and although his brawn should have been sufficient, he employed psychological tactics as a means of bringing his team to victory. On the occasion of the 1879 Princeton-Yale game, Remington reputedly dipped his jersey in blood at a local slaughterhouse "to make it look more businesslike." *Frederick Remington: Paintings, Drawings, and Sculpture in the Amon Carter Museum and the Sid W. Richardson Foundation Collections* (New York: Harry N. Abrams, 1973), p. 19. Also see p. 101.

For a grouping of some of Remington's sporting works see the sections entitled "He Knew Horses," "Football," "Bull Fighting," and "Hunting and Fishing" in *The Illustrations of Frederic Remington* with a commentary by Owen Wister and edited by Marta Jackson (New York: Crown, 1970).

13. Lowe, p. 62.

14. See, for example, the catalogs of the following recent exhibitions: *Forms in Sport* (1842-1978) arranged by Terry Dintenfass, 50 West 57th Street, New York, N.Y. 10019 and *Play Ball! A Century of Sports in Art*, arranged by the Queen's Museum, New York City Building, Flushing Meadow, Corona Park, Flushing, N.Y. 11368. For information and materials on the many recent exhibits of Bill Goff, write him at Spectrum Fine Art Ltd., 50 West 57th Street, New York, N.Y. 10019.

15. Gilbert Seldes, *The 7 Lively Arts* (New York: Sagamore, 1957), p. 114.

16. Wiley Lee Umphlett, *The Sporting Myth and the American Experience* (Lewisburg, Pa. and London: Bucknell University Press), p. 20.

17. Ibid., p. 21.

18. Christian Karl Messenger, *Sport and the Spirit of Play in American Fiction* (New York: Columbia University Press, 1981), p. 313.

19. Robert Cantwell, "A Sneering Laugh with the Bases Loaded," *Sports Illustrated*, 23 April 1962, p. 69.

20. Ibid., p. 67.

21. Ibid., p. 68.

22. Robert Boyle, *Sport: Mirror of American Life* (Boston: Little Brown & Co., 1963), p. 241.

23. Burt L. Standish [Gilbert Patten], *Frank Merriwell's "Father": An Auto-biography* (Norman: University of Oklahoma Press, 1964), p. 178.

24. Boyle, p. 243.

25. Michael J. Halberstam, "Stover at the Barricades," *American Scholar* 38 (Summer 1969), 480.

26. Arthur Prager, *Rascals at Large; or, The Clue in the Old Nostalgia* (New York: Doubleday, 1971), p. 286.

27. Ibid.

BIBLIOGRAPHY

Art Index. New York: H. W. Wilson Company, 1929-.

Berman, Neil D. *Playful Fiction and Fictional Players: Games, Sport, and Survival in Contemporary Fiction.* Port Washington, N.Y.: Kennikat Press, 1980.

Bellows, Emma S. *The Paintings of George Bellows.* New York: Alfred A. Knopf, 1929.

Bellows, George. *Drawings of George Bellows.* Edited by Charles Morgan. Alhambra, Calif.: Borden, 1979.

Boyle, Robert. *Sport: Mirror of American Life.* Boston: Little, Brown, & Co., 1963.

Brown, Joe. *Joe Brown: Retrospective Catalog, 1932-1966.* Introduction by Norman Thomas and Red Smith.

Cantwell, Robert. "A Sneering Laugh with the Bases Loaded." *Sports Illustrated,* 23 April 1962, pp. 68-76.

Clark, Sir Kenneth. *The Nude: A Study in Ideal Form.* New York: Doubleday, 1956.

Conningham, Frederic A. *Currier and Ives Prints: An Illustrated Check List.* New York: Crown, 1970.

Coover, Robert. *The Universal Baseball Association, Inc. J. Henry Waugh, prop.* New York: Random House, 1968.

Culross, Michael. *The Lost Heroes.* Pittsburgh: The University of Pittsburgh, 1974.

Drees, Ludwig. *Olympia: Gods, Artists, and Athletes.* New York: Frederick A. Praeger, 1967.

Elder, Donald J. *Ring Lardner: A Biography.* Garden City, New York: Doubleday, 1956.

Encyclopedia of Associations, 16th ed. Detroit: Gale Research Company, 1981.

Fitzgerald, F. Scott. "Ring," in *The Crack-Up.* Edited by Edmund Wilson. New York: New Directions, 1945.

Forms in Sport (1842-1978). Catalog of the sports-art exhibition arranged by Terry Dintenfass, 50 West 57th St., New York, N.Y., 10019.

Gardiner, E. Norman. *Athletics of the Ancient World.* London: Oxford University Press, 1930.

————. *Greek Athletic Sports and Festivals.* 1910. Reprint. Dubuque, Iowa: William C. Brown, 1970.

Gardner, E. A. *Handbook of Greek Sculpture.* London: Macmillan & Co., 1929.

Goodrich, Lloyd. *Thomas Eakins: His Life and Work.* 1933. Reprint. New York: AMS Press, 1970.

Gold, Robert S., ed. *The Roar of the Sneakers.* New York: Bantam Books, 1977.

Halberstam, Michael J. "Stover at the Barricades." *American Scholar* 38 (Summer 1969), 470-80.

Haley, Bruce E. *The Healthy Body and Victorian Culture*. Cambridge, Mass.: Harvard University Press, 1978.

Harris, George Washington. *High Times and Hard Times*. Edited by M. Thomas Inge. Nashville, Tenn.: Vanderbilt University Press, 1976.

_____. *The Sut Lovingood Yarns*. Edited by M. Thomas Inge. New Haven, Conn.: College and University Press, 1966.

Harrison, William. *Roller Ball Murder*. New York: Morrow, 1974.

Hassrick, Peter H. *Frederic Remington: Paintings, Drawings and Sculpture in the Amon Carter Museum and the Sid W. Richardson Foundation Collections*. New York: Harry W. Abrams, 1973.

Hawker, Peter. *Instructions to Young Sportsmen in All that Relates to Guns and Shooting*. Reprint from 9th London edition, 1844. Philadelphia: Lippincott, 1922.

Hendricks, Gordon. *The Life and Work of Thomas Eakins*. New York: Grossman Publishers, 1974.

Higgs, Robert J. *Laurel and Thorn: The Athlete in American Literature*. Lexington: University Press of Kentucky, 1981.

Huizinga, Johan. *Homo Ludens: A Study of the Play Element in Culture*. Translated by R. F. C. Hull. Boston: Beacon Press, 1960.

The Illustrations of Frederic Remington. Commentary by Owen Wister and edited by Marta Jackson. New York: Crown, 1970.

Isaacs, Neil D. *Jock Culture U.S.A.* New York: W. W. Norton, 1978.

Johannsen, Albert. *The House of Beadle and Adams*. 2 vols. Norman: University of Oklahoma Press, 1950.

Johnson, Owen. *Lawrenceville Stories*. New York: Simon and Schuster, 1967.

_____. *Stover at Yale*. 1911. Reprint. New York: Macmillan Co., 1968.

Knudson, P. R., and P. K. Ebert, eds. *Sports Poems*. New York: Dell, 1971.

Koch, Kenneth. *Ko; or, A Season on Earth*. New York: Grove Press, 1960.

Kozar, Andrew J. *R. Tait McKenzie: The Sculptor of Athletes*. Knoxville: University of Tennessee Press, 1975.

Lowe, Benjamin. *The Beauty of Sports: A Cross-disciplinary Inquiry*. Englewood Cliffs, N.J.: Prentice-Hall, 1977.

Marshall, Joe. "Heroes with Feet of Clay." *Sports Illustrated*, 5 November 1973, pp. 42-46.

Messenger, Christian Karl. *Sport and the Spirit of Play in American Fiction*. New York: Columbia University Press, 1981.

_____. "Sport in the Dime Novel." *Journal of American Culture* 3 (Fall 1978), 494-505.

Monro, Isabel Stevenson, and Kate M. Munro. *Index to Reproductions of American Paintings*. New York: H. W. Wilson, 1948.

_____. *Supplement to Index to Reproductions of American Paintings*. New York: H. W. Wilson, 1964.

Morrison, Lillian, ed. *Sprints and Distances: Sports in Poetry and the Poetry of Sports*. New York: Crowell, 1965.

Music Index. Detroit: Information Coordinators. Beginning date, 1949.

Nye, Russel B. *The Unembarrassed Muse: The Popular Arts in America*. New York: Dial, 1970.

Oriard, Michael. *Dreaming of Heroes: American Sports Fiction, 1868-1980.* Chicago, Nelson-Hall, 1982.

Palmer, Melvin D. "Mythic Heroes and Natural Men." *Quest* 19 (Winter 1973), 49-58.

Patten, Gilbert [Burt L. Standish], *Frank Merriwell's "Father": An Autobiography.* Ed. Harriet Hinsdale Norman: University of Oklahoma Press, 1964.

Play Ball! A Century of Sports in Art. Catalog of the exhibition of The Queen's Museum, New York City Building, Flushing Meadow, Corona Park, Flushing, New York 11368.

Porter, William T., ed. *The Big Bear of Arkansas and Other Stories.* 1845. Reprint. New York: AMS Press, 1978.

_____. *A Quarter Race in Kentucky and Other Sketches.* 1846. Reprint. New York: AMS Press, 1978.

_____. *The Spirit of the Times: A Chronicle of the Turf, Agriculture, Field Sports, Literature and the Stage.* New York, 1831-1861. Available through University Microfilms International, Ann Arbor, Michigan.

Prager, Arthur. "Edward Stratemeyer and His Book Machine." *Saturday Review,* 10 July 1971, pp. 15-17, 52-53.

_____. *Rascals at Large; or The Clue to the Old Nostalgia.* New York: Doubleday, 1971.

Reynolds, Quentin. *The Fiction Factory or from Pulp Row to Quality Street.* New York: Random House, 1955.

Robinson, Rachel S. *Sources for the History of Greek Athletics.* 1955. Reprint. Chicago: Ares, 1980.

Rice, Grantland. *Only the Brave and Other Poems.* New York: A. S. Barnes, 1941.

_____. *The Tumult and the Shouting: My Life in Sport.* New York: A. S. Barnes, 1954.

Rondon, Stewart. "Sports, Sporting Codes, and Sportsmanship in the works of Ring Lardner, James T. Farrell, Ernest Hemingway, and William Faulkner." Ph.D. dissertation, New York University, 1961.

Schulman, L. M. *Winners and Losers.* New York: Macmillan Co., 1968.

Scott, Jack. *Athletics for Athletes.* Oakland, Calif.: Another Ways Book, 1969.

Seldes, Gilbert. *The 7 Lively Arts.* New York: Sagamore, 1957.

Snyder, Eldon E., ed. *Sports: A Social Scoreboard.* Bowling Green, Ohio: Bowling Green University Popular Press, 1975.

Standish, Burt L. [Gilbert Patten]. *Frank Merriwell's "Father:" An Autobiography.* Ed. Harriet Hinsdale Norman: University of Oklahoma Press, 1964.

Thorpe, Thomas Bangs. *The Mysteries of the Backwoods; or, Sketches of the Southwest: Character, Scenery, and Rural Sport.* 1845. Reprint. Upper Saddle River, N.J.: The Gregg Press, 1970.

Umphlett, Wiley Lee. *The Sporting Myth and the American Experience.* Lewisburg, Pa. and London: Bucknell University Press, 1975.

Veblen, Thorstein. *Theory of the Leisure Class.* 1899. Reprint. New York: New American Library, 1953.

West, James L. W. III. *Gyascutus: Studies in Antebellum Southern Humorous and Sporting Writing.* Atlantic Highlands, N.J.: Humanities Press, 1978.

Woolf, Virginia. "American Fiction." In *The Moment and Other Essays*. New York: Harcourt, Brace, 1948.

Yalouris, Nicolaos. *The Eternal Olympics: The Art and History of Sport*. New Rochelle, N.Y.: Caratzas Brothers, 1979.

Yates, Norris W. *William T. Porter and the Spirit of the Times: A Study of the "Big Bear" School of Humor*. Baton Rouge: Louisiana State University Press, 1957.

CHAPTER 4

Sports and Popular Culture: Sports Language, Photography, Film, Comics, Cartoons, Popular Music, Philately

Just as some are reluctant to call juvenile literature art, so are some hesitant to consider sportswriting as an art. Yet the sportswriter, who is a recurring figure in both juvenile and adult fiction, does precisely what the authors of *epiniciia* did in ancient Greece: he supplies us with a version of the actual event. Although the quality and mode of expression have changed since the days of Pindar, anyone noticing the endless parade of metaphors in the sports pages would find it difficult to deny that there is not at least an attempt at artful expression. The sportswriter, in fact, must make this attempt for he is the recorder of dramatic spectacles. The box score gives the results, but only the sportswriter tells how the game was played. The question becomes not whether sportswriting is an art but the degree or level of the art. In the views of many, including sportswriters themselves, the art is severely lacking in quality.

The basic stylistic problem facing the sportswriter is one of repetition: How does one describe the same event day after day without boring readers? In trying for variety, the sportswriter faces a problem of equal magnitude. In their article: "Sportugese: A Study of Sports Page Communication" in *Sport, Culture and Society: A Reader on the Sociology of Sport* edited by John W. Loy, Jr., and Gerald S. Kenyon, Percy N. Tannebaum and James E. Noah point out that the simple expression of a fact has disappeared: "No one wins today. Teams rock, sock, roll, romp, stagger, swamp, rout, decision, down, drop, eke out, topple, top, scalp, and trounce opponents, but no one wins a game."[1] The authors refer to a delightful article in the June 21, 1958, *New Yorker* on "the science or art of baseball-headline verbs," which provided rules for the selection of appropriate terms covering a range of possibilities:

Rule: Any three-run margin, provided the winning total does not exceed ten, may be described as a vanquishing. If, however, the margin is a mere two runs and the losing total is five or more, "OUT-

SLUG," is considered very tasty. You will notice, S.F., the trend called Mounting Polysyllabism, which culminates, at the altitude of double digits, in that trio of Latin-root rhymers, "ANNIHILATE," "OBLITERATE," and "HUMILIATE." E.g., "A'S ANNIHILATE O's."[2]

Edwin Newman in *Strictly Speaking* seems to imply that a lot of people have simply given up trying for variety and have settled on a few dependable phrases like "pretty good":

> I have an additional reason for watching football fade out without much regret. That reason is a protective interest in the English language. The phrase "pretty good," as in "He hit him pretty good," and "We stopped them pretty good," and "He moves pretty good for a big man," gets worked out pretty good from late September to mid-January. After which it should be given a pretty good rest, or allowed to rest pretty good, or at any rate left to basketball where they hit the backboards pretty good.
>
> Basketball, of course, cannot be played without referees, and generally they do the officiation pretty good, but not always. Said K. C. Jones, coach of the Capital Bullets of the NBA, explaining why he would not comment on the officiating in a play-off game against New York: "No sense in risking a $2,000 fine. To hell with it. They read the papers pretty good for our remarks."[3]

While "pretty good" and "great" ("great" kick, "great" catch, "great" pass, "great" hands) are having their finest hour, William Eben Schultz in "Football Verbiage" proves that sportswriters are probably as inventive as any other group in their efforts to avoid triteness. Schultz lists approximately ninety headline action verbs from the weekend editions of metropolitan and small-town presses during a football season. The verbs range from *annexes* ("Duke annexes victory") to *yields* ("Iowa yields to Minnesota").

Sportscasters have the same problem as sportswriters, and "mounting polysyllabism" seems to be ascendant. Singling out Howard Cosell, Edwin Newman points to his unquenchable supply of bromides and ability to range from "relative paucity" to "veritable plethora" without, says Newman, "drawing a breath."[4] Even Cosell's relative erudition can cause problems, for example, when he commented that "the mist is drifting over the stadium like a description in a Thomas Hardy novel."[5] Not surprisingly, Cosell has been the sports announcer most subject to attack both for his polysyllabism and his volume. As Larry Merchant states in . . . *And Everyday You Take Another Bite*: "Cosell doesn't clarify or amplify, he CLARI-

FIES and AMPLIFIES. What comes at you is: THIS IS ME, HOWARD COSELL, WHO JUST THIS AFTERNOON HAD LUNCH WITH CHOU ENLAI, TELLING YOU THAT THAT PASS WAS OVER-THROWN ! ! ! yes, we know, Howard, we just saw it."[6] Because he is so frequently attacked, it is not surprising that one of the questions Cosell is most often asked concerns his reaction to the criticism he receives from sportswriters. Cosell's answer, contained in *Like It Is*, should provide his critics with enough food for thought to last through a Monday night game:

> In the first place, no one is above being knocked. In the second place, many sportswriters have a built-in antipathy toward television as a medium. The medium, itself, has stolen much of their thunder. People see the event as it happens, know for themselves what did happen and often, by way of post-event interviews, get the inside of what happened right on the spot. For those writers who are assigned to cover the event, it has changed the whole nature of their job. They have to be more thoughtful, more creative. A mere recital of what happened in the game on the day after most people have seen it constitutes a redundancy. The sportswriter is materially reduced not just in his function, but in his importance. This has caused many a sportswriter to feel bitterness and envy: Bitterness over the fact that he has a declining significance, envy in the fact that his pay scale is far less than that of the average announcer.[7]

Sportscasters are living redundancies. Why is it, then, that they have achieved such eminence? Perhaps it is because they have provided not the best version but the first version. Heroic deeds must be talked about first before they are recorded. It has always been so. In the beginning was the word: the typewriter came later.

Newman's chapter on language of sports, "Is Your Team Hungry Enough, Coach?" and Schultz's essay, "Football Verbiage," are reprinted in *Language Awareness* edited by Paul Eschholz, Alfred Rosa, and Virginia Clark. Bill Gilbert's fine and funny *Sports Illustrated* article, entitled "Fast as an Elephant, Strong as an Ant," is also included in this volume. With Tannebaum and Noah's "Sportugese," these articles are available under one cover and make a good introduction to the basic problems of sportswriting. Another helpful piece is "Sports Page" by Frederick W. Cozens and Florence S. Stumpf in *Sport and Society: An Anthology* edited by John H. Talamini and Charles H. Page. "Sports Page" originally appeared in a fine book on sports also by Cozens and Stumpf entitled simply *Sports in American Life*. A superb article of the growth of sportswriting entitled "The Writing of Sports" by Randall Poe appeared in the *Esquire* "Super Sports Issue" of October 1974. In championship form himself, Poe looks at the developments and styles of "six champ scribes," Red Smith, Jim Murray, Dick Young, Larry Merchant, Wells Twombly, and Roger Kahn. Equally impressive are the reminiscences of "the most influential" of all, that is, Red Smith, contained in *Esquire* a year later ("Special Issue: The Joy of Sports!") in an article entitled "My Press-Box Memoirs" with this endearing epigraph: "Old sportswriters never die. Few, in fact, even grow up." A truly classic book on the milieu of the sportswriter is Stanley Woodward's highly enjoyable and nostalgic *Sports Page*. The last sentence of it could serve as the motto of every sports editor in the world: "I think it is better to abjure promotions and concentrate on getting out a sports page."

The Tumult and The Shouting: My Life in Sport by Grantland Rice should not be forgotten in any study of the history of sports journalism, especially because of the picture of his colleagues he gives in a chapter called "Writers and Pals." His discussion of the switch in emphasis on the sports page from verse to prose recalls a major change in sports reporting, one that in Rice's view brought "sorrow to many, many people." That shift, when recognized, points to a visible pattern of change in the manner of praising athletes and epic heroes. First there was the oral tradition of the tall tale, then there were writers such as Frank Adams ("Tinker to Evers to Chance") of sporting verse, then writers of prose, in Rice's words, "the Peglers and the Winchells, the Brouns and the Ed Sullivans," and today an army of TV commentators, many of whom are ex-athletes. The sportswriter is still alive, but he works in relative obscurity compared to the fame of the TV commentator. If modern sportswriters want to see what has happened to them, they should look back a generation and see what effect the prose writers of that day had upon versifiers and epigrammatists.

A rarity who survived both the world of sportswriting and television and lived to tell about them is Heywood Hale Broun. *Tumultuous Merriment*, a title taken from Dr. Johnson's definition of sport, is not about newspapers nor is it about television. It is, however, about the effects these institutions, especially television, have had upon American attitudes toward sports and play. Told with characteristic wit and humor, the book contains some expressions of genuine regret. Of his part in bringing the National Wrist-Wrestling Championships to ABC's Wide World of Sports, he writes, "I'm sorry I helped to turn arm games into Armageddon." Reminded that a college friend warned him that if he didn't choose between athletes and aesthetes he would fall into a "patternless existence," Broun discovers that this "patternless existence" is analogous to change, the occasional fruit of which is "tumultuous merriment." He ends on an optimistic note, expressing the belief that the pendulum in the sports world will swing away from official control with huge TV audiences and back toward a freer structure. If he is correct, perhaps some day Dr. Johnson, brilliantly described by Broun as "a great laughing brown ball," who set himself rolling down a grassy hill and at the bottom "arose hay-streaked and refreshed," will be regarded not only as the great champion of literature but of sport as well.

Michael Novak's chapter on "Jocks, Hacks, Flacks, and Pricks" in his *The Joy of Sports: End Zones, Bases, Baskets, Balls and the Consecration of the American Spirit* contains a thoughtful analysis of sportswriting and sportscasting, especially in the sportsreel sections on Grantland Rice, Vince Sculley, and Howard Cosell that bracket the chapter. In graceful prose Novak points to the power of the metaphor in Rice, for example, "the Four Horsemen," the beauty of clarity in Scully, and the error of Cosell in regarding sports as entertainment. Of Cosell, he writes:

> Having done so well in cracking the crust of unreflective pieties, Cosell fails at the most radical level to "tell it like it is." He leaves out the inner power of sports, the power of the human spirit, without which crowds could not be attracted and so much love and energy could not be inspired. In trying to be secular, dry, abrasive; above all, in trying to entertain, he neglects the living roots. Left to his care alone, therefore, one would expect sports to wither on the vine, to begin to bore him, and many others with him.[8]

The special problems of black sportswriters are identified in *The Revolt of the Black Athlete* by Harry Edwards, who distinguishes between the "Negro sports reporter" and "The Black sports reporter" among whom he finds some white reporters such as Robert Lipsyte and Pete Axthelm. Hal Blythe and Charlie Sweet present a humorous and perceptive analysis of the language of the sportscaster in an article entitled "Some Simple Steps to Stardom in the TV Sports Booth" in the Lexington, Kentucky, *Herald Leader*. For earlier works on the sporting press and the language of sports, Norris W. Yates's *William T. Porter and the Spirit of the Times: A Study of the Big Bear of Humor* and *Frank Forester (William Henry Herbert): A Tragedy in Exile* by William S. Hunt are useful, as are the sections on sport in *American Journalism: A History, 1660-1960* by Frank Luther Mott. For earlier information on sporting slang the authoritative works are H. L. Mencken's *The American Language* and its second supplement, and Eric Partridge's *Slang, To-day and Yesterday*. The beginner who wishes to comprehend the lingo of the fifteen most popular sports should see *The Encyclopedia of Sports Talk*, edited by Zander Hollander.

Along with the words on the sports page, there are invariably a lot of pictures; and if there is doubt about whether or not sportswriting is art, so there is too about photography. The problems facing the sportswriter also face the photographer, and sometimes in small-town weeklies one person does both jobs. Again, repetition is the major danger. How many ways are there to show a player sliding into second, striking out, or hitting a home-run? Admittedly, there are probably an infinite number of variables in each sporting event that the photographer can work with, but it would be a dull photographer who did not feel the need for innovation in an endeavor that is basically repetitive.

There are really only a handful of truly significant developments in sports photography. One is the result of the work of Eadweard Muybridge whose achievements are outlined in *Photography and the American Scene: A Social History, 1839-1899* by Robert Taft. Muybridge's photographs of the horse in motion, which confirmed that at a certain instant the horse took all four feet from the ground, not only extended man's knowledge about the horse but influenced artists as well. According to Taft,

> It is not at all unlikely that the best known American portrayer of the horse in action, Frederic Remington, was influenced by these photographs. It is a fact that Remington's artistic career dates from 1880, practically the same time that the Muybridge photographs were becoming well known. Remington was a close student of the horse, and while no positive information is available, it seems almost inevitable that Remington was familiar with, and influenced by, these striking photographs of the horse. If true of Remington, it was still truer of the later portrayers of the horse in action, especially of the Western horse—including such artists as Russell and Schreyvogel. Certain it is that a comparison of sketches in the popular illustrated journals before and after the Muybridge photographs became well known shows that the depiction of horses underwent a marked change in form at this time.[9]

In addition to his pioneering photographic work, Muybridge assisted Thomas Eakins in his lecture "History of a Jump," which is reproduced in *The Life and Works of Thomas Eakins* by Gordon Hendricks. "Eakins' interest in—and contribution to—photography," says Hendricks, "is at once more conspicuous and more notable than that of any other painter in the history of American art. He is America's greatest artist, and, at least, one of her excellent—perhaps great—photographers."[10] Whether Eakins was America's greatest artist depends perhaps upon one's taste, but his achievements are large. Like Walt Whitman, whom he photographed and painted, he extended the domain of art. In photography, painting, and sculpture Eakins made Americans see scenes that previously had been considered outside the realm of art, and many of these scenes were scenes of sporting life. While there has always existed an aristocratic bias against anything that masses of people enjoy, Eakins fought against that prejudice with his scenes of popular sports.

In a chapter on football in *The Astonished Muse*, Reuel Denney astutely observes that Muybridge's motion studies for Leland Stanford came at a time when the pressures and rhythms of industrialism were having a subtle yet profound effect upon American consciousness:

> Spurred by interest in the analysis of the athletic motions of men and animals, photographer Eadweard Muybridge was setting out his movie-like action shots of the body motion (more preoccupied even than Vesalius or Da Vinci with the detailed anatomy of movement) at about the same time that Coach Woodruff of Pennsylvania (1894) was exploring the possibilities for momentum play: lineman swinging into motion before the ball is snapped, with the offensive team forming a wedge, charging toward an opposition held waiting by the offside rule. In Philadelphia the painter Eakins, self-consciously following the tenets of naturalism and his own literal American tradition, was painting the oarsmen of the Schuylkill. Nearby, at the Midvale plant of the American Steel Company, efficiency expert Frederick Winslow Taylor was experimenting with motion study and incentive pay geared to small measurable changes in output-pay that would spur but never soften the workman.[11]

The motion picture, which Muybridge was instrumental in developing if not directly responsible for, is perhaps the most appropriate art form for highly industrialized societies. In a sense, it is also an art form ideally suited for sport, which detractors claim have become industrialized. Several sports editors, in fact, now speak matter-of-factly of "the sports industry." Sports always involve motion, and an art form that has the inherent ability to reflect motion would seem to be far more able to capture the essence of sports than one that cannot. Unfortunately, however, most critics feel that motion pictures have only rarely successfully portrayed the essential drama of sports.

There are many reasons why the apparent potential of the motion picture has not been utilized more creatively, but a major problem is the same one that faces the individual with a still camera: what material is to be selected and how is it to be shot? Before Leni Riefenstahl's *Olympische Spiele* in 1936, there had been little attention paid to aesthetic matters in sports films. As Ken Wlaschin has observed in "The Olympics of Film": "In truth all the Olympic films until 1936 were essentially newsreels, or, at best, documentary records filmed in a flat and relatively dull manner."[12] Riefenstahl, instead of merely recording, interpreted, and while her interpretations have been the subject of controversy because many believe that she deliberately promoted the Aryan ethos (though not so blatantly here as in her earlier film *Triumph of the Will*), few have disputed her artistic skills. In displaying the possibilities of film in sports, Riefenstahl raised the age-old dilemma between art and didacticism. When and under what circumstances are there limits to artistic expression? It is a problem that has manifested itself many times, from the case of Ezra Pound during World War II to the revolt of the black athletes at the Mexico Olympics in 1968. Art, like sports, can be used for many ends, religious, political, and commercial, and it is not always easy to determine when such is taking place. In the case of Leni Riefenstahl, it is only fair to point out, as Wlaschin does, "that the star of the film is the black American athlete Jesse Owens, winner of four gold medals, not Hitler (an ironic comment on the Nazi theories of Aryan superiority)."

Riefenstahl's still photography in her book *The Last of the Nuba* is as impressive as her film, especially the scenes on wrestling in chapter four. Just as she did in her films, she again captures the spirit of strength and beauty, the athletic ideal. Whether filming or photographing, however, she is unable to escape the charge of fascism which Susan Sontag accused her of in an article entitled "Fascinating Fascism," that appeared in the *New York Review of Books* for February 6, 1975. Those wishing to pursue the matter further should look at the letter from David B. Hinton, lecturer in film, at Schiller College, Heidelburg, in the September 8, 1975, issue of the *New York Review of Books* and Sontag's response in the same issue. Even more detail can be found in the book *Leni Riefenstahl: The Fallen Film Goddess* by Glen B. Infield. Infield unfortunately fails to list Hinton's response in his bibliography.

Another notable aesthetic achievement in film is that of Kon Ichikawa, director of the documentary on the 1964 Olympics in Tokyo. Yet the question of why in a highly technical age, and one in which sport is flourishing as never before, there have not been more distinguished accomplishments is still unanswered. The question becomes even more pressing in the case of dramatic films about sports heroes and sports. There really are only a handful of notable Hollywood productions about sports, for example, *Raging Bull, Chariots of Fire, Bang the Drum Slowly, Rocky,* and *Roller Ball.*[14] It would seem the alliance between Hollywood and sports can only be termed a failure, which is the thesis of a well-researched and enjoyable article by Robert Cantwell entitled "Sport Was Box Office Poison" that was reprinted in *Sport and Society,* edited by Talamini and Page. Cantwell claims to have looked at approximately one hundred old movies and come away with one strong impression: "The shows were by and large entertaining when they were comedies—or melodramas—and disasters when they were tragic or sentimental." Even the comedies, he states, cannot redeem the losses, and critics and the public alike know it. Cantwell observes that of about 200 movies projected each week on television in the Los Angeles area, no more than a dozen will concern sports. Why does Hollywood have such a poor batting average not just on baseball films but all sports films? Cantwell says simply that "Hollywood was never able to fuse hoke and sports in the way it fused hoke and every other human activity."[15] This is undeniable, of course, but there must be other reasons as well. I believe that the other very complex reasons can be best understood by comparing and contrasting the movies with other media.

Consider, for example, the correlation between photography and movies and single cartoons and comic strips. A cartoon, like a photograph, arrests a situation forever. The cartoonist, like the photographer, stops time and makes a statement with his subject, sometimes in satire, sometimes in praise as Deobold B. Van Dalen has shown in his article "Political Cartoons Employing Sports as a Communications Media." The cartoon and the photograph, then, exist in sacred time, while the film and the comic strip exist in entropy, or passing time. The motion picture and comic strip deal with the flow of events and tell a story. Hence both are more attuned to the harsh rhythms of the industrial age. The fact that people and objects in cartoons and photographs are still invites analysis and judgment, both of which require time on the part of the beholder. Movies and strips, however, ask not for judgment but for a suspension of disbelief, a totally irrelevant consideration as far as photographs are concerned. Thus, cartoons and photographs inherently possess greater potentials for evoking outrage, sentiment, admiration, amazement, piety, wonder, and finally meaning than do dramatic movies and strips. For example, no Hollywood spectacle of the life of Christ can evoke the feeling experienced by a single crucifixion scene by El Greco or Thomas Eakins or the description of the power of the *Pieta* in Chaim Potok's *My Name is Asher Lev*. The more color that is added in religious movies, as Hollywood invariably does, the more removed the movies become from anything sacred. It would seem that the sublime exists in black and white, a fact long lost on modern filmmakers. Sports, belonging to the kingdom of ends as Michael Novak has argued in *The Joy of Sports*, will not be mocked. Games, in the view of Marshall McLuhan's *Understanding the Media: The Extensions of Man*, are also a form of media, but media closer to the kingdom of ends than that of the movies. It is possible that sports can be served by the movies just as it is possible that the Bible can be, but it has never happened with the Bible and only rarely and recently with sports.

In his forthcoming book *The Movies Go to College: Hollywood and the World of the College-life Film*, Wiley Lee Umphlett takes a broader and more generous view of the significance of the movies on sports. The movies served, Umphlett argues, as a bridge between popular sports fiction at the turn of the century and the ubiquitous medium of television today. They prepared us, in other words, for the spectacle of the Big Game. Beyond that, though, and more importantly, they humanized the hero, usually a football player, by dramatizing the conflict between him and the system. Temporarily the hero may suffer setbacks at the hands of the system but eventually he wins out over all odds, his inherent worth finally visible to all just as had been the case with the young heroes of Gilbert Patten and others. Not only did the steady stream of college-life films from the twenties up into the forties, films such as *The Freshman* (1925) and *The Big Game* (1936), prepare Americans for the spectacle of the Big Game but they also filled us with the faith that the participants were essentially heroic individuals who would not sell out under any circumstances.

The truth is that neither movies nor television can do justice to the sports hero, a point well made in a superb book, entitled *Photographing Sports: John Zimmerman, Mark Kauffman, and Neil Leifer*, in the section entitled "Sharing the Life of the Hero" written by Sean Callahan, Gerald Astov, and the Alskog editors.

> The work of sports photographers is unique in that it compels us to look again at what we have seen before and know to be true. The game is familiar to all. The rules never change, the costumes are familiar, the route to victory is clear. Only the inevitable result is in doubt.
>
> Yet, in an era when more and more prime time television hours beam sports to millions, over two million people turn to *Sports Illustrated* magazine a week after the event to see how Mark Kauffman, John Zimmerman, Neil Leifer and their colleagues saw it. Sports pages sell many more million newspapers every day, especially when there is nothing more newsworthy on the front page. Smart editors of tabloids give sports photographs big play on the back page, where the reader automatically begins his perusal of the paper.[16]

While movies and video can show an event, they cannot tell the inner story. For that we need words to read and pictures to hold in our hands. Instant replay can help to recall what happened, but the significance of the action comes only with emotions recalled in tranquility, preferably with the aid of photographs by people who know what to look for, people like Zimmerman, Kaufman, and Leifer. Their work is an experience to behold.

Photographs and cartoons, much like print, serve to judge and indict, to celebrate and honor. Movies and strips may on occasion do the same, but their principal purpose is to entertain, perhaps to instruct. Their mode is ironic and mimetic while that of the cartoons and photographs is sentimental and romantic. "All photographs," says Susan Sontag in the introduction to *Portraits in Life and Death* by Peter Hujar, "embody a 'romantic' relation to reality." So does the cartoon. The romanticism Sontag has in mind is that of the poet Novalis, that which makes "the familiar appear strange, marvelous appear commonplace." She also says in a very quotable line: "Life is a movie. Death is a photograph." The statement suggests other parallels: Life is oral speech; death is the written word; life is a comic strip; death is a cartoon. It is the idea of death, as Ernest Becker has so brilliantly shown in *The Denial of Death*, that reminds us of tragedy and religion and inspires heroism. Photography, like literature, sobers us, announces us to ourselves, though stranger selves, but movies for the most part distract and deceive. All movies are staged, even those by Alain Robbe-Grillet, but the photograph, especially the sports photograph, is authentic. A good photograph may require hours of waiting for the right combination of hero and events, but the results are honest in contrast to the mimetic tricks of the movie director. The effects that a superb sports photographer like John Zimmerman achieves may appear sensational, for example an eight or ten feet arm of Dr. J. making a shot, but the attempt is not to create illusion for the sake of illusion but to reveal the marvel of athletic action.

Their romanticism and their attempt to reveal athletic action help to explain somewhat the role and place of cartoons, photographs, and comic strips in newspapers. Cartoons usually appear on the editorial page, which in turn is usually devoid of photographs. It is here that the social and political world is examined and contrasted with concepts of a better one. For this reason, cartoons are often expressions of outrage. When satirical, cartoons reflect a displacement from some center, from the combination of strength, beauty, and sanity.

Because of their traditional satiric role, cartoons derogating sports would be out of place on the sports pages, which reflect a world that is far from perfect but perhaps superior to that found in the "serious" part of the paper. When cartoons of sporting figures and scenes do appear on the sports page or elsewhere, they are usually kind and gentle, especially when compared to the running iconoclasm found on the editorial page. The cartoons in "Sports: Indoor and Outdoor" in *Comic Art in America* by Stephen Becker tend to confirm this observation. The satiric spirit of sports cartoons is usually Horatian, while the spirit of those on the editorial page is Juvenalian. Because we feel sports should be as free and pure as possible we separate them from the turmoil depicted elsewhere and and shield them whenever we can from the methods usually used to attack abuses in other fields. In fact one of the major criticisms of sports editors and writers is that they tend to ignore the abuses in their area of coverage in order to keep the benefits. Some years ago Ring Lardner proposed a simpler reason in a story entitled "Champion" in *How to Write Short Stories*. People, Lardner claimed, simply don't like to see the sports world dirtied up. The athlete hero of this bizarre tale, Midge Kelly, is a monster, but the story and the picture lay-out in the Sunday edition of the "New York News" make him appear to be an all-American boy. According to Lardner, had the reporter presented a more accurate version, the sports editor would have objected: " 'Suppose you can prove it,' that gentleman would have said, 'it wouldn't get us anything but abuse to print it. The people don't want to see him knocked. He's champion.' "[17]

It is not, then, so much that sportswriters want free tickets as it is that the public needs at least one part of the paper to reflect an idealized world free of war, politics, arson, and murder. Sports, we feel, *ought* to be clean, and most of us want them that way. We want some field of human enterprise that remains decent and relatively pure as a relief from the daily wear and tear. No one has expressed this need better than Robert Frost in "A Day of Prowess:"

> Prowess of course comes first, the ability to perform with success in games, in the arts and, come right down to it, in battle. The nearest of kin to the artists in college where we all become bachelors of arts are their fellow performers in baseball, football, and tennis. That's why I am so particular college athletics should be kept from corruption. They are close to the soul of culture. At any rate the Greeks thought so.[18]

For the most part, society wants all athletics, amateur and professional, kept free of corruption, which is why the picture lay-outs in Sunday papers almost invariably attempt to depict some degree of heroism. Even face shots are meaningful. The picture of a Joe Dimaggio or Pete Rose during a hitting streak has a significance for the sports fan, and so does the picture of the starting quarterback for a Class A high-school football team. In other words, the photographs on the sports page deal with heroes who are engaged in the drama of ring, diamond, gridiron, turf, or whatever. Sports photography praises and records the deeds of performers; it elevates, as it were, the moment of action to the status of epiphany. A look at any daily newspaper will, I believe, support this contention, but if additional evidence is needed, one need only to look at the photographs appearing in *An Illustrated History of the Olympics* by Dick Schapp or in *Man in Sport: An International Exhibition of Photography* directed by Robert Riger and published by the Baltimore Museum of Art.

The comic strip is another medium with its own peculiar message. The characters again provide variations on a mode, but the mode is invariably low mimetic as opposed to the romanticism of photography. While comic heroes may be ageless and have eternal life in their strips, they live one day at a time like the rest of us. Hence, the worlds they inhabit are flawed, a world diametrically opposed to that of sports where rules are clear, the umpires always just, and the grounds clean and well kept. Still there is an overlap between sports and comics, and in *Jock Culture, U.S.A.*, Neil D. Isaacs notes the encroachment of the one on the other.

As pervasive as sports are in the substance, texture, and framework of written narrative, they are even more influential in the fictions of movies, television, and comic strips. The most casual glance at these forms should register their preoccupation with sports. Here too the three phases of mythologizing, demythologizing and remythologizing exist simultaneously. On the same page, for example, one may find crew-cut Gil Thorpe applying the ancient verities of sport to his contemporary social problems, the on target satire of "Tank McNamara" shooting holes in all the pious traditions of the norts spews, and a primitive attempt to encompass a contemporary sports ethic in the unlikely figure of Milton Caniff's Stalky Schweisenberg.[19]

What Isaacs says about mythologizing, demythologizing, and remythologizing is certainly true, and no better example of the process can be found in literature and comics than in the polar relationship of Burt L. Standish's (Gilbert Patten) Frank Merriwell and Ring Lardner's Busher Keefe, one a school boy hero, the other a parody of the hero. Both were at one time comic strip figures as well as literary ones. Standish, believing the dime novel to be on its way out, wrote the first Merriwell story in 1896 and thus gave impetus to the new American mythology of the athlete hero. In 1914 at about the same time that Frank disappeared from the pages of *Tip Top Weekly* after a seventeen-year run, Lardner brought out Busher Keefe. Intentionally or unintentionally, Lardner was demythologizing the cult of the all-round man that had been symbolized by Frank Merriwell, Teddy Roosevelt, Jack London and others. In 1934 Patten resurrected Frank in the comics, drawn by Jack Wilhelm,[20] but with no more real success in remythologizing than Lardner had with Busher Keefe, drawn by Dick Dorgan in the same medium.[21] Frank Merriwell and Busher Keefe are the antithesis of each other, their fortunes waxing and waning with public taste, yet neither could endure in the comics. Indeed the appearance of any celebrity, athlete or not, in the comics generally is the last step in the mythologizing, demythologizing, and remythologizing cycle.

One can almost count on one hand the number of athletes that have been comic strip heroes, although almost all heroes are in some way athletic. A perusal of *The Great Comic Book Heroes* by Jules Feiffer shows just how athletic the super heroes really are. The comic strip Superman has a torso close to that of Michelangelo's Adam; the movie Superman is closer to that of his David. Both have strength, beauty, and goodness. The same can be said of Captain Marvel, who embodies the ancient epic ideal of wisdom and strength (*sapientia et fortitudo*), which is evident in Billy Batson's magic acronym, SHAZAM, "S" for the wisdom of Solomon, "H" for the strength of Heracles, and so forth. Superman is born strong (by earthly standards), and Captain Marvel has his strength bestowed upon him, but Bruce Wayne must develop his own strength. Spurred by the horror of seeing his parents murdered by a robber, he prepares himself to be a scientist and "trains his body to physical perfection until he is able to perform amazing athletic feats."[22] The same formula of strength, beauty, speed, and goodness holds for all the others. Beneath all the flames, Torch has a superb physique, and when the Flash slows down enough for ordinary mortals to see him, he too is something to behold. He may not be as strong as Superman, but he is just as fast, and his intentions are just as honorable. The Green Lantern, the Spectre, and the Hawk are superb specimens. All of them would be winners in decathlons with members of the ordinary race of men. When he is not stretched out, Plastic Man fits the familiar mold and so do the Spirit, Captain America, and Sub-Mariner. The most beautiful of all is Wonder Woman, who is just as strong as any of her male counterparts. In the selection given in the Feiffer book she is pitted against Mammotha, who looks like the Farnese Hercules come to life. Wonder Woman wins not because she is a woman but because she personifies strength and beauty. Unlike Mammotha, her muscles do not get in her way. As he fans the air, she gets "on her bicycle" out of harm's way until she is ready for the knockout punch. She too "floats like a butterfly and stings like a bee." Muhummad Ali may be the greatest but he was not the first. There is no way of judging how much good the comics have done for mankind. Any child who took them seriously—and many children did—wanted to be strong and brave and fair.

Still athletes *qua* athletes are a minor breed in comics. In the section entitled "The Sports Strip" in *The Comics: An Illustrated History of Comic Strip Art*, Jerry Robinson states:

> Sports, like the movies and the comics, had its golden age, and this was it. Each sport seemed to produce a towering figure that dominated the era. Baseball had Babe Ruth; golf, Bobby Jones; football, Red Grange; tennis, Bill Tilden; and boxing, Jack Dempsey. The comics would seem to be the perfect medium for a sports adventure story, yet no strip had emerged with an athlete as its central figure. In 1930, Ham Fisher after years of trying to sell a boxing strip, launched Joe Palooka.[23]

Later Robinson adds, "Despite the success of Palooka, no rash of sports strips followed, as often happens in syndication." There were other strips featuring athletes, *Curley Kayoe, Ned Brandt, Ozark Ike,* and *Big Ben Bolt,* but Joe Palooka was "the greatest" until Muhummad Ali entered the scene with his own television cartoon and movies.

In "A Champ for All Time," which appears in *Sport and Society,* edited by Talamini and Page, Robert Boyle says Palooka is "the American dream come true. He is strong but modest, manly but virtuous, tolerant but principled. He would never think of wrestling cops much less of drinking."[24]

Joe, perfect as he is, has problems, as Boyle states near the end of his article:

> Joe is still heavyweight champ, but he hasn't put on the gloves in years. He leads a nice suburban life, but it is a dull one to many readers. Instead of boxing, he goes skiing with Knobby or bluefishing with Leemy. Sometimes he takes the kids sledding. Joe still looks as fit as he did in the past—if anything, his shoulders have broadened—but he lacks the zip. Gone are the plots of the prize ring. The villains of yesteryear are no more. Life seems drab for Joe and even for Ann. The strip is stale. Happily, there is some talk that Joe may soon return to the ring.[25]

Anyone with some understanding of media and modern life will understand the situation immediately. Joe has joined the dreary world with the rest of us, and while we would allow this for most comic strip characters, we won't allow it for athletes. Joe must either return to the ring or die.

The ring, not suburbia, is a place for heroes, and while the ring itself is out of place in a comic strip because it belongs to the idealized world of sport, its champions may occasionally move into another genre to battle with villains attempting to make the sporting milieu like the rest of the world. Joe did return to the ring after Boyle's article, and while that decision was enough to save him, it was not really enough to count. "The strip," says Bill Blackbeard in *The World Encyclopedia of Comics*, edited by Maurice Horn, "has now reached an even keel, on a minor level of popularity...."[26] Even Joe Palooka cannot constantly bridge the basically antagonistic gap between the world of comics and the world of sport; nor can Muhummad Ali. Ali now has been in at least two movies. He also has been the subject of a TV cartoon and comic strip in which he is pitted against Superman in the ring.[27] But Ali truly remains "the greatest" in the astounding photography in *Muhammad Ali: A Portrait in Words and Photographs* by Wilfred Sheed.

Although every high school and college in America has a fight song and a few tunes, such as "Take Me Out to the Ball Game," have become popular classics, there has not been a strong relationship between sports and music. John R. Betts lists several popular songs with sporting themes in his *America's Sporting Heritage, 1850-1950* but concludes that "popular music has paid only passing attention to sport...."[28] The fact that sports and music have not had a happy marriage is ironic since in ancient Greece music was a symbol for half of the Greek ideal of education in which the other half was "gymnastic."

Still, from one point of view, music and sports, especially football, are inseparable, for better or for worse. We simply do not know and probably will never know what effect each has had upon the other. The half-time band show is an American tradition, and we can only imagine what other directions high-school band music might have taken if football had not been so popular. Without football there might have been no band at all in many places. The cultural implications of the kinship between band and football would be worth extended study if one could determine an approach to the problem or even define the problem. A number of studies have been done on this subject and other aspects of music and sports and can be discovered in *The Music Index* under the heading of "Sports" and related topics. It is surprising, however, that there has not been a major study of these two art forms that virtually engulf us every day. Only the weather is more pervasive.

Researchers interested in popular music and other popular art forms such as cartoons, comics, and films, should consult the standard reference works discussed in the appropriate sections of *Handbooks of American Popular Culture*, edited by M. Thomas Inge, and the in-depth refererence series, also edited by Inge, of which this work is one. Works on the relationship between sports and other popular arts are surprisingly few in many cases, but it is always desirable to approach an area of interest from as many different angles as may be productive.

It is far too easy to overlook philately in a discussion of sports and popular culture. The themes depicted on stamps are invariably intended to be representative of the achievements or aspirations of nations. Almost without exception the athletes depicted on stamps have had the same physiques as comic book heroes or the athletes of Myron or Polyclitus. They carry the implied message of strength, beauty, health, courage, prowess, prosperity, and the good life.

They are created not only to honor the athlete or sports in general but also to inspire the citizens in the country of issue to be stronger, faster, and better. To the best of my knowledge there is only one book on the subject of stamps and sports, *Sports Stamps* by Carl-Olaf Enhagen. It appears to be an extremely thorough book, but it is more of a manual or a catalog for collectors. As such it is invaluable. If there is a flaw in the book, it is the absence of any interpretation of the themes and the symbolism depicted on the stamps. There have been, he says, "many articles on the subject" in the philatelic press, which he has attempted to collect and present as fairly as possible. A bibliography of the more important of these articles, which he says have been "various" and "contradictory," would be a great help to his readers. However, a serious sports stamp collector would not want to be without this book and probably would want to join Sports Philatelists International. This organization publishes the *Journal of Sports Philately* and sponsors other activities (see section 13 of *Encyclopedia of Organizations*). Sports philately is a recent hobby, as Enhagen points out. The first issue appeared in 1896 in Greece in connection with the reopening of the

Olympic Games, but it is a form of sports art that is growing steadily with the interest in games. Collectors should not forget, however, that the postage stamp can be a special and powerful form of propaganda, or what Jürgen Moltmann calls a "drilled-in morality." According to Moltmann in his *Theology of Play*, "Modern dictators are fond of sponsoring sports events; they subsidize highly trained professionals with whom the people can identify and who can become an object of the people's pride. For the more peace-loving there is stamp collecting with a wide assortment of special issues in constant supply."[29] What is on stamps makes a difference, and it would be well if buyers remembered this as well as those who design them.

What is evident in a survey of sports and related arts is that the alliance between sports and sculpture is alive, though certainly not flourishing; that both adult and juvenile literature abound with sporting themes; that movies and comics as a rule have not successfully used the heroic materials of sports; and that sports have had suprisingly little impact on popular music. The art forms most successful in capturing the heroics in sports are the sports articles and pictures that make up the sports pages, which are in turn reflections of an idealized world with clear-cut rules and clean, enthusiastic players. This is also true of sports philately, an expanding art form related to the sports picture. Because movies and comics are realistic modes, especially when compared to photographs and cartoons, they tend to cheapen the purer art forms of sports. Movies and comics succeed best in mirroring ordinary life, which is not art at all but pure chaos. Sports are not chaotic, but artistic. As Erich Segal said in an excellent review entitled "Strength Not Art obtains the Prize" of H. D. Harris's book *Greek Athletes and Athletics* in *The Yale Review*, "athletics is more than history. It is also philosophy and art."[30]

The fact that sports are art does not mean that they cannot be degraded and dehumanized. José Ortega y Gasset did not posit sports against art because they are different modes of activity but because he believed that modern sports have become a dehumanized form of art. In *Velasquez, Goya, and The Dehumanization of Art* he writes:

Modern art begins to be understandable, acquiring a certain element of greatness when it is interpreted as an attempt to instill youthfulness into an ancient world. Other styles insisted on being associated with dramatic social or political upheavals or with profound philosophical or religious currents. The new style, on the contrary, asks to be associated with the triumph of sports and games. It shares the same origins with them.

In the space of a few years, we have seen the tidal wave of sport all but overwhelming the pages of our newspapers that bear serious news. Articles of depth threaten to sink into the abyss their name implies, while the yachts of the regattas skim victoriously over the surface. The cult of the body eternally speaks of youthful inspiration, because it is only beautiful and agile in youth, while the cult of the mind implies an acceptance of growing old, because it only achieves full maturity when the body has begun to fail. The triumph of sport signifies the victory of the values of youth over the values of old age. The same is true of cinema, which is *par excellence* a group art.[31]

It is interesting to note that Ortega y Gasset associates the rise of mass sport with the emergence of the cult of youth and the prominence of the cinema. All three have one thing in common—mindlessness, or the orgiastic celebration of life. To lament this trend is to reveal one's age and to raise the suspicion of elitism. Although Ortega is an aristocrat, he is definitely not fascistic. Nor is he stodgy. The idea of "sport" is central to his concept of life, as Nelson Robert Orringer points out in the abstract of his Brown University dissertation in 1969:

> Like Huizinga's *Spel*, "sport" possesses both Dionysian and Apollonian attributes. But play as described in *Homo Ludens* is separated temporally and spatially from the sphere of routine; whereas "sport" may take place in any arena of life. Ortega thereby denotes a "program of living" dedicated to the cheerful but disciplined translation of existent fatality into liberty. . . .
>
> At its root, Ortega's ludic conception of life is a moral one. When man lives in continued fidelity to his personal destiny, he is "noble," always surmounting his own accomplishments and spontaneously attracting others by his example. Sportive excellence gives rise to norms in every sphere of life and to such institutions as the tribe, the polis, the nation-state, and liberal democracy. Currently, though, the masses threaten to stifle the spontaneous efforts of their superiors. To save the Western world, Ortega proposes a "United States of Europe," a new discipline like those of old, which align the multitudes behind their true captains and keep them all "in trim."[32]

To read such phrases as keeping the multitudes "in trim" and "aligned" behind their "true captains" causes one to shudder when considering the tyrannies of the twentieth century. Like Nietzsche, who worshipped the ancient and aristocratic ideal of strength and beauty and by whom Ortega was influenced, Ortega is easily misunderstood. For this reason, it is essential to remember his dedication to individualism, his reputation as a humanist, and his concern for the quality of life. There are two types of sports for Ortega' the concept of sports and the actual "tidal wave" of sports that has uprooted the older traditions. The clear implication is that Europe and the world would be better if the two, concept and actuality, were not so estranged.

NOTES

1. Percy N. Tannebaum and James E. Noah, "Sportugese: A Study of Sports Page Communication," in *Sport, Culture, and Society: A Reader on the Sociology of Sport*, ed. John W. Loy, Jr. and Gerald S. Kenyon (London: Macmillan & Co., 1969), p. 328.

2. "Talk of the Town," *New Yorker* 34 (June 21, 1958), 21.

3. Edwin Newman, *Strictly Speaking* (Indianapolis: Bobbs-Merrill, 1974), pp. 149-50.

4. Ibid., p. 156.

5. Ibid.

6. Larry Merchant, . . . *And Every Day You Take Another Bite* (New York: Doubleday, 1971), p. 167.

7. Howard Cosell, *Like It Is* (Chicago: Playboy Press, 1974), pp. 204-5.

8. Michael Novak, *The Joy of Sports: End Zones, Bases, Baskets, Balls, and the Consecration of the American Spirit* (New York: Basic Books, 1976), p. 280.

9. Robert Taft, *Photography and the American Scene: A Social History, 1839-1889* (New York: Dover Publications, 1938), p. 410.

10. Gordon Hendricks, *The Life and Works of Thomas Eakins* (New York: Grossman Publishers, 1974), p. 217.

11. Reuel Denney, *The Astonished Muse* (Chicago: University of Chicago Press, 1974), pp. 111-12.

12. Ken Wlaschin, "The Olympics on Film," in *The Olympic Games: 80 Years of People, Events, and Records*, eds. Lord Killanin and John Rodda (New York: Macmillan Co., 1976), p. 165.

13. Ibid.

14. The ten best sport movies of all time, according to Rex Reed, are: *The Stratton Story, Visions of Eight, Pride of the Yankees, Pat and Mike, Fat City, Bang the Drum Slowly, Requiem for a Heavy weight, Champion, Downhill Racer* and *The Hustler*. The ten worst are: *Take Me out to the Ball Game, Jim Thorpe—All American, One on One, Slap Shot, The Babe Ruth Story, The Endless Summer, Golden Boy, Knute Rockne—All American, Angels in the Outfield*, and *The Great American Pastime*. See Phil Pepe and Zander Hollander, "A List of Lists that Will Delight, Tease, and Even Infuriate," *Sports Illustrated*, 30 April 1979, p. 80.

15. Robert Cantwell, "Sport was Box Office Poison," in *Sport and Society: An Anthology*, ed. John H. Talamini and Charles H. Page (Boston: Little, Brown, & Co., 1973), pp. 450, 454.

16. *Photographing Sports: John Zimmerman, Mark Kauffman, and Neil Leifer*, text by Sean Callahan and Gerald Astor with the editors of Alskog (New York: Alskog/Crowell, 1975), p. 14.

17. Ring Lardner, *How to Write Short Stories* (New York: Scribner, 1925), p. 178.

18. Robert Frost, "A Day of Prowess," in *Selected Prose of Robert Frost*, ed. Hyde Cox and Edward Connery Lathem (New York: Collier Books, 1966), p. 91.

19. Neil D. Isaacs, *Jock Culture U.S.A.* (New York: W. W. Norton, 1978), pp. 78-79. For a comprehensive and enjoyable picture of Tank McNamara's encounter with the sports world, see *The Tank McNamara Chronicles* by Jeff Millar and Bill Hinds (Kansas City, Kan.: Sheed Andrews and McMeel, 1978).

20. Albert Johannsen, *The House of Beadle and Adams*, 2 vols. (Norman: The University of Oklahoma Press, 1950), 2: 223.

21. See Donald J. Elder, *Ring Lardner: A Biography* (New York: Doubleday,

1956), pp. 176-77. See also *Ring Lardner's You Know Me Al: The Comic Strip Adventures of Jack Keefe* (New York: Harcourt, Brace, Jovanovich/Bruccoli Clark, 1979).

22. Jules Feiffer, *The Great Comic Book Heroes* (New York: Bonanza Books, 1965), p. 70.

23. Jerry Robinson, *The Comics: An Illustrated History of Comic Strip Art* (New York: G. P. Putnam's Sons, 1974), pp. 122-23.

24. Robert Boyle, "A Champ for All Time," in *Sport and Society*, p. 433.

25. Ibid., p. 441.

26. Bill Blackbeard, *The World Encyclopedia of Comics*, 2 vols. (New York: Chelsea House, 1976), vol. 1, ed. Maurice Horn, p. 344.

27. See *Superman vs. Muhammad Ali: The Fight to Save Earth from Star-Warriors* (New York: DC Comics, Inc., 1978).

28. John R. Betts, *America's Sporting Heritage, 1850-1950* (Reading, Mass.: Addison-Wesley Publishing Co., 1974), p. 368.

29. Jürgen Moltmann, *Theology of Play* (New York: Harper and Row, 1971), p. 7.

30. Erich Segal, "It is Not Strength, But Art, Obtains the Prize," *The Yale Review* 46 (June 1967), 608.

31. José Ortega y Gasset, *Velazquez, Goya, and the Dehumanization of Art* (New York: W. W. Norton, 1972), pp. 81-82.

32. Nelson Robert Orringer, "Sport and Festival: A Study of Ludic Theory in Ortega y Gasset," Ph.D. diss., Brown University, 1969. Quotation from *Dissertation Abstracts International*, 31-A (Ann Arbor: University Microfilms, 1970), p. 364.

BIBLIOGRAPHY

Becker, Ernest. *The Denial of Death*. New York: Free Press, 1973.

Becker, Stephen. *Comic Art in America*. New York: Simon and Schuster, 1959.

Betts, John R. *America's Sporting Heritage, 1850-1950*. Reading, Mass.: Addison-Wesley Publishing Co., 1974.

Blythe, Hal, and Charlie Sweet. "Some Simple Steps to Stardom in the TV Sports Booth." Lexington (Ky.) *Herald Leader*, 3 September 1978, sec. C, p. 1.

Broun, Heywood Hale. *Tumultuous Merriment*. New York: Richard Marek, 1979.

Cosell, Howard. *Like It Is*. Chicago: Playboy Press, 1974.

Cozens, Frederick W., and Florence S. Stumpf. *Sports in American Life*. 1953. Reprint. New York: Arno Press, 1976.

Denny, Reuel. *The Astonished Muse*. Chicago: University of Chicago Press, 1974.

Edwards, Harry. *The Revolt of the Black Athlete*. New York: Free Press, 1969.

Elder, Donald. *Ring Lardner: A Biography*. New York: Doubleday, 1956.

Encyclopedia of Associations. 16th ed. Detroit: Gale Research Co., 1981.

Enhagen, Carl-Olaf. *Sports Stamps*. New York: Arco Publishing Co., 1961.

Eschholz, Paul, Alfred Rosa, and Virginia Clark, eds. *Language Awareness*. New York: St. Martin's Press, 1978.

Esquire. Super Sports Issue. October 1974.

Esquire. Special Issue: The Joy of Sports. October 1975.

Feiffer, Jules. *The Great Comic Book Heroes*. New York: Borranga Books, 1965.

Frost, Robert. "A Day of Prowess." In *Selected Prose of Robert Frost*, edited by Hyde Cox and Edward Connery Lathem. New York: Collier Books, 1966.

Hendricks, Gordon. *The Life and Work of Thomas Eakins.* New York: Grossman, 1974.

Hinton, David B., and Susan Sontag. "An Exchange on Leni Riefenstahl." *New York Review of Books*, 18 September 1975, pp. 58-60.

Hollander, Zander, ed. *The Encyclopedia of Sports Talk.* New York: Corwin Books, 1976.

Horn, Maurice, ed. *The World Encyclopedia of Comics.* 2 vols. New York: Chelsea House, 1976.

Hujar, Peter. *Portraits in Life and Death.* Introduction by Susan Sontag. New York: Da Capo Press, 1976.

Hunt, William S. *Frank Forester (William Henry Herbert): A Tragedy in Exile.* Newark, N.J.: Carteret Book Club, 1933.

Infield, Glen B. *Leni Riefenstahl: The Fallen Film Goddess.* New York: Crowell, 1976.

Inge, M. Thomas, ed. *Handbook of American Popular Culture.* 3 vols. Westport, Conn.: Greenwood Press, 1978-1981.

Isaacs, Neil D. *Jock Culture U.S.A.* New York: W. W. Norton, 1978.

Johannsen, Albert. *The House of Beadle and Adams.* 2 vols. Norman: University of Oklahoma Press, 1950.

Journal of Sports Philately. Indianapolis: Sports Philatelists International, 1962-.

Killanin, Lord, and John Rodda, eds. *The Olympic Games: 80 Years of People, Events, and Records.* New York: Macmillan Co., 1976.

Lardner, Ring. *How to Write Short Stories.* New York: Scribner, 1925.

Loy, John W., Jr., and Gerald S. Kenyon, eds., *Sport, Culture and Society: A Reader on the Sociology of Sport.* London: Macmillan & Co., 1969.

McLuhan, Marshall. *Understanding Media: The Extensions of Man.* New York: New American Library, 1964.

Mencken, H. L. *The American Language: An Inquiry into the Development of English in the United States*, Supplement II. New York: Alfred A. Knopf, 1965-67.

Merchant, Larry. *....And Every Day You Take Another Bite.* New York: Doubleday, 1971.

Millar, Jeff, and Bill Hinds. *The Tank McNamara Chronicles.* Kansas City, Kan.: Sheed Andrews and McMeel, 1978.

Moltmann, Jürgen. *Theology of Play.* New York: Harper and Row, 1973.

Mott, Frank Luther. *American Journalism: A History, 1660-1960.* 3d ed. New York: Macmillan Co., 1962.

Newman, Edwin. *Strictly Speaking.* Indianapolis: Bobbs-Merrill, 1974.

Novak, Michael. *The Joy of Sports: End Zones, Bases, Baskets, Balls, and the Consecration of the American Spirit.* New York: Basic Books, 1976.

Orringer, Robert Nelson. "Sport and Festival: A Study of Ludic Theory in Ortega y Gasset." Ph.D. dissertation, Brown University, 1969.

Ortega y Gasset, José. *Velazquez, Goya, and The Dehumanization of Art.* Translated by Alex Brown, with an introduction by Philip Troutman. New York: W. W. Norton, 1972.

Partridge, Eric. *Slang, Today and Yesterday.* 4th ed., New York: Barnes and Noble, 1970.

Pepe, Phil, and Zander Hollander. "A List of Lists that Will Delight, Tease, and Even Infuriate." *Sports Illustrated*, 30 April 1979, pp. 76-80.

Photographing Sports: John Zimmerman, Mark Kauffman, and Neil Leifer. Text by
    Sean Callahan and Gerald Astor. New York: Alskog/Crowell, 1975.

Rice, Grantland. *The Tumult and the Shouting: My Life in Sport.* New York: A. S.
    Barnes, 1954.

Riefenstahl, Leni. *The Last of the Nuba.* New York: Harper and Row, 1974.

Riger, Robert. Director. *Man in Sport: An International Exhibition of Photography.*
    Baltimore: The Baltimore Museum of Art, 1969.

Ring Lardner's You Know Me Al: The Comic Strip Adventures of Jack Keefe. New
    York: Harcourt, Brace, Jovanovich/Bruccoli Clark, 1979.

Robinson, Jerry. *The Comics: An Illustrated History of Comic Strip Art.* New
    York: G. P. Putnam's Sons, 1974.

Schaap, Dick. *An Illustrated History of the Olympics.* New York: Alfred A. Knopf,
    1975.

Segal, Erich. "It is not Strength, But Art, Obtains the Prize." *The Yale Review* 46
    (June 1967), 605-9.

Sheed, Wilfrid. *Muhammad Ali: A Portrait in Words and Photographs.* New York:
    Crowell, 1975.

Sontag, Susan. "Fascinating Fascism." *New York Review of Books*, 6 February
    1975, pp. 23-30.

Superman vs. Muhammad Ali: The Fight to Save Earth from Star-Warriors. New
    York: DC Comics, 1978.

Taft, Robert. *Photography and the American Scene: A Social History, 1839-1889.*
    New York: Dover Publications, 1938.

Talamini, John T., and Charles H. Page, eds. *Sport and Society: An Anthology.*
    Boston: Little, Brown, & Co., 1973.

"Talk of the Town." *The New Yorker* 34 (June 21, 1958), 21.

Umphlett, Wiley Lee. *Hollywood and the World of the College-life Film The Movies
    Go To College.* Madison, N.J.: Fairleigh Dickinson University Press (A divi-
    sion of Associated University Presses), 1982.

Van Dalen, Deobold B. "Political Cartoons Employing Sports as a Communication
    Media." *Canadian Journal of History of Sport and Physical Education*, 47
    (October 1976), 39-57.

Woodward, Stanley. *Sports Page.* 1949. Reprint. Westport, Conn.: Greenwood
    Press, 1968.

Yates, Norris W. *William T. Porter and the Spirit of the Times: A Study of the "Big
    Bear" School of Humor.* Baton Rouge: Louisiana State University Press,
    1957.

CHAPTER 5

Sports and Education

What José Ortega y Gasset calls the "triumph of sport" has occurred in large measure through the schools. Although today the media is probably the most obvious promoter of sport, American sports in their early days, especially in the last part of the nineteenth century, would never have become so widespread and accepted had it not been for the influence, good or bad, of the academies. Sports and education like sports and art, have had an uneasy relationship through the centuries, but one can understand that relationship it is necessary to understand the attraction and repulsion that exist between them.

In his novel, *Joiner*, James Whitehead coins the terms "mod" and "bindy" in his attempt to show that *body* and *mind* are bound inseparably. Thus, the question for societies has always been, what is the best way or ways for opposites (or *apparent* opposites) of body and mind to coexist? That there is a tension between them is undeniable, but there is also a clear desire for harmony.

To the Greeks of the fifth century B.C. the best combination could be attained through the application of severe standards for both body and mind, which in turn serve the soul. As Socrates explained to Glaucon in the *Republic*:

> "And as there are two principles of human nature, one the spirited and the other the philosophical, some God, as I should say, has given mankind two arts answering to them (and only indirectly to the soul and body), in order that these two principles (like the strings of an instrument) may be relaxed or drawn tighter until they are duly harmonized."
>
> "That appears to be the intention."
>
> "And he who mingles music with gymnastic in the fairest proportions, and best attempers them to the soul, may be rightly called the true musician and harmonist in a far higher sense than the tuner of the strings."
>
> "You are quite right, Socrates."[1]

This dialogue is one of the most important in the Western world, for from it derives the ideal of Western education: the integration of the body and the mind in the service of the soul. Indeed, this tripartite concept of the essence of man has been the subject of thousands of lectures in school chapels throughout the Western world.

The Greek ideal of education, "music and gymnastic," was, as E. Norman Gardiner has shown in *Athletics of the Ancient World*, inseparable from the athletic ideal, "strength and beauty." These terms bear a striking similarity to the epic formula *sapientia et fortitudo* (wisdom and strength) and Juvenal's *mens sana in corpore sano*. All reveal the desirability of uniting the body and mind through the right combination of gymnastic and music, which included, as Rachel Sargent Robinson points out in *Sources for the History of Greek Athletics*, "reading, writing, mathematics, harmony, poetry, drawing, and music in its narrowest sense."[2] Music and gymnastics together formed not just the goal of Greek education but the Greek view of the world.

The degree to which the Greeks succeeded in integrating the mind and body depends upon one's point of view. There was certainly a divergence of views on exactly what role sports should play in education and society, and there were a number of dissenters. Isocrates claimed:

> Many times have I wondered at those who first convoked the national assemblies and established the athletic games, amazed that they should have thought the power of men's bodies to be deserving of so great bounties, while to those who had toiled in private for the public good and trained their own minds so as to be able to help also their fellow men, they apportioned no reward whatsoever, when in all reason they ought rather to have made provision for the latter, for if all the athletes would acquire twice the strength they now possess, the rest of the world would not be better off, but let a single man attain to wisdom and all men will reap the benefit who are willing to share his insight.[3]

The attitude toward sports in school and society from the fifth century B.C. to the present rarely has been based on antipathy toward them but on the concept of balance. Galen (A.D. 130-200), the most distinguished physician of antiquity, pointed out beneficial results of a variety of exercises for developing strength, speed, and agility. He was also one of the first to find great worth in a game of ball in which players on opposite sides of a playing area worked to prevent a man in the middle from "snatching the ball away." Robinson's *Sources for the History of Greek Athletics* identifies several passages on athletics in Galen who in typical Greek fashion believed that exercise and games "not only exercise the body but bring delight to the mind"; that moderation should be practiced at all times ("Lack of moderation I everywhere condemn, and I maintain that every art should practice moderation; whatever lacks moderation is not good. Therefore I do not approve of running, for it wears a man down thin and furnishes no training in bravery''); and that games should be democratic and should develop mental excellence as well as physical. Most important of all, however, was his absolute insistence that games should not become ends in themselves and that the participant should not degenerate into an athlete.[4]

Galen viewed sports as an art only up to the point of specialization. After this point he felt that they became a spectacle rather than an art. Although, as Robinson states, Galen's rabid denouncement of athletes may have been "an exaggerated, sarcastic account of current tendencies in athletics,"[5] some of his ideas, even if they appear exaggerated and superseded in some ways, are still astonishingly relevant in other ways. According to E. Norman Gardiner in *Greek Athletic Sports and Festivals,*

> When we come to Galen, we seem to pass from the free and open atmosphere of the playing-field and country into the artificial air of the town gymnasium. The simple exercises of the earlier period... have given place to a scientific system of physical training based on the teaching of generations of gymnastai.... There is little in our modern systems of physical education which we will not find anticipated in Greek medical writings.[6]

Unlike the Greeks, the Romans, as Eugene W. Nixon and Frederick W. Cozens point out in *An Introduction to Physical Education,* contributed little to physical education. Their sports were almost entirely spectator sports or were designed for the military service of the state. They helped to provide bread and circuses and hardened legions for the emperors. As far as sports were concerned, the Middle Ages were indeed a "dark" time. Although during this period archery, football, and tennis began to develop into popular sports and pastimes, scholasticism and asceticism, as Nixon and Cozens observe, dominated medieval life. Scholasticism, while glorifying the achievements of the mind, pays little attention, or disdains totally, the possibilities of the body. Similarly, asceticism, as Nixon and Cozens state, "sets the soul and body in opposition and finds it necessary to degrade the latter in order to glorify the former."[7]

The Renaissance is noted for its rediscovery of the past, of art and learning, in short the mind. It also is noted for its rediscovery of the body, as even a cursory study of Renaissance painting and sculpture will indicate. As the glorification of the body began to reappear in the art of the time, it gradually assumed its old place in the scheme of education, which was principally for aristocrats. By the sixteenth century Roger Ascham in *The Schoolmaster* was lamenting the stereotyping that had come to be associated with scholars, the legacy of scholaticism:

And how can a comely body be better employed, then to serve the fairest exercise of God's greatest gift and that is learning. But commonly, the fairest bodies are bestowed on the foulest purposes. I would it were not so.... For, if a father have four sons, three fair and well formed both mind and body, the fourth, wretched, lame, and deformed, his choice shall be to put the worst to learning, as one good enough to become a scholar. I have spent the most part of my life in the university, and therefore I can bear good witness that many fathers commonly do thus....[8]

Indirectly Ascham was calling for the rebirth of *mens sana in corpore sano*, as John Milton did directly in his essay "Of Education" almost a century later. Milton's curriculum included "necessary rules of some good grammar," readings from the ancients for imitation and example, the study of agriculture, medicine, and a series of exercises and recreations that "may but agree and become these studies."[9] The exercises, which were to be performed an hour and a half before lunch, began with the use of weapons and wrestling. Milton also wanted to reinstitute the ancient concept of music and gymnastics in its most literate sense. In Milton's plan music was a part of education, especially after the exercise and before and after the noon meal.

> The interim of unsweating themselves regularly, and convenient rest before meat, may both with profit and delight be taken up in recreating and composing their travailed spirits with the solemn and divine harmonies of music, heard or learned; either while the skillful organist plies his grave and fancied descant in lofty fugues, or the whole symphony with artful and unimaginable touches adorn and grace the well-studied chords of some choice composer; sometimes the lute or soft organ-stop waiting on elegant voices, either to religious, martial, or civil ditties; which, if wise men and prophets be not extremely out, have a great power over dispositions and manners, to smooth and make them gentle from rustic harshness and distempered passions. The like also would not be unexpedient after meat to assist and cherish nature in her first concoction, and send their minds back to study in good time and satisfaction.[10]

Thus, the *mens sana in corpore sano* philosophy began to come into bloom in the late Renaissance in England, but it did not fully flower until the Victorian period, as Bruce E. Haley shows in *The Healthy Body and Victorian Culture*. Even during the Victorian era, there was disagreement over what proportions of body and mind should make up the whole person. Haley, for example, points to the erroneous twentieth-century belief that

Thomas Arnold supported athleticism and believed in the psychological value of sport. "Nowhere in *Tom Brown* is it suggested that he actively promoted games or saw any moral value in them.... [T]he ultimate goal of Arnold's system of education, was to develop manliness, by which he meant maturity of mind, not body."[11]

Dr. Arnold may not have been an advocate of sporting values, but others in positions of influence felt that sports were indeed necessary for the complete man and the well-rounded life. For example, in his inaugural address at Harvard College on October 19, 1869, President Charles William Eliot, almost as if he had Theodore Roosevelt in mind, called for the education of "the aristocracy which excels in manly sports, carries off the honors and prizes of the learned professions, and bears itself with distinction in all fields of intellectual labor and combat; the aristocracy which in peace stands for the public honor and renown, and in war rides first into the murderous thicket."[12]

Thus, in less than a decade after its revival in England the philosophy of *mens sana in corpore sano* found its way across the seas. With it arrived the belief that if Waterloo had been won on the playing fields of Eton, American wars might yet be won on the playing fields of Harvard and Yale, West Point and Annapolis. With the president of Harvard championing the manly sports and slightly later the president of the United States, a Harvard graduate, ardently advocating them, the triumph of sports was assured. Yet the report of the Physical Training Conference of 1889 was not quite as definite. According to Frederick W. Cozens and Florence S. Stumpf in their chapter on "The Role of the School in the Sports Life of America" in *Sports in American Life*:

> In the entire discussion of the thirty-three participants mention was made of athletic sports only twice, once by Hartwell of Johns Hopkins and once by Hitchcock of Amherst. Sports were valued only as pastimes, and systematic gymnastics were considered to be the forms of exercise yielding the best results in the physical training of school children and college students. This represents a reasonably accurate point of view regarding the place of sports in the school curriculum just prior to the turn of the century, since it came from men who were considered the authorities.[13]

Although the authorities in 1889 generally did not acknowledge a place for sports in the schools, intercollegiate contests were already flourishing in eastern colleges, and a new trend in physical activity was on the way, as Cozens and Stumpf reveal in their excellent survey. The debate in the schools then as today was between the values of gymnastics and those of sports and play. While there was strong opposition to sports and play both

from within academe and without, time was on the side of play. In the view
of Cozens and Stumpf some new theories of education also added to the
debate:

> Widespread changes in the school curriculum were a part of the ad-
> justment of the culture to the new ideas of play. School playgrounds,
> lessened homework loads, Montessori methods in the kindergarten,
> President Theodore Roosevelt's support of the idea of play in the
> school curriculum, and recess game periods were all evidences of
> cultural interaction which made way for a new philosophy of educa-
> tion in America.[14]

Among other factors contributing to the rise of sports in schools and therefore in the nation were the development of sports for women, the demand
for intramural sports as well as interscholastic and intercollegiate com-
petitions, and compulsory physical education programs, which were
developed when World War I revealed the poor physical condition of the
draft age population and were further developed during World War II. By
the middle of the twentieth century sport had become a national institution
with its own bureaucracy, scandals, and resilience to mounting criticism.

How did sports and games overcome the objections to play, frivolity, and
violence and completely vanquish gymnastics and calisthenics? How did the
cultural situation develop in which in any freshman class in any American
college students will, if given a short test, be able to identify only a few of
the major contemporary artists, writers, intellectuals, and scientists but
most if not all of the current stable of athletic heroes and even sports
announcers? An answer such as "because of the media" is too simple.
Sports attracted people, as Cozens, Stumpf, and others have suggested,
because they are "fun," certainly more fun than exercises and running
merely to keep the body in shape. This explanation is, of course, true, but it
too overlooks the real appeal of sports both to participants and observers:
its potential for heroism. The phenomenon of heroism and the sports
superstar will be discussed in a subsequent chapter, but it is essential to
understand that sports evolved into their dominant position in the world not
merely because they are enjoyable but because they provide a genuine sense
of drama and meaning for millions of people. The question then becomes,
especially for educators, how can the heroism inherent in sports and games
be made to serve humanistic ends?

Answers are not easy, for the problem goes right to the heart of the
dilemma of Western culture. Traditionally heroes have not undertaken
great deeds in expectation of material compensation, yet today success for
athletes and others is often measured by worldly gain. Heroic acts have been
performed for the glory and honor of one's self, school, village, city, race,

or tribe but not for financial reward. Money has a way of defiling everything with which it comes into contact, or so prophets, philosophers, and
scholars have claimed since time out of mind. "When money enters into
sport," says E. Norman Gardiner in *Athletics of the Ancient World*, while
discussing the results of professionalism among the Greeks, "corruption is
sure to follow." There are many who deny that money automatically cor-
rupts sports, that it is not money but greed. Defenders of this position might
point to the adage that Gardiner refers to, *"Aidos* [sense of right] is stolen
away by secret gain," and argue that the key word is "secret," that there is
nothing at all wrong with "gain" from sports or any other human activity
that is not inherently vicious. This is a valid point of view, but how much
gain is enough? A dazzling college player, for example, attracts large
crowds and generates publicity for his university. Because of his talents he
becomes a moneymaker for others, should he then get some of the cash for
himself? In *Athletes for Sale*, Kenneth Denlinger and Leonard Shapiro
quoted from Wilt Chamberlain's autobiography to illustrate how extensively the exceptional athlete is courted by college and exploited by them.
Chamberlain, like many other young athletes, took some of the inducement
money offered him during recruiting season for the following reason: "with
me playing basketball, Kansas University, the City of Lawrence, the state of
Kansas, and all these alums got richer.... Why should I let them exploit
me, without reaping at least a little bit of the profit myself?"[15] Ability,
especially athletic ability, draws attention, and anything that attracts not
only can be sold but will be sold.

Over the years sports in colleges have been plagued by violence, sexism,
and racism, but the one problem underlying all others is that of money. For
this reason in recent years there have been more and more attempts to
define "amateur" and "professional." Paul Weiss also makes this attempt
in *Sport: A Philosophic Inquiry*. Weiss explains why the old, simplistic
definitions will no longer suffice:

> The oldest and easiest definitions are that an amateur is an "amator,"
> "a lover," one who gives himself to an activity without reserve and
> for no further end, whereas a professional engages in the activity only
> to make money. These definitions overlook the truth that many pro-
> fessionals love their sport, and that many an amateur has money in
> mind. More important, perhaps, is the fact that no one ever gives
> himself absolutely to any one type of activity; if he did, he would have
> neither time for, nor interest in, food, sex, art, or social affairs.[16]

In a conclusion that is not as revolutionary as it might at first appear, Weiss
states that he "would allow players to switch back and forth in their status
as amateurs and professionals" but goes on to acknowledge that both still

ought "to be segregated . . . when their distinctive abilities, tasks, and objectives would be perverted. . . ."

In the view of many, the perversion that Weiss would inhibit already exists on a wide scale in American schools, particularly colleges and particularly in the major college sports of football and basketball. Recommendations for preventing this are often extreme. James A. Michener, for example, would build up part of the athletic establishment even more, a proposal as revolutionary in a way as that to abolish the major sports altogether. There is no surprise when Michener writes in *Sports in America* that "a scandal of nationwide proportions threatens to break over the athletic establishment," but astonishment begins to mount when he goes on to say:

> The way to avoid it is to make playing for the super-league a strictly professional affair, with no emphasis on academic suitability. Let the boy be drafted in an orderly procedure without regard to his academic ability; let him be offered a decent salary with the opportunity of acquiring a degree if he wants one and has the capacity to do the work, and then let him move on to the professionals in accordance with the rules of their draft."[17]

Michener is not speaking of athletes like Bill Bradley, Jerry Lucas, O. J. Simpson, and Calvin Hill, who are intelligent as well as athletic, but of a group far more numerous, those young athletes physically able to play for any college but mentally prepared for nothing more advanced than the fourth grade. It is these, he says, who must be protected. Under Michener's system these young men can pursue an education on the side, but their main goal will be to play for pay in a supervised system.

Under his scheme, the athlete in the super league can return to college tuition free at any point during the fourteen years after he has left the super league. Professional teams would be called upon to help reimburse the colleges for the athlete's expense while enrolled. This system would operate for what Michener calls Group I schools, schools that would be openly professional. There would also be three other groups defined in terms of professional or amateur emphasis. Group IV would play for fun and love of the game. Group III would receive some coaching, while Group II would not be quite as good as Group I.

Considering the problems of intercollegiate athletics, Michener's proposal and his provisions for those who would want to participate in sports more for fun and enjoyment than for national recognition seem sensible to many people. It seems likely that spectator sports will move in the direction of Michener's recommendations as the coaches at such football powers as Alabama, Michigan, Notre Dame, Ohio State, Oklahoma, Texas, and

USC, would be financially well served by such an arrangement. Denlinger and Shapiro in their chapter "What Should Be Done" in *Athletes for Sale* appear to support such a structure, or in fact any structure that a particular school feels it can support financially:

> Why not simply allow each school to determine its own athletic destiny? Let a school decide the size and scope of its athletic program, whom it chooses to play, what standards its players must meet, and for what price they will play.
>
> The NCAA has been moving in that direction by splitting into three divisions, and the future is likely to produce an even greater gap between colleges obsessed with winning national championships and colleges content to train student-athletes.[18]

John R. Rooney, Jr. in *The Recruiting Game: Toward a New System of Intercollegiate Athletics* also endorses the idea of a super league and bases his proposals on a vast amount of information on all aspects of the current system. Whether or not one agrees with Rooney, he has done his homework well. The essence of "the practical solution" that Rooney sets forth is the open and honest professionalization of big-time college football and basketball.

There is understandably (and fortunately) considerable opposition to the recommendations for more professionalism and for more autonomy for colleges. A wide variety of suggestions are coming forth, most of which lie between Michener's proposals for a grouping based on a choice of professional involvement and those calling for complete deemphasis. This is the solution advocated by Roger M. Williams in his article "Away with Big-Time Athletics," which appeared in the *Saturday Review* for March 6, 1976. According to Williams, we should:

> (1) Eliminate all scholarships awarded on the basis of athletic ability *and* those given to athletes in financial need. Every school should form its teams from a student body drawn there to pursue academic interests.
>
> (2) Eliminate athletic dormitories and training tables, which keep athletes out of the mainstream of college life and further their image as hired guns. Also eliminate special tutoring, which is a preferential treatment of athletes, and "red shirting," the practice of keeping players in school an additional year in the hope that they'll improve enough to make the varsity.
>
> (3) Cut drastically the size and the cost of coaching staffs. Football staffs at Division I schools typically number 12 or 14, so that they are larger than those employed by professional teams. . . .

(4) Work to eliminate all recruiting of high-school athletes. It has produced horrendous cases of misrepresentation, illegal payments, and trauma for the young men involved.[19]

These same recommendations are a part of a more detailed plan set forth by J. Robert Evans in *Blowing The Whistle on Intercollegiate Sports*. Evan's book is an important, constructive one. In a simple, straightforward fashion he identifies the problems facing collegiate sports, makes a compelling, no-nonsense case for change, and then presents a wide range of solutions. In Evans's view the restructuring would consist of six phases. The first would be the creation of an organization known as the National Awareness Program for Collegiate Athletic Reform (NAP-CAR), which would arrange and coordinate publicity. Publicity campaigns would be similar to those pointing out the need for social change in other areas of American life. The other five phases would require concerted action on the part of presidents and athletic boards genuinely dedicated to reform. The measures that might be adopted are many, but the following three are perhaps the most crucial:

A. Require that intercollegiate athletic programs be financed through a student activities budget and/or the regular university budget.

B. Require that all income from intercollegiate athletics, such as game receipts, radio and TV rights, etc. go directly into the student activity fund or the regular university budget and not into athletic departments or into a single sports coffer.

C. Require that all athletics scholarships be renamed *activity scholarship grants* and awarded through the university's financial aid office....[20]

Obviously there would be much opposition to these proposals, and a great deal of education would be required on the part of faculty, administration, students, and alumni before such measures could be adoptd. Evans also has a set of excellent suggestions for regulating a deemphasized program.

Another list of fifteen recommendations concludes the *Sports Illustrated* article by John Underwood entitled "Student-Athletes: The Sham, the Shame." The article shocked some readers, but did not surprise those familiar with athletics in the schools. The suggestions that Underwood constructively sets forth were culled from coaches and academicians. The best solution to the matter, as Underwood rightly concludes, is a sense of "caring" about the education of the young on the part of coaches, faculty and administrators.

George Leonard, author of *The Ultimate Athlete*, suggests an approach quite at odds with Michener's plan. His book may well be the most thought-provoking book on sports yet written. Leonard identifies the ills of the present order but rather than concentrating on cures and operations, he suggests leaving it to its own destiny and launching out in other directions.

> By all means let us cherish the traditional sports for their many beauties, their unplumbed potential, and for the certainty they afford. But we have signed no long-term contract to suffer their extremes. The time has come to move on, to create new games with new rules more in tune with the times, games in which there are no spectators and no second-string players, games for a whole family and a whole day, games in which aggression fades into laughter—*new* games.[21]

Some new games can be found in the appendix to *The Ultimate Athlete* and in the October 1974 "Super Sports" issue of *Esquire* in the article entitled "The Games People Should Play."

Whereas Michener would widen the gap between sport and physical education yet retain wide provisions for each, Leonard would try to close the gap or at least to restore some balance. "Proponents of new physical education certainly are not asking that athletics be done away with," he writes, "They are asking for a balance between programs for the few and for the many." Leonard's credo seems to be that of Jefferson as imagined by Henry Adams, that progress will come when every man is potentially an athlete in body and an Aristotle in mind. The outcome from such an imaginative physical education could almost be utopian. One of the great ironies of the current situation, as Leonard and Dr. George Sheehan, a cardiologist and medical editor for *Runner's World*, see it, is that those who play the major sports are not in good physical condition. Leonard points out that Dr. Sheehan, who calls football "an act between consenting adults," ran a mile in four minutes and forty-seven seconds, which, Leonard claims, few professional players would be able to do.

"Eventually," says Leonard, "what we now call physical education... may well stand—as it did in ancient times—at the center of the academy, providing the strong foundation from which all education can rise."[22] It is doubtful, though, that Leonard would go as far as Dr. George Sheehan, who would like to give grants-in-aid for sports but not for academic achievement. Sheehan outlines this startling proposal in the *New York Times* sports section, for November 10, 1974. His basic rationale is:

> ...the athlete provides a much better model than the scholar. The athlete restores our common sense about the common man. He re-vitalizes old faults and instructs us in the old virtues. However modest

his intellectual attainments, he is a whole person, integrated and fully functioning. And in his highly visible pursuit of a highly visible perfection, he illustrates the age-old desire to become the person you are.[23]

Surely he jests at least in part. If he is serious in what he has said, he demonstrates an incredible myopia about the college sports scene as well as a questionable philosophy of life. Anyone who reads this article should certainly read the responses that appeared on December 1, 1974, under the headline "Thoughts on Scholarships: Should a Collegian Major in Football?" by those less famous but no less wise.

Michael Novak's *The Joy of Sports: End Zones, Bases, Baskets, Balls, and the Consecration of the American Spirit* also recognizes the need for change and advances. In chapter 17, entitled "Some Burkean Reforms," Novak lists eleven reforms, some of which deal with professional sports. The most important of these is number eight, which calls for the reimbursement of the colleges by professional teams for the training of players. These payments could be assessed annually on each professional team and "levied by law, as part of the cost for the privilege of a franchise."[24] Novak quotes Red Smith in support of this recommendation and again discusses the idea in chapter 15, "The Universities and the Professionals": "A mandatory contribution to a National Collegiate Athletic Association (NCAA) sports fund of, say $250,000 by each professional team every year would go a long way toward reducing the deficits of college athletic departments."[25]

One of the most startling proposals to be made in recent years calls for the total and complete separation of competitive sports from the university. In the fall of 1977 the Arts and Sciences faculty at Tulane University voted 101 to 10 drop football, whereupon the football team voted 90 to 0 for the university to drop the College of Arts and Sciences. Tulane still plays a major schedule, which is not to say that the Arts and Sciences faculty did not have a valid point. That basic argument is best presented in a compelling paper by Phebe M. Scott entitled *Reflections*, the thirteenth lecture in the Amy Morris Homans Series sponsored by the National Association for Physical Education of College Women. Scott is quite serious in her ideas but not messianic by any means. She points out the need for a sense of humor in all human enterprises and step by step engages each point that might be raised against removing competitive sports from the academic world. In her view, competitive sports and physical education have little in common. As others have done, she questions the character-building argument of competitive sports and the assertion that athletic scholarships are the only means by which some students can go to college. She argues that schools do not now have control over their sports programs, and states that there are many other organizations that could and would take over competitive sports if they were taken out of the schools. Such organizations, she feels, would be fine administrators for these programs.

While extreme, this proposal is modest compared to Michener's and makes a great deal more sense, although one still wonders why it is not possible to throw out the bathwater of intercollegiate sports and still keep varsity athletics. This could be accomplished merely by deemphasis. Public money could be spent with good conscience on a wide range of varsity athletics rather than an elite few. The results would expand the opportunities for personal heroism for large numbers of young men and women who find intramurals not enough. Ideally, a university is not merely dedicated to the pursuit of truth but also to the creation of beauty and the cultivation of the good. The first of these can be pursued in the classroom and laboratory, but the last two require a stage, a studio, and a playing field where discipline and talent can come to fruition in aesthetic achievement.

In addition to remembering the dangers of extremes in either direction, one should also remember when reading the new criticism of sports that it is not especially new. This is a point well made by John A. Lucas and Ronald A. Smith in *Saga of American Sport*:

> The new sport humanists, Stuart Miller, George Leonard, Bil Gilbert, Neil Amdur, and many others may be unfamiliar with the older philosophies of R. Tait McKenzie, Clark Hetherington, Jay B. Nash, and Arthur H. Steinhaus. A close analysis of the modernists reveals a sport-for-all attitude precisely the same as those of the traditional educators. There is no essential philosophical difference in Esalen Institute's Stuart Miller and that of the late physical education scientist, Arthur Steinhaus. Miller's "new" directions sees sport as "a powerful psychological searchlight, teaching the player about himself ...consciously used in the development of the whole personality...." Steinhaus' classic essay, "Fitness beyond muscle," concluded that "for the highest human accomplishments man must be strong in totality." The laudable message of the new sport humanists is old, very old.[26]

If sports do not change in some significant direction in the next few years, it will not be for lack of criticism and study. Courses in the humanistic values of sports are now established in many colleges, not just within the department of physical education but within the college of arts and sciences as well. In "The Changing Room," an analysis of David Storey's play of the same name, J. R. Schleppi calls upon physical educators to interpret the playwright's views—and by implication that of other artists as well—toward sports. In Schleppi's view, physical educators must move away from their "how-to" approaches to a broader understanding of sports. The reverse of this is equally true. Those in the humanities must broaden their view to see man as a living, breathing creature and not just as an abstraction.

Changing attitudes and new interest have brought forth a number of anthologies in sociology and literature that can also serve as textbooks. Among the best arranged primarily along sociological themes are: *Sociology of American Sport*, edited by D. Stanley Eitzen and George H. Sage; *Sociology of Sport* by Harry Edwards; *Sport and American Society: Selected Readings*, edited by George H. Sage; *Sport, Culture, and Society: A Reader on the Sociology of Sport*, edited by John W. Loy and Gerald S. Kenyon; *Sport and Society: An Anthology*, edited by John T. Talamini and Charles H. Page; and *Sport in the Socio-Cultural Process*, edited by M. Marie Hart. To this list should be added *Social Philosophy of Athletics* by Hans Lenk and *Handbook of Social Science of Sport* edited by Günter Lüschen and George Sage. This valuable tome refers to anthropological, historical, psychological, and philosophical approaches in the study of sport and games and contains a classified international bibliography of over 3,000 items. Two journals devoted to the study of sport in social context are *Journal of Sports Behavior* and *Journal of Sport and Social Issues*.

Valuable texts on the history of physical education are *Chronicle of American Physical Education: Selected Readings (1855-1930)* by Aileene S. Lockhart and Betty Spears and *Innovators and Institutions in Physical Education* by Ellen W. Gerber, both books representing a Carlylean approach in that the focus is upon those individuals who have shaped the history of physical education. A leading name to look for on the history and philosophy of physical education is Earle F. Zeigler, editor of *Physical Education and Sport in the United States and Canada* and author of *A History of Sport and Physical Education to 1900*.

Recent texts on the literature of sports include *Sports Literature*, edited by John Brady and James Hall, *Sports in Literature*, edited by Henry B. Chapin, *A Literature of Sports*, edited by Tom Dodge, and *The Sporting Spirit: Athletes in Literature and Life*, edited by Robert J. Higgs and Neil D. Isaacs. Also available is a text entitled *Sports in Modern America*, edited by two sports historians, William J. Baker and John M. Carroll. In addition to addressing such familiar areas as blacks and women in sports and violence, Baker and Carroll treat the frequently neglected subjects of the Olympics and the expansion of American sports abroad. Another history book suitable as a classroom text is *American Sports: From the Age of Folk Games to the Age of the Spectator* by Benjamin G. Rader. Rader examines the social and cultural matrix from which the transformation indicated in the title sprang. *Saga of American Sport* by Lucas and Smith is also a fine text both for a course on sports history or a more general approach. There is also a wide range of sports fiction in paperback and a growing number of articles on the teaching of sports, for example, "Sports in the English

Classroom," by Connie Brannen, Mary F. Vincent, and Teri Walton; "A Humanistic Physical Education Course," by Louie Crew; and "Getting It All Together: The Integrated Learning Semester," by Barbara J. Kelley, as well as two dissertations that deal with the reading and/or teaching of sports fiction at the high-school level. The dissertations, one by Edna Earl Edwards and the other by Robert W. Reising, can be found in the bibliography at the end of this chapter.

There is a wide choice of sports films available for classrooms. *Guides to Educational Media* by Margaret I. Rufsvold is a basic reference to them. Also helpful is *Educational Film Locator of the Consortium of University Film Centers and R. R. Bowker Company*. As its preface claims, this hefty volume is "a union list of the titles held by member libraries of the Consortium of University Film Centers, and a compilation and standardization of their 50 separate catalogs, representing about 200,000 film holdings with their geographic locations." Films can be accessed by title and/or subject. Physical education, recreation, and sports related subjects include 22 headings. The most comprehensive film guide of all, however, is that known as *NICEM* (National Information Center for Educational Media). In addition to the basic volume, which is a subject guide, there are three additional volumes of alphabetic guides. The topic to look under in *NICEM* is "Physical Education and Recreation." Also available through *NICEM* are thirteen volumes of indexes, including one entitled *35 mm Educational Materials*. A surprising number of films are free, although many of them are of the "how-to" variety.

What *NICEM* is to film, *Current Index to Journals in Education* (*CIJE*) is to articles. This cumulative index is compiled according to title and contains articles from approximately 600 journals. It is a source that the sports researcher should never overlook, but the researcher should look under "athletics" rather than "sports." *Education Index* is also helpful. Although it is an index only and does not review as many periodicals as *CIJE*, it is probably more popular with students then *CIJE*, which is oriented more toward research. An attractive feature of the *CIJE* is its article reprint service available through University Microfilms in Ann Arbor, Michigan. Educational Resources Information Center (ERIC) publishes *Resources in Education*, which is a voluminous listing of studies and reports that are available on microfiche, which many libraries have on file. The entry is "Athletics." Rather surprisingly, commercial books are sometimes listed in the index, but they are not always issued in microfiche. The old familiar *Reader's Guide to Periodical Literature* should also be on every researcher's checklist. A companion series, *Cumulative Index to Periodical Literature*, lists all articles in the *Reader's Guide* for 1959 to 1970, conveniently under topic. There are hundreds of articles listed under "Athletics," "Sports," and individual sports such as "Baseball" and

"Basketball" and there are scores of subtitles. For any research on topics in the 1960s, the scholar has a handy periodical bibliography already prepared and waiting to be used. It is a tremendous research aid, as is the *Subject Cross Reference Guide*, which lists scores of topics.

On the matter of the general problem of athletics in colleges, the most extensive work is *An Inquiry into the Need for and Feasibility of a National Study of Intercollegiate Athletics*, edited by George H. Hanford. It is an indispensable reference that contains a superb bibliography on all aspects of intercollegiate sports. Denliger's and Shapiro's *Athletes for Sale* traces the dismal consequences of a recruiting season at the University of Maryland, which, since it is a large metropolitan university with a major sports program, serves as a mirror of the college sports empire. The idea of a college sports empire is also established in "The Graves of Academe" in Neil D. Isaacs' *Jock Culture, U.S.A.* The works of Denlinger and Shapiro and Isaacs are informative, but they are not the exposés that *Out of Their League* by Dave Meggyesy and *Meat on the Hoof* by Gary Shaw tend to be. Meggyesy and Shaw describe athletic programs at the University of Syracuse and the University of Texas. John F. Rooney's *The Recruiting Game* deals with the practices observed at Oklahoma State. It is a book designed not to raise eyebrows but to change minds on the basis of hard information and the moral imperatives of American education.

All works on recruiting and scholarships stress the dire need for a change in the manner in which sports are conducted in many American institutions of higher learning. The malaise, however, is not universal, and those wishing to look at a working model entirely different from those of the "football factories" should consult John Underwood's "Beating Their Brains Out" in the May 26, 1976, *Sports Illustrated*. Underwood describes the sports program at MIT. He points out that with a budget of $820,000 MIT fields intercollegiate teams in twenty-two sports and supports five women's teams, as well as its physical education and intramural programs and club sports, all in contrast with the $4.1 million budget of the University of Michigan and $3.3 million budget of UCLA. Although there is no chance of breaking even, there is no complaint, for a big expense that plagues other universities is nonexistent at MIT.

> There is no MIT football team. Nor is there evidence that anyone wants one. Athletic Director Ross H. (Jim) Smith says that the subject is broached "in cycles, every five years or so," usually by fiery-eyed stars of the Class A intramural football league (the ones who are coordinated) itching to get their mitts on the likes of Colby and Bates. At MIT this cyclic phenomenon is treated as if it were an open jar of smallpox virus, and soon routed. Peter Close, the sports information director, notes that the school fielded a football team from 1882 to 1893. In 13 games with Harvard it was outscored 555-5.[27]

MIT may have fumbled at football, but its contributions to science, technology, and all fields of knowledge are immeasureable and sufficient to remove all doubt that winning college football and basketball games isn't the only thing of importance.

Regardless of what plan of change is undertaken, there are many complex matters to keep in mind. Good arguments have been advanced on all sides, but there is a special caveat that I would like to make in the case of Michener's proposal. While *Sports in America* definitely should be read, it is anything but the "blockbuster" its publishers claim. It is a book that harms no one, makes no charges, and in point of fact calls for more of the same. Thus, it is not surprising that Michener seems to admire Bear Bryant and Bryant's incredible confession, not of shame but of pride:

> I used to go along with the idea that football players on scholarship were "student-athletes," which is what the NCAA calls them. Meaning a student first, an athlete second. We were kidding ourselves, trying to make it more palatable to the academicians. We don't have to say that and we shouldn't. At the level we play, the boy is really an athlete first and a student second.[28]

Although the term "student-athlete" has lost all meaning at Alabama and most other places as well, reversing the term does nothing except to place the education of the athlete in an even lower priority than before with all the doleful consequences for the athlete and society that misplaced emphasis encourages. Michener's proposal for a super league of college football powerhouses reflects a victimization by the "super" syndrome, which is brilliantly criticized by John Updike in "Superman" in *The Carpentered Hen and Other Tame Stories*. The Bloomsbury intellectuals, as Bruce E. Haley has observed, blamed the English decline in the twentieth century on the English worship of games and the failure of English institutions to turn out truly enlightened young men. No thoughtful American should dismiss that same possibility in our own land.

Still it will not do to end on a dismal note. College football powerhouses such as Alabama and Ohio State may become more and more specialized until there is no distinction whatever between them and professional teams, but the sports-for-all attitude is here to stay as Lucas and Smith observe. In 1976, for example, over 15 million Americans played over 300 million rounds of golf. This figure alone suggests what we all know, that Americans are playing and amusing themselves on a scale unparalleled in all of history. Because of this fact Lucas and Smith conclude with a quotation from Sebastian de Grazia's *Time, Work, and Leisure*: " 'Through leisure man may realize his ties to the natural world and so free his mind to rise to divine reaches.' "[29] This was also the hope of Walt Whitman who loafed and invited his soul and based his optimism on the cultivation of a "divine average," which can only occur when large numbers of men and women develop both mind and body for the sake of the soul.

Among the number would be the handicapped, both physically and mentally, a group easy to overlook in discussing education of the body. Fortunately, many individuals and organizations have not overlooked them, and there is a wide range of publications addressing problems of special populations. Among these are *Physical Activities for Individuals with Handicapping Conditions* by Dolores Geddes and *Special Olympics Instructional Manual—From Beginners to Champions* by Julian A. Stein and Lowell A. Klappholz. Indeed, it may well be that growth of the soul has far less to do with development, exercise, and recreation of our own minds and bodies than with the concern shown for others less fortunate.

NOTES

1. Plato, *Republic: Book III, Five Great Dialogues*, trans. Benjamin Jowett (New York: Walter J. Black, 1942), p. 300.

2. Rachel Sargent Robinson, *Sources for the History of Greek Athletics* (Cincinnati: University of Cincinnati Press, 1955), p. 125.

3. *Isocrates*, translated by George Norlin, 3 vols. (London: Oxford University Press, 1928), 3: 121.

4. Robinson, pp. 185-88.

5. Ibid., p. 191.

6. Quoted in ibid., p. 177.

7. Eugene W. Nixon and Frederick W. Cozens, *An Introduction to Physical Education* (Philadelphia: W. B. Saunders Co., 1952), p. 30. Before completely condemning asceticism as an enemy of sports, one should consider the subtle but profound point emphasized by John P. Sisk in his article "Hot Sporting Blood":

> Helen Waddell writes in *The Desert Fathers* that "asceticism had not traveled far from the *ascesis*, the training of the athlete, and the Fathers themselves to their contemporary biographers are the *athletae Dei*, the athletes of God." Austerity was not an end in itself, however it was cultivated. Waddell quotes Dorotheus the Theban's ancient formula, "I kill my body, for it kills me." To the Fathers the killing of the body meant the liberation of the spirit for holy living and holy dying; to the Greek Olympic athlete it meant a triumphant return home and possibly celebration by Pindar; to the Green Bay Packers, Vince Lombardi's ascetics, it meant two Super Bowls.

Intellectual Digest 4 (November 1973), pp. 46-47. Some regard asceticism as a natural ally of sports.

8. Roger Ascham, *The Schoolmaster*, ed. Lawrence V. Ryan (Ithaca: Cornell University Press, 1967), p. 28.

9. John Milton, *Areopagitica and Of Education*, ed. George H. Sabine (New York: Appleton-Century-Crofts, 1951), pp. 63-68.

10. Ibid., pp. 69-70.

11. Bruce E. Haley, *The Healthy Body and Victorian Culture* (Cambridge, Mass.: Harvard University Press, 1978), p. 154.

12. Charles William Eliot, *A Turning Point in Higher Education: The Inaugural Address of Charles W. Eliot as President of Harvard College, October 19, 1869* (Cambridge, Mass.: Harvard University Press, 1969), p. 17.

13. Frederick W. Cozens and Florence S. Stumpf, *Sports in American Life* (New York: Arno Press), p. 63.

14. Ibid., p. 65.

15. Kenneth Denlinger and Leonard Shapiro, *Athletes for Sale* (New York: Crowell, 1975), pp. 5-6.

16. Paul Weiss, *Sport: A Philosophic Inquiry* (Carbondale: Southern Illinois University Press, 1969), pp. 195-96.

17. James A. Michener, *Sports in America* (New York: Random House, 1976), pp. 149-50.

18. Denlinger and Shapiro, pp. 253-54.

19. Roger M. Williams, "Away with Big-Time Athletics," *Saturday Review*, 6 March 1976, pp. 10, 46.

20. J. Robert Evans, *Blowing the Whistle on Intercollegiate Sports* (Chicago: Nelson-Hall, 1974), p. 141.

21. George Leonard, *The Ultimate Athlete* (New York: Avon, 1977), p. 125.

22. Ibid., p. 164.

23. George Sheehan, "Athletic Scholarships Yes, Academic Scholarships No," *New York Times*, sports section, 10 November 1974, p. 2.

24. Michael Novak, *The Joy of Sports: End Zones, Bases, Baskets, Balls, and the Consecration of the American Spirit* (New York: Basic Books, 1976), p. 330-31.

25. Ibid., p. 281.

26. John A. Lucas and Ronald A. Smith, *Saga of American Sport* (Philadelphia: Lea and Febiger, 1978), p. 422.

27. John Underwood, "Beating Their Brains Out," *Sports Illustrated* 42 (May 26, 1975), 86.

28. Quoted in Michener, p. 254.

29. Quoted in Lucas and Smith, p. 422.

BIBLIOGRAPHY

Ascham, Roger. *The Schoolmaster*. Edited by Lawrence V. Ryan. Ithaca: Cornell University Press, 1967.

Baker, William, and John Carroll, eds. *Sports in Modern America*. Saint Louis, Mo.: River City Publishers, 1981.

Brady, John, and James Hall, eds. *Sports Literature*. New York: McGraw-Hill, 1975.

Brannen, Connie, Mary F. Vincent, and Teri Walton. "Sports in the English Classroom" *English Journal* 64 (February 1975), 104-5.

Chapin, Henry B., ed. *Sports in Literature*. New York: David McKay Co., 1976.

Cozens, Frederick W., and Florence S. Stumpf. *Sports in American Life*. New York: Arno Press, 1976.

Crew, Louie. "A Humanistic Physical Education Course." *Journal of Physical Education* 71 (January/February 1974), 70-71.

Cumulative Index to Periodical Literature, 1959-1970. Princeton, N.J.: National Library Service Corporation, 1976.

Current Index to Journals in Education. Phoenix, Arizona: Oryx, 1969-.

Denlinger, Kenneth, and Leonard Shapiro. *Athletes for Sale.* New York: Crowell, 1975.

Dodge, Tom, ed. *A Literature of Sports.* Lexington, Mass.: D. C. Heath, 1980.

Education Index. New York: H. W. Wilson, 1978-.

Educational Film Locator of the Consortium of University Film Centers and R. R. Bowker Company. New York: R. R. Bowker, 1979.

Edwards, Edna Earl. "A Comparison of Factors Affecting the Success of Athletes in Selected Junior Novels and Biographies." Ph.D. dissertation, Florida State University, 1969.

Edwards, Harry. *Sociology of Sport.* Homeward, Ill.: The Dorsey Press, 1973.

Eitzen, D. Stanley, and George H. Sage, eds. *Sociology of American Sport.* Dubuque, Iowa: William C. Brown, 1978.

Eliot, Charles W. *A Turning Point in Higher Education: The Inaugural Address of Charles W. Eliot as President of Harvard College, October 19, 1869.* Cambridge, Mass.: Harvard University Press, 1969.

Evans, J. Robert. Blowing The Whistle on Intercollegiate Sports. Chicago: Nelson-Hall, 1974.

Gardiner, E. Norman. *Athletics of the Ancient World.* London: Oxford University Press, 1930.

_____. *Greek Athletic Sports and Festivals.* 1910. Reprint. Dubuque, Iowa: William C. Brown, 1970.

Geddes, Dolores. *Physical Activities for Individuals with Handicapping Conditions.* St. Louis: Mosby, 1978.

Gerber, Ellen W. *Innovators and Institutions in Physical Education.* Philadelphia: Lea and Febiger, 1971.

Haley, Bruce E. *The Healthy Body and Victorian Culture.* Cambridge, Mass.: Harvard University Press, 1978.

Hanford, George H., ed. *An Inquiry into the Need for and Feasibility of a National Study of Intercollegiate Athletics.* 2 vols. Washington, D.C.: American Council on Higher Education, 1974.

Hart, M. Marie, ed. *Sport in the Socio-Cultural Process.* Dubuque, Iowa: William C. Brown, 1972.

Higgs, Robert J., and Neil D. Isaacs, eds., *The Sporting Spirit: Athletes in Literature and Life.* New York: Harcourt, Brace, Jovanovich, 1977.

Isaacs, Neil D. *Jock Culture, U.S.A.* New York: W. W. Norton, 1978.

Isocrates. Translated by George Norlin. London: Oxford University Press, 1928.

Journal of Sport and Social Issues. New York: Institute of Sport and Social Analysis, 1977-.

Journal of Sports Behavior. Mobile, Ala.: U.S. Sports Academy, 1974-.

Kelley, Barbara J. "Getting it All Together: The Integrated Learning Semester." *Journal of Health, Physical Education, and Recreation* 45 (October 1974), 32-35.

Lenk, Hans. *Social Philosophy of Athletics.* Champaign, Ill.: Stipes Publishing Co., 1979.

Leonard, George. "The Games People Should Play." *Esquire* (Super Sports Issue) 82 (October 1974): 214-17, 254.

_____. *The Ultimate Athlete.* New York: Avon, 1977.

Lockhart, Aileen S., and Betty Spears, eds. *Chronicle of American Physical Education: Selected Reading, 1855-1930.* Dubuque, Iowa: William C. Brown, 1972.

Loy, John W., and Gerald S. Kenyon, eds. *Sport, Culture, and Society: A Reader on the Sociology of Sport.* London: Macmillan & Co., 1969.

Lucas, John A., and Ronald A. Smith. *Saga of American Sport.* Philadelphia: Lea and Febiger, 1978.

Lüschen, Günther, and George Sage. *Handbook of Social Science of Sport.* Champaign, Ill.: Stipes, 1981.

Meggyesy, Dave. *Out of Their League.* Berkeley, Calif.: Ramparts Press, 1970.

Michener, James A. *Sports in America.* Greenwich, Conn.: Fawcett, 1976.

Milton, John. *Areopagitica and Of Education.* Edited by George H. Sabine. New York: Appleton-Century-Crofts, 1951.

NICEM (National Information Center for Educational Media). *Index to 16mm Educational Films.* 6th ed. Los Angeles: National Information Center for Educational Media, 1977.

Nixon, Eugene W., and Frederick W. Cozens. *An Introduction to Physical Education.* Philadelphia: W. B. Saunders Co., 1952.

Novak, Michael. *The Joy of Sports: End Zones, Bases, Baskets, Balls, and the Consecration of the American Spirit.* New York: Basic Books, 1976.

Plato. *Republic: Book III, Five Great Dialogues.* Translated by Benjamin Jowett. New York: Walter J. Black, 1942.

Rader, Benjamine G. *American Sports from the Age of Folk Games to the Age of the Spectator.* Englewood Cliffs, N.J.: Prentice-Hall, 1982.

Reader's Guide to Periodical Literature. New York: H. W. Wilson Co., 1960-.

Reising, Robert W. "A High School Text book Employing a Thematic Approach to the Study of Literature." Ed.D. dissertation, Duke University, 1969.

Resources in Education (ERIC). Washington, D.C.: HEW/National Institute of Education, 1968-.

Robinson, Rachel Sargent. *Sources for the History of Greek Athletics.* Reprint. Chicago: Ares, 1980.

Rooney, John F. *The Recruiting Game: Toward a New System of Intercollegiate Athletics.* Lincoln, Neb.: University of Nebraska Press, 1981.

Rufsvold, Margaret I. *Guides to Educational Media.* 4th ed. Chicago: American Library Association, 1977.

Sage, George H., ed. *Sport and American Society: Selected Readings.* Reading, Mass.: Addison-Wesley Publishing Co., 1974.

Schleppi, J. R. "The Changing Room." *Physical Educator*, October 1974, pp. 143-44.

Scott, Phebe M. *Reflections.* The Thirteenth Amy Morris Homans Lecture. Champaign, Ill.: Human Kinetic Publishers, 1979.

Shaw, Gary. *Meat on the Hoof.* New York: St. Martin's Press, 1972.

Sheehan, George. "Athletic Scholarships Yes, Academic Scholarships No." *New York Times.* Sports section, 10 November 1974, p. 2.

Sisk, John P. "Hot Sporting Blood." *Intellectual Digest* 4 (November 1973), 46-47.

Stein, Julian A., and Lowell A. Klappholz. *Special Olympics Instructional Manual—from Beginners to Champions.* Washington, D.C.: American Alliance for Health, Physical Education, and Recreation and the Joseph P. Kennedy Jr. Foundation, 1972.

Subject Cross Reference Guide. Princeton, N.J.: National Library Service Co., 1976.

Talamini, John T., and Charles H. Page, eds. *Sport and Society: An Anthology.* Boston: Little, Brown & Co., 1973.

"Thoughts on Scholarships: Should a Collegian Major in Football?" *New York Times,* 1 December 1974, p. 2.

Underwood, John. "Beating Their Brains Out." *Sports Illustrated,* 26 May 1976, pp. 86-96.

_____. "Student-Athletes: The Sham, the Shame." *Sports Illustrated,* 19 May 1980, pp. 36-72.

Updike, John. *The Carpentered Hen and Other Tame Creatures.* New York: Harper and Row, 1958.

Weiss, Paul. *Sport: A Philosophic Inquiry.* Carbondale: Southern Illinois University Press, 1969.

Whitehead, James. *Joiner.* New York: Avon, 1973.

Williams, Roger M. "Away with Big-Time Athletics." *Saturday Review,* 6 March 1976, pp. 10, 46.

Zeigler, Earle F., ed. *A History of Physical Education and Sport in the United States and Canada.* Champaign, Ill.: Stipes, 1975.

_____. *A History of Sport and Physical Education to 1900.* Champaign, Ill.: Stipes 1973.

CHAPTER 6

Sports, Money,
and Social Values

Something happened to American sports in the 1960s, or perhaps it would be more correct to say that something happened to the perception of American sports. In the view of many, the problems then identified by critics have remained unsolved. Others, however, maintain that changes that have occurred have been significant. Whatever the outcome, the American sports establishment came under the heaviest attack in its history in the late 1960s and early 1970s. While there had been earlier scattered salvos from such disaffected intellectuals and educators as Thorstein Veblen, Lewis Mumford, and the authors of the Carnegie report of 1929, by the end of the Vietnam War a small army of athletes and writers were besieging the sacred citadel of sports. The rallying cry was for the humanization of sport, but the specific targets were racial and sexual discrimination and the exploitation of athletes and the general public for money. Jack Scott in a book of the same title called the new criticism "the athletic revolution," a revolution that grew out of a number of other forces:

By the late 1960's the revolt in the athletic world had escalated to such an extent that some coaches, only half jokingly, talked about asking for combat pay. Coaches who were hardened to the criticism from fans and alumni that came with a losing season were not prepared to be told by faculty, students, and human rights commissions that they were racist, insensitive, and lacked the ability to communicate. Coaches wondered aloud since when was sensitivity a quality they were supposed to possess. Sensitivity was effeminate: the coach's job was to make men out of boys and to produce winning teams. But the criticism kept mounting, and in the fall of 1969 *Sports Illustrated* came to the defense of coaches with a special three part series entitled "The Desperate Coach."[1]

If substantive changes did not result from the revolution, a barrage of books did. Invariably the books were critical, ranging from irony and lament to outrage and iconoclasm. Harry Edwards's *The Revolt of the Black Athlete*, Dave Meggyesy's *Out of Their League*, Chip Oliver's *High for the Game* and Jack Scott's *The Athletic Revolution* signaled the start of a new war on an old subject. Among other blasts by athletes were Jim Bouton's *Ball Four*, Bernie Parrish's *They Call It a Game* and Gary Shaw's *Meat on the Hoof*. In still another wave came the volleys of the sports-writers, who, perhaps out of guilt, turned some of their fire upon themselves. The belief that sportswriters will not bite the hand that feeds them was certainly not true after 1970. Among the most effective and best aimed shots are Glenn Dickey's *The Jock Empire: Its Rise and Deserved Fall*, Jerry Izenberg's *How Many Miles to Camelot?* Larry Merchant's . . . *And Every Day You Take Another Bite*, and the late Leonard Shecter's *The Jocks*. In general the books by the sportswriters were less missionary than those by the athletes or former athletes, but the indignation over the state of sports was still present, whether in the spirit of humorous debunking or straight invective. Though styles and approaches differed considerably, the message common to all is found in the foreword of Glenn Dickey's *The Jock Empire*:

Nowhere in society is male chauvinism more rampant than in sports, as we are just beginning to realize. From Little League to professional ranks, sports are a male affair, with women permitted in only as secretaries, as quiet and stupid spectators and as bed partners. Especially as bed partners.

All the problems of society, from drug-taking to racism, are writ extralarge in sports. The Winning Is Everything Syndrome which is the basis of the Watergate affair orginated in sports. Nowhere is power politics more blatantly practiced than in the Olympics, which were started as an antidote to politics.

There are rotten spots in the sports apple wherever you look. The Little League program, designed to promote baseball, often has the opposite effect because boys are bored, ruined or heartbroken by the time they're 13. Intercollegiate sports encourage lying and cheating because of the pressure to win and unrealistic rules. Professional sports have problems ranging from hubris to senility. The specter of fixed games hangs over all sports, and many fans seem convinced the exposed cases are only the tip of the iceberg.[2]

Larry Merchant's . . . *And Every Day You Take Another Bite* is not at all apocalyptic and certainly not concerned about the evils of gambling. What he does fault is the tendency to use football as a metaphor of war, politics, and manhood. Merchant finds no connection between the NFL (National Football League) and Vietnam, the decline of the West, or sophisticated theories of aggression. What he does find is a lot of "snake oil" and ballyhoo about patriotism and razor blades. "The NFL," Merchant says, "has a beautiful product. Running, throwing, jumping, catching, smiting, fighting. People can hardly get enough of it. Why does the NFL have to over-sell and hard-sell itself? Because the NFL has a problem, not unlike everyone else in football—what to do the other six days of the week?"[3]

Merchant obviously believes that the "revolution" made hardly a whimper much less a bang in the busy camp of the NFL. He is even slightly critical of the four NFL dropouts, Meggyesy, Rick Sortun, Chip Oliver, and George Sauer for finding in football a mirror of society and nature. Football mirrors football, Merchant seems to say, and everyone would be wiser to regard it as an exciting, brutal game that sometimes approaches art rather than metaphor. It provies no theories except that people like action and like to bet, and it is hardly a barometer of anything. Merchant's view is compelling but such anti-intellectual stances play havoc with the study of sports or anything else.

The conclusion that the sports apple, big and shiny on the outside, has a lot of soft, dark places just beneath the surface, was reached in numerous works of fiction during the same period. Among the best of this period are two novels, Pete Gents's *North Dallas Forty* and Dan Jenkins's *Semi-Tough*. Both authors are in a good position to know whereof they speak, for Gent was an athlete and Jenkins, a sportswriter. While the main purpose of Jenkins's book is to entertain, behind the ribaldry is a world as censurable as that more soberly described by Gent.

Merchant's pragmatic reasoning closely resembles that of Christopher Lasch, a historian, who in "The Corruption of Sports" criticizes Paul Hoch, Jack Scott, Dave Meggyesy and other "cultural radicals" for their naive theory of sports. Lasch finds their position objectionable because it is arrogant and outdated. The left-wing critics, Lasch claims, do not necessarily "understand the needs and interests of the masses better than the masses themselves," and their reductionist approach "makes no allowance for the autonomy of cultural traditions."[4] In Lasch's view, "the reactionary values" allegedly perpetuated by sport no longer reflect the dominant needs of American capitalism at all. A society of consumers has no need for the support of an ideology of manliness and martial valor. The athletes' businesslike approach to their craft has undermined loyalty to old-school ties. Lasch has a convincing case, but he speaks with the advantage of nearly a decade of hindsight. Max Rafferty's view of the coach's job, which Lasch discusses, is now dated, but it wasn't when Jack Scott first published *The Athletic Revolution*. It should be recognized that Lasch's argument is not original. For instance, many years ago Thomas Wolfe, speaking of the demise of loyalty brought on by professionalism, said: "It is hard to get excited about the efforts of the hired men."[5]

Still Lasch has examined the contemporary scene intelligently and has said many things well, even memorably, including the following:

The degradation of sport, then, consists not in its being taken too seriously but in its subjection to some ulterior purpose, such as profit-making, patriotism, moral training, or the pursuit of health. Sport may give rise to these things in abundance, but ideally it produces them only as by-products having no essential connection with the game. When the game itself, on the other hand, comes to be regarded as incidental to the benefits it supposedly confers on participants, spectators, or promoters, it loses its peculiar capacity to transport both participant and spectator beyond everyday experience—to provide a glimpse of perfect order uncontaminated by commonplace calculations of advantage or even by ordinary considerations of survival.[6]

Discrimination, racial and sexual, is a manifestation of the larger issue of money, or what in Joseph Durso's *The All-American Dollar: The Big Business of Sports* is called, "Greed." Undoubtedly some distinctions between amateurism and professionalism ought to be preserved, even if some colleges admit to their own professionalism, but professionalism does not mean specialization and acquisitiveness. As Paul Weiss has pointed out in *Sport: A Philosophic Inquiry*, the athlete does not necessarily sell his soul when he turns professional, but he leads himself into temptation. Most of us are never in a position to be tempted by the big money that top athletes and other performers can command. If we were, few of us would perform any differently, which is the point stressed by Tommy John as reported in the second part of a three-part series, "Money in Sports" by Ray Kennedy and Nancy Williamson that appeared in *Sports Illustrated*. Kennedy and Williamson report that during a question and answer session after a banquet a man accused players who jumped clubs of being greedy, and they record John's reply:

John replied, "If you were offered a job by a competitor of your present employer, and the competitor said he would give you a $50,000 raise, a new car and a new home, would you leave your company?" The man said no. John recalls, "I told him he was either dumb or drunk, perhaps a little of both, and the rest of the people laughed him down."[7]

The response of John, who has since left the Dodgers to join the Yankees, is well taken, but so is that of the man who made the accusation. Loyalty to a team or place sometimes does seem to be a thing of the past, a problem compounded by the standardization of places. As Wright Morris has said in *The Territory Ahead*, "No matter where we go in America today, we shall find what we just left."[8] Although this statement is true enough to give us pause, even in the age of big money many sports fans want their heroes to remain loyal to their teams.

The tradition of loyalty is as old as heroism itself. In ancient Greece, heroes, including athlete heroes, made sacrifices and performed great deeds for the glory and honor of their town or village as well as their own personal fame. The more that money entered the picture, particularly if it were "secret" money (today's hidden bonuses), the more loyalty was subverted. For the Greeks, specialization was another natural enemy of the aesthetic-ethical ideal of *kalos kagathos*, the ideal combination of beauty and goodness. An athlete who turns from amateur to professional certainly retains the "beauty" of his skills, but it becomes exceedingly difficult for him or her to remain "good," or untarnished, when the development of a specialty for money becomes the primary concern. Since we don't have the ability the athlete has, we pay to look on, and it is a rare person indeed who will not be bribed by both flattery *and* money. Thus, the athlete tends to raise or lower himself to the moral level of his admirers. If he surrounds himself with opulence, he merely reinforces the perverted taste of his worshippers through his status as a role model, and the cycle becomes more and more vicious until "goodness" is banished altogether.

This is one possibility; another is the development of so many teams because of the greed of owners that the beauty of the athlete will become so commonplace no one will take notice of him, much less pay to see him perform. In February 1975, *Forbes* carried an article entitled "The Sports Boom is Going Bust" with the following observation:

> Ancient Rome taxed its brothels to support its sports arenas. For better or worse, modern America has driven this particular middleman underground, and it looks as though our taxpayers will have to reach into their own pockets to keep many of our new sports arenas in business.
>
> Since 1960 an estimated $1 billion worth of municipally supported arenas have been built. Now with numerous stadiums half filled at best, and many professional teams about to fold, taxpayers will have to shell out close to $1 billion to cover their new arenas' financing cost and operating deficit for the next 20 years.[9]

The *Forbes* article suggests we allow our stadia to follow the example of the Roman Colosseum, that is, crumble and then advertise them as tourist attractions. If the stadium, as Arnold Toynbee observed in his study of the decline of civilizations, is a symbol of decadence, then the collapse of some might be a sign of hope, which is a point that the *Forbes* article is quick to acknowledge: "Sports isn't dying; it is merely shrinking to a more healthy size."[10]

Certainly the sports boom has not burst yet, but concern is widespread. In October 1975 *Esquire* devoted a special issue to the proposition that sports can survive money and assigned Roger Kahn to the lead-off position. In an article of the same title Kahn asks, "Can sports survive money?"

"Quite simply," he says, "it always has. Can sport survive network promotion and television's babbling belief that money is, all by itself, proof of
merit?"[11] This, Kahn implies, is the real question and proceeds to indict
sports journalists, especially the newer breed, for drawing attention to the
staggering salaries without really investigating the truth of the claims. With
men like Roger Kahn and Red Smith in their lineup, *Esquire* presents a good
case for survival and asserts with the gusto of a beer ad: "SPORTS CAN
SURVIVE MONEY, DAMMIT!" Yet in the summer of 1981 ball fans were
still asking that question. For all its assurance *Sports Illustrated* also had
asked that question in the Kennedy and Williamson three-part series.
Pressing questions appeared on the title page: "Are all those O.J.'s and Dr.
J's overpaid? Are the team owners headed for the poorhouse or the count-
inghouse? Is the faithful fan being ripped off? Should all of our programs
be renamed moneyball?" There seems to be no answer to the question, How
much is enough? but most people are likely to agree with Elvin Hayes when
he said, "No athlete is worth the money he is getting—including me."[12]

Yet, it is possible to justify and rationalize the salaries athletes receive.
The editors of the October 1975 special issue of *Esquire* give a list of such
reasons and so do Kennedy and Williamson. The reasons are based on the
same arguments that highly paid athletes offer to the charge that they are
overpaid ingrates. The two lists make a good case on the athlete's behalf,
for they draw upon an appeal to the Protestant work ethic, the child in us
all, and plain sympathy.

Esquire List

Heroes have a price to pay

Muscles do not come cheap

Winning and losing are their
own rewards

The athlete's heart is never
negotiable

Risk can hardly be measured
in dollars

Eternal boyhood is as free as
the air[13]

Sports Illustrated List

There's no biz like show biz—
except sports biz (If Paul
Newman can get rich, why
can't I?)

Nobody knows the trouble
we've seen

One in a million deserves a
million

You only go around once, and
it's a short trip

Don't blame us, blame de massa

Put yourself in our Adidases[14]

With all the hullabaloo over money in sports and the threat of the collapse of the "jock empire," one certainly can appreciate the argument that
there never was an "athletic revolution" to begin with, which is not to
berate the efforts of those who thought that there was or hoped for better
things. In a section entitled "The Counterculture" in *An Inquiry into The
Need for and Feasibility of a National Study of Intercollegiate Athletics*,
George H. Hanford concludes, as Emerson did about society, that there is
the establishment and the movement. In the case of modern sport, the
movement did not, in Hanford's view, ever constitute a serious threat to the
prevailing order:

> Early on in the course of the project, when the chief inquirer was
> attempting to read himself into the literature of sports generally and
> intercollegiate athletics in particular, it appeared that the popular
> books fell into two classifications: those that favored the athletic
> establishment or culture and those that were against the establishment
> or culture—that were anti-establishment or counter-culture in out-
> look. In retrospect and in review near the end of the inquiry, it would
> appear that there is no single counter-culture as such, that *there is no
> unified front committed to bringing down the athletic establishment*,
> and indeed that that establishment is pretty well entrenched and
> secure.[15]

If there has not been "a sports liberation movement" per se, there has
emerged, in the view of Burling Lowrey, "a body of floating ideas" that
constitute the goals of those attempting to humanize sports. Lowrey delin-
eates these ideas of his article "The Dehumanization of Sport" in *The
Virginia Quarterly Review* for autumn 1976:

> 1. One should play to win while avoiding the excesses of the "win-
> ning is everything" philosophy.
> 2. Athletes should be given a voice in the hiring of coaches and in
> the conditions under which they are expected to play.

3. Athletes should be made conscious of the potential destructiveness of the machismo role which has been imposed upon them.

4. Women should be encouraged to participate more fully in sports.

5. Institutional racism should be eliminated. Talented blacks should be employed in managerial positions and as coaches.

6. The use and abuse of drugs should be scrutinized carefully, especially as it applies to athletes playing with injuries and getting "up" for key games.

7. College athletic departments should be placed into the academic mainstream. They should be made responsible to the central authority of the institution along with other departments.

8. Recruiting abuses and the emphasis on acquiring "superstars" should be eliminated.

9. College athletic programs should benefit all the students rather than being used primarily as training grounds for professional athletes.

10. Children should be eased out of organized sports and away from authoritarian coaches into free spontaneous play.[16]

These ideas have been around in one form or another for a long time, but they did not receive widespread attention until a handful of people like Jack Scott, Harry Edwards, and George Leonard began the rallying cries for change in the late 1960s and early 1970s. The net effect of their efforts and those of others carrying on the fight may prove to be minor after all, but that is not yet known.

Most of the works by sportswriters in the 1970s devote some attention to the pervading influence of money in sports, but the most comprehensive treatments of the rise of the dollar are probably Paul Hoch's *Rip Off the Big Game: The Exploitation of Sports by the Power Elite* and Joseph Durso's *The All-American Dollar: The Big Business of Sport*. Hoch's book reveals the social ramifications of corporate manipulations, but constrained as it is by an almost Marxist point of view, his effort appears somewhat Procrustean. Durso's book is a type of exposé but it is superior to his later, hastily written *The Sports Factory: An Investigation into College Sports*, which apparently was thrown together in an effort to show how the commercialism of the professionals also flourishes in some American universities. The intent of *The Sports Factory* is admirable, but instead of presenting the wealth of information that *The All-American Dollar* does, it becomes a compilation of recorded interviews with players recruited and abused by colleges and long excerpts from *An Inquiry Into the Need for and Feasibility of a National Study of Intercollegiate Athletics*. Both Hoch and Durso, however, deserve plaudits for breaking new ground in their attempt to show in detail the complex connections in our society between money and sports, especially from moral and social points of view.

Also deserving of plaudits is Lee Ballinger, whose *In Your Face: Sports for Love and Money* is one of the most refreshing books on sports in recent years. In Ballinger outrage is alive and well. He is "mad as hell" as he says in his introduction over "what's being done to sports in the United States"[17] and he goes on to show the reason for his anger in a very compelling way. The villains, in Ballinger's view, are those who run the present system of sports in Academe and out, and the victims are most of the rest of us, especially the poor, minorities, and women. Ballinger, a steel worker in Warren, Ohio, is perhaps the strongest sports advocate on the scene at present of sports for all, and he never eases his attack on those who in his view stand in the way of that happy condition. *In Your Face!* is a little book, but it packs a wallop in its disturbing depiction of the profit motive behind contemporary sports. It also contains a bibliography with a number of items not usually listed in most works on the subject. Ballinger is also the author of *In Your Face: America's Bluecollar Sport Letter* in which he continues to vent his indignation, often with humor, at the way things are in sportsworld, U.S.A.

One of Ballinger's concerns is that of the exploitation of many college athletes who get neither adequate compensation for their hard work nor an education. This too is one of the concerns of CARE (Center for Athletes' Rights and Education). Sponsored by Sports for the People and cosponsored by the NFL Players Association and National Conference of Black Lawyers, CARE has stated its role as follows:

> In the world of professionalized college sports, our task is to defend the men and women who comprise the athletic workforce. The owners of professionalized collegiate sports have their organization, the NCAA. The managers have their organizations, the College Football (and Basketball) Coaches Association. Justice demands that the athletes have theirs, the Center for Athletes' Rights and Education.
>
> As employees, professionalized college athletes deserve fair compensation for the time and effort their sport requires. Scholarship athletes have a right to share in the allocation of the millions of dollars they generate. CARE proposes that a percentage of their revenues be placed in an Academic Trust Fund (ATF) to help scholarship athletes finish their educations when their college sports careers are over. All scholarship athletes, including those in so-called "non-revenue producing sports" have earned these benefits.[18]

Whether one agrees or disagrees with CARE's approach, the analysis of the problem is both honest and realistic. Understandably, CARE has encountered opposition from officials within the sports establishment but the "nationwide scandal" that constantly hangs over the scene of big-time college athletics calls for extreme measures in one of two directions, major de-emphasis or, as CARE proposes, a sharing in some fashion of the revenue of college sports by the young people who actually produce it.

The economics of sports is a dismal science. It is necessary to keep an eye on contracts and wheeling and dealing behind the scenes, since what goes on in the offices of owners, commissioners, and television executives will ultimately affect the social values exhibited by all sports, amateur as well as professional. The boring half-time pass and punt contests for children, for example, seem like harmless forms of collusion between the NFL, the network, and the sponsor, but its intent is not so much to promote good health among the nation's youth as to keep those footballs in the air and the fans coming to the stadia. Money may be behind all things, yet it is painful to read about the commercial aspects of sports. It is sad, for instance, to read a book like Ralph Andreano's *No Joy in Mudville: The Dilemma of Major League Baseball*, which has much to recommend it, if the author's business point of view is accepted. In chapters entitled "Money and the Folk Hero," "Exporting the FHF [Folk Hero Factor]," and the "Supply of Folk Heroes," Andreano implies that such things can be regulated by manipulation, rather than natural demand. Heroes, we are asked to believe, are commodities, and this is a hard pill to swallow. The business side of baseball, however, need not be a drab and uninteresting subject as Lee Lowenfish and Tony Lupien reveal in *The Imperfect Diamond: The Story of Baseball's Reserve System and the Men Who Fought to Change It*. Both dramatic and factual, *The Imperfect Diamond* shows that while major-league baseball players have always been commodities both before and after the reserve clause was declared illegal in 1976, they themselves now have some voice in shaping their careers. Some fans may object to the free agent system and the unionization of baseball, but it is necessary to keep in mind that unions, like baseball, are as American as apple pie. So too is the right to seek the highest pay for one's own services.

It is astonishing that more has not been written about gambling, that ubiquitous activity. Gambling itself is a form of play, what Roger Caillois in *Man, Play, and Games* calls *alea* (chance). Chances taken in sports, however, differ considerably from those taken on the sidelines. Contests and dramatic performances legitimize chance (*alea*) as well as competition (*agon*), role playing (*mimicry*) and vertigo (*ilinx*). Although in contests athletes engage in one or more of these aspects of play on a regular basis, something is wrong when the spectator becomes too involved in any of them, especially in chance. It is usually an attempt to get much for little, a blatant violation of the law of compensation. An even greater wrong than the spectator's exploitation (or hopes of exploitation) of the sweat of others is gambling by the participant, or worst of all, the manipulation of the out-come by the participant (point shaving) for financial gain. The effects that these practices have had upon individuals and American sports in the last quarter of a century have been disruptive and demoralizing as Stanley Cohen shows in *The Game They Played* and Charles Rosen shows in *Scandals of 1951: How the Gamblers almost Killed College Basketball.* Both deal with the basketball scandals of the 1950s, which occurred at the New York City schools and the University of Kentucky. Both serve to remind us where we've been and where, as far as values are concerned, we might be returning.

In spite of books like *Man, Play, and Games* by Caillois and Thorstein Veblen's *Theory of the Leisure Class*, we still know little about the phe-nomena of chance and the belief in luck. Indeed, the field is relatively unexplored. Stephen Longstreet has made a contribution to the field in *Win or Lose*, a history of the popularity of gambling in sports, but much more needs to be done not only on the history of gambling but also on the philos-ophy behind it. There are major issues to be resolved. For example, if gambling, like competition, role-playing, and intoxication, is a natural instinct and if sports legitimize these instincts by rules and a system of open rewards, then would it not make some sense to allow some forms of gam-bling? Instead of the constant and exhausting effort to keep spectator gam-bling out of sports and especially out of the hands of players, which means total corruption, it might be wiser to carry the principles of sports—its emphasis upon fair play—to the larger arena of society. Perhaps we should recognize gambling as the natural form of play that it is and establish clear-cut rules for controlling it for the general welfare of society. Like the Greeks, we have learned that sports and money do not easily mix, especially money and gambling, but the case for gambling on sports remains to be presented. Just as there has to be a better way to recruit athletes for college play, so too there has to be a better system of gambling than the illegal one that undergirds both college and professional athletics. Open gambling on college football games with betting windows in the stadia might be the *coup de grâce* for the game as many would contend; it might also be the most honest, profitable, and genuinely beneficial course of action imaginable. The possibilities and ramifications of gambling are vast.

NOTES

1. Jack Scott, *The Athletic Revolution* (New York: Free Press, 1971), p. v.

2. Glenn Dickey, *The Jock Empire: Its Rise and Deserved Fall* (Radnor, Pa.: Chilton Book Co., 1974), p. vii.

3. Larry Merchant, *...And Every Day You Take Another Bite* (New York: Doubleday, 1971), p. 49.

4. Christopher Lasch, "The Corruption of Sports," *New York Review of Books* 24 (April 28, 1977), 28.

5. Thomas Wolfe, *The Web and the Rock* (New York: Harper and Row, 1939), p. 122.

6. Lasch, p. 26.

7. Ray Kennedy and Nancy Williamson, "For the Athlete, How Much is Enough?" *Sports Illustrated* 49 (July 24, 1978), 38.

8. Wright Morris, *The Territory Ahead* (New York: Harcourt, Brace and Company, 1958), p. 22.

9. "The Sports Boom is Going Bust," *Forbes* 115 (February 15, 1975), 26.

10. Ibid., p. 24.

11. Roger Kahn, "Can Sports Survive Money?" *Esquire* 84 (October 1975), 108.

12. Quoted in Kennedy and Williamson, p. 36.

13. Editorial, *Esquire* 84 (October 1975), 109.

14. Kennedy and Williamson, p. 38.

15. George H. Hanford, *An Inquiry into the Need for a Feasibility of a National Study of Intercollegiate Athletics*, 2 vols. (Washington, D.C.: American Council on Higher Education, 1974), p. 60.

16. Burling Lowrey, "The Dehumanization of Sports," *The Virginia Quarterly Review* 52 (Autumn 1976), 556-57.

17. Lee Ballinger, *In Your Face: Sports for Love and Money* (Chicago: Vanguard Books), p. 1.

18. *Athletes' Rights Bulletin: A Newsletter of the Center for Athletes' Rights and Education* 1, No. 1 (Winter 1982), 2.

BIBLIOGRAPHY

Andreano, Ralph. *No Joy in Mudville: The Dilemma of Major League Baseball.* Introduction by Jim Brosnan. Cambridge, Mass.: Schenkman Publishing Company, 1965.

Ballinger, Lee. *In Your Face: Sports for Love and Money.* Chicago: Vanguard Books, 1981.

———. *In Your Face: America's Bluecollar Sport Letter.* Published monthly by author. All-Star Features, Box 1041, Warren Ohio, 44481.

Bouton, Jim. *Ball Four.* Edited by Leonard Shecter. New York: Dell, 1971.

Caillois, Roger. *Man, Play, and Games.* Translated by Meyer Barash. New York: Free Press, 1961.

Cohen, Stanley. *The Game They Played.* New York: Farrar, Straus, and Giroux, 1977.

Dickey, Glenn. *The Jock Empire: Its Rise and Deserved Fall.* Radnor, Pa.: Chilton Book Company, 1974.

Durso, Joseph. *The All-American Dollar: The Big Business of Sport.* Boston: Houghton Mifflin, 1971.

———. *The Sports Factory: An Investigation into College Sports.* Boston: Houghton Mifflin, 1971.

Edwards, Harry. *The Revolt of the Black Athlete.* New York: Free Press, 1969.

Esquire. Special Issue: The Joy of Sports. 84 (October 1975).

Gent, Pete. *North Dallas Forty.* New York: Morrow, 1973.

Hanford, George H. *An Inquiry into the Need for and Feasibility of a National*

Study of Intercollegiate Athletics. 2 vols. Washington, D.C.: American Council on Higher Education, 1974.

Hoch, Paul. *Rip Off the Big Game: The Exploitation of Sports by the Power Elite.* New York: Anchor, 1972.

Izenberg, Jerry. *How Many Miles to Camelot?* New York: Holt, Rinehart, and Winston, 1972.

Jenkins, Dan. *Semi-Tough.* New York: New American Library, 1973.

Kahn, Roger. "Can Sports Survive Money?" *Esquire* 84 (October 1975), 105-9.

Kennedy, Ray, and Nancy Williamson. "Money: The Monster Threatening Sports." *Sports Illustrated*, 17 July 1978, pp. 19-88; "For the Athlete, How Much is Enough?" 24 July 1978, pp. 34-49; "The Fans: Are They up in Arms?" 31 July 1978.

Lasch, Christopher. "The Corruption of Sports." *New York Review of Books* 24 (April 28, 1977), 24-30. Revised and reprinted as "The Degradation of Sport," in *The Culture of Narcissism.* New York: W. W. Norton, 1978.

Longstreet, Stephen. *Win or Lose.* Indianapolis: Bobbs-Merrill, 1977.

Lowenfish, Lee, with Tony Lupien. *The Imperfect Diamond: The Story of Baseball's Reserve System and the Men Who Fought to Change It.* New York: Stein and Day, 1980.

Lowrey, Burling. "The Dehumanization of Sports." *The Virginia Quarterly Review* 52 (Autumn 1976), 545-59.

Meggyesy, Dave. *Out of Their League.* Berkeley: Ramparts, 1970.

Merchant, Larry. *. . . And Every Day You Take Another Bite.* New York: Doubleday, 1971.

Morris, Wright. *The Territory Ahead.* New York: Harcourt, Brace and Company, 1958.

Oliver, Chip. *High for the Game.* Edited by Ron Rapoport. New York: Morrow, 1971.

Parrish, Bernie. *They Call It a Game.* New York: Dial Press, 1971.

Rosen, Charles. *The Scandals of 1951: How the Gamblers Almost Killed College Basketball.* New York: Holt, Rinehart, and Winston, 1978.

Scott, Jack. *The Athletic Revolution.* New York: Free Press, 1971.

Shaw, Gary. *Meat on the Hoof.* New York: St. Martin's Press, 1972.

Shector, Leonard. *The Jocks.* New York: Paper Library, 1969.

"The Sports Boom is Going Bust." *Forbes* 115 (February 15, 1975), 24-28.

Veblen, Thorstein. *Theory of the Leisure Class.* 1899. Reprint. New York: Macmillan Co., 1953.

Weiss, Paul. *Sport: A Philosophic Inquiry.* Carbondale, Ill.: Southern Illinois University Press, 1969.

Wolfe, Thomas. *The Web and the Rock.* New York: Harper and Row, 1939.

CHAPTER 7

Sports, Race, and Sex

If there has not been a revolution in sports, in the opinion of Harry Edwards, author of *The Revolt of the Black Athlete*, there has been the development of a "new consciousness among people not only in America but throughout the world about what sports *is* and what it *should be*."[1] A year before Edwards's book appeared, Jack Olsen wrote a series of articles entitled "The Black Athlete: A Shameful Story" that appeared in *Sports Illustrated* in 1968 and were published in book form the following year, when Edwards' work also appeared. Both men were pioneers in the development of the new consciousness on aspects of race, and both books must now be considered as milestones of moral outrage over racial inequality. The series of articles by Olsen evoked more responses than any other series in the history of the magazine, according to Donna Mae Miller and Kathryn R. E. Russell in *Sport: A Contemporary View*. Both *The Black Athlete: A Shameful Story* and *The Revolt of the Black Athlete* are more than catalogs of shameful practices; they constitute a call for the elimination of racial prejudice not just on the playing fields but in every corner of life. While Edwards's work is more political than Olsen's, both are reminders that the athlete cannot and should not exist *in vacuo*. If he is a symbol of the tastes, beliefs, and attitudes of a particular society, then he should be able to help shape that society toward more democratic practices.

Needless to say, Edwards's promotion of a black boycott of the 1968 Olympics did not meet with universal support, even among blacks. Other men of good will, including Jesse Owens, disagreed with the idea of a boycott. Their attitude in Edwards's view was fostered by the "controlled generation" of which they were a part. Edwards believes that Owens was exploited, which he claims Owens admitted to friends, but the boycott in Owens's view was too severe. His approach to the problem is best defined in his autobiography *Blackthink* (written with Paul G. Neimark), especially in the chapter entitled "An Open Letter to a Young Negro." In this chapter he calls upon Edwards to moderate not his ideals but his solutions.

As influential as the works of Olsen and Edwards have been, they pale in comparison with the influence exerted through the dramatic successes of a long line of athletic champions whose triumphs quite often have been victories for democracy itself. Notable among these have been the accomplishments of Jesse Owens, Joe Louis, and Jackie Robinson. As always, actions have spoken louder than words, although words too have had an effect, especially when they have served to recall the obstacles overcome by several great black champions and their contribution to fair play.

Regardless of what methods brought the best results, in the last decade there has been a tremendous improvement in the situation of the black athlete, amateur and professional, if one judges from statistics alone. A *Time* article, "The Black Dominance," argues that blacks possess an inherent athletic superiority over whites and by way of proof points to the percentages of black athletes in professional and collegiate sport. As of 1977, nearly 65 percent of the NBA (National Basketball Association), 42 percent of the NFL (National Football League), and 19 percent of major league baseball players were black. These same proportions were found in the college ranks and among U.S. Olympic athletes.

"The Black Dominance" and an earlier, much-discussed essay, "An Assessment of 'Black is Best' " by Martin Kane, build a strong case for black athletic superiority, but before accepting the conclusion of either article one should read "The Myth of the Racially Superior Athlete" by Harry Edwards, which appeared in *The Black Scholar* in 1971. According to Edwards, Kane's article implies that whites are intellectually superior, a myth that has been used to justify a multitude of sins.

Dr. Alvin F. Pouissant, professor of psychiatry at Harvard University, agrees with Edwards that the idea of innate black physical ability or capacity should not be accepted. In an *Ebony* article entitled "Are Black Athletes Naturally Superior?" Pouissant is quoted as saying, "I don't think it's safe and I don't think that notion should be promoted at all—for a number of reasons. Frequently there is this whole business implied that blacks are better in athletics because they are 'mere animal'; therefore they can excel in sports but aren't much good at doing things with the brain."[2] He goes on to say that the inordinate number of black participants (in proportion to black population) is the result of cultural and environmental influences.

Through his excellence in sports, the black athlete has become a folk hero to millions of Americans—particularly young black Americans. Arthur Ashe noted in an article entitled "Send Your Child to the Library" that such a situation is fraught with subtle but familiar problems:

> So your child gets a massive dose of O. J. Simpson, Kareem Abdul-Jabbar, Muhammad Ali, Reggie Jackson, Dr. J., and Lee Elder and other pro athletes. And it is only natural that your child will dream of being a pro athlete himself.

> But consider these facts: For the major professional sports of hockey, football, basketball, baseball, golf, tennis, and boxing there are roughly only 3,170 major league positions available (attributing

200 positions to golf, 200 to tennis and 100 to boxing). And the annual turnover is small.

We blacks are a subculture of about 28 million: Of the 13½ million men, 5 to 6 million are under 20 years of age, so your son has less than one chance in 1,000 of becoming a pro. Less than one in a thousand. Would you bet your son's future on something with odds of 999 to 1 against you? I wouldn't.[3]

Ashe's advice is simple, when one considers the odds against anyone, black or white, becoming a successful athlete: Go some other route. Find other talents. Says Ashe, "We have been on the same roads—sports and entertainment—too long. We need to pull over, fill up at the library, and speed away to Congress and the Supreme Court, the unions and the business world." Noting that much will be gained and nothing lost, Ashe writes: "Don't worry: we will still be able to sing and dance and run and jump better than anybody else."[4] It is interesting to note that what Ashe has turned to here in his advice to black parents to stress education is the noblest of all ideals, *mens sana in corpore sano*, which unfortunately has come to seem like an empty platitude, or worse, a white front for the exploitation of athletes of all colors under the guise of character building, developing the whole man, or the importance of winning.

Black leaders as well as white have seen through this ruse and are calling, like the Reverend Jesse Jackson, for excellence, not just in one field but in all, what the Greeks called *aretê*. Ashe is not the first black to make this particular call to action. In fact, practically every point that Ashe makes was made at least a decade earlier by a number of other black athletes. It is a point that is emphasized and reemphasized throughout Olsen's *The Black Athlete: A Shameful Story*, especially in the chapter entitled "Oh, I Can Read, but It's Such a Burden." After pointing out the depressing statistics on the black athletes who have graduated from college, Olsen quotes Harry Edwards who succinctly states the problem, which as any honest professor will admit, has not gone away: "They [black college athletes] don't get an education. Their primary responsibility is to the athletic department, and at the end of four years they wind up with no degree, no job and no references."[5] This same unfortunate fact is equally true of white college athletes. They aren't educated; and the common enemy to both black and white is overemphasis of the body at the expense of the mind. The solution is not to eliminate academic requirements for outstanding athletes, as Michener suggests, but, as Arthur Ashe advises, to reemphasize the value of learning.

Discrimination against women, like that against blacks, has been a prominent issue in sports in recent years. If the word "revolution" applies anywhere in the world of sports, it does so most deservedly in the case of women athletes. In June 1978 the title of the *Time* cover story was "Comes the Revolution," and as *Time* put it, "they have come a long, long way."[6]

While prejudice directed toward women in sport has often been as blatant as that directed toward minorities, the issues are more complex. Prejudice grows out of, or at least is fostered by, cultural attitudes, but in the case of women there are physiological considerations as well, although the considerations once frequently cited, primarily menstruation, parturition, lactation, and fear of injury to reproductive organs and breasts, are now recognized to be not as inhibiting as previously believed. It is now generally believed that "the normal healthy female may participate in any athletic endeavor for which her training and experience prepare her." This view, expressed by Clayton L. Thomas in "The Female Sports Participant: Some Physiological Questions," is essentially supported by Dr. Tenley Albright, who is an athlete as well as a surgeon: ". . . doors are continuing to open for women in sports, and the limit should be what the girl sets for herself. The safeguards are pretty much built in." Both of these essays are contained in an important book on the subject entitled *DGWS* [The Division for Girls and Women's Sports] *Research Reports: Women In Sports* and edited by Dorothy V. Harris of Pennsylvania State University, a leading authority in the field. The myths surrounding the physiology of women as an inhibiting factor in sports and play are being systematically exploded and the possibilities for the involvement of women in sports are greater than ever before. Any researcher interested in this field certainly should read and study such works as *DGWS Research Reports* and *The Female Athlete: Conditioning, Competition, and Culture* by Carl E. Klafs and M. Joan Lyon.

What games women are biologically capable of playing is one matter— and there would seem to be none based on physiological considerations alone—and what games they should play in the view of society is another matter. Cultural and social attitudes exert powerful influences on the determination of the role of women in sport. Eleanor Metheny has given considerable thought to this subject in her book, *Connotations of Movement in Sport and Dance.* She centers her approach around the roles of mythological figures in sport, for example, Heracles, Hippolyta, and Theseus. Metheny believes the basic question revolves around the degree of force a women may use in overcoming the inertia of mass, either in the form of another person or an object. Although, as Klafs and Lyon remark, some combative sports like judo are finding a degree of cultural acceptance, there is still strong social opposition to the idea of women attempting, in the words of Metheny, "to overcome an opponent by direct application of bodily force." Metheny feels that a clue to this prohibition "may lie in the difference between the ways in which males and females may use their own bodily forces in the mutual act of procreation."[7]

The role or image of women in sports will become increasingly important in light of the opportunities presented under Title IX of the Education Amendments Act, which was passed by Congress in 1972 and specifically forbids sexual discrimination in any educational institution receiving federal funds. Many people believe that this act, perhaps the most important in the history of American athletics, ultimately may change sports as we know them. If this does happen, it will be for the good; in fact, nothing else bodes so well for the democratization of sports. While equal rights for blacks in sports was a simple matter of justice, the fact remains that black athletes by their very excellence, especially in spectator sports, have unwittingly reinforced a system of spectacle that is unrelentingly exploited for purely commercial ends. While professional opportunities also are opening up for women on a scale previously unequaled, women also are drawing attention to a wide range of less popular amateur sports, such as rowing, lacrosse, rugby, and fencing. These sports require money from the athletic budget just as the far more costly sports do. The pie must be shared now, and while it will be some time before it is divided equally, change is inevitable. Women in sports may lead to greater democratization, or they may fall into the same trap that men did and overemphasize recruiting and winning. As early as 1931 Mable Lee, one of the pioneers in women's physical education, offered a cautionary note in her article on "The Case For and Against Intercollegiate Athletics for Women and the Situation Since 1923":

It is interesting to note the rising tide of condemnation of men's intercollegiate athletics. It has grown from a mild protest, voiced by a few in the study of 1923, to most emphatic statements of disapproval, voiced by a large number in this present study of 1930. There exists a great fear that once intercollegiate athletics for women gain a foothold, college women might become involved in the same athletic predicament of their brothers. The director who replies in the following strain seems to voice the opinion of the great majority when she says, "I would approve of a program of intercollegiate athletics for women if it would actually be conducted as amateur sports should be conducted but not as men's intercollegiate athletics are conducted in this country." There is ever present the alarming thought that women might become involved in something equally undesirable. Directors for women seem to feel that these fears are not altogether idle fancies, judging from the pressure being brought to bear in yearly growing force from certain sources.[8]

In the view of Michigan Athletic Director Donald Canham, the worse has already happened. Quoted in "Comes the Revolution," he laments, "The women had a golden opportunity to establish an athletic program with the men's mistakes as a guide. I think women will regret the change. They now have almost an exact copy of men's sports—with all the mistakes."[9]

Women, like men, deserve the right to make mistakes, but it is to be hoped that they will not continue to do so in sports, especially because the mistakes in the past have been so flagrant.

So much has been written on the issues of race and sex in sports that an entire book would be required merely to list the bibliographic items. A good survey of the situation can be found in Jack Scott's *The Athletic Revolution*. For more detail on the issue of race, one should begin with *The Black Athlete: A Shameful Story* by Jack Olsen and *The Revolt of the Black Athlete* by Harry Edwards. Other noteworthy works on the subject are *The Black Athlete: His Story in American History* by Jack Orr and *Pioneers of Black Sport* by Ocania Chalk. A marvelous work on baseball during the years of Jim Crowe is Robert Peterson's *Only The Ball Was White*. On the same topic and equally informative is *Josh W. Gibson: A Life in the Negro Leagues* by William Brashler. Still another contribution to this relatively neglected aspect of American sporting culture is "Reading the Hops: Recollections of Lorenzo Piper Davis and the Negro Baseball League," an interview with Theodore Rosengarten that appears in "Long Journey Home: Folklife in the South," a special issue of *Southern Exposure*. Although he never made it to the big leagues, Davis was the third black ball player of modern times to sign a major league contract after Jackie Robinson and Larry Doby. Edwin Bancroft Henderson offers a general history that ends with the beginning of World War II in *The Negro in Sports*. The story of racial prejudice in boxing is found in John Lardner's superb book, *White Hopes and Other Tigers*. Lardner reports that one talent scout, Walter (Good Time Charlie) Friedman went to China "to look for a white hope among the Chinese peasants." According to Lardner, "the last publicist to invoke the idea—or rather to paraphrase it—was Dr. J. P. Goebbels, when he billed Max Schmeling's second fight with Louis, in 1938, as a mission to restore the championship to Aryan control."[10] The themes of white and black hopes have been utilized in three movies in recent years, *The Great White Hope*, *The Greatest*, and *Rocky*. Numerous books deal with the black man's struggle for equality in sports. *The Dictionary Catalog of the Schomburg Collection of Negro Literature and History* of the New York Public Library lists over seventy titles on the general subject in basic publications and supplements. *The Chicago Afro-American Union Analytic Catalog* lists over eighty articles from such magazines as *Time*, *Crisis*, and *Opportunity*. The *Bibliographic Guide to Black Studies*, published annually by G. K. Hall and based upon materials catalogued during the previous year by the New York Public Library Schomburg Center for Research in Black Culture, also contains entries under sports and athletes. Items on blacks in the major professional sports can be found in *Black Athletes in the United States: A Bibliography of Books, Articles, Autobiographies, and Biographies on Professional Black Athletes, 1880-1981* by Lenwood G. Davis and Belinda S. Daniels.

In addition to the authorities on women's sports that have already been mentioned, there are Pearl Berlin, Ellen Gerber, M. Marie Hart, and Celeste Ulrich, to name only a few. H. A. Harris has a brief account of women in sports in antiquity in his *Greek Athletes and Athletics*, and Paul Weiss has devoted a chapter to the subject in *Sport: A Philosophic Inquiry*, a book that is often referred to in other studies. An excellent survey on women in sports with an extensive bibliography can be found in *Sport: A Contemporary View* by Donna Mae Miller and Kathryn R. E. Russell. Although not as recent as the *Time* article "Comes the Revolution," the three-part series in *Sports Illustrated* by Bill Gilbert and Nancy Williamson beginning May 28, 1973 with the title "Sport is Unfair to Women" provides a wider coverage. Mary Mckeown is the author of Appendix 4 on women in intercollegiate sport in *An Inquiry into the Need for and Feasibility of a National Study of Intercollegiate Athletics* by George H. Hanford, which is a solid treatment of the subject and a plea for more decisive action as well. Still other recommendations can be found in "Athletics and Equality: How to Comply with Title IX without Tearing down the Stadium" by George R. LaNoue which appeared in *Change* for November 1976.

Penetrating insight and incisive commentary can be found in Lee Bal-linger's *In Your Face: Sports for Love and Money*, especially in the chapter entitled "Three Times a Lady: Bench Press, Deadlift, Squat." In fact, Ballinger lays down a hard challenge to everyone involved in sports, both women and men.

> The women's sports movement has two paths open to it. It can continue to focus on the athletic and business success of a small group of women or it can shift its emphasis to the vast majority of women who are generally left out of American political life: women in the ghettos and the barrios; on the reservations and in the backwaters of the South, the Southwest, and Appalachia. Sports must be made available to the women who work in the fields from California to the Rio Grande Valley to Florida; to the women who labor in the textile mills of Georgia and the Carolinas; to the women who create our electronic hardware in the silicon valleys of California, Texas, and Massachusetts; and to the countless women who wait on tables, work in offices, or clean other people's homes.[11]

Women in sports today tends to be a popular subject, but for those wishing to delve into the history of it, Earle F. Zeigler's article, "A Brief Chronicle of Sport and Physical Activity for Women," is a good place to start for a capsule introduction and information on sources. A bibliography of eighty-three items is appended to the article. The article appears in *A History of Physical Education and Sport in the United States and*

Canada, which Zeigler edited. Other informative articles in the collection are "The Effect of Some Cultural Change upon the Sports and Physical Education Activities of American Women, 1860-1962" by Marianna Trekell and "The History of Physical Education in Colleges for Women (U.S.A.)" by Dorothy S. Ainsworth. The section on equality and its notes in chapter 2 of *From Ritual to Record: the Nature of Modern Sports* by Allen Guttman are also valuable. The *Bibliography of Theses and Dissertations Concerning Intercollegiate Athletics* prepared by Dale Meggas, research assistant for the National Collegiate Athletic Association, contains a listing of sixteen dissertations on women's athletics from 1970-1977. Perhaps the most comprehensive reference work on the subject is edited by Mary L. Remley and entitled *Women in Sport: A Guide to Information Sources*. One wishing to research women in the modern Olympics should read *A Historical Analysis of the Role of Women in the Modern Olympic Games* by Uriel Simri and the review by Mary L. Leigh in *Journal of Sport History* (Summer 1978) as well as the subsequent exchange between the author and reviewer in the *Journal* (Fall 1978). Women in sport is a comparatively easy topic to research. A publication devoted entirely to the subject is *Women Sports* which is published by Bille Jean King. Many of the studies available are recent and well indexed in various sources, including most of the data base feeding computer systems. Within thirty minutes I have been able to retrieve over fifty references on women and Title IX legislation from one computer system. Although many humanists may recoil at the idea of computer search, it is a prejudice that must be overcome.

If one wants some comic relief from the scholarly dissertations on women in sports, a little jewel to turn to is *The Athletic Snowball* by Charles B. Corbin with illustrations by Jim Raatz. The satire is directed not so much at women or men but at the aggrandizing tendencies of all humans. Once there was an innocent little snowball that young people made to have fun. Slowly the snowball grew and grew and grew until finally it came to rest at the edge of a precipice and had to be supported by all kinds of structures contrived by the college president, athletic directors and boards, and the alumni to keep it from rolling off. On a nearby hill, the women can be seen pushing another snowball down the hill, still having fun but headed in the same direction. This fine little book is not necessarily a prophecy, but it should at least be read as a warning.

NOTES

1. Harry Edwards, *The Revolt of the Black Athlete* (New York: Free Press, 1969), p. xxiii.

2. Quoted in Bill Rhoden, "Are Black Athletes Naturally Superior," *Ebony* 30 (December 1974), 138.

3. Arthur Ashe, "Send Your Children to the Library," *New York Times*, 6 February 1977.

4. Ibid.

5. Jack Olsen, *The Black Athlete: A Shameful Story* (New York: Time-Life Books, 1968), p. 87.

6. "Comes the Revolution," *Time*, 26 June 1978, p. 54.

7. Eleanor Metheny, *Connotations of Movement in Sport and Dance* (Dubuque, Iowa: William C. Brown, 1965), p. 52.

8. Mable Lee, "The Case For and Against Intercollegiate Athletics for Women and the Situation Since 1923," *Research Quarterly* 2 (May 1931), 124-25.

9. "Comes the Revolution," p. 59.

10. John Lardner, *White Hopes and Other Tigers* (Philadelphia: J. B. Lippincott, 1956), pp. 20-21.

11. Lee Ballinger. *In Your Face: Sports for Love and Money* (Chicago: Vanguard Books), p. 102.

BIBLIOGRAPHY

Ashe, Arthur. "Send Your Child to the Library." *New York Times*, 6 February 1977. Section 5.

Ballinger, Lee. *In Your Face: Sports for Love and Money*. Chicago: Vanguard Books, 1982.

Bibliographic Guide to Black Studies. Boston: G. K. Hall, 1975-.

"The Black Dominance." *Time*. 9 May 1977, pp. 56-60.

Brashler, William. *Josh W. Gibson: A Life in the Negro Leagues*. New York: Harper and Row, 1978.

Chalk, Ocania. *Pioneers of Black Sport: The Early Days of the Black Professional Athlete in Baseball, Basketball, Boxing, and Football* New York: Dodd, Mead, 1975.

The Chicago Afro-American Union Analytic Catalog. Boston: G. K. Hall, 1972.

"Comes the Revolution." *Time*, 26 June 1978, pp. 54-60.

Corbin, Charles B. *The Athletic Snowball*. Champaign, Ill.: Human Kinetics Publishers, 1977.

Davis, Lenwood G., and Belinda S. Daniels. *Black Athletes in the United States: A Bibliography of Books, Articles, Autobiographies, and Biographies on Professional Black Athletes, 1880-1981*. Westport, Conn.: Greenwood Press, 1981.

The Dictionary Catalog of the Schomberg Collection of Negro Literature and History. 9 vols. Boston: G. K. Hall, 1962; 2 supplements, 1972.

Edwards, Harry. "The Myth of the Racially Superior Athlete." *Black Scholar* 3 (1971), 16-28.

_____. *The Revolt of the Black Athlete*. New York: Free Press, 1969.

Gerber, Ellen W., Jan Felshin, Pearl Berlin, Waneen Wyrick, eds. *The American Woman in Sport*. Reading, Mass.: Addison-Wesley Publishing Company, 1974.

Gilbert, Bill, and Nancy Williamson, "Sport is Unfair to Women." *Sports Illustrated*, 28 May 1973, pp. 88-98; "Are You Being Two-Faced? *Sports*

Illustrated, 4 June 1973, pp. 44-54; and "Programmed to Be Losers." *Sports Illustrated*, 11 June 1973, pp. 60-73.

Guttman, Allen. *From Ritual to Record: The Nature of Modern Sports*. New York: Columbia University Press, 1978.

Hanford, George H. *An Inquiry into the Need for and Feasibility of a National Study of Intercollegiate Athletics*. 2 vols. Washington, D.C.: American Council on Higher Education, 1974.

Harris, Dorothy V., ed. *DGWS Research Reports: Women In Sports*. Washington, D.C.: American Association for Health, Physical Education, and Recreation, 1971.

Harris, H. A. *Greek Athletes and Athletics*. Bloomington: Indiana University Press, 1966.

Hart, Marie M., ed. *Sport in the Socio-Cultural Process*. Dubuque, Iowa: William C. Brown, 1976.

Henderson, Edwin Bancroft. *The Negro in Sports*. Washington, D.C.: Associate Publishers, 1939.

Kane, Martin. "An Assessment of 'Black is Best'." *Sports Illustrated*, 18 July 1971, pp. 72-76.

Klafs, Carl E., and M. Joan Lyon. *The Female Athlete: Conditioning, Competition, and Culture*. Saint Louis, Mo.: C. V. Mosby, 1978.

LaNoue, George R. "Athletics and Equality: How to Comply with Title IX without Tearing Down the Stadium." *Change* 8 (November 1976), 27-30, 63-64.

Lardner, John. *White Hopes and Other Tigers*. Philadelphia: J. B. Lippincott, 1956.

Lee, Mable. "The Case for and Against Intercollegiate Athletics for Women, and the Situation Since 1923." *The Research Quarterly* of the American Physical Education Association 2, No. 2 (May 1931).

Leigh, Mary L. Review of *A Historical Analysis of the Role of Women in the Modern Olympic Games*. *Journal of Sport History* 5 (Summer 1978), 98-100.

Meggas, Dale. *Bibliography of Theses and Dissertations Concerning Intercollegiate Athletics*. 1978. Available through office of National Collegiate Association, P.O. Box 1906, Shawnee Mission, Kansas 66222.

Metheny, Eleanor. *Connotations of Movement in Sport and Dance*. Dubuque, Iowa: William C. Brown, 1965.

Miller, Donna Mae, and Katherine R. E. Russell. *Sport: A Contemporary View*. Philadelphia: Lea and Febiger, 1971.

Olsen, Jack. *The Black Athlete: A Shameful Story*. New York: Lions Press, 1969.

Orr, Jack. *The Black Athlete: His Story in American History*. Introduction by Jackie Robinson. New York: Pyramid Books, 1969.

Owens, Jesse, with Paul G. Neimark. *Blackthink*. New York: Putnam, 1970.

Peterson, Robert. *Only the Ball Was White*. Englewood Cliffs, N.J.: Prentice-Hall, 1971.

"Reading the Hops: Recollections of Lorenzo Piper Davis and the Negro Baseball League," an interview with Theodore Rosengarten. *Southern Exposure* 5 (Summer and Fall 1977), 62-79.

Remley, Mary L., ed. *Women in Sport: A Guide to Information Sources*. Detroit: Gale Research Co., 1980.

Rhoden, Bill. "Are Black Athletes Naturally Superior?" *Ebony* 30 (December 1974), 42-46, 136-40.

Simri, Uriel. *A Historical Analysis of the Role of Women in the Modern Olympic Games.* Wingate, Israel: The Wingate Institute of Physical Education and Sport, 1977.

Ulrich, Celeste. *To Seek and Find.* Washington, D.C.: American Alliance for Health, Physical Education, and Recreation, 1977.

Weiss, Paul. *Sport: A Philosophic Inquiry.* Carbondale, Ill.: Southern Illinois University Press, 1969.

Women Sports. Magazine published monthly by Women's Sports Publications, Palo Alto, California. Beginning year, 1974.

Zeigler, Earle F., ed. *A History of Physical Education and Sport in the United States and Canada.* Champaign, Ill.: Stipes Publishing Company, 1975.

CHAPTER 8

The Sports Hero

It has often been said that heroes are dead and we live in an antiheroic age. The sports world belies such assertions. Here the hero is alive and well. It is not a question of whether or not heroes are dead but rather what *type* of heroism is popular at any particular time in history. The fact that the athlete always has been a popular hero suggests that there is something inherently heroic about sports. What is it about sports that engenders heroism and hero-worship? First it is necessary to define the hero, or at least to outline various theories of the hero.

All theories of the hero come back to or are related in some way to the monomyth, a term coined by James Joyce and explained by Joseph Campbell in the opening chapter of *The Hero with a Thousand Faces*. "A Hero ventures forth from the world of common day into a region of supernatural wonder: fabulous forces are there encountered and a decisive victory is won: the hero comes back from this mysterious adventure with the power to bestow boons on his fellow man."[1] The hero, then, is one who achieves distinction in action. He or she through superhuman action performs deeds that others admire but cannot themselves perform. One should not be charged with Procrusteanism or a tendency to mythologize in drawing parallels between the athlete and the hero of myth. An equally valid interpolation of Campbell's definition might well be as follows: The athlete ventures forth from the world of profane time (training and practice) into the region of supernatural wonder, that is, sacred time in special places (Soldier Field, Yankee Stadium, Wimbledon). Fabulous forces are encountered, and a decisive victory is won. The athlete comes back from this mysterious adventure with the power to bestow boons on his fellow man, that is a sense of identity and self-worth.

The challenge of hitting a baseball or golf ball or an elusive foe in the ring provides a natural setting for the heroic, the dramatic, and the spectacular. The athlete, however, as Neil D. Isaacs points out in *Jock Culture, U.S.A.*, achieves the status of hero not just through action but through a mysterious charisma as well.

In the presence of three athletes I have experienced a sense of presences that extended beyond the physical dimensions of their bodies. It was clearly not a matter of size, though two of the athletes were large men, Muhammad Ali and Westley Unseld. The third was Bill Shoemaker. These men seemed to me larger than life. Their energy bodies, as George Leonard might put it, filled the space around them and dominated large rooms. I felt what was almost the pressure of a power that radiated from within them. And in each case the feeling was strongest when the men were quiet and their bodies still. In repose, these figures projected a sense of enormous energy and strength and will.[2]

Isaacs goes on to say that such experiences may appear to be "romantic blather," but he has made every effort to state his impressions as objectively as possible. His testimony is not "blather," but it is "romantic," and an experience shared by many people at many times, including F. Scott Fitzgerald whose romanticism sensitized him to the unusual qualities in others. Fitzgerald, for example, stood in raptured awe of Hobie Baker, the Princeton All-American who was killed in France in 1918. According to John Davies in his *Esquire* article, "It's Baker!...Going for Another Touchdown!" Baker served as a model for Allenby and to some extent Amory in *This Side of Paradise*. As Davies points out, Fitzgerald remembered Baker as "an ideal worthy of everything in my enthusiastic admiration, yet consummated and expressed in a human being who stood within ten feet of me."[3] It is a distinction in itself to be aware of a "presence."

In the view of many the existence of this "presence" in our society is rare. It is this view with which Joe McGinnis in *Heroes* would tend to agree. McGinnis searched for heroes almost like a medieval knight in quest of the holy grail or Good Time Charley Friedman in search of a Great White Hope during the reign of Jack Johnson, or John J. McGraw beating the bushes for a Jewish Babe Ruth. McGinnis talked with successes in all walks of American life from politicians and generals to poets and playwrights and even to Joseph Campbell, but the story was always the same—*Götterdämmerung!* Sports fared no better in his evaluation than any other activity:

In sports, another traditional breeding ground for American heroes, mythic dimension seemed lost. One could note, perhaps, the difference between the tumultuous public enthusiasm for Babe Ruth and the respectful but basically disinterested attitude it maintained toward Henry Aaron as he moved inexorably toward the moment when he would surpass Ruth's greatest statistical feat. Aaron was black, of course, and possessed of a distinctly uncharismatic personality; but underlying these differences was what seemed a more central fact: the hero as home-run king was no more—due, at least in part, to television and to the overexposure of sports by television throughout the Sixties. "Every hero becomes a bore at last," Emerson said, and, with the relentless televising of seemingly endless, interchangeable, and heavily sponsored seasons, "at last" was here before we knew it.[4]

Every hero may bore at last as Emerson says, but the heroic never bores, which is another way of saying heroism never dies. As in the days before television, the atomic bomb, and the Vietnam War, young and old alike still ask for autographs. Even when heroes disappoint us, as they always do, or vanish, we never stop hoping.

McGinnis was looking for a hero of long ago who, in the view of critic Victor Brambert, "provided a transcendental link between the contingencies of the finite and the imagined realm of the supernatural."[5] This is the same type of hero that Eric Bentley describes in *A Century of Hero-Worship*:

> There are three groups of circuits: those which run between one center and another within the individual; those which run between individuals; and those which run between an individual and the non-human cosmos. The Lawrentian theory of the hero should now be more exactly comprehended. The hero is a necessity because most people lack the third kind of circuit, that which runs between a man and the cosmos. The hero is the man who is most fully alive because he possesses all three groups of circuits. He is necessary because other people do not. Carlyle said that while the law of master and man is inexorable, every man may be in his degree heroic. The act of worshiping a master puts a man in a vital rapport with the heart of the cosmos. "Give homage and allegiance to a hero," says Lawrence, "and you become yourself heroic, it is the law of men."[6]

The image of circuitry well explains the mysterious bond between hero and admirer, neither of whom can exist alone. The maintenance of the bond is a constant process of transmitting and receiving, and when the circuit is broken by age or apathy, the result is sterility and death. Things stop happening. With the spirit dormant, nothing crackles or pops or even goes bump in the night. Coaches have always realized this, which is why they talk so much about leadership, give trophies for spirit, and make pep talks at halftime. If McGinnis did not find any heroes in the traditional mold, perhaps he set his sights too high and looked too hard. The heroic is truly all around us and so obvious that it can be overlooked daily. The demise of the hero is only apparent and for a number of reasons.

The distrust of the romantic view of the hero was a result in part of the holocaust wrought by fascism in the 1930s and forties, of the ideas of Aryan supremacy, the talk of the "master race," and other such racist notions. Like any other principle, the law of men can be perverted toward narrow and inhuman ends. Since this is possible, it is much better to understand the law and how it works so that barbarism will be minimized rather than to say that such a law does not exist or merely is romantic tripe. The explicit claim of the Lawrentian theory of the hero is that heroic vitalism is a fact of life, applicable for all people at all times. The fact that "the golden people" of "the golden age" were all white males with one or two exceptions, does not mean that the law would not work for others, but merely that others have not had the opportunity to try it for themselves. The universality of personal magnetism and charisma has been illustrated over and over again in recent years not only by such blacks as Jesse Owens, Joe Louis, Jackie Robinson, and Muhummad Ali, all of whom brought boons to their own people as well as others, but also by women. At one time, women could be only heroines with all the implications of that term, but lately it has been realized that they can be heroes as well. A good example of this is Billie Jean King but not merely by her victory in a silly contest with Bobby Riggs. Part of her success, as Robert Lipsyte points out in his chapter "Designated Heroes, Ranking Gods, All-Star Holy Persons" in *Sports World: An American Dreamland*, is due to the efforts of others. She in turn has brought boons that are subtle but widespread for tennis and for women and men alike.

> The animus/anima that gave soul to the trend was Billie Jean. She personalized this bringing of tennis—classiest of sports—to the people. And she was the only one who could have done it, male or female. Others grumbled about the hypocrisy of the United States Lawn Tennis Association, about the humiliation of having to accept secret payments from the very officials who had solemnly ruled them illegal, about having to dance attendance upon wealthy patrons, of playing under poor conditions, of slipping into a dependent life instead of being allowed to sweat and fight for independence and wealth. But nobody who had as much to lose from the old way and as much to gain from a new way stepped up and spoke as boldly as Billie Jean.[7]

The hero receives, and the hero gives. The gifts lavished upon him or her may be material ones, but money is never the primary purpose. If it is, the athlete's soul becomes darker than that of Cerberus. Money is an unpoetic, unimaginative way of repaying the athlete for the delight, wonder, and other spiritual gifts he or she bestows upon us. Even in a world without money, people would play, and heroes would emerge simply because of their skill and their largeness of soul. Billie Jean King, according to Lipsyte, wanted "lots and lots of money," but she also wanted to be an "honest person" and wanted to "hear the fans hoot and holler so she'd know they cared."[8] Over and above the money and the cheers is another reward, the most elusive but perhaps most meaningful. Lipsyte quotes King in regard to her feelings after a perfect shot: "My heart pounds, my eyes get damp, and my ears feel like they're wriggling, but it's also just totally peaceful. It's almost just like having an orgasm—it's exactly like that."[9] If we look carefully, we may find that sports provide the best chance of all for creating "that transcendental link between the contingencies of the finite and the imagined realm of the supernatural," as long as questions of sex, national boundaries, and even philosophy do not obstruct our view.

Campbell's *Hero with a Thousand Faces* is a work of tremendous intellect that deals with the hero from mythological, historical, anthropological, and psychological perspectives, but Ernest Becker's *The Denial of Death* extends the concept of the hero even beyond the wide psychological dimensions staked out by Campbell. One of the truly important books of our time, it is a work of probing analysis and stunning synthesis that provides its readers with the shock of recognition of the essence of the human condition, that is, our lifelong battle with death. Becker's preface begins: "The prospect of death, Dr. Johnson said, wonderfully concentrates the mind. The main thesis of this book is that it does much more than that: the idea of death, the fear of it, haunts the human animal like nothing else; it is the mainspring of human activity—activity designed to avoid the fatality of death, to overcome it by denying in some way that it is the final destiny of man."[10] Another name for this ceaseless activity is heroism. Says Becker, "In times such as ours there is great pressure to come up with concepts that help men understand their dilemma." One such concept, Becker says, is "the idea of heroism; but in 'normal' scholarly times we never thought of making much out of it. . . . Yet the popular mind always knew how important it was: as William James remarked at the turn of the century: 'Mankind's common instinct for reality has always held the world to be essentially a theater for heroism.' "[11]

According to Becker, since all conscious endeavors on earth are attempts at transcendence of the body, individuals and societies are eternally caught in the dilemma of nature (death) and art (meaning). Man, Becker believes, needs a "second" world, "a world of humanly created meaning, a new reality that he can live, dramatize, nourish himself in."[12] History, in Becker's view, can be read easily against ideologies—"how embracing they are, how convincing, how easy they make it for men to be confident and secure in their personal heroism."[13]

Although Becker does not discuss the athlete in his theory of heroism, he argues that neurosis is a problem of illusion, of "creative cultural play" and that "the quality of cultural play varies with each society and historical period."[14] In a sense Becker is writing about *homo ludens* (man at play), but a more appropriate term might be *homo faber*, man the maker or artist.

No one can condense an idea as the poet can. Robert W. Hamblin, who had never read Becker when he wrote his powerful ode in memory of the Evansville basketball team, mirrored precisely Becker's theory in a remarkable elegy.

ON THE DEATH OF THE EVANSVILLE UNIVERSITY BASKETBALL TEAM IN A PLANE CRASH, DECEMBER 13, 1977

And now we know
why coaches rage,
kick benches,
curse rivals and referees.

Here, on this corpse-strewn hill
where grief smothers hope
with an obscene fog,
finality the only prize,
the orphaned heart knows
that every contest is do or die,
that all opponents are Death
masquerading in school colors,
that each previous season
is mere preliminary for encounter
with this last, bitter cup.

Yet we would not have it so,
it must not be so:
man is not made for death.
Cry foul. Shriek protest.
Claim a violation.
Even in losing, dying,
herald the perfect play.

So scream, all-knowing coaches,
admonishing priests, scream.
Swear, chew asses, make us work.
Never quit.
What else sustains
in nights when dreams
plummet downward in darkness
to question the betraying earth?

For any thinking, feeling person the task is not to deny the athlete his obvious heroism, since attempts at heroism are inescapable for all of us, but to examine the quality of that heroism, or in Becker's terms, "the quality of cultural play, of creative illusion."

But what is quality? An attempt to answer this question can be found in another great book of our time, *Zen and the Art of Motorcycle Maintenance: An Inquiry into Values* by Robert Pirsig, which has now become a best seller. Quality, according to Pirsig is the coming together of mind and matter, the third event in the universe, the union of energy and form, the mathematical beauty that is wrought from the subliminal self. Quality depends on caring and is analogous to the Greek concept of excellence, or *aretê*. The best, or quality, cannot be defined, but Pirsig believes that we know it exists and we know that it involves the union of opposites or apparent opposites.

While quality cannot be defined, it can be described. It also can be embodied in various degrees. Hence the need for models and modes, which are another justification for the hero and heroic. Models help us to see, and what we behold makes a great deal of difference. Saul Bellow explains why in *Mr. Sammler's Planet*:

> Greatness without models? Inconceivable. One could not be the thing itself—Reality. One must be satisfied with the symbols. Make it the object of imitation to reach and release the high qualities. Make peace therefore with intermediacy and representation. But choose higher representations. Otherwise the individual must be the failure he now sees and knows himself to be.[15]

Models, like heroes, should represent some type of synthesis of opposites. The Greek word *heros* meant "the embodiment of composite ideals." It would be hard to overemphasize that point, "a composite of ideals." This is why the ancient world demanded its heroes have both strength and wisdom, strength and beauty, and a sound mind in a sound body. Quality, which Pirsig equates with *aretê* or excellence, is the harmonious blending of mind and matter. Quality equals *aretê* (excellence) equals *heros* (heroism) equals *aristoi* (the best). Superlatives, as Tolstoy said of happy families, are all alike. The best, said Socrates, is he who mingles music and gymnastic and best attempers them to the soul. This is the so-called all-round man.

If the best in the Greek mind was the composite ideal, the worst was the one-dimensional man, the isolated intellectual, the *idiotes* (a private person who is not involved in political activity) or the *banausos* (one who uses some professional skill of expertise for private gain). These were the great nemeses of the ancient world, and they may be the nemeses of the modern world. Arnold Toynbee in *A Study of History* defined the *banausos* as "a person whose activity [is] specialized through a concentration of his energies upon some particular technique, at the expense of his all-round development as a 'social animal.'" According to Toynbee:

In our latter-day Western World ... [the] attempt to adjust life to Industrialism through Sport has been partially defeated because the spirit and the rhythm of Industrialism have become so insistent and so pervasive that they have invaded and infected Sport itself—just as the *Banausia* which the Spartans sought so earnestly to keep at bay eluded their vigilance after all by capturing their own peculiar profession of arms. In the Western World of to-day professional athletes—more narrowly specialized and more extravagantly paid than the most consummate industrial technicians—now vie with the professional entertainers in providing us with horrifying examples of *Banausia* at its acme.[16]

Orrin E. Klapp makes the same charge in *Heroes, Villains, and Fools: The Changing American Character* when he notes that the specialist is the man of the hour; he has become the narrow successor of the Renaissance man:

There have been and still are, incredibly versatile people (Goethe, Cellini, Leonardo, Bacon, Franklin, Schweitzer, Churchill)—"whole men" fitting Carlyle's specification: "I have no notion of a truly great man that could not be all sorts of men." But opposite—almost a caricature—are favorites of today whose appeal consists of one thing (often trivial): pinups and profiles; movie and television stars; crooners and spellbinders; playboys, headliners, and other splendid performers. The athlete comes onto the field for the big sock, the politician gives his great speech, the evangelist thrills twenty thousand people in a stadium—what are these but specialists in a certain kind of impression? What do they have aside from the ability to give the crowd this moment? The specialist appears to be the man of the hour. Considering that both "expert" and "specialist" have univocally heroic ratings, and looking at the current array of American heroes (both as types and as personalities), there seems little reason to say that men of broad ability—"whole men"—are entering the top places of popular choice. On the contrary, what the public seems to be getting—and enthusiastically receiving—most of the time are half-men, quarter-men, or only the surfaces of men.[17]

Why did the modern world, especially America, choose the specialist and give homage and allegiance to him? As Toynbee has pointed out, one candidate for the villainy that has been wrought upon us is industrialism. This too is the view of Lewis Mumford in his chapter "Sport and the Bitch Goddess" in *Technics and Civilization*:

Instead of being looked upon as a servile and ignoble being, because of the very perfection of his physical efforts, as the Athenians in Socrates' time looked upon the professional athletes and dancers, this new hero represents the summit of the amateur's effort, not at pleasure but at efficiency. The hero is handsomely paid for his efforts, as well as being rewarded by praise and publicity, and he thus further restores to sport its connection with the very commercialized existence from which it is supposed to provide relief—restores it and thereby sanctifies it. The few heroes who resist this vulgarization—notably Lindbergh—fall into popular or at least into journalistic disfavor, for they are only playing the less important part of the game. The really successful sports hero, to satisfy the mass-demand, must be midway between a pander and a prostitute.[18]

Industrialism set the scene for the arrival of the mass hero and his subsequent commercialization, but we honor him at first because he does something very well, as Mumford puts it. As Pirsig might say, we honor the quality of his act. The money an athlete eventually will make may turn some heads in his or her direction, but these are materialistic minds to start with. What originally attracts us to the athlete is his skill or prowess.

A medical doctor once related how often he had been struck by what an absolutely marvelous thing a cadaver was. Everything is there except life. If a cadaver is mind-boggling, how much more so is the living body? Yet, the living body is not the end point on the scale of the miraculous. The most miraculous thing of all is the *performing* body, the athlete or dancer. This is the wonder that from the chaos of star stuff should emerge a Nadiâ Comaneci, a Mark Spitz, an Edward Villella, an Arnold Palmer, a Dr. J., an O. J., and an Ali. There is only one other marvel to compare with the performing body and that is the *performing* mind, a Newton, Tolstoy, Freud, or Hannah Arendt. For me the greatest mystery of all is consciousness manifested by mind, or ultimately spirit. No matter what one's taste is in the marvelous, there is no denying that the athlete is an object of admiration in and of himself whether he is a saint or sinner.

The hero, then, achieves distinction through deeds of body and mind, and the reverence accorded to him or her depends upon the taste of a particular society. An individual might have a special talent or potential that would be revered and cultivated in one age and yet go unnoticed in another. There is simply no accounting for taste in heroes; there is only a wide variety of possibilities or models. In *Man and His Symbols* Carl G. Jung refers to male and female models as animus and anima figures, and in his classification they range from the physical to the spiritual as follows:

	Man	*Woman*
The Physical or Biological	Tarzan	Eve
The Romantic	Hemingway	Helen of Troy
Bearer of the "Word"	Lloyd George	Virgin Mary
The Wise Guide to Spiritual Truth	Gandhi	Athena or Mona Lisa[19]

One thing has remained the same over the centuries: the felt need for a synthesis of body and soul. If one could somehow combine the body of Tarzan and the spirit of Gandhi or the qualities of Eve and the Mona Lisa, he might glimpse what the ancients sought in the ideal called *sapientia et fortitudo*, wisdom and strength.

In dealing with the subject of the sports hero, it is essential not to dismiss the subject of heroism, as the behaviorists have done. Yet it is also necessary to avoid the romantic trap of *Götterdämmerung*, the belief that all heroes have departed the scene as Joe McGinnis has done in *Heroes*, Tom Wolfe in "Junior Johnson is the Last American Hero. Yes!," and Daniel J. Boorstin to some extent in *The Image: A Guide to Pseudo-Events in America*. McGinnis's book is reflective reading, but the causes of his dismay are sometimes questionable and sometimes ludicrous. He sees Eugene McCarthy's appeal diminished considerably, for example, by the mere fact that he didn't keep a drinking appointment with the author and Howard Cosell. The heroic may belong to ages past, but we certainly will want more evidence than this. McGinnis does provide other evidence in his book, some of it disturbing indeed, but he seems to forget the millions of children, for example, who under the spur of their parents are trying, as Paul says in his letters to the Thessalonians, to "hold fast to that which is good," and their efforts quite often are more heroic than we realize.

Michael Oriard is closer to the truth of the current condition, (and the eternal condition), with his assertion in *Dreaming of Heroes* that the star athlete may be "a diminished hero" but remains our only link with the heroes of earlier myths, the Adonises and Galahads. Similarly, Leverett T. Smith, Jr. in *The American Dream and The National Game* understands the eternal appeal of "camaraderie" among athletes and why Jerry Kramer could compare the Packer situation at the time with Camelot. "Vince Lombardi's world," the title of Smith's chapter (chapter V), is an old world made up of leaders and followers. As cliché-ridden as that heroic world often is, we may abandon it at our peril. A composite picture of that world by one who lived in it appears in *Instant Replay* by Jerry Kramer.

It simply will not do to generalize too much about heroism. The death of heroism has been lamented by romantic minds throughout the ages. Note, for example, the following refrain, "Though he was strong of arm he will not rise again; / He had wisdom and a comely face, he will not come again."[20] These lines are from one of the oldest literary works known to man, *The Epic of Gilgamesh*. But some things simply never change. One is the need for heroes, and another is the certainty that they never stay around long enough to redeem us.

In fact the heroic is never dead, which is why the student of sports should explore the subject in some depth and not be content with the sociological observations of a single decade. To do this thoroughly, the researcher will need to consult works such as those by Campbell and Jung as well as such equally impressive works as *The Hero* by Lord Raglan and *The Myth of the Birth of the Hero* by Otto Rank. It is difficult to see mythical patterns in today's cultures but discernible parallels frequently emerge. The book that best provides the framework for understanding heroism in the modern world is Ernest Becker's *The Denial of Death*, which traces the trauma and glory of heroism from womb to tomb and leaves one aghast both with terror and possibilities.

NOTES

1. Joseph Campbell, *The Hero With a Thousand Faces* (Cleveland: World Publishing Co., 1965), p. 30.

2. Neil D. Isaacs, *Jock Culture, U.S.A.* (New York: W. W. Norton, 1978), p. 37.

3. John Davies, "It's Baker!...Going for Another Touchdown!" *Esquire* 66 (September 1966), 135.

4. Joe McGinnis, *Heroes* (New York: Viking Press, 1976), pp. 18-19.

5. Quoted in ibid., p. 26.

6. Eric R. Bentley, *A Century of Hero-Worship* (Philadelphia: J. B. Lippincott, 1944), p. 246.

7. Robert Lipsyte, *Sports World: An American Dreamland* (New York: Quadrangle, The New York Times Book Co., 1975), p. 228.

8. Ibid.

9. Ibid., p. 280.

10. Ernest Becker, *The Denial of Death*. New York: Free Press, 1973), p. ix.

11. Ibid., p. 1.

12. Ibid., p. 189.

13. Ibid., p. 190.

14. Ibid.

15. Saul Bellow, *Mr. Sammler's Planet* (New York: Viking Press, 1970), p. 149.

16. Arnold Toynbee, *A Study of History*, vol. 4, *The Breakdowns of Civilizations* (New York: Oxford University Press, 1939), p. 242.

17. Orrin E. Klapp. *Heroes, Villains, and Fools: The Changing American Character* (Englewood Cliffs, N.J.: Prentice-Hall, 1962), pp. 102-3.

18. Lewis Mumford, *Technics and Civilization* (New York: Harcourt, Brace and World, 1978), pp. 306-7.

19. C. G. Jung, *Man and His Symbols* (New York: Doubleday, 1964), pp. 184, 194.

20. *The Epic of Gilgamesh*, trans. N. K. Sanders (New York: Penguin Books, 1979), p. 118.

BIBLIOGRAPHY

Becker, Ernest. *The Denial of Death*. New York: Free Press, 1973.

Bellow, Saul. *Mr. Sammler's Planet*. New York: Viking Press, 1970.

Bentley, Eric R. *A Century of Hero-Worship*. Philadelphia: J. B. Lippincott, 1944.

Boorstin, Daniel J. *The Image: A Guide to Pseudo-Events in America*. New York: Atheneum, 1975.

Campbell, Joseph. *The Hero with a Thousand Faces*. Cleveland: World Publishing Company, 1965.

Davies, John. "It's Baker!... Going for Another Touchdown!" *Esquire* 66 (September 1966), 132-35, 171.

_____. *The Legend of Hobie Baker*. Boston: Little Brown & Co., 1966.

Isaacs, Neil D. *Jock Culture, U.S.A.* New York: W. W. Norton, 1978.

Hamblin, Robert W. "On the Death of the Evansville University Basketball Team in a Plane Crash, December 13, 1977." *The Cape Rock* 14 (Winter 1978), 42.

Jung, Carl G. *Man and His Symbols*. New York: Doubleday, 1964.

Klapp, Orrin E. *Heroes, Villains, and Fools: The Changing American Character*. Englewood Cliffs, N.J.: Prentice-Hall, 1962.

Kramer, Jerry and Dick Schaap. *Instant Replay*. New York: New American Library, 1968.

Lipsyte, Robert. *SportsWorld: An American Dreamland*. New York: Quadrangle, New York Times Book Co., 1975.

McGinnis, Joe. *Heroes*. New York: Viking Press, 1976.

Mumford, Lewis. *Technics and Civilization*. New York: Harcourt, Brace and World, 1963.

Oriard, Michael. *Dreaming of Heroes: American Sports Fiction, 1868-1980*. Chicago: Nelson-Hall, 1982.

Pirsig, Robert. *Zen and the Art of Motorcycle Maintenance: An Inquiry into Values*. New York: Morrow, 1974.

Raglan, Lord. *The Hero*. 1956. Reprint. Westport, Conn.: Greenwood Press, 1975.

Rank, Otto. *The Myth of the Birth of the Hero and Other Writings*. Edited by Philip Freund. New York: Vintage Books, 1959.

Sanders, N. K., trans. *The Epic of Gilgamesh*. New York: Penguin Books, 1979.

Smith, Leverett T., Jr. *The American Dream and The National Game*. Bowling Green, Ohio: Bowling Green University Popular Press, 1975.

Toynbee, Arnold. *A Study of History*. 6 vols. New York: Oxford University Press, 1939.

Wolfe, Tom. "Junior Johnson is the Last American Hero. Yes!" *Esquire* 80 (October 1973), 211, 222, 436-38.

CHAPTER *9*

The Sports Fan and Hero-Worshiper

The types of heroes that a society develops are determined in part not only by the individual will and character of the hero but also by public attitudes. The admired and the admirers mirror each others's tastes. In other words, the quality of the hero is shaped somewhat by the quality of the hero-worshipers, which often can leave something to be desired.

In recent years, fan behavior and fan violence have become problems that disrupt games and even cause injury in some instances. There are even soccer wars in Latin America. In a sad but funny book entitled *Fans! How We Go Crazy over Sports*, sportswriter Mike Roberts reveals myriad forms of crowd insanity and clearly demonstrates that violence is not limited to ethnic groups or places. Not only does Roberts more than adequately survey the silliness and brutality in the American scene, that is, *how* we go crazy, but also without even attempting to do so, he explains why our heroes are often flawed and frequently even bizarre. According to Roberts, the taste for blood simply is in us, and some promoters exploit that taste at every turn:

> Infected with the Christmas spirit in 1975, one arena billed a Holiday Holocaust 20-man Yuletide Wrestling Free-for-All. It featured Haystack Calhoun, "600 pounds of meanness and muscle," and Ivan Putski, "nastier than a swarm of bees." Another card offered Andre the Giant. "7 '4 " tall, weighs 444 pounds and can destroy people with his hands, his feet, his elbows, and his breath . . . See Andre the Giant *do terrible things to* Cowboy Bob Duncum. . . ."[1]

All of this seems very humorous until it is viewed in a larger context. In that context the pertinent remarks of Wilhelm Stekel's classic work *Sadism and Masochism* come to mind:

> Who would deny that the need for the expression of savagery has increased rather than diminished? Our epoch, which likes to call itself

an epoch of humanity, is in truth one of barbarousness. What do we see if we look at art, politics, life? Coarse, atavistic impulses awakened to new power; everywhere joy in the repulsive, ugly, common.

Books which treat of horrible themes . . . have the greatest success, reach the stage, and are filmed. People crowd everywhere where there is something gruesome to be seen. . . . It is really no better than in the Middle Ages, when public executions were a favorite spectacle. Bull fights are becoming popular even outside of Spain, and in the centers of civilized countries bloody boxing matches are fought daily.[2]

Stekel goes on to argue that "the group sinks to the standpoint of the lowest member in it" and "always becomes cruel, even if it performs its barbarousness in the service of a higher idea."[3]

In the case of sports this "higher idea" may be invoked either in the name of nationalism or religion, which may help to explain the conservative cast of most sports heroes. It is difficult to imagine Socrates, Jesus, Augustine, Leonardo, Newton, Beethoven, Tolstoy, or Einstein in the stands cheering a team, which may tell us something about the phenomenon of mass spectacle. Unfortunately no matter how badly spectators have behaved in the past at a contest, one must remember they can always do worse. One may be tempted to paraphrase Benjamin Franklin's remark on religion: If people are as bad as they are with mass spectator sports, think how much worse they would be without them. Of course, there is also the opposite view to which many subscribe, that the display of violence, whether on TV, a football field, or a hockey rink, increases the tendency toward violence in the beholder. Proof for either position probably is not obtainable.

In fact, good words about fans are few and far between these days. Sports announcers and even athletes frequently register their dismay over the excess of fan reaction. It takes a brave soul to stand up for fans even in a general way, and Michael Novak is to be congratulated for doing so in his *The Joy of Sports: End Zones, Bases, Baskets, Balls, and the Consecration of the American Spirit.* "Rooting" in his view is the fourth of seven seals that lock the inner life of sports. "The fan," Novak points out, " 'roots.' " He goes on to say that since the enlightenment the tendency has been toward the attainment of universality, but that "a human goal more accurate than enlightenment is 'enhumanment.' " The "enhumaned" man, he argues, is "a rooted beast." "To be a fan is totally in keeping with being a man. To have particular loyalties is not to be deficient in universality."[4] Novak points out that a root word of fan is "fantastic" as well as "fanatic," and he notes the relationship of the word "fan" to *fanun*, "the temple of the god of the place."[5] Novak's whole thesis in regard to the fan might be summed up as: To cheer is human: to play divine. His generous opinions must be music to the ears of fans.

Any mention of the word "fan" brings to mind one of the most remark-able books on the subject, *A Fan's Notes: A Fictional Memoir* by Frederick Exley, a most unusual fan indeed. Like Michael Murphy's *Golf in the King-dom*, *A Fan's Notes* is fiction, but as in the case of *Golf*, one has to be informed of that fact to know for sure. It is a marvelous work about two of the oldest truths of all, the inevitability of human suffering and the need for heroes. It is done with crystal clarity and dazzling erudition that would have been the envy of both James Boswell and Edmund Wilson.

The son of a football star in Watertown, New York, the narrator (Exley) grows up with a longing for fame that is attributable to his father's in-fluence, which wanes as the son grows older and becomes a haunting memory with the father's death from cancer at the age of forty. At the University of Southern California where the narrator majors in English, he fastens upon another gridiron hero, Frank Gifford, and follows his pro-fessional career with the zeal of any young, truly devoted NFL fanatic. What distinguishes Exley from other fans is his ability to articulate his fantasies and failures. *A Fan's Notes*, however, is not simply a story of failures and successes. It is principally a discovery of reality. Exley discovers that heroes fail and also die but more importantly "that of itself longevity is utterly without redeeming qualities, that one has to live the contributive, the passionate, life and this can as well be done in twenty-six (hence Keats) as in a hundred and twenty-six years, done in no longer than the time it takes a man to determine whether the answer is *yea* or *nay*."[6] By the end of the novel, the narrator has ceased to be a fan and at least in his dreams is involved in action defending ideals. He proves the dictum from *Apocalypse* by D. H. Lawrence, "Give homage and allegiance to a hero, and you your-self become heroic."[7] As Joseph Campbell noted in *The Hero with a Thou-sand Faces*, the hero comes back from his mysterious adventure bringing with him a boon. In the case of Exley the boon is a searing glimpse into the human aspiration.

A Fan's Notes is the subject of a splendid paper by Don Johnson entitled "*A Fan's Notes* and the Concept of Heroism in the Literature of Sports," which appears in *Southern Humanities Review* in 1979. Johnson begins by observing:

> Despite the increasing capacity of the media to demythologize the athlete, sports—barring an increased emphasis on the human element in the space program or the commencement of a popular war—pro-vide almost the only consistently available arena for the performance of the visible heroic enterprises traditionally associated with the *agon* figure in myth and literature.[8]

Drawing upon Michael Novak's *The Joy of Sports* and Ernest Becker's *The Denial of Death*, Johnson argues that *A Fan's Notes* is the most complete and provocative examination of the sports hero as an immortality figure in contemporary literature. It is this serious theme that in Johnson's view elevates *A Fan's Notes* far above those works that "are merely about sports."

The admiration of Gifford by Exley's narrator illustrates a puzzling aspect of the modern scene, and that is the complete abdication of the man of letters to the man of action. Norman Mailer and George Plimpton also seem to surrender to this impulse, Mailer in boxing, Plimpton in everything. Plimpton, in fact, has become a symbolic figure as seen in *Paper Lion* and other such texts. With every book on his sojourn into the world of sports, Plimpton, no matter how much he entertains us, in effect apologizes for the *Paris Review* and shows how irrelevant such a publication is in a world where sports have triumphed completely.

No one is more aware of this transformation than Mailer, which he proves in *Presidential Papers*, *Cannibals and Christians*, and *Armies of the Night*. Leverett T. Smith, Jr. has perceptively analyzed his work in "Norman Mailer and the NFL: A Reading of *The Armies of the Night*," which appeared in *Journal of Sports History*. There is, in Smith's view, a sign of growth and even recovery in Mailer's treatment of professional football:

> In his [Mailer's] prophecy football stands for an entirely different set of values than those he understands the American establishment to find in it. Organization and specialization give way to spontaneity and self-fulfillment as Mailer images himself a halfback, his children pass receivers and linebackers. In sum, professional football in *The Armies of the Night* is a symbol which unites the two warring Americas. It is an image which at once signifies the absence of the "mind of the passionate artist" in America and an assertion that that mind is in the process of being reborn.[9]

Smith ends his article with a brilliant quotation from Emerson's journal entry for October 1837 in which Emerson advises us to be "a football to time and chance, the more kicks, the better, so that you inspect the whole game and know its uttermost law."[10] It is a statement on the failure of American education, the total repudiation of everything Emerson advised in "The American Scholar," that we have to be reminded of basic wisdom through a book on national schizophrenia. Every age, as Emerson said, "must write its own books," and no American writer is more typical of his age than Norman Mailer and to a lesser extent George Plimpton. Both are fans and representative men.

Fans are either parents (or adults in general) or children, and for children, as Exley in a sense has demonstrated, the problems of heroism and hero-worship are compounded enormously. Not only are children filled with impossible dreams from watching the deeds of their idols, but far too many are pushed beyond their limits either by themselves, their parents, or their coaches whose own values have become reversed in a society in which achievement is principally physical or materialistic. One can well appreciate the quiet outrage of Robert Lipsyte in *Sports World: An American Dreamland* when he writes:

> A million Little Leaguers stand for hours while a criminally obese "coach" drills the joy of sports out of their souls, makes them self-conscious and fearful, teaches them technique over movement, emphasizes dedication, sacrifice, and obedience instead of accomplishment and fun. And their mothers and fathers "Jog for Health" and "Swim for Your Life" in grim and dogged programs without ever sighing in ecstasy at the wind touching the sweaty roots of their hair, without moaning at the water's stroke on their gliding bodies.[11]

No one would deny the value of play or even the necessity of play in the life of the child, but how much is enough? This is a vital question that must be dealt with if society ever intends to elevate the quality of heroism. What Arthur Ashe has recommended for parents of black children, two hours in the library for children for every hour of play, is sound advice for all, considering the staggering odds against even financial success in sports for any individual. There are joys of the mind as well as the body for children, and among these are two activities, reading and writing, that unlike many athletic skills can bring boons that will last a lifetime. Considering the crisis in reading and writing that is daily remarked by educators all across the country, it would seem to be time to shift the emphasis from the physical to the intellectual in the composite ideal of modern heroism.

The subject of children in sports is analogous to that of women in sport and just as complex. Children are a minority. There are physiological factors as in the case of women in sports and these factors frequently are not understood or are ignored. For this reason alone it is imperative to learn as much as possible about sports for the young. Books that help to meet this need are *Children in Sport: A Contemporary Anthology*, edited by Richard A. Magill, Michael J. Ash, and Frank L. Small, *Child in Sport and Physical Activity*, edited by J. G. Albinson and G. M. Andrews, and *Joy and Sadness in Children's Sports*, edited by Rainer Martens.

For a history of the rise of children's sports, the definitive work, at least for the participation of boys, is Jack Berryman's article, "From the Cradle to the Playing Field: America's Emphasis on Highly Organized Competitive Sports for Preadolescent Boys" in *Journal of Sport History*. This carefully documented essay more than adequately proves the author's thesis that "the growth and development of highly competitive sports programs for boys below the age of twelve was a phenomenon of the first half of the twentieth century and was indicative of the fact that sports had finally penetrated all levels of the American population."[12] Among several conclusions drawn by Berryman is the following: "The sporting ideals of Americans which were already established by the late 1920's and the subsequent sponsorship of boy's sport by boy's work groups were therefore the two most important factors leading to the highly competitive situation we have today."[13] This overemphasis has led to two persistent themes in American literature: the youthful idolizing of sports heroes and the subsequent disappointment. J. F. Powers's "Jamesie" and Sherwood Anderson's "I Want to Know Why" best embody the first theme, while the second theme, that of the "has been," the former star who cannot mature, can be found in Irwin Shaw's "Christian Darling," John Cheever's "O Youth and Beauty," and in John Updike's novels, *Rabbit, Run* and *Rabbit Redux.*

The best nonfiction book dealing with the subject of great expectations of young athletes is *Destiny's Darlings: A World Championship Little League Team Twenty Years Later* by Martin Ralbovsky. The title comes from Mel Allen's description of the Schenectady, New York, world champions of little league baseball in 1954. Ralbovsky, who interviewed the players on the team twenty years later, presents his information and leaves conclusions up to the reader. Though some of the lives of players may be judged successes, depending on definitions, in most cases the inescapable feeling is one of frustration, disappointment, and even sadness. They are no longer "destiny's darlings." There emerges the conviction that the cruellest compliment that one can bestow on youth is the mantle of promise. Baseball, as some know, was never meant to be a barometer of anything; certainly it is no measure of future performance either on the field or off.

Ralbovsky is also the author of *Lords of the Locker Room: The American Way of Coaching and its Effects on Youth*, which describes and documents the questionable practices of coaches of young athletes. Ralbovsky is one who doubts that any genuine revolution has occurred in the world of sports. Not much, if anything at all, has changed in his view, except appearance. Much, however, needs to be done, and Ralbovsky makes two contributions toward this goal in his concluding chapters, "A Modest Proposal: From Tots to Teens, Why not Soccer?" and "A General Guide for Parents: What to Look for in a Coach (or How to Preserve Your Son's Health and Sanity)."

Anyone beginning research in youth in sports or anyone establishing a sports program for youth would want to know about the work of Dr. Jack Hutslar, Director of NAYSI (North American Youth Sport Institute), located at Kernersville, North Carolina (see Appendix 2). The key goals for youngsters in sport that NAYSI promotes are: participation, fun, learning, safety, social development, effort, physical growth, school studies, sportsmanship, fitness, mental control, maturation, persistence, life-time participation, and Aristotle's golden mean of nothing to excess. The "Resources List" published by the Institute contains a wealth of information on all aspects of youth programs, books, films, and periodicals and a wide range of services offered by the Institute. Hutslar's own publications constitute an impressive resource list, especially the "Youth Sport Bibliography" contained in his article, "Sources of Information for Youth Sport Leaders."

James A. Michener's *Sports in America* also has a section on children and sports. In his chapter "Children and Sports," Michener presents his view that "Destiny's Darlings" is only one side of the coin. As he does on many topics, he presents junior league football and little league baseball in their "most favorable light." To his credit his treatment of the subject is fairly balanced. There is much good to be said for the games of modern youth. The reservations one does have about Michener's views on children in sports occur in his discussion of the college super-league in which he argues, "Let the boy be drafted [by college super-league teams] in an orderly procedure without regard to his academic ability."[14] Michener is not referring to the bright athlete but to a much larger group, those "mentally prepared for nothing more advanced than the fourth grade."[15] The key phrase here is "mentally unprepared." Why not, rather than easing or eliminating academic standards for superior athletes to play in a super-league, prepare them both physically and mentally at the earliest age possible for the demands of living? Why not, as Arthur Ashe recommends, send the child to the library? Why not teach all how to read, write, and do arithmetic? Why not teach all to think for themselves? This, after all, has been the goal of education of the young since time out of mind. Perhaps it is time to deemphasize the role of spectator sports in our lives and recommit ourselves to quality education. What promising young superstar, applauded by peers and parents, is going to prepare himself mentally for anything when he knows that under Michener's plan he will receive a big salary in college with, in Michener's words, "No emphasis on academic suitability."[16] Few grownups could resist such temptation and even fewer among the young. It is true that Michener would make provisions for the opportunity of a free education up to "fourteen years after departure from college," but this is a little late for learning so many basic things that could have been learned much earlier if distorted social values had not prevented it. Genuine quality in a society stems from a composite ideal, the development of mind *and* body. There will always be heavy prices to pay as long as that fundamental fact is widely ignored.

Somehow a more realistic, informal approach needs to be taken with children. Athletic heroism and winning need to be put in perspective. There should be as much concern for the psyche of the child as for his body. The overriding consideration in the implementation of any program for children should be the benefits for the participants. Toward this end, Thomas Tutko and William Bruns in *Winning is Everything and Other American Myths* have formulated "The Young Athlete's Bill of Right," which parallels nicely the ten points set forth by Martin Ralbovsky in "A General Guide for Parents" in *Lords of the Locker Room*. Tutko and Bruns's bill of rights summarizes well the intent of Ralbovsky's: "The right to freedom from physical and emotional punishment by the parents and by the coach. Punishment leads only to fear and constriction of behavior, whereas the purpose of sports should be to help a child grow, feel expansion, and realize his or her potential."[17] There are those who disagree with this philosophy on punishment and those who claim that most sporting programs for children already meet this aim. In any event one thing is certain—the attitudes fostered in children today will determine to a large extent the quality of the fans and heroes of tomorrow. This is essentially the conclusion of Arnold R. Beisser in the chapter entitled "The Sports Fan and Recreational Violence," in his book *The Madness in Sport*. After reminding the modern reader of the actions of the fans in Rome during the years of decline, he writes:

> Hope rests on whether people's active participation or their identification with the active participants can be restored. Such a sense of involvement is necessary for people to be willing to support society's institutions by lending strength to their maintenance and revision. The stadium not only is the mirror of society but also its mentor. Attitudes learned in sports strongly affect the ways in which the young will view society, and those attitudes are continually reinforced by what adults and young people alike experience when they visit the stadium.[18]

If our age in the view of Wilhelm Stekel is no better than the Middle Ages, and in some instances similar to Rome during its worst days, what can be expected of the future? If an improvement in the quality of heroism is ever to come, the widespread sports programs of children must be evaluated in terms of their balance with the development of the mind. Raise up a child in the way he should go and when he is old he will not depart from it. The best is he who mingles music and gymnastics and best attempers them to the soul.

NOTES

1. Michael Roberts, *Fans! How We Go Crazy Over Sports* (Washington, D.C.: The New Republic Book Co., 1976), p. 161.

2. Wilhelm Stekel, *Sadism and Masochism: The Psychology of Hatred and Cruelty*, 2 vols. (1929; rpt. New York: Grove Press, 1965), 1: 32.

3. Ibid., p. 35.
4. Michael Novak, *The Joy of Sports: End Zones, Bases, Baskets, Balls, and the Consecration of the American Spirit* (New York: Basic Books, 1976), pp. 142-43.
5. Ibid., p. 144.
6. Frederick Exley, *A Fan's Notes: A Fictional Memoir* (New York: Random House, 1968), p. 385.
7. D. H. Lawrence, *Apocalypse* (New York: Viking Press, 1960), p. 25.
8. Don Johnson, "The Hero in Sports Literature and Exley's *A Fan's Notes*," *Southern Humanities Review* 13 (Summer 1979), 233.
9. Levrett T. Smith, Jr., "Norman Mailer and the NFL: A Reading of *The Armies of the Night*," *Journal of Sport History* 3 (Spring 1976), 33.
10. *Selections from Ralph Waldo Emerson*, ed. Stephen E. Whicher (Boston: Houghton Mifflin, 1957), p. 81.
11. Robert Lipsyte, *SportsWorld: An American Dreamland* (New York: Quadrangle, New York Times Book Co., 1975), p. 281.
12. Jack Berryman, "From the Cradle to the Playing Field: America's Emphasis upon Highly Organized Competitive Sports for Preadolescent Boys," *Journal of Sport History* 2 (Fall 1975), p. 112.
13. Ibid., p. 131.
14. James Michener, *Sports in America* (Greenwich, Conn.: Fawcett, 1976), pp. 249-50.
15. Ibid., p. 250.
16. Ibid.
17. Thomas Tutko and William Bruns, *Winning is Everything and Other American Myths* (New York: Macmillan Co., 1976), p. 233.
18. Arnold R. Beisser, *The Madness in Sport*, 2d ed. (Bowie, Md.: Charles Press Publishers, 1977), p. 198.

BIBLIOGRAPHY

Albinson, J. G., and G. M. Andrews, eds. *Child in Sport and Physical Activity*. International Series on Sport Sciences. Vol. 3. Baltimore: University Park Press, 1976.
Becker, Ernest. *The Denial of Death*. New York: Free Press, 1973.
Beisser, Arnold R. *The Madness in Sport*. 2d ed. Bowie, Md.: Charles Press Publishers, 1977.
Berryman, Jack W. "From the Cradle to the Playing Field: America's Emphasis upon Highly Organized Competitive Sports for Preadolescent Boys." *Journal of Sport History* 2 (Fall 1975), 112-31.
Campbell, Joseph. *The Hero with a Thousand Faces*. Cleveland: World Publishing Company, 1965.
Exley, Frederick. *A Fan's Notes: A Fictional Memoir*. New York: Random House, 1968.
Hutslar, Jack. "Sources of Information for Youth Sport Leaders." *North Carolina Libraries* 38, no. 2 (Summer 1980), 37-40.
Johnson, Don. "The Hero in Sports Literature and Exley's *A Fan's Notes*." *Southern Humanities Review* 13 (Summer 1979), 233-44.
Lawrence, D. H. *Apocalypse*. New York: Viking Press, 1960.

Lipsyte, Robert. *Sports World: An American Dreamland*. New York: Quadrangle, New York Times Book Co., 1975.

Magill, Richard A., Michael J. Ash, and Frank L. Small, *Children in Sport: A Contemporary Anthology*. Champaign, Ill.: Human Kinetics Publishers, 1978.

Martens, Rainer. *Joy and Sadness in Children's Sports*. Champaign, Ill.: Human Kinetics Publishers, 1978.

Mailer, Norman. *The Armies of the Night*. New York: Signet, 1971.

_____. *Cannibals and Christians*. New York: Dell, 1970.

_____. *The Presidential Papers*. New York: Putnam, 1963.

Michener, James A. *Sports in America*. Greenwich, Conn.: Fawcett, 1976.

Murphy, *Golf in the Kingdom*. New York: Viking Press, 1972.

Novak, Michael. *The Joy of Sports: End Zones, Bases, Baskets, Balls, and the Consecration of the American Spirit*. New York: Basic Books, 1976.

Plimpton, George. *Paper Lion*. New York: Harper and Row, 1966.

Ralbovsky, Martin. *Destiny's Darlings: A World Championship Little League Team Twenty Years Later*. New York: Hawthorne, 1974.

_____. *Lords of the Locker Room: The American Way of Coaching and Its Effects on Youth*. New York: Peter H. Wyden, 1974.

Roberts, Michael. *Fans! How We Go Crazy Over Sports*. Washington, D.C.: The New Republic Book Co., 1976.

Smith, Leverett T., Jr. "Norman Mailer and the NFL: A Reading of *The Armies of the Night*." *Journal of Sport History* 3 (Spring 1976), 20-34.

Stekel, Wilhelm. *Sadism and Masochism*. 2 vols. New York: Grove Press, 1965.

Tutko, Thomas, and William Bruns. *Winning is Everything and Other American Myths*. New York: Macmillan Co., 1976.

Updike, John. *Rabbit, Run*. New York: Alfred A. Knopf, 1960.

_____. *Rabbit Redux*. New York: Alfred A. Knopf, 1971.

CHAPTER 10

Sports and Aggression

The behavior of fans, even more than the performance of athletes, raises a pressing question about the nature of man: Is he inherently aggressive? If history confirms that man is either a hero or hero-worshiper, it also confirms his aggression. Yet, there are valid arguments that man, at least in the beginning, was not predominantly warlike. Most religions, if not all, posit the existence of an original paradise or a golden age that for one reason or another fell. Similarly, Rousseau in his refutation of Thomas Hobbes argued that man in his natural state was good and peaceful and that "civilization" was the cause of all ills. In *Inequality Among Mankind* Rousseau wrote:

> But above all things let us beware concluding with Hobbes, that Man, as having no idea of Goodness, must be naturally bad, that he is vicious because he does not know what Virtue is; that he always refuses to do any service to those of his own Species, because he believes that none is due them.... This author to argue from his own principles, should say that the State of Nature, being that where the Care of our own Preservation interferes least with the Preservation of others, was of course, the most favourable to peace, and most suitable to Mankind."[1]

The impact of this attitude has been immeasurable. In America the Transcendentalists, Emerson, Thoreau, and Whitman, reflected this essential optimism by proclaiming the inherent worth of every individual and disdaining the doctrine of original sin. Emerson even went so far in his journal entry for February 16, 1838, to refer to original sin and related ideas as the "soul's mumps and measles and whooping-coughs." The guide for all was nature, which for Emerson, however, took on more somber aspects as he grew older. While Thoreau was never the sentimentalist that Rousseau was about external nature, he did believe that in wildness lay the hope of the world. Hence there were other alternatives to Hobbes's acquisitiveness. Thoreau illustrated these by example and in so doing had a direct influence upon such nonviolent men of this century as Gandhi and Martin Luther King. For those who insist that Transcendentalism is a romantic myth, there are the arguments of social scientists like Thorstein Veblen and natural scientists like Richard Leakey. Veblen, to be sure, did not believe in an original paradise, but he did believe that primitive societies evolved from peaceful savagery to barbarian temperment primarily because of the division of labor and honorific distinctions based on combat and the hunt. Men always have fought, Veblen acknowledges in *Theory of the Leisure Class*, but the conditions of war have *evolved*, an important distinction indeed:

> It may therefore be objected that there can have been no such initial stage of peaceable life as is here assumed. There is no point in cultural evolution prior to which fighting does not occur. But the point in question is not as to the occurrence of combat, occasional or sporadic, or even more or less frequent and habitual; it is a question as to the occurrence of an habitual bellicose frame of mind—a prevalent habit of judging facts and events from the point of view of the fight.[2]

Contemporary anthropologists have been even more generous in their view of early man. For example, Richard E. Leakey and Roger Lewin argue in *Origins*:

> The core of the aggression argument says that because we share a common heritage with the animal kingdom we must possess and express an aggressive instinct. And the notion is elaborated with the suggestion that at some point in our evolutionary history we gave up being vegetarian ape-like creatures and became killers, with a taste not only for prey animals but also for each other. It makes a good gripping story. More important, it absolves society from attempting to rectify the evil in the world. But it is fiction—dangerous fiction.[3]

The authors go on to say that killing is not necessarily "in our genes," and they see farming as more a cause for invidious distinction than the hunt. Thus, they agree, in effect, with Thoreau and Veblen that conspicuous wealth is the cause of much of our trouble.

It is too shortsighted a view to argue that man is violent by nature, although evidence to the contrary sometimes may seem overwhelming. It is probably closer to the truth to say that man is a creature of energy that sometimes erupts in destructive ways but other times flows harmoniously and creatively. It is not a matter of viewing man as either good or bad but of finding the right amount of control and timely release of energy for the purpose at hand.

Sporting competition is a means of discharging this energy, and the rules of the contest are a means of control. Aside from professional wrestling and possibly roller derby, there is no sport involving contestants that does not have rules, which is what distinguishes sports from war. Although violence in some sports such as football, hockey, and recently college and professional basketball seems to be increasing, still they are games with rules. In other words, the aggression, both that of players and fans, is controlled. This is one reason why sports have attracted the attention of philosophers, psychologists, and scientists. They offer an alternative to apathy and inactivity on the one hand and rage and unchecked energy on the other. Bertrand Russell, for instance, in "Social Cohesion and Human Nature" in *Authority and the Individual*, the title of the Reith lectures for 1948-49, points out the desirability of nondestructive competition.

I do not think that ordinary human beings can be happy without competition, for competition has been, ever since the origin of Man, the spur to most serious activities. We should not, therefore, attempt to abolish competition, but only to see to it that it takes forms which are not too injurious. Primitive competition was a conflict as to which should murder the other man and his wife and children; modern competition in the shape of war still takes this form. But in sport, in literary and artistic rivalry, and in constitutional politics it takes forms which do very little harm and yet offer a fairly adequate outlet for our combative instincts. What is wrong in this respect is not that such forms of competition are bad, but that they form too small a part of the lives of ordinary men and women.[4]

Perhaps the most noted exponent of sports as a means of channeling aggression is Konrad Lorenz whose *On Aggression* has been hailed as "revolutionary" and "epoch-making." While some would question the appropriateness of such phrases since many of Lorenz's ideas have been advanced before by others, there is no doubt that it is an important book and a hopeful one as the following extract illustrates:

The value of sport . . . is much greater than that of a simple outlet of aggression in its coarser and more individualistic behavior patterns, such as pummeling a punch-ball. It educates man to a conscious and responsible control of his own fighting behavior. Few lapses of self-control are punished as immediately and severely as loss of temper during a boxing bout. More valuable still is the educational value of the restrictions imposed by the demands for fairness and chivalry which must be respected even in the face of the strongest aggression-eliciting stimuli.[5]

There is, of course, another side to this belief, that is, the more man participates in or even observes violence the more prone he is to practice it. Some believe that ferocious sports make a bellicose temperament habitual and that the widespread practice of such sports is not a surrogate of war but another form of it. Both sports and combat in this theory exist along a spectrum of aggression that is *acquired*, not natural. Therefore, they are interdependent and cannot be distinguished from each other. According to Thorstein Veblen's *Theory of the Leisure Class*:

> Sports of all kinds are of the same general character, including prize-fights, bull-fights, athletics, shooting, angling, yachting, and games of skill, even where the element of destructive physical efficiency is not an obtrusive feature. Sports shade off from the basis of hostile combat, through skill, to cunning and chicanery, without its being possible to draw a line at any point. The ground of an addiction to sports is an archaic spiritual constitution—the possession of the predatory emulative propensity in a relative high potency. A strong proclivity to adventuresome exploit and to the infliction of damage is especially pronounced in those employments which are in colloquial usage specifically called sportsmanship.[6]

Veblen views all athletes, sportsmen, and fans as adults who have failed to mature; and while he generalizes wildly, sweeping away all platitudes about the value of sports, there is this much about his theory that is hopeful—man, though emulative, is not inherently aggressive. Thus, if hostility has been learned, it could be unlearned with different social values and orientation. Veblen is in essence a behaviorist, and as such the appeal of his implicit cures, as well as his explanation of the causes of aggression, is limited. He is also a neo-Puritan, and the noninvidious world he obviously prefers would be as dreary as any heavenly city of the Calvinist or any utopia of the Marxist. Lorenz does a better job of acknowledging the mystery in the origins of aggression than either Veblen or Richard Leakey. Farming and the beginning of honorific distinction may well be results and not causes. Common sense tells us that the seeds of strife had to be there from the beginning, thus insuring a crop of bitter fruit for each generation upon the earth. Perhaps the flaw is not in one system or another such as farming, for example, or capitalism, but in man himself. The left-wing critic sees as the solution to world problems the elimination of competition, which would have to include sports: the right-wing critic advocates the substitution of sports for war. Although governments and businesses frequently manifest the very abuses in regard to sports that left-wing critics accuse them of, the latter seems more realistic. As Christopher Lasch's essay "The Corruption of Sports" pointed out, the problem may not be so much the exploitation of sports by a power elite, such as the aristocracy of ancient Greece or Victorian England, but the degeneration of sport into spectacle for commercial reasons entirely. Admittedly this could be regarded as a capitalistic rip-off, but the connections between such ventures and an aggressive foreign war seem remote. Furthermore, the Marxist solution to any fascist problem, and vice versa, is never an appealing prospect for anyone who looks at it carefully. A spectacle, as Johan Huizinga clearly implies in *Homo Ludens: A Study of the Play Element in Culture*, is a spectacle whether at the Olympics in Moscow or Super Bowl in Miami.

"Catharsis and War," a chapter in *From Ritual to Record: The Nature of Modern Sports* by Allen Guttman, surveys both sides of the controversy well, and the relevance of the matter can be perceived immediately when Guttman asks about the Vietnam War: "Did the aggression stimulated by the game [football] increase the desire to unleash emotion in a socially sanctioned (up to a point) act of war or did a mounting frustration with guerrilla warfare send the citizenry to the stadium, where one was at least able to shout and scream with one's equally frustrated peers? Research into such questions as these has barely begun."[7] Guttman goes on to say that the neo-Marxists claim combative games bring about an "interventionist foreign policy." Perhaps there is some truth to this, but sports competition has never been the bugaboo that some have made of it. Vince Lombardi, though an admirer of General Patton, did not cause the Vietnam War, as someone has said, and Muhummad Ali, an aggressive man in a brutal sport, and his followers certainly did not encourage it. In the study of aggression, as anything else, the paradox abounds at every turn.

In spite of the complexity of aggression in sports, the problems desperately need solutions. One of the most disturbing books to read in recent years, "a bone-jarring autobiography" as *Time* called it, is *They Call Me Assassin* by Jack Tatum, the former Oakland Raiders safety who left New England Patriots safety Darryl Stingley paralyzed from the neck down after a tackle in a 1978 game. The book has been controversial for several reasons. For one thing, Tatum in his own defense points out that the violence he wreaks on the field is totally within the rules. His defense should remind us that part of the fault lies within all of us who applaud too much not when injured players leave the field but when they are legally assaulted in the first place.

Obviously something needs to be done, and Robert C. Yeager in *Seasons of Shame: The New Violence in Sports* sets forth recommendations in four distinct areas: (1) game rules and penalties, (2) playing gear and equipment, (3) the legal system, and (4) attitudes and expectations of the fans. This last may be the most difficult challenge of all, since we are attracted to violence in ways that we can't even begin to comprehend. Indeed Norman Mailer in *The Presidential Papers* noted that brutality partakes of the horror sublime when he described the death of Benny Paret:

And Paret? Paret died on his feet. As he took those eighteen punches something happened to everyone who was in psychic range of the event. Some part of his death reached out to us. One felt it hover in the air. He was still standing in the ropes, trapped as he had been before, he gave some little half-smile of regret, as if he were saying, "I didn't know I was going to die just yet," and then, his head leaning back but still erect, his death came to breathe about him. He began to pass away. As he passed, so his limbs descended beneath him, and he sank slowly to the floor. He went down more slowly than any fighter had ever gone down, he went down like a large ship which turns on end and slides second by second into its grave. As he went down, the sound of Griffith's punches echoed in the mind like a heavy ax in the distance chopping into a wet log.[8]

Still it happens. On July 7, 1980 following his bout with Gaetan Hart in Montreal, Cleveland Denny became, as Boston *Herald American* sportswriter George Kimball observed, the 340th boxer to die from injuries since 1946. Deaths in automobile accidents are often cited in comparison and contrast, as they are in discussions of casualities in war, as if this somehow excuses the need for reform in sports or politics. While there are obviously some similarities in the causes of all violent deaths, in sports there is the presence of the paying spectator.

Because of the high salaries commanded by athletes and the new violence in sports, a whole new field, sports law, has blossomed overnight. Complex contract negotiations between players and owners have opened new opportunities for lawyers, and brutality in the games demands not just new rules but posibly new interpretations of law. Among a number of recent books addressing these issues and others are *Sports and the Courts* by Herb and Thomas Appenzeller, *Sports Violence: The Interaction Between Private Lawmaking and the Criminal Law* by Richard B. Horrow, and *Law and Sport* by Gary Nygaard. Students doing research on this subject should check the "Sport and Law" section under "Book Notes" in the *Journal of Sport History*, court and congressional records, and also the Wes-Law Computer System.

In spite of the violence in modern sport, the inherent values of competition remain. Perhaps the most important of these values is the synthesis competition offers between cooperation and aggression. In ideal competition both the reward and rules are clearly understood. Cooperation without any *agon* (competition) might finally be as objectionable as aggression without principle or restraint. Man is not just a being but a becoming as well and must have an agony of spirit as well as dreams of rest and peace. Sports provides a means for this struggle, for they represent a middle way between play and war, similar to each but fundamentally different from both. Nature is at play, as Rousseau believed, and at war as Hobbes believed.

Man cannot fall into either extreme without dire consequences sooner or later. With their emphasis upon rules, sports provide systems of checks and balances upon the human predilection toward extremes. Involvement in sports or other types of art represents a quest for a better life, a higher form of being achieved through effort, a finer proportion or balance of mind and body and soul than what one has known before.

To find the best balance between materialistic and transcendental goals, however, is not an easy undertaking, as matters of human aggression never are. There is even disagreement between scholars over the definition of aggression and assertion, which have been classified in a number of ways. Clearly, the definition of assertion is important as it may stand as an alternative to aggression, especially if aggression is seen as "an act whose intent is to do harm." The subject is much too complex even to begin to survey, and the reader, therefore, is referred to a number of respected studies providing definitions. Among those dealing with aggression are *Aggression: A Social Psychological Analysis* by Leonard Berkowitz and *Frustration and Aggression* by John Dollard and others. A disturbing picture of the ramifications of violence in professional football is contained in John Underwood's three-part series, "Brutality: The Crisis in Football," which began in the August 14, 1978, edition of *Sports Illustrated*. On the subject of violence, as on almost all other aspects of sports, Arnold Beisser's *The Madness in Sports* is a must, especially the concluding chapters on "The Sports Fan and Recreational Violence." Among the helpful books on "assertion" are *Your Perfect Right: A Guide to Assertive Behavior* by R. E. Alberti and M. L. Emmons, "Development and Validation of an Athletic Assertion Scale" by Jacki Daily, and *Responsible Assertive Behavior* by Arthur J. Lange and Patricia Jakubowski. All of these studies note the difficulty in making distinctions between assertion and aggression, as well as the difficulty in measuring them. The terms are, in fact, frequently used interchangeably, but while they have something in common, there is significant difference between them, and to define this difference is a worthy goal of scholarship. Nothing on earth is so important as man's understanding of aggression, especially in view of the fact that it frequently takes the form of war.

NOTES

1. Jean Jacques Rousseau, *Inequality Among Mankind* (1761; reprint ed., New York: Lenox Hill, 1971), pp. 68-69.

2. Thorstein Veblen, *Theory of the Leisure Class* (1899; reprint ed., New York: Macmillan Co., 1953), pp. 31-32.

3. Richard E. Leakey and Roger Lewin, *Origins* (New York: Dutton, 1977), p. 10.

4. Bertrand Russell, *Authority and the Individual* (London: George Allen and Unwin Ltd., 1949), p. 22.

5. Konrad Lorenz, *On Aggression*, trans., Marjorie Kerr Wilson (New York: Harcourt, Brace and World, 1966), p. 72.

6. Veblen, p. 170.

7. Allen Guttman, *From Ritual to Record: The Nature of Modern Sports* (New York: Columbia University Press, 1978), p. 136. For further discussion and additional information on sources see Guttman's article, "Sports Spectators from Antiquity to the Renaissance," *Journal of Sport History* 8 (Summer 1981), pp. 5-27.

8. Norman Mailer, *The Presidential Papers* (New York: G. P. Putnam's Sons, 1963), pp. 244-45.

BIBLIOGRAPHY

Alberti, Robert E., and M. L. Emmons. *Your Perfect Right: A Guide to Assertive Behavior*. San Luis Obispo, Calif.: Impact, 1974.

Appenzeller, Herb, and Thomas Appenzeller. *Sports and the Courts*. Charlottesville, Va.: Michie, 1980.

Beisser, Arnold R. *The Madness in Sports*. 2d ed. Bowie, Md.: The Charles Press Publishers, 1977.

Berkowitz, Leonard. *Aggression: A Social Psychological Analysis*. New York: McGraw-Hill, 1962.

Daily, Jacki A. "Development and Validation of an Athletic Assertion Scale." Ph.D. dissertation, University of North Carolina at Greensboro, 1978.

Dollard, John, Leonard V. Doob, Neal E. Miller, G. H. Mowrer, and Robert R. Sears. *Frustration and Aggression*. New Haven, Conn.: Yale University Press, 1974.

Guttman, Allen. *From Ritual to Record: The Nature of Modern Sports*. New York: Columbia University Press, 1978.

_____. "Sports Spectators from Antiquity to the Renaissance." *Journal of Sport History* 8 (Summer 1981), 5-27.

Horrow, Richard B. *Sports Violence: The Interaction Between Private Lawmaking and the Criminal Law*. Arlington, Va.: Carrollton Press, 1981.

Huizinga, Johan. *Homo Ludens: A Study of the Play Element in Culture*. Translated by R. F. C. Hull, Boston: Beacon Press, 1960.

Lange, Arthur J., and Patricia Jakubowski. *Responsible Assertive Behavior*. Champaign, Ill.: Research Press, 1976.

Lasch, Christopher. "The Corruption of Sports." *New York Review of Books* 24 (April 28, 1977), 24-30. Revised and reprinted as "The Degradation of Sport," in *The Culture of Narcissism*. New York: W. W. Norton, 1978.

Leakey, Richard E., and Roger Lewin. *Origins*. New York: Dutton, 1977.

Lorenz, Konrad. *On Aggression*. Translated by Marjorie Kerr Wilson. New York: Harcourt, Brace and World, 1966.

Mailer, Norman. *The Presidential Papers*. New York: Putnam, 1963.

Nygaard, Gary. *Law and Sport*. New Brighton, Minn.: Brighton Publishing Co., 1981.

Rousseau, Jean Jacques. *Inequality Among Mankind*. 1761. Reprint. New York: Lenox Hill, 1971.

Russell, Bertrand. *Authority and the Individual*. London: George Allen and Unwin Ltd., 1949.

Tatum, Jack, with Bill Kushner. *They Call Me Assassin*. New York: Everest House, 1980.

Underwood, John. "Brutality: The Crisis in Football, an Unfolding Tragedy," *Sports Illustrated,* August 14, 1978, pp. 68-72; "Punishment is a Crime," August 21, 1978, pp. 32-56; and "Speed is All the Rage," August 28, 1978, pp. 30-41.

Veblen, Thorstein. *Theory of the Leisure Class*. 1899. Reprint. New York: Macmillan Co., 1953.

Yeager, Robert C. *Seasons of Shame: The New Violence in Sports*. New York: McGraw-Hill, 1979.

CHAPTER II

Sports and War

Sports would appear to be an alternative to war; but paradoxically through-out history sports and war have fed each upon the other. The kinship between them is at least as old as the *Odyssey* where, according to E. Norman Gardiner in *Athletics of the Ancient World* the word "athlete" appears for the first time.[1] Stung by the taunt of the Phaeacian spielman that he is no athlete, Odysseus proceeds to prove that he is. In early Greek culture it was unthinkable for a warrior not to be an athlete. Athletic training not only prepared the Greek for battle but also was essential in the development of the whole man. It is difficult to separate the Greek love of art from the Greek love of sports and love of country. All three in com-bination have born remarkable results for democracy and civilization, as Chief Justice Byron White noted in his essay, "Athletics: . . . Unquenchably the Same?"

[I]t is said in the books that Darius, the Persian king in the sixth and fifth centuries B.C., determined to conquer the Greeks, considering them to be an inferior race. He accordingly sent a spy among them to see how they trained for battle and to determine their capabilities. This spy disguised himself as a merchant and infiltrated the Greek army. What he saw was Greek soldiers, their bodies naked and oiled, practicing a variety of athletics. They did much dancing, too, clad only in a bronze shield. And they walked together, arm in arm, hand in hand. These soldiers seemed strong enough, but they sat and paid close attention when Greek poets were read aloud to them. The spy reported to Darius that the Greeks spent their time cavorting around in the nude or sitting, partially clothed, while listening to idiots pro-pound ridiculous ideas about freedom and equality for the individual citizen.

Darius and his luxurious court were greatly amused and thought conquest of Greece would be a terribly easy job. What a rude shock it was when at Marathon the Persian army was driven out to sea. All of this was beyond the comprehension of the powerful emperor.[2]

Strong bodies within sound minds make an excellent defense against outside enemies, but the composite ideal also carries with it an inherent danger: The overdevelopment of either body or mind at the expense of the other. According to Arnold Toynbee this is what happened when the Spartans allowed *banausia* (specialization) to capture their peculiar profession of arms. It also has occurred in the modern world to a degree never imagined by the ancients. Professional armies have become more and more professional until ironically some forms of specialization have ceased to depend upon athletic ability altogether, as thousands of technicians around the world prove.

Historically the English, like the Greeks, have placed great faith in the sports-war metaphor. Joseph Strutt's *Sports and Pastimes of the People of England* carefully distinguishes between sports for the people as a whole and those practiced by the aristocracy in preparation for war from the Middle Ages to the first quarter of the nineteenth century. Sports were not merely for fun and entertainment but also were of practical value in the defense of the state. By the Victorian age the English went so far as to claim that the battle of Waterloo was won on the playing fields of Eton. For an unforgettable picture of the legacy of this belief one should read Paul Fussell's *The Great War and Modern Memory* in which he points out that British soldiers sometimes were inspired to attack by considering war a game. "One way of showing the sporting spirit," says Fussell, "was to kick a football toward the enemy lines while attacking. This feat was first performed by the 1st Battalion of the 18th London Regiment at Loos in 1915. It soon achieved the status of a conventional act of bravado and was ultimately exported far beyond the western front."[3]

In America the sports-war metaphor also gained wide support in part as a result of Theodore Roosevelt's pronouncements and articles, for example, "The Value of an Athletic Training." Frank Norris in his short story "Travis Hallet's Halfback," published in 1894, summed up the popular feeling when he had the father of the girl saved by the halfback pronounce, " 'I think you would find that the same qualities that make a good football man will make a good soldier. . . .' "[4] Football seems to have been the sport most frequently singled out. Stephen Crane in his letters even attributed his ability to write about war to his experiences on the football field.[5]

Part of the popular association of sports and war grew out of the cult of versatility that gripped the nation around the turn of the century and the decades immediately following. It was America's answer to the Victorians' *mens sana in corpore sano*, and its leading exponents were, in addition to Theodore Roosevelt, Jack London, and Burt L. Standish in the guise of

Frank Merriwell. One had to be manly and ready for war, and if one did not measure up, the results were nothing less than traumatic, at least in the case of F. Scott Fitzgerald as he reported in *The Crack-Up*.

> The old dream of being an entire man in the Goethe-Byron-Shaw tradition, with an opulent American touch, a sort of combination of J. P. Morgan, Topham Beauclerk, and St. Francis of Assisi, has been relegated to the junk heap of the shoulder pads worn for one day on the Princeton freshman football field and the overseas cap never worn overseas.[6]

Yet the alliance between sports and war is not due entirely to the cult of versatility nor, in Thorstein Veblen's view, should it surprise anyone. Veblen, in *Theory of the Leisure Class*, posited that both proceeded from the barbarian temperament that seeks honor above all else. The theory is said to apply wherever a division of labor occurs, which is just about everywhere. Furthermore, the other two principal forms of distinction, politics and religion, also reflect a predatory impulse, especially in nations or religions that are particularly messianic. Sports do provide a ready and effective means for proselytizing for any cause as the Soviets, for example, well know. In *Sport in Soviet Society: Development of Sport and Physical Education in Russia and the USSR*, James Riordan writes: "The Soviet Union is keenly aware of the advantages that are thought to accrue from international sporting success and, of course, deliberately prepares its athletes for international events."[7] The West undertakes essentially the same practices, although the aims are never so blatantly stated. As in Russia and China, organized sports in America are invested with a high dignity that almost invariably exhibits the trapping of civil religion and nationalism. In the West the pregame prayers and national anthems and the half-time ceremonies, which usually celebrate patriotism in one way or another, are all attributable to the conscious or unconscious threat of war. Until a world without threat of war arrives, the notion of national defense and national honor will continue to exert a powerful influence upon American sports and that of other countries as well.

Now that several years have passed since the Vietnam War, the tie between sports and military preparedness may seem slim, but the linkage is always felt and is as strong as ever underneath the surface of appearances. Should another localized conflict such as Korea and Vietnam erupt, the old alliances will once again be manifest. At the various service academies the kinship between sports and battle is never out of sight. It is believed that every cadet and midshipman must be an athlete to be ready for the larger struggle.

The press as well as the military establishment itself never tires of promoting the role of sports in battlefield heroism, especially during times of war. The American public has been reminded again and again that not only do great generals play sports (Eisenhower, MacArthur, Stillwell, and Patton) but also that great athletes go to war. In the April 6, 1966, issue of *Life*, Pete Dawkins, Heisman Trophy winner and Rhodes scholar, appears as the apotheosis of the all-round man and the final argument against those who doubt that football helps in the training of the warrior. Dawkins managed to sanctify both sports and battle when he said, "This is the varsity. I want to be in it."[8] Shown in one picture strumming his guitar, Dawkins became the modern example of a tradition running back to Rupert Brooke, Philip Sidney, Beowulf, and the democracy-loving Greeks. In June 1966 Bill Carpenter, Dawkins's All-American teammate, called for an air strike on his own position. News media carried Carpenter's heroism around the world, and it is probably safe to assume that the headline of the June 10, 1966, Knoxville *News-Sentinel* did not differ substantially from that of newspapers in other American cities: "LONESOME END'S NAPALM SAVED MEN."[9] Carpenter was nominated for the Congressional Medal of Honor for his action and was presented the first distinguished American award by the National Football Foundation and Hall of Fame.

While the sports-war metaphor received a great deal of attention and praise in both the Korean and Vietnam wars, it almost became a combat casualty itself. For the first time in its history, the United States found itself engaged in wars it could not win in any traditional sense, and out of the increasing frustration the faithful old clichés took on strange new twists. MacArthur's celebrated "There is no substitute for victory," which applied principally to war, became extremely popular in sports as "Winning is the only thing." The saying usually is attributed to Vince Lombardi but was ardently subscribed to by the late Jim Tatum of Maryland and Paul (Bear) Bryant of Alabama. (Larry Merchant in . . . *And Every Day You Take Another Bite* points out that it wasn't Lombardi at all who came up with "Winning is not everything; it is the only thing" but "Hurry-Up" Yost, a famous coach at the University of Michigan in the early 1900s.)[10] In fact the emphasis on the importance of winning in sports was dominant in the fifties and sixties as the country moved toward its first tie in Korea and loss in Vietnam. Paul Bryant, among many others, desperately tried to hold on to the old football-war parallel when at the end of the 1966 season he was quoted as saying, "Here in our area, particularly in Alabama, I think our football players have a far-reaching influence on young people. Some of these young folks are going off for Vietnam every day, and I hope they aren't going over there to fight for any tie."[11] But it was becoming clear to some in high places that football was of no worth whatever in the conduct of war. Admiral Hyman G. Rickover, father of the atomic submarine, indicated in an interview before the 1965 Army-Navy football game that he could not have cared less who won and ridiculed the philosophy contained in the alleged words of the Duke of Wellington: "The Battle of Waterloo was won on the playing fields of Eton." According to Rickover, " 'There is no evidence that the Duke ever made such a statement: he probably learned the spirit of adventure by jumping over a ditch on horseback.' "[12] Rickover, who either never read Tennyson's ode to Wellington or was not impressed by it, even thought that the Duke might have acquired his athletic training by " 'tobagganing around corridors, drawn by a bevy of young women.' " It is not surprising, therefore, that Rickover in the same article agreed with General Thomas D. White who, as chairman of the board investigating cheating at the Air Force Academy, found no significant relationship between excellence of football and air force officers.

This was the unkindest cut of all, for it flew in the face of a cherished tradition. In "Football's Biggest Show" (The Army-Navy Game) Harry T. Paxton stated that as of 1950 eighty former Navy players had become admirals including Bull Halsey, Jonas Ingram, and Richard E. Byrd. Ninety-eight Army players had become generals including Omar Bradley, Joe Stillwell, James Van Fleet, and Dwight Eisenhower. How did football men compare with other students? According to Paxton, no precise figures were available but it was "the belief of officials that the football men do just as well, if not better. The number who have been decorated for heroism is high."[13]

Behind new apostasy is the disturbing evidence that future wars will be won in classrooms and laboratories rather than playing fields, which, of course, was the essence of Admiral Rickover's argument and reason for his insistence upon high academic standards. Wars now involve killing at a distance and depend upon such technological marvels as the nuclear submarine and the high-speed aircraft, described by Tom Wolfe in his "The Truest Sport: Jousting with Sam and Charlie." The traditional comparison between sports and war has less and less application as time goes on. War has become intellectual. Under these circumstances the football player on scholarship at Alabama or Ohio State is not likely to be regarded as a symbol of hope for national survival, nor will it contribute to patriotism or the security of the country to allow the service academies to compete with behemoths around the country as James Michener recommends in *Sports in America*. Instead, the service academies should deemphasize football and join some conferences like the Ivy League where they can compete without endangering their basic mission, which is, of course, to train young men and women to defend democracy. The symbiotic relationship between sports and war may be eternally valid for West Point graduates going into the infantry, but it does not require participation at the semiprofessional level to acquire any lessons that football is supposed to provide for the man with the gun.

Something besides the sheer technological complexity of modern methods of war took its toll of the sports-war metaphor and that was the repudiation of the idea of victory by the counterculture. War has always appeared absurd to those who think, but for the first time in history a war became absurd not to a few but to millions and not only absurd but unjust. In 1973 George Leonard's essay "Winning Isn't Everything. It's Nothing," which was part of an Esalen Sports Symposium, appeared in *Intellectual Digest.* Leonard was speaking principally of sports, but thousands of youths had already extended that same philosophy to war and politics and, instead of going to Vietnam to fight for a win as Bear Bryant wanted them to do, chose to go either to jail or to Canada. It was a bad time for the sports-war metaphor and a bad time for the country. America's attitudes toward winning would never be exactly the same again.

After the 1968 elections and during the peak of the controversy over Vietnam, *Time* ran an essay on the subject entitled "The Difficult Art of Losing." It carefully identified the poles the country was torn between and admirably placed winning and losing, both in politics and war, in a sane perspective.[14] It is a noteworthy piece as is John P. Sisk's "Hot Sporting Blood," a superb counter argument to George Leonard's article. Much like Michael Novak, Sisk recommends a realistic approach to games, politics, and life.

> It would be far better to face up to the fact that all play is for the prize, and that until we are huddled fraternally into the global village there will always be, for better or worse, two games: the one the individual player or team is playing and the one each nation is playing against competitor nations. Thus there will always be two prizes.[15]

In Sisk's view, having accepted a sense of limits and the necessity of individual and group competition, one can then strive for the classic virtue:

> Hugo Rahner's *Man At Play* proposes the Aristotelian virtue of *eutrapelia* as the informing virtue for his playful man. The *eutrapelos* man is the happy mean between the frivolous man who is incapable of commitment and the zealous boor who is unaware of points of view other than the one he is fixed in. Maybe if there are enough *eutrapelos* men at the Twenty-First Olympiad, such impulses toward world unity as are present may have a better chance to do their salvational work.[16]

Edwin Cady's *The Big Game: College Sports and American Life* has numerous references to winning and losing both in sports and war. Cady looks at primitive groups such as the Kwakiutl and the Kurelu in Peter Matthiessen's *Under the Mountain Wall: A Chronicle of Two Seasons in the Stone Age* and discusses similarities and differences between their forms of play and war and ours. He concludes that "the struggle-play-gamble pattern characteristic of our Big Game [college football] seems preferable (in as far as we stick to it) to their fight-murder-war patterns. We are not so far, and what withholds us not so indestructible, from relapsing that we can afford to rip up the fabric of custom and consolation which holds us to the possibility of our pattern. And we need urgently to promote *homo frater-nales*, the citizen of the world."[17] Admirable words indeed but just how much do we need to stick to our patterns and what kind of world citizen is one who sedulously attends the big game? Furthermore, how big is big? The University of Tennessee, the institution that published Cady's book, is presently considering expanding Neyland Stadium to 106,000, thus making it the largest college stadium in the country.

The danger of the big game and the mesmerized crowd are well identified by Wilma Dykeman in *Return the Innocent Earth*. In a few pages describing the big game between Jackson (read the University of Tennessee) and the University of Alabama, Dykeman identifies every reprehensible facet of the do-or-die game: the bromidic mentality of the alumni, the postseason bowl lust, the swelling arrogance sure to come with victory, and most of all "the dark malevolent growl" that "moves through the multitude." Is this sub-limation or the incipient weening of an awakening monster? Deborah Einemann (Dykeman's character), a Jew and a citizen of the world, "had heard this crowd before"—in Germany, of course. Clearly the road to hell runs in two directions, back to the tribes of Kwakiutl and Kurelu and forward to corporate and fascist states. Cady is aware of limits, as his learned study clearly reveals, but once again it is necessary to ask, "How big is Big?"

Cady's book is troublesome not because of the "arcane and sesquipeda-lian" vocabulary that Jonathan Yardley points to in his *Sports Illustrated* review of January 15, 1979, but because of its imbalance. There is not, for instance, even the mention of any significant book left of center such as Jack Scott's *Athletic Revolution*, Dave Meggyesy's *Out of Their League* or Paul Hoch's *Rip Off the Big Game: The Exploitation of Sports by the Power Elite* or even Gary Shaw's innocent but funny *Meat on the Hoof*, almost as if these books and scores of others were beneath comment. All of his references are "solid" or "respectable," which perhaps is another reason the book is boring. *The Big Game* is a pat on the back from one arm of the establishment to the other. Cady does not seem to realize that the athletic department no longer needs any vote of confidence; it needs a long, hard look at itself.

Even if the big game sublimates aggression in ourselves, which is debat-able, it may at the same time (and probably does) distract us from the dangers of such naked aggression as the Russian invasion of Afghanistan. This is clearly the implication of novelist Josiah Bunting, a Rhodes Scholar, former Virginia Military Institute First Captain, Marine Corps major in Vietnam, and now president of Hampden-Sydney whom Hugh Sidey quotes in "The Presidency" in *Time* magazine for January 14, 1980: "For the first time in years there exists in the world a power stronger than we are and deeply hostile to us. . . . But failure of our will, the failure to act quickly and decisively, is evidence of the values in our society. We have become a nation of spectators—football, basketball, and now the world." Sidey adds, "Bunting is not calling for a careless military adventure. He had that. His is a call for strength, for purpose, for meaning."[18] The big crowd at the big game is not apt to have the powers of discrimination needed to determine the wars that should be fought nor the will to wage those that should be. Sports can help save the state as in ancient Greece in battles against the Persians or undermine it as in the case of Rome before its fall. Sports, being inherently value free, can serve any end we wish. The task is to make them serve the purposes of humanity and civilization as much as possible.

It might appear that the sports-war metaphor to some degree is another victim of the Vietnam War and the credibility gap of the late 1960s and early 1970s, but taps have not yet been played for that age-old analogy. It still survives in a hundred subtle forms in America as it does more blatantly in Russia, China, and countries of the Eastern bloc. It is found in the spectacle of sports everywhere. It surfaces during Olympics when television networks and wire services count up medals, and it comes home to us again in startling ways when commentators provide little tidbits of news about the athletic backgrounds and involvements of congressmen and commanders-in-chief. What is needed is not the faith that the relationship between sports and war will finally fade away but a close look at the problem in history and on the contemporary scene.

Paul Weiss has made perhaps the best contribution in "The Urge to Win" in *Sport: A Philosophic Inquiry.* While both sports and war have much in common, they differ in many important respects. As Weiss says, "Wars begin with a disagreement precluding the acceptance of rules," which is where sports begin.[19] Arnold Beisser also emphasizes rules in his discussion of winning in *The Madness of Sport.* "The explicit goal of all competition is . . . to win within the rules."[20] There are other things, however, that must moderate the goal of victory at least in sports. "Good sportsmanship," says Beisser, "is thus an integration of our hopes and fears in relationship. It also represents the integration of the Lombardi and Rice purposes in sports: winning as the only thing, and fairness and goodwill as an equal value."[21] War is clearly the horrible alternative to all the marvelous possibilities of sports.

The matter comes down to one simple question: How can man achieve heroism without annihilating his fellow man? Common sense, in which the world has never placed much stock, tells us that sports provide a marvelous opportunity to do just that. To tap this potential, however, it is necessary to regard competition as a means for achieving an abstract and aesthetic excellence (*aretê*) rather than as an arena for proving the superiority of one political system over another. Eleanor Metheny in *Connotations of Movement in Sport and Dance* has defined this higher and nobler system of competition as follows:

> The concept of "the good strife" is implicit in the word competition, as derived from cum and pedere—literally, to strive with rather than against. The word contest has similar implications being derived from con and testare—to testify with another rather than against him.[22]

Paul Weiss feels that Methany exaggerates, that the "with" includes and supplements an "against." Even with this qualification, the attitude is far superior to that seen in practice so often today. Even with all its problems the Olympics perhaps offers the best arena for "the good strife."

NOTES

1. E. Norman Gardiner, *Athletics of the Ancient World* (London: Oxford University Press, 1930), p. 19.

2. Byron R. White, "Athletics: . . . Unquenchably the Same?" in *The Sporting Spirit: Athletes in Literature and Life*, ed. Robert J. Higgs and Neil D. Isaacs (Harcourt, Brace, Jovanovich, 1977), p. 152.

3. Paul Fussell, *The Great War and Modern Memory* (New York: Oxford University Press, 1975), p. 27.

4. Frank Norris, "Travis Hallet's Halfback," *Overland Monthly* 23 (January 1894), 27.

5. See *Stephen Crane: Letters*, ed. R. W. Stallman and Lillian Gilkes (New York: New York University Press, 1960), p. 58.

6. F. Scott Fitzgerald, *The Crack-Up* ed. Edmund Wilson (New York: New Direction, 1945), p. 84.

7. James Riordan, *Sport in Soviet Society: Development of Sport and Physical Education in Russia and the USSR* (Cambridge: Cambridge University Press, 1977), pp. 377-78.

8. Sam Angleoff, "Pete Dawkins Takes to the Field," *Life* (8 April 1966), 100.

9. For a more objective account of the event, see S. L. A. Marshall, "The Truth About the Most Publicized Battle of Vietnam," *Harper's* 234 (January 1967), 67-78.

10. Larry Merchant, *. . . And Every Day You Take Another Bite* (New York: Doubleday, 1971), p. 109.

11. Quoted by George Leonard in his column "Sideline" under the title "Meaty Quote," *Nashville Banner*, December 5, 1966, p. 29.

12. "Admiral Rickover 'Kicks' at Football as Military Aid," Knoxville *News-Sentinel*, November 27, 1965, p. 6. On the matter of Waterloo, Admiral Rickover is ironically echoing E. M. Forester. See Bruce E. Haley, *The Healthy Body and Victorian Culture* (Cambridge, Mass.: Harvard University Press, 1978), p. 261. On the origin of the Waterloo myth, see also Haley, p. 170.

13. Harry T. Paxton, "Football's Biggest Show," *Saturday Evening Post* 228 (26 November 1955), p. 124.
14. "The Difficult Art of Losing," *Time* (15 November 1968), 48.
15. John P. Sisk, "Hot Sporting Blood," *Intellectual Digest* 4 (November 1973), 47.
16. Ibid.
17. Edwin Cady, *The Big Game: College Sports and American Life* (Knoxville: The University of Tennessee Press, 1978), pp. 61-62.
18. Quoted in *Time* (14 January 1980), p. 35.
19. Paul Weiss, *Sport: A Philosophic Inquiry* (Carbondale, Ill.: Southern Illinois University Press, 1969), p. 177.
20. Arnold Beisser, *The Madness in Sport.* 2d ed. (Bowie, Md.: The Charles Press Publishers, 1977), pp. 159-60.
21. Ibid., p. 151.
22. Quoted in Weiss, p. 151.

BIBLIOGRAPHY

Angleoff, Sam. "Pete Dawkins Takes the Field." *Life* 40 (April 8, 1966), 91-100.
Beisser, Arnold R. *The Madness in Sport.* 2d ed. Bowie, Md.: The Charles Press Publishers, 1977.
Cady, Edwin. *The Big Game: College Sports and American Life.* Knoxville: The University of Tennessee Press, 1978.
"The Difficult Art of Losing." *Time*, 15 November 1968, pp. 47-48.
Dykeman, Wilma. *Return the Innocent Earth.* New York: New American Library, 1974.
Fitzgerald, F. Scott. *The Crack-Up.* Edited by Edmund Wilson. New York: New Directions, 1945.
Fussell, Paul. *The Great War and Modern Memory.* New York: Oxford University Press, 1975.
Gardiner, E. Norman. *Athletics of the Ancient World.* London: Oxford University Press, 1930.
Hoch, Paul. *Rip Off the Big Game: The Exploitation of Sports by the Power Elite.* New York: Anchor Books, 1972.
Leonard, George. "Winning Isn't Everything. It's Nothing." *Intellectual Digest* 4 (October 1973), pp. 45-47.
Marshall, S. L. A. "The Truth About the Most Publicized Battle of Viet Nam." *Harper's* 234 (January 1967), 67-78.
Matthiessen, Peter. *Under the Mountain Wall: A Chronicle of Two Seasons in the Stone Age.* New York: Ballantine, 1969.
Meggyesy, Dave. *Out of Their League.* Berkeley, Ca.: Ramparts, 1970.
Merchant, Larry. . . . *And Every Day You Take Another Bite.* New York: Doubleday, 1971.
Metheny, Eleanor. *Connotations of Movement in Sport and Dance.* Dubuque, Iowa: William C. Brown, 1965.
Michener, James. *Sports in America.* Greenwich, Conn.: Fawcett, 1976.
Norris, Frank. "Travis Hallett's Halfback." *Overland Monthly* 23 (January 1894), 20-27.

Paxton, Henry T. "Football's Biggest Show." *Saturday Evening Post* 228 (November 26, 1955), 28-29, 120, 122-24.

Rahner, Hugo. *Man at Play*. New York: Herder and Herder, 1972.

Riordan, James. *Sport in Soviet Society: Development of Sport and Physical Education in Russia and the USSR*. Cambridge: Cambridge University Press, 1977.

Roosevelt, Theodore. "The Value of an Athletic Training." *Harper's Weekly* 37 (December 23, 1893), 1236. Reprinted in *Sporting Spirit: Athletes in Literature and Life*, ed. Robert Higgs and Neil D. Isaacs. New York: Harcourt, Brace, Jovanovich, 1977.

Scott, Jack. *The Athletic Revolution*. New York: Free Press, 1971.

Shaw, Gary. *Meat on the Hoof*. New York: St. Martin's, 1972.

Sidey, Hugh. "The Presidency." *Time*, 14 January 1980.

Sisk, John P. "Hot Sporting Blood." *Intellectual Digest* 4 (November 1973), 46-47.

Stallman, R. W., and Lillian Gilkes, eds. *Stephen Crane: Letters*. New York: New York University Press, 1960.

Strutt, Joseph. *Sports and Pastimes of the People of England*. 1801. Reprint. New York: Augustus M. Kelley, 1970.

Veblen, Thorstein. *Theory of the Leisure Class*. 1899. Reprint. New York: Macmillan Co., 1953.

Weiss, Paul. *Sport: A Philosophic Inquiry*. Carbondale, Ill.: Southern Illinois University Press, 1969.

Wolfe, Tom. "The Truest Sport: Jousting With Sam and Charlie." *Esquire* 84 (October 1975), 157-59, 228-37.

Yardley, Jonathan. "Let's Give a Sesquipedalian Cheer for the Old Synergistic Ball Game." *Sports Illustrated* (19 January 1979), p. 4.

CHAPTER 12

Sports and World Order

Whether communist, democratic, or fascist, modern governments have one thing in common—a reliance upon sports to help define and bolster national pride. The physical health of the citizenry and the conditioning of the armed forces depend to some extent upon the promotion of sports, but these are not the only reasons for nationally endorsed sports programs.

Nations not only wish to survive but also to attain glory, no matter how dubious the forms of glory may be to an objective observer. Nations, or rather the ruling classes with their endless bureaucratic ranks, wish for places in the sun. Veblen claims in *The Theory of the Leisure Class* that the four activities of a ruling class—sport, government, warfare, and religion—reinforce one another in many ways. Just as civil or nationalistic religions can take many forms, including Leninism, Maoism, Christianity, Zionism, and Mohammadanism, any form, that is, of true believing, so can sports take many forms from professional football to Ping-Pong. Sports provide a ready and dependable means of reaching masses with propaganda that promotes the national religion of the state in its quest for power. Sports equate with prowess and hence symbolize not only a strong defense but also honor. Moreover, sports rarely suggest humility, which, as Flannery O'Connor has so aptly remarked in *Mystery and Manners*, is "not a virtue conspicuous in any national character."[1]

Because sports offer the possibility for a display of prowess and the gain of glory, sports, war, and politics constantly interact and have an astonishing impact upon each other. Here are a few modern examples:

1. On October 16, 1968, during the Olympics in Mexico City, black sprinters Tommie Smith and John Carlos of the American team stood on the victory stand after their 200 meter dash and defiantly rasied the gloved fist as the national anthem was played. For this action they were suspended by the U.S. Olympic Committee but were regarded as heroes by the Mexicans and by black and brown athletes from all over the world. As Jack Scott says in *The Athletic Revolution*, "The U.S.

Olympic Committee realized that it was no longer the sole spokesman of the U.S. Olympic team."[2]

2. On July 14, 1969, El Salvador invaded Honduras following the riots and disruptions that stemmed from the preliminary round of soccer games in the World Cup competition. According to Neil D. Isaacs in *Jock Culture, U.S.A.*, possibly as many as 2,000 people were killed in the "Soccer War" and perhaps as many as 100,000 were made refugees.[3]

3. On April 9, 1971, the U.S. government allowed fifteen members of the U.S. table tennis team to accept an invitation for a match with the People's Republic of China. The event was instrumental in establishing relations between the two countries and helped to end more than twenty years of cold war between them. It paved the way for President Nixon, a football fan, to meet with Chairman Mao, an avid supporter of Ping-Pong. Just as President Nixon believed that the lesson of sports was applicable to politics and war ("When the going gets tough, the tough get going."), so Chairman Mao believed that war provided instruction for sports. According to Shih Pen-Shan in "I Fought in Red China's Sports War":

> The Communist cadre didn't have to tell us how important sports were in the Chinese communist scheme. Sports training was entrusted to the highest and most respected men in the government. Mao Tse-tung himself was the source of the "ideological instruction" which was to arm us for victory. So, twice daily, we pored over Mao's *Problems of Strategy in China's Revolutionary War* which, we were told, contained universal truths applicable to table tennis (or to basketball or whatever). One Mao "truth" was that we'd win if we "despised the enemy strategically" (regarded him as a paper tiger) "but respected him tactically" (equipped ourselves to cope with him technically).[4]

4. On September 5, 1972, during the Olympic games in Munich, Germany, for political purposes Palestinian commandos broke into the Israeli compound, capturing and holding hostage most of the Israeli team. Eleven of the Jewish athletes were killed in an act of such stunning horror that many questioned not only the future of the Olympics but also of the world itself. It was recalled with irony that the massacre occurred in Munich where Hitler, who presided over the 1936 Berlin Olympics in which he hoped to demonstrate through the medium of sports the superiority of the Aryan race, had risen to power.[5]

5. On May 17, 1976, the Trudeau government of Canada received a note from the People's Republic of China stating that to allow the Tai-

wanese to participate in the Olympics under the name of the Republic of China would violate the terms of Canada's recognition of Peking. The Canadian government was late in notifying both the IOC (International Olympic Committee) and the Taiwanese of its intention to honor the request, and the Taiwanese came to Montreal. Indignation was widespread; Lord Killanin pointed out that even the Nazis in 1936 had not officially tampered with the games by imposing political bans. Following the threat of withdrawal of the U.S. team, a compromise was attempted whereby the Taiwanese athletes would keep their flag and anthem so long as the name Republic of China was dropped. The compromise was rejected. In the same Olympiad, Tanzania, along with five Arab neighbors, withdrew in protest over the IOC refusal to ban New Zealand, which had sent a Rugby team to South Africa, a country which had been banned from competition since 1968 because of its system of apartheid.[6]

6. In February 1978, Vanderbilt University in Nashville, Tennessee, came under attack by civil rights groups for hosting the zone finals of the Davis Cup tennis matches between the United States and South Africa. Irony was added to the situation when Peter Lamb, a South African Vanderbilt sophomore, was added to the South African Davis Cup team and became the first nonwhite ever to represent his country in that event. Critics called the selection of Lamb, who is of mixed blood, "tokenism." During the controversy Richard E. Lapchick, a student of race and international sports, claimed that as a result of his stand on the issue at Vanderbilt and elsewhere, he was assaulted in his office at Virginia Wesleyan College by two masked men who beat him and scratched the word "NIGER" [sic] into his skin with the reminder "that you have no business in South Africa." Opponents of Lapchick, who would not take a polygraph test on principle, said the racial epithet was self-inflicted, but Lapchick's doctor did not believe it was.[7]

7. In January 1981, the United States served notice to the Soviet Union that U.S. athletes would not participate in the summer Olympics in Moscow unless the Russians withdrew their troops from Afghanistan. It was suggested that the Olympics should be held elsewhere, postponed, or cancelled. The Russians did not call home their troops, and the United States refused to participate, creating a controversy among its own athletes.

These instances are but a few illustrating the dilemma of modern sports and world peace and the delicate relationship that has come to exist between them. As the *U.S. News and World Report* article "World Athletes: Victims of Political Games" puts it, "the question is turning from whether the

Olympics can survive to whether they should."[8] After the experience of the
summer Moscow Olympics the question is more pressing than ever before.

Although the Olympics offer great hope for international harmony, they
inevitably, and increasingly of late, create conflict. These two opposing
points of view are succinctly expressed by Pierre de Coubertin and George
Orwell, who are quoted by Richard E. Lapchick in his introduction to *The
Politics of Race and International Sport: The Case of South Africa*:

> The aims of the Olympic Movement are to promote the development
> of those fine physical and moral qualities which are the basis of ama-
> teur sport and to bring together the athletes of the world in a great
> quadrennial festival of sports thereby creating international respect
> and goodwill and thus helping to construct a better and more peaceful
> world.
>
> Pierre de Coubertin, 1894

> It is bound up with hatred, jealousy, boastfulness, disregard for all
> rules and sadistic pleasure in witnessing violence—in other words, it is
> war minus the shooting.
>
> George Orwell [1959][9]

This is, of course, the irreconcilable conflict between the idealist and the
realist. Coubertin is speaking in terms of the "aims" of the movement,
while Orwell is speaking of the results, which have become even more dis-
tressing in the last two decades.

Should the Olympics be abolished? There is a compelling case against
international games of any sort. Certainly we could get along without the
term "World-Class Athlete," which makes one wonder if Tolstoy was a
"World-Class Writer." To eliminate the Olympics and regional games such
as the Pan-American Games would be a simple remedy, but such a course of
action might be analogous to cutting out the heart of a patient when surgery
was required only in the limbs. The Olympics and regional games provide
arenas for individual heroism that can serve either the goals of totali-
tarianism or liberty. Both Pope John XXIII and former President Eisenhower believed that sports definitely contributed to international good will,
but both, possibly as a result of the offices they held, were disposed to look
kindly upon the future of man. A more realistic view is that of the diplomat
quoted by Lloyd Garrison in his New York *Times* article, "Gabon Expels
3000 in Soccer Dispute."

> There are two things every diplomat, no matter what his nation-
> ality, dreads more than anything else short of war. . . . One is for your
> country to dispatch a goodwill naval visit and give 3000 of your sailors
> shore leave. The other is to try to build international friendship
> through football.[10]

Studies of the incidents of discord related to the Olympic games do not seem to support the optimistic opinions of the former president and the ecumenical pope, although they do not entirely negate those expectations. Philip Goodhart and Christopher Chataway in *War without Weapons* have produced the single most comprehensive study of this subject as well as the most authoritative, even without footnotes and bibliography. Goodhart and Chataway write:

> [T]he games are not, as de Coubertin intended, a gentle *exposé* of chauvinism, but one of the main manifestations of it. There is probably no regular occasion when so many people identify so aggressively with their own nation as during the fortnight in which millions follow *their* champion's struggles against the foreigner. Does this invalidate every former hope that the Olympics would make some contribution towards world peace? Or is the nationalistic fervour of the modern Games a kind of safety valve? Do they perhaps cater harmlessly and vicariously to some deep human instinct to be a member of a group locked in conflict with another? Could it be that in describing the odd phenomenon of twentieth-century international sport as "war minus the shooting," Orwell was producing, not a condemnation as he thought, but its ultimate justification?[11]

Sports, like other art forms, can be used for any number of purposes. It is just as bad to make sports a means to some end as it is to make sports an end in themselves. They must be kept in some sort of perspective, and it is not an easy thing to do. It is convenient to draw political lessons from athletic achievements, but it is almost essential for world peace not to do so. An even greater danger, however, may lie in removing the opportunity for competition altogether. In spite of the many failures, there are, Donald E. Fuoss concluded in 1952 in his Columbia University dissertation, "An Analysis of the Incidents in the Olympic Games from 1924 to 1948, with Reference to the Contribution of the Game to International Good Will and Understanding," some successes and the potential for harmony. Although Fuoss's study covered a period of a world war and all the attendant tensions before and after the war, the author found evidence that the games did appear to have some beneficial effects. These results were summarized by Richard H. Blair in his 1971 East Tennessee State University master's thesis, "International Integration through International Sports," which updates and supplements Fuoss's:

> Athletes from different countries might observe how much they have in common, the average man might gain an appreciation and a perspective of people in other countries, athletes usually appeared for the next Olympic Games, the games spread the idea of support, the

games did not prove that all the nations were friendly toward each other or were willing to make sacrifices for each other, and the games gave nations an opportunity to display national pride by means other than war.[12]

Blair's hypothesis that international sports from 1952 to 1968 contributed to international goodwill and understanding was "neither proved nor disproved." More research, he concluded, was needed before one could make a statement one way or another. Research certainly will help in reaching an understanding of the motives of men and nations, but simple goodwill on the part of participants and participating nations will be an even greater help.

Although much that is depressing has happened since the 1948 games, the fact is they are still going on. As long as the Olympics continue, nations are faced with practical problems concerning their own degree of participation. There are four approaches that individual countries can take in regard to international competition.

Out of moral conviction a country can refuse to compete altogether or engage in bans and interdicts toward those countries that limit basic human rights. Moral outrage, however, is not the exclusive possession of democracies. Tyrannical regimes have resorted to the expression of it time and time again. Regardless of who is showing the indignation, it is a simplistic hard-line approach that, from the Western point of view, has been summed up admirably by Sir Arthur Lund in "Sports and Politics," an essay that appears in *Sports in the Socio-Cultural Process*, edited by M. Marie Hart.

The slogan "sport has nothing to do with politics" is always invoked to justify surrender to totalitarians, but it was not a political difference which separated civilized people from the Nazis and Communists. In civilized countries politicians are not divided into those who do and those who do not advocate genocide, as practiced both by the Nazis in their liquidation of the Jews and by the Communists in their liquidation of whole classes who opposed them, the Kulaks for instance. The gulf which separates civilized people from Nazis or Communists is the same gulf which separated the Hellenes from the Barbarians. . . .

In the modern world sport has a prestige and an influence comparable to that of the Church in medieval Europe and the Olympic Committee should have the same power as had the medieval Church to place a country which offends against the basic laws of humanity under an interdict. The Hellenes refused to compete against Barbarians and were right. While the last sparks of heroic resistance were being extinguished by Russian tanks in Budapest I saw a photograph in the press of American and Russian athletes exchanging jokes during the Olympic Games in Australia. It made me sick.[13]

An entirely opposite tack is to participate even while disagreeing and deploring the practices of the sponsoring government. This view was well expressed by Chancellor Alexander Heard of Vanderbilt University during the controversy over the zone finals of the Davis Cup matches in 1978. He is quoted by Saundra Ivey in her article "Dilemma at Vanderbilt," which appeared in the February 27, 1978, issue of *Chronicle of Higher Education*:

> We would not prohibit a ballet company from the Soviet Union, a Ping-Pong team from the People's Republic of China, or a theater troupe from Uganda from appearing here because of political policies of the home government. . . . Tennis play by a team from South Africa on our campus does not represent a support or endorsement of apartheid by the university or its officers any more than the appearance of controversial speakers on campus constitutes support or endorsement of what those speakers say.[14]

Some 200 faculty members at Vanderbilt supported this position with a petition that stated it would be folly to mix politics and athletics unless they wished "to protest all athletic contests involving athletes from countries with oppressive regimes." In that case the petition said, "there would be an end to athletic competition as we have known it."

A similar but more optimistic view is to participate in hopes of improving the character of all involved by behaving like gentlemen and good sports at all times, as Olympic contestants are supposed to do. This is the advice of Allan J. Ryan in his article, "The Future of the Olympics," which appeared in the *Journal of Health, Physical Education and Recreation*:

> Quite simply, it would seem, since the participation of United States teams is supported entirely by public contributions, that a feeling of obligation should underlie the actions of the United States Olympic Committee and all members of its Olympic and Pan-American teams. This obligation should not be to pay off the public in terms of so many medals won, so many other countries overcome or so many individual stars established or confirmed. It should be expressed by all support elements in terms of providing the best possible circumstances for the participating athletes to put forward their best performances. On the part of the athletes it should be expressed in their manner of conducting themselves with the dignity as well as the exuberance, which befits the occasion; by earning the respect of others through respecting themselves; and by making their best possible effort so that they win honor for themselves, whether or not they win a victory.[15]

This is a splendid article by Dr. Ryan, who points out the variety of opinions toward the Olympics and who also reminds us of the intentions of the Olympics in the first place. He is a man after Coubertin's own heart.

Another approach, proposed by Michael Novak in "War Games: Facts and Coverage," is to get tough and beat them at their own game. Novak argues against the philosophy of "one-worlders" whom he equates with the agnostics. We are, says Novak, limited by time and place and the more uniformity that appears on the surface of things the deeper the divisions underneath. Hence in the Olympics especially "rootedness and spirit are at stake." Novak sees no reason why free societies cannot prevail in fair competition and goes on to state the moral advantages of victory:

> Perhaps my competitive instincts are overdeveloped (perhaps it is merely an East European seriousness about such things); but I would prefer to win before I tried to make my moral points. I would like to see the U.S. go to Moscow in 1980 and come home with the highest point total of any nation in the world. If the Eastern bloc wants a fight, let's stick it to them right in Moscow. Frank Merriwell would have done no less. What cheers would echo through the world, even to the farthest cell of the Gulag Archipelago![16]

Erich Segal also favors winning first to show that winning in politics is not the only thing. In "Black, White, and Very Blue," he laments the fact that the Africans withdrew from the Montreal games before the contests, which some of them would have won. As it was, he feels no one really noticed their departure, but had they won and then protested, there would have been a difference:

> The slogan of the 60's "The whole world is watching," often turned out to be accurate. For a gesture to engrave itself on the conscience of mankind, it needs a giant theater and a global audience. This means the winners' stand, not an airport departure lounge.
>
> In retrospect, we admire all the more the sheer brilliance of Tommie Smith's tactics in Mexico. Here at Montreal the whole world would again be watching as black Africans mounted the podium to be acknowledged Olympic champions. *Then* the glove of protest, *then* the dramatic refusal to accept a tarnished goal. And a chance to discourse at length to an avid collection of sensation-loving international press. There is no message without media.[17]

Protest of any sort is anathema to the Olympic authorities. Lord Killanin, president of the IOC (International Olympic Committee), stated that any athlete making a political gesture in the 1980 Olympics would be stripped of his medal. Responding to the rumor that NATO nations might possibly boycott the 1980 Olympics in Moscow because of the Russian invasion of Afghanistan, Lord Killanin in January 1980 pronounced, "Athletes come first, and in *no way* should be prevented from competing in international competition by political, racial, or religious discrimination."[18] President Jimmy Carter obviously had a different opinion.

From ancient times to the present the Olympics have constituted a vast enigma of human aspirations and failure. In spite of the failures and ironies, wisdom suggests that nations should continue to try. History will not provide simple solutions, but it will remind us of wrong tacks and tragedies of one kind or another. *The Olympics: The First Thousand Years* by M. I. Finley and H. W. Pleket, will provide some of this information, although the authors advise against drawing any parallels between the old games and the new. There is also a good book on the revival of the Olympics by Richard D. Mandell, entitled *The First Modern Olympics. The Olympic Games: 80 Years of People, Events, and Records*, edited by Lord Killanin and John Rodda, provides an overall view of the modern games and so does *The Story of The Olympic Games* by John Kieran and Arthur Daley. One wishing to study some of the more controversial Olympics should look at such works as *The Nazi Olympics* by Richard Mandell and *The Blood of Israel: The Massacre of the Israeli Athletes, the Olympics, 1972* by Serge Groussard. Lapchick's *Politics of Race and International Sport* is a thorough analysis of the problem of international competition in general and South Africa in particular. Because the subject is so controversial, one should check other sources, and a good place to begin is the review of Lapchick's book by Maxine Grace Hunter in the spring 1976 issue of *Journal of Sport History*. The black protest in Mexico City in 1968 is outlined in Harry Edwards's *The Revolt of the Black Athlete*. For an analysis of how the Soviet Union uses the Olympics, including the 1980 Moscow Olympics, see *Olympic Sports and Propaganda Games: Moscow 1980* by Baruch A. Hazan. Also discussed in the book is the Soviet counteroffensive to the American boycott. Perhaps the most compelling case for the continuation of the Olympics is chapter fourteen, "The Need for Reform in a New Olympic Era," in the *Modern Olympic Games* by John A. Lucas, though some, such as Randy Roberts in his review in *Journal of Sport History*, may question the basis of his optimism. In a decalogue of Olympic Games Lucas offers suggestions of reform that strike a compromise in his view between utopianism and the abolition of the games. The first of these suggestions is the call for a permanent Olympic site such as central Switzerland, Helsinki, or Athens.

The most comprehensive book on Russian sports is *Sport in Soviet Society* by James Riordan, but an earlier book of value on the subject is *Soviet Sport* by Henry W. Morton. Although somewhat dated, *Sport and Society: A Symposium*, edited by Alex Natan, presents views of sports from the perspectives of Great Britain, France, Italy, Germany, Hungary, Denmark, Switzerland, and Finland and sensitively examines a number of issues. A more recent treatment of international sports is *Sport and Physical Education Around the World*, which was edited by William Johnson. This is a huge and exhaustive work with notes, references, and tables. It contains vast amounts of information by various authorities around the world, but as Mary Lou LeCompte points out in her review in *Journal of Sport History* for spring 1981, it suffers from a lack of index and synthesizing information.

One of the works most critical of modern sports is *Sport: A Prison of Measured Time* by Jean-Marie Brohm. The twenty essays that make up the book evaluate sports in France, East Germany, Great Britain, and other countries from a Marxist perspective. Brohm may be accused by apologists for modern sports of grinding an ax in his thesis, but his indignation is marvelous. I know of no book that contains so much outrage directed against modern sports as Brohm's.

> Our critique of sport is not nihilist or intellectualist as the Communist Party claims. If today we criticise sport, the dominant capitalist and bureaucratic form of physical education, as repressive and alienating, *it is precisely because competitive sport does not evaluate the body but mutilates it.* (To see this you only have to look at some of the monsters produced by the Olympic Games.) The charge levelled against competitive sport stems from this very concrete fact. . . .
>
> For athletes from Eastern Europe the policing and administrative control goes to grotesque lengths, reminiscent of certain well known passages in George Orwell's *1984*. Soviet athletes for example may only be interviewed when accompanied by their "trainers," who are in turn supervised by an "interview officer".[19]

In Brohm's view virtually the whole industrialized world is imprisoned by sports, the East as well as the West. The mottoes coming out of Moscow and Eastern Europe bear a striking resemblance to clichés of Victorian culture and Nietzschean Romanticism: "The Communists and Soviet ideologues even go so far as to claim that the sportsman is a forerunner of the 'complete man' Marx wrote about. However reality is different." "In fact," adds Brohm, "the opposite is true." Brohm concludes with twenty devastating theses on modern sports, one of which ends with a sentence that could have served as the epigraph of this remarkable book: "Sport must be smashed, like the state machine."[20]

Outside of *Sports, Politics, and Theology in China*, by Jonathan Kolatch, little exists, especially in recent years, on sports in China. Kolatch's book came out slightly before the thawing of relations between the United States and China, but it is still the work to begin with for understanding the role and scope of sports in China. Among many other features, it is remarkable in tracing the surprising influence of the YMCA upon Chinese sports in the early decades of this century. A later article that adds significantly to the subject is "The People's Republic of China" by Roy A. Clumper and Brian B. Pendleton, which appears in *Sports Under Communism* edited by James Riordan. The essay is full of valuable information, as are the other essays on Communist countries, but one senses almost an advocacy of the Chinese development of sports. The authors appear to report accurately what they see, but they also rather seem to approve of what they see. How much the highly structured party sports apparatus is designed to serve the state rather than "serve the people" is a question the authors do not raise. Unfortunately, comments by Western observers are limited, since most observations, if not all, are determined by what the government wishes visitors to see. The complimentary pictures drawn in "Ping-Pong Diplomat" by Judy Bochenski and in "My China Visit as a Ping-Pong Diplomat" by George Brathwaite should be contrasted with the scenes reported in "I Fought in Red China's Sport War" by Shih Pen-Shan. Two different Chinas emerge from these observations, and two different governments appear in the essays "The People's Republic of China" by Clumper and Pendleton and "Red China and the IAAF-Collusion and Conspiracy" by Vince Reel. In Clumper and Pendleton's essay the government is indulgent and benign, in Reel's scheming and conspiratorial. In Reel's view, the People's Republic of China has succeeded by machinations in "eliminating Taiwan from ever existing in the athletic world."[21] This same problem in reporting arises in other countries as well. Though he has words of praise for Doug Gilbert's *The Miracle Machine*, which deals with sports in East Germany, Gerald A. Carr in his review of the book for the spring 1981 issue of *Journal of Sport History* states:

An irritation in reading *The Miracle Machine* is the feeling that Gilbert is often excessive in his praise of all things East German. This reviewer became progressively annoyed by the heroic dimensions given to many East German athletes. They are persistently charming and modest—as opposed to many from the West—and they win repeatedly in spite of sickness and other adversity. In opposition to this, the negative aspects of the East German system are seldom mentioned and no effort is made to interview the athletes who preferred to leave the G.D.R. and settle in West Germany. Some comments from these people would have added greatly to the value of *The Miracle Machine*.[22]

Gilbert's tone in *The Miracle Machine* should be contrasted with that of Jean-Marie Brohm in *Sport: A Prison of Measured Time.*

E. Germany resembles a vast, "democratic" concentration camp, cut off by the Berlin wall, that symbol of so-called "socialist" freedom in the East. A look at the sports system brings to mind a sports factory or a sports barracks: sport has become an essential productive force. Such a penetration of competition into all spheres of society has turned E. Germany into a vast sports laboratory or sports enterprise— some would go as far as to say a sports prison.

Brohm sees sports in East Germany as an example of Stakhanovism, a term derived from the Soviet miner Aleksey Grigoriyevich Stakhanov who allegedly mined 102 tons of coal in one shift. Those who successfully responded to the government's propaganda to go and do likewise received special privileges and rewards. Quoting M. Castaing of *Le Monde*, Brohm concludes as follows: "It must be said that this striving after 'the inhuman work pace' when the object of sport is supposed to be relaxation and joy can only be described as a form of Stakhanovism."[23]

This obviously was not the East Germany Gilbert visited.

Considering the ramifications of politics in sports, it is surprising that not more has been written on the subject. Most sociological anthologies deal with the topic to some extent, and the most successful in this regard is *Sport in the Socio-Cultural Process*, edited by M. Marie Hart. In addition, there are approximately 100 books on sports in different countries listed in volume 47 of the *Library Catalog of the Hoover Institution on War, Revolution, and Peace* and in volume 5, which contains the supplements thereto. The Hoover Institution is located at Stanford University. Any scholar dealing with the aspects of international sport should be aware of the publications of the Wingate Institute in Israel, for example the following: *Proceedings of the First International Seminar on Comparative Physical Education* and *Sport and History of Physical Education and Sport in Asia* (1972, 1974, 1976). Descriptions of traditional Asian games can be found in *Games of the Orient: Korea, China, Japan* by Stewart Culin. Although dated because of the immense changes in the social life and sporting scene of Asia, it is still valuable to the folklorist and historian.

Unfortunately, there are no books on U.S. Olympic involvement that can compare with Riordan's *Sport in Soviet Society*. With this fact in mind, the next best book for current information is *The Final Report of the President's Commission on Olympic Sports: 1975-1977*, which consists of two volumes and an executive summary. It is available through the government printing office. The documents, like all government documents, generally are weak on philosophy, although the *Executive Summary* contains recommendations by the Commission on Organization of the U.S. Olympic Teams that are both practical and imaginative. The basic proposal calls for a

self-regulating association of sports administrations, a final merging of the diverse directions of American sport. Such a banding together is common in protection of professional integrity and independence. In the law, medicine, accounting and communications such associations have been crucial to maintaining free, responsible and professional practice. The sports groups of America have never had the unity to form such an association. However, it is apparent to the Commission that such unity is essential if the American sports system is to continue along its traditional lines. In its absence, the sports community can only drift more deeply into ineffectiveness and chaos—inviting government intervention.[24]

To get governments out of sports is a noble cause. If this would occur in the United States and elsewhere, the Olympics could be conducted in peace, as men have long dreamed. The concept of the "good strife" should not be an ideal beyond the search of man.

NOTES

1. Flannery O'Connor, *Mystery and Manners* (New York: Noonday Press, 1970), p. 35.
2. Jack Scott, *The Athletic Revolution* (New York: Free Press, 1971), p. 86.
3. Neil D. Isaacs, *Jock Culture, U.S.A.* (New York: W. W. Norton, 1978), p. 14.
4. Shih Pen-Shan, as told to Lester Velie, "I Fought in Red China's Sports War," *Reader's Digest* 90 (June 1967), 75.
5. See Serge Groussard, *The Blood of Israel: The Massacre of the Israeli Athletes, the Olympics, 1972*, trans. Harold J. Salemson (New York: William Morrow Co., 1975).
6. "Game Playing in Montreal," *Time* 108 (July 26, 1976), 32, 39.
7. Saundra Ivey, "Dilemma at Vanderbilt," *The Chronicle of Higher Education* 16 (February 27, 1978), 12.
8. "World Athletes: Victims of Political Games," *U.S. News and World Report* 81 (July 26, 1976), 52.
9. Richard E. Lapchick, *The Politics of Race and International Sport: The Case of South Africa* (Westport, Conn.: Greenwood Press, 1975), p. xv.
10. Lloyd Garrison "Gabon Expels 3,000 in Soccer Dispute," *New York Times*, 23 September 1962, p. 43.
11. Philip Goodhart and Christopher Chataway, *War Without Weapons* (London: W. H. Allen, 1968), p. 19.
12. Richard H. Blair, "International Integration through International Sport" (M.A. thesis, East Tennessee State University, 1971), p. 7.
13. Sir Arthur Lund, "Sports and Politics," in *Sports in the Socio-Cultural Process*, ed. M. Marie Hart (Dubuque, Iowa: W. C. Brown, 1972), p. 484.
14. Ivey, p. 1.
15. Allen J. Ryan, M.D. "The Future of the Olympics," *Journal of Health, Physical Education and Recreation* 43 (November-December 1972), 20.
16. Michael Novak, "War Games: Facts and Coverage," *National Review* 28 (September 1976), 954.

17. Erich Segal, "Black, White, and Very Blue." *New Republic* 175 (July 1976), 7.
18. "Lord Killanin Denounces Plan for Olympic Boycott," Johnson City (Tennessee) *Press Chronicle*, 3 January 1981, p. 12. Italics added.
19. Jean-Marie Brohm, *Sport: A Prison of Measured Time*, trans. Ian Fraser (London: Ink Links, 1978), pp. 110-11.
20. Ibid., p. 110.
21. Vince Reel, "Red China and the IAAF—Collusion and Conspiracy," *Women's Track World* 1 (December 1978), 23.
22. Gerald A. Carr, review of *The Miracle Machine*, by Doug Gilbert, *Journal of Sport History* 8 (Spring 1981), 93.
23. Brohm, p. 176.
24. *The Final Report of the President's Commission on Olympic Sports*, 2 vols. (Washington, D.C.: U.S. Government Printing Office, 1977), 1: 29.

BIBLIOGRAPHY

Blair, Richard H. "International Integration Through International Sports." M.A. thesis, East Tennessee State University, 1971.
Bochenski, Judy. "Ping-Pong Diplomat." *Seventeen* 30 (October 1971), 142-74.
Brathwaite, George. "My China Visit as a Ping-Pong Diplomat." *Ebony* 27 (November 1971), 84-86.
Brohm, Jean-Marie. *Sport: A Prison of Measured Time*. Translated by Ian Fraser. London: Ink Links, 1978.
Carr, Gerald A. Review of *The Miracle Machine*, by Doug Gilbert. *Journal of Sport History* 8 (Spring 1981), 92-93.
Culin, Stewart. *Games of the Orient: Korea, China, Japan*. 1895. Reprint. Rutland, Vt., Tokyo, Japan: Charles E. Tuttle Co., 1958.
Edwards, Harry. *The Revolt of the Black Athlete*. New York: Free Press, 1969.
Finley, M. I., and H. W. Pleket. *The Olympics: The First Thousand Years*. New York: Viking Press, 1976.
Final Reports of President's Commission of Olympic Sports, 1975-1977. 2 vols. Washington, D.C.: U.S. Government Printing Office, 1977. Vol. 1: *"Executive Summary and Major Conclusions and Recommendations."* Vol. 2: *Finding of Fact and Supporting Material* Vol. 3. *Executive Summary.*
Fuoss, Donald E. "An Analysis of the Incidents in the Olympic Games from 1924 to 1948, with Reference to the Contribution of the Games to International Good Will and Understanding." Ph.D. dissertation, Teachers College, Columbia University, 1952.
"Game Playing in Montreal." *Time* 108 (July 26, 1976), 32, 39.
Garrison, Lloyd. "Gabon Expels 3,000 in Soccer Dispute." *New York Times*, 23 September 1962, pp. 1, 43.
Gilbert, Doug. *The Miracle Machine*. New York: Coward, McCann and Geoghegan, 1980.
Goodhart, Philip, and Christopher Chataway. *War Without Weapons*. London: W. H. Allen, 1968.
Groussard, Serge. *The Blood of Israel: The Massacre of the Israeli Athletes, the Olympics, 1972*. Translated by Harold J. Salemson. New York: William Morrow Co., 1975.

Hart, M. Marie, ed. *Sports in the Socio-Cultural Process.* Dubuque, Iowa: W. C. Brown, 1972.

Hazan, Baruch A. *Olympic Sports and Propaganda Games.* New Brunswick, N.J.: Transaction Books, 1982.

Hunter, Maxine Grace. Review of *Politics and Race and International Sport* by Richard E. Lapchick. *Journal of Sport History* 3 (Spring 1976), 105-8.

Isaacs, Neil D. *Jock Culture, U.S.A.* New York: W. W. Norton, 1978.

Ivey, Saundra. "Dilemma at Vanderbilt." *Chronicle of Higher Education* 16 (February 27, 1978), 1, 12.

Johnson, William, ed. *Sport and Physical Education Around the World.* Champaign, Ill.: Stipes Publishing Co., 1980.

Kieran, John, and Arthur Daley. *The Story of the Olympic Games 776 B.C. to 1968.* Philadelphia: J. B. Lippincott, 1969.

Killanin, Lord, and John Rodda, eds. *The Olympic Games: 80 Years of People, Events, and Records.* New York: Macmillan Co., 1976.

Kolatch, Jonathan. *Sports, Politics, and Theology in China.* Middle Village, N.Y. Jonathan David, 1972.

Lapchick, Richard. *The Politics of Race and International Sport: The Case of South Africa.* Westport, Conn.: Greenwood Press, 1975.

LeCompte, Mary Lou. Review of *Sport and Physical Education Around the World.* *Journal of Sport History* 8 (Spring 1981), 93-95.

LeViness, Richard D. *The Happy Highway to Peace.* Boston: The Christopher Publishing House, 1957.

Lucas, John A. *The Modern Olympic Games.* New York: A. S. Barnes, 1980.

Mandell, Richard D. *The Nazi Olympics.* New York: Macmillan Co., 1971.

――――. *The First Modern Olympics.* Berkeley: The University of California Press, 1976.

Morton, Henry W. *Soviet Sport.* New York: Collier Books, 1963.

Natan, Alex, ed. *Sport and Society: A Symposium.* London: Bowes and Bowes, 1958.

Novak, Michael. "War Games: Facts and Coverage." *National Review* 28 (September 1976), 953-54.

O'Connor, Flannery. *Mystery and Manners.* New York: Noonday Press, 1970.

O'Leary, Jeremiah. "Soccer: The Undeclared War that Never Ends." *Washington Post,* 7 June 1970, p. 65.

"Pope Calls Sports Aid to Brotherhood." *New York Times,* 30 August 1960, p. 33.

"President Says Games Diminish World Strife." *New York Times,* 16 February 1960, p. 2.

Proceedings of the First International Seminar on Comparative Physical Education and Sport. Israel: The Wingate Institute for Physical Education and Sport.

Proceedings of the International Seminar on the History of Physical Education and Sport in Asia (1972, 1974, 1976). Israel: Wingate Institute for Physical Education and Sport.

Reel, Vince. "Red China and the IAAF—Collusion and Conspiracy." *Women's Track World* 1 (December 1978), 15-16, 23.

Riordan, James. *Sport in Soviet Society.* Cambridge, England: Cambridge University Press, 1977.

_____, ed. *Sport Under Communism*. Montreal: McGill-Queen's University Press, 1978.

Roberts, Randy. Review of *The Modern Olympic Games*. *Journal of Sport History* 9 (Spring, 1982), 95-96.

Ryan, Allan J., M.D. "The Future of the Olympics." *Journal of Health, Physical Education and Recreation* 43 (November-December 1972), 18-20.

Scott, Jack. *The Athletic Revolution*. New York: Free Press, 1971.

Segal, Erich. "Black, White, and Very Blue." *New Republic* 175 (July 1976), 7.

Shih Pen-Shan, as told to Lester Velie. "I Fought in Red China's Sports War." *Reader's Digest* 90 (June 1967), 75-78.

"300 Dead in Lima as Rioting Erupts at Soccer Match." *New York Times*, 25 May 1964, p. 1.

Veblen, Thorstein. *Theory of the Leisure Class*. 1899. Reprint. New York: Macmillan Co., 1953.

"World Athletes: Victims of Political Games." *U.S. News and World Report* 81 (July 26, 1976), 52.

CHAPTER *13*

Sports Psychology

In the preceeding chapters, sports have been examined in a social or cultural context, but this chapter will survey the material dealing with sports and their relationship to the mind and spirit in their quest for the Good, the True, and the Beautiful. Athletes in recent years have adopted a wide variety of mental states in their struggle for material success or meaning, and at the same time psychologists, philosophers, and others have discovered in sports not only mirrors of social values but potential clues to the deeper understanding of the mystery of man. What is man? asks the psalmist, Shakespeare, and B. F. Skinner. Sports may not prove to be any more successful in answering this question than psychology, philosophy, and theology have been but coupled with these traditional disciplines sports offer exciting new dimensions to the study of man. Whatever else man is, he *is* a physical being; and he is more than that.

The word "control" is crucial in the psychology of sports as well as in all other endeavors. How much force is required to control kinetic energy? Who is to do the controlling and for what purposes? While the sports psychologist as a scientist must examine the relationship between the mind and body of an athlete, he should never overlook crucial humanistic questions. This is one of Jack Scott's objections to the book *Problem Athletes and How to Handle Them* by Bruce C. Ogilive and Thomas A. Tutko, two pioneers in modern sports psychology. In his chapter "Sport Psychologists—Friend or Foe" in *The Athletic Revolution*, Scott prefaces his charges with a single reminder that remains as relevant at any time in history as it was during the counterculture days of the late 1960s:

> Before getting into an analysis of *Problem Athletes and How to Handle Them* I'm going to discuss briefly a matter that will have relevance to that analysis. What I want to talk about is the willingness, in fact many times the eagerness, of some social scientists to brand any individual that represents a threat to the status quo as a "problem."

These social scientists feel that there must be something wrong with anyone who would have the audacity to challenge an authority figure. They are especially apt to feel this way if they happen to support and agree with the values of the authority figure who is being challenged. The most blatant use of this technique is in the Soviet Union where those individuals who represent a threat to the existing social order are declared mentally ill by the State's social scientists. After being declared mentally ill, they are then "hospitalized" for their own protection![1]

In retrospect the suggestion that Tutko and Ogilive could be even inadvertently in the service of a regime as oppressive as that of the USSR may appear extreme and unfair, but Scott makes an important point. Not all uncoachable athletes are problems, and the whole issue of administering psychological tests is as debatable in sports as it is in all other fields. We have become a nation of test-takers and the conscious person, the healthy skeptic, can scarcely keep at bay the same doubts raised by Scott.

There is, however, another side to the argument. There is always a place in a democracy for inquiry and the gathering of empirical data. Epistemology depends upon statistics. After establishing the Institute for the Study of Athletic Motivation in 1963, Ogilive and Tutko expanded their research and arrived at conclusions surprisingly similar to what Scott and others had maintained all along. Their findings, which are outlined in "Sport: If You Want to Build Character, Try Something Else" and appeared in *Psychology Today*, do anything but salve the mind of the traditionalist:

In the midst of the controversy psychologists find themselves being asked what personal, social or psychological significance can be attributed to organized sport. For the past eight years we have been studying the effects of competition on personality. Our research began with the counseling of problem athletes, but it soon expanded to include athletes from every sport, at every level from the high-school gym to the professional arena. On the evidence gathered in this study, we can make some broad-range value judgments. We found no empirical support for the tradition that sport builds character. Indeed, there is evidence that athletic competition limits growth in some areas. It seems that the personality of the ideal athlete is not the result of any molding process, but comes out of the ruthless selection process that occurs at all levels of sport.[2]

They also pointed out that they "quickly discovered" the coach was a crucial factor and that in the changing society of the 1960s the coach, too, was a problem whether or not he realized it:

Value changes that involve drugs and politics put the coach under strain. Most coaches believe that a truly good athlete is also, by definition, a red-blooded, clean-living, truth-telling, prepared patriot. A top-notch competitor who disagrees with national policy is a heavy thing for a coach who undoubtedly believes that the wars of England were indeed won on the playing fields of Eton.[3]

Ogilive and Tutko predicted that many coaches would not be able to adapt to the changing values and attitudes and that as many as one third of them would be forced out of business. Although no statistics are available that I know of, it seems safe to say that few coaches since 1971 have been forced to leave their profession because of the strain of changing values. A coach usually is forced out of his job for one main reason—failure to win. This is true at almost all levels of competition. It is also questionable how far athletes have gone toward the joyous pursuit of esthetic experience that sport psychologists recommend. It is true that sports today are somehow different than they were before the "athletic revolution," but the more things change the more they stay the same. Drugs and violence remain problems, but the pressure to win, even for nonprofessional teams, remains the greatest problem, in spite of numerous books and articles stressing other goals and values. Tutko, a leading contibutor to this trend as he continues to examine and question the traditional assumptions surrounding sports, has published two books on this subject in the same year (1976): *Sports Psyching: Playing Your Best Game All the Time* (with Umberto Tosi) and *Winning Is Everything and Other American Myths* (with William Bruns). *Winning Is Everything* contains a noteworthy epilogue entitled "The Young Athlete's Bill of Rights," which fully absolves Tutko of the charge of neglecting humanistic concerns in his earlier work.

Sports may not build "character," but most experts feel that positive results can be gained from participation. According to Dr. George Sheehan in his discussion of the Ogilive and Tutko article in *On Running*, "Sport will not build character; it will do something better. It will make a man free."[4] It will also make a woman free at least according to Dr. William Morgan: ... "Athletes are less depressed, more stable and have higher psychological vigor than the general public. This is true of both men and women athletes." Although the layman may question what Dr. Morgan means by "psychological vigor," it is undoubtedly true that there are obvious benefits to be derived from a sanely administered sports program. Indeed common sense refutes any argument to the contrary.

Dr. Arnold R. Beisser also has had considerable experience working with athletes, and many of his cases are reported in *The Madness of Sport*. Since Beisser is a psychiatrist and not a psychologist, his orientation is different from that of Tutko and Ogilive but no less restrictive. His book is clearly one of the best produced in recent years. He claims with apparent validity in the preface to the second edition of his work that his book is the only one that "deals with the issues from the intrapsychic perspective of the athlete and fan as well as from the psychological and social observations that can be made from viewing sports."[6] The book is organized into two parts, case histories in the first part and "psychological theories about play and work" in the second. Beisser explains his title as follows: "We have come to realize that in order to get along in the world you have to be 'a little bit crazy' and that those of us who unquestionably accept the convictions of our society may be more irrational that those who do not."[7]

The closest to Beisser's book as far as understanding both the inner drive of athletes and the external goals is Peter Fuller's *The Champions: The Secret Motives in Games and Sports*. Fuller may occasionally fall into a Procrustean trap in his efforts to fit certain events in the lives of superstars into the framework of Freudian analysis, but his work is stimulating. Secret motives are only part of the picture, since to a large measure motives are derived from what we expect of champions. There are two notable works dealing with the various aspects of motivation: *Motivation in Play, Games, and Sports*, edited by Ralph Slovenko and James A. Knight and *Psychology of Sport: The Behavior, Motivation, Personality, and Performance of Athletes* by Dorcas Susan Butt. Butt's work has a good general discussion of aggression and sex roles in sports with excellent supporting bibliographies. An important new concept in motivation is logotherapy, which is set forth in Viktor E. Frankl's superb book, *The Unheard Cry for Meaning: Psychotherapy and Humanism* in his section entitled "Sports—the Asceticism of Today." "Logotherapy" means "*therapy through meaning*" as opposed to "*meaning through therapy*."[8] Frankl's work combines three disciplines, sports, psychotherapy, and humanism into one sane, unified approach to healing. For the imaginative mind, the possibilities are almost endless.

Almost as if the psychological aspects of sports were not already complex and challenging enough, Michael Murphy and Rhea A. White in their book *The Psychic Side of Sport* have extended the boundaries even further to include such unexplored subjects in sports as mysticism, time alteration, ESP, psychokinesis, and evolutionary possibilities. It is a unique book on sports that is completely fascinating and done with enthusiasm. It is also a superb reference on psychic phenomena, for it contains a 538 item bibliography. The only hesitation one might have over the book is that it does not deal with the spirit and soul of man as the authors imply but rather with the potential powers of body and mind. Although the words "spirit" and "sacred" are used frequently in the book, the connection between the moral, or divine, life and the events the authors describe, even "stigmata" and "rings of espousal," is thin. One can believe that such things have happened without believing that the acceptance of the fact of occurrence is

a condition of faith. It is also difficult to see the connection between stigmata and sports, and there is the inevitable question of the role and value of
such phenomena as psychokinesis and levitation in sports. Even if we knew
enough about all forms of psychic power to enable coaches to use them in
games, what ends would they be made to serve? It seems likely that coaches
would abuse them as much as they have recruiting, which would lead to the
need for a psychic regulatory agency in the NCAA. These moral questions
are not even implied in the book except indirectly in the comparison or
contrast to what the Russians are doing in this area. The main interest in
psychic phenomena to begin with is often a negative interest, that is, fear of
what others might do with such extraordinary powers. Perhaps the one inescapable flaw in all sports "psyching" is the preoccupation with self, an
undeniably Eastern influence that pervades the book by Murphy and White.
One could almost paraphrase Isocrates and say, "If all the sports mystics
had twice the power they now have, the world would not be any better off,
but let a single man attain unto wisdom and all can reap his benefit who are
willing to share his insight." *The Psychic Side of Sports* should be read, but
while it is a book of strange accounts, it is not a book about spiritual things.

Whereas the work of Ogilive and Tutko has centered on problem solving
and that of Murphy and the Esalen Institute on "psyching" and social
issues, Dr. William P. Morgan has focused upon the empirical branch of
sports psychology and the interrelationship of complex factors like health,
speed, endurance, strength, accuracy, and coordination. Sports psychology,
like sports medicine, immediately reveals what a marvelously complex
machine the human body is and how little we know about it. While the
preponderance of articles in *Contemporary Reading in Sport Psychology*,
which Morgan edited, is based on empirical data, the socialization process is
not neglected in the section called "cogent commentaries." One of the best
there is the last called "Fitness Beyond Muscle" by Arthur H. Steinhaus,
which has now achieved the status of classic.

The problems posed by artificial stimulants have been a growing concern
to psychologists, sports physicians, and others. According to many reput-
able accounts, the use of drugs in sports is widespread and raises pressing
ethical questions. "The Stimulants," Bill Gilbert writes in the second of a
three-part *Sports Illustrated* series entitled "Drugs in Sports," "are medi-
cally risky because, like every other drug, they are to some degree toxic.
They are particularly dangerous for athletes because they artificially
increase the strain on various physiologic systems, ones that are already
under stress because of exertion. The drugs also artificially prolong the period of stress by masking fatigue."[9] Because of the pressure to win, "some of
the pros," says one trainer, "need almost a full week to get over getting
pepped up for Sunday. Afterward, they must either have tranquilizers or
whiskey to bring them down. So they move through a cycle: pepped up,
drunk, hung over, depressed and then pepped up again."[10]

Gilbert quoted this unidentified trainer in 1969, and in 1975 Dr. Arnold
J. Mandell, a research pharmacologist and the NFL's first psychiatrist-in-
residence (for the San Diego Chargers), confirmed in "Pro Football Fumbles the Drug Scandal" basically the same pattern, that is, "psych up on
speed, come down on grass."[11] Mandell, like Gilbert, is not especially
critical of the athletes but sympathetic. He found professional football was
a hard world and participants in order to survive and entertain us apparently needed all the help they could get from drugs, God, It, or even the team
shrink. Says Mandell,

> Faced with early losses, the pain and the need to win, most players
> reached for common antidotes adopted by football players years ago.
> By the fourth regular season game, I had realized that there was no
> way to discuss or manipulate the psychological aspects of pro football
> without grappling with the pervasive, systematic use of mood-altering
> drugs: uppers, grass, booze. From both common knowledge and the
> public press it was clear that the League knew about it, but, like most
> official bodies, tried first to deny reality and later to suppress it. Few
> laymen like to wrestle with the tangled roots of drug use.[12]

There is no attempt in any of these discussions to equate drugs with God
or Buddha or to imply that religion is merely an opiate or stimulant. It is
only suggested that the athlete frequently needs some sort of "outside" help
for his encounter. Some sports psychologists and physicians object on good
grounds to equating psychological doping with administering drugs (see, for
example, "Report: The Psychological Doping Concept must be Rejected"
by José Ferrer-Hombravella in *Contemporary Psychology of Sport: Proceedings of the Second International Congress of Sport Psychology*) and
Tom Powers who has coached both high school and college teams, including Notre Dame under Frank Leahy, makes an interesting distinction. In an
interview with Robert J. Bueter entitled "The Use of Drugs in Sports: An
Ethical Perspective," which appeared in *Christian Century*, Powers states:

> At one time it was considered part of the coach's job to motivate
> athletes to perform to the best of their abilities. But it seems that in the
> past decade or so, use of words to motivate people has more and more
> come to be considered unsophisticated and passé. It may be that, in
> the absence of the old-fashioned pep talk, some of the kids who need
> to be motivated are turning to other forms of "pep." I wonder if this
> is part of our affluent and sophisticated society. When I played high
> school football and college ball—and even when I was in the Navy—I
> never saw any type of drug used or even heard it suggested. But in the
> past 15 years all that has changed. Players seem to be substituting pills
> for the motivation that the coach's words used to provide.[13]

John Underwood suggests in his last article in the series on violence for *Sports Illustrated* that speed has not replaced words but merely supplemented them: "Coaches know the game is ideally played in controlled anger. They hang up clippings, and talk vendettas. Players get half crazy anyway, and if 60% of them have their heads half filled with amphetamines, the injury projection is enormous."[14]

In a more recent article co-authored by Underwood and former NFL player Don Reese, the drug situation in the NFL appears to be worse than ever. If the problem in the seventies was amphetamines, the problem now is, in Reese's view, cocaine or "the lady." Entitled "I'm Not Worth a Damn," the controversial article charges on the front page of the June 14, 1982 issue of *Sports Illustrated* in the form of a special report that "cocaine can be found in quantity throughout the NFL." It also indicts the NFL for failing to deal with the drug problems realistically.

Everyone who has studied the drug problem in sports is calling for reforms, but as of the present major sporting organizations have taken limited action. Although the problem is admittedly complex, we could, as Gilbert has convincingly argued, learn a lot from horses and horse racing. According to Gilbert in the third article in his series, "High Time to Make Some Rules," the racing establishment took that crucial step by first defining doping. Until the same is done for men, we must live with Gilbert's sobering reminder:

> The mystery and drama of sport, for both participants and spectators, has always been the unfolding action that occurs when men match these intangible elements of their characters. It is the thing that elevates sport to an art form, perhaps our oldest. However, the motive for using drugs is to remove both the drama and the mystery by literally fixing the outcome in the most subtle of all ways, by changing the character of the performers. Any use of drugs, no matter how benign they may be, is an attempt to destroy what is sporting about sport, to reduce sport to the status of an entertainment, a demonstration, a spectacle.[15]

Drugs pose a threat to sports similar to that posed by government, business, and even religion—the manipulation of the athlete for some particular purpose. To be sure, sports are not an end in themselves and, like business, government, and religion, should exist to serve human goals. It is this fact that administrators, coaches, psychologists, psychiatrists, other doctors and scientists should keep in mind above all else.

As Dr. Morgan points out in his introduction to *Contemporary Readings*, sports psychology as a formal discipline is both recent and multidimensional. It is an extremely complex field, bewildering and even intimidating to the layman. For this reason the beginning researcher should start with survey articles such as the one by Dr. Morgan entitled "Sport Psychology" in *Psychomotor Domain: Movement Behaviors*, edited by Robert N. Singer. Another article by Dr. Morgan, "Sport Personology: The Credulous-Skeptical Argument in Perspective," published in *Proceedings of the Third Symposium on Integrated Development: Psycho-Social Behavior of Sport and Play*, is also a good survey of some of the claims of sports psychology as well as its limitations. Anyone doing research into motivation, aggression, or any topic under the broad spectrum of sports psychology should check on the wealth of material identified in *Psychological Abstracts*. A survey of articles relative to one's work can be made quickly through the use of the *Cumulated Subject Index to Psychological Abstracts, 1927-1974*. There are hundreds of articles on sports and related topics listed in this helpful guide, an indication of the staggering expansion of sports psychology within the last few decades. Further proof of growth, if any were needed, is the increasing attention given to the subject by professional journals. The *Journal of Sport Psychology* was established in 1979, and *Psychiatric Annals*, for instance, devoted its entire March 1980 issue to the psychological aspects of sports. Guest editor, Michael H. Sacks, M.D., included in the issue articles on five sports, football, hockey, basketball, tennis, and sailing, by psychiatrists as well as an article entitled "A Behavioral Method for Improving Sport Performance" by Herbert Fensterheim, a psychologist. The essays can be read and understood by the layman, which makes the special issue a good introduction in itself to sports psychology.

NOTES

1. Jack Scott, *The Athletic Revolution* (New York: Free Press, 1971), p. 135.

2. Bruce C. Ogilive and Thomas A. Tutko, "Sport: If You Want to Build Character, Try Something Else," *Psychology Today* 3 (October 1971), 61.

3. Ibid., p. 63.

4. George Sheehan, M.D., *On Running* (New York: Bantam, 1978), p. 202.

5. Quoted in "Comes the Revolution," *Time*, 26 June 1978, p. 59.

6. Arnold R. Beisser, *The Madness in Sport*. 2d ed. (Bowie, Md.: The Charles Press Publishers, 1977), p. x.

7. Ibid., p. 2.

8. Viktor E. Frankl, *The Unheard Cry for Meaning: Psychotherapy and Humanism* (New York: Simon and Schuster, 1978), p. 19.

9. Bill Gilbert, "Something Extra on the Ball," *Sports Illustrated*, 30 June 1969, p. 38.

10. Ibid.

11. Arnold J. Mandell, "Pro Football Fumbles the Drug Scandal," *Psychology Today* 9 (June 1975), p. 39.

12. Ibid., p. 40. For more on the controversy following Mandell's disclosures, see his book *Nightmare Season* (New York: Random House, 1976), and the third article in John Underwood's *Sports Illustrated* series, "Speed is all the Rage," 28 August 1978, pp. 30-41.

13. Robert J. Bueter, "The Use of Drugs in Sports: An Ethical Perspective," *Christian Century* 89 (April 5, 1972), p. 397.

14. John Underwood, "Speed is All the Rage," *Sports Illustrated*, 28 August 1978, p. 33. The pressures to win in competitive sports, the proliferation of athletic injuries, and the desire for enhancing the performance of the human body without incurring abuse has led to a tremendous growth and expansion in the field of sports medicine in recent years. For an introduction to the subject, see *What is Sportsmedicine?* by Ernst Jokl, *Medical Care of the Athlete* by Allan J. Ryan, *Encyclopedia of Athletic Medicine* by George Sheehan, and *A Bibliography of Sports Medicine* by Jack C. Hughston and Kenneth S. Clark. The McGraw-Hill publication, the *Physician and Sports Medicine* is devoted exclusively to the subject.

15. Bill Gilbert, "High Time to Make Some Rules," *Sports Illustrated*, 7 July 1969, p. 32.

BIBLIOGRAPHY

Beisser, Arnold R. *The Madness in Sport*. 2d ed. Bowie, Md.: The Charles Press Publishers, 1977.

Bueter, Robert J. "The Use of Drugs in Sports: An Ethical Perspective." *Christian Century*, 5 April 1972, pp. 394-97.

Butt, Dorcas Susan. *Psychology of Sport: The Behavior, Motivation, Personality, and Performance of Athletes*. New York: Van Nostrand Reinhold, 1976.

"Comes the Revolution." *Time*, 26 June 1978, pp. 54-60.

Cumulated Subject Index to Psychological Abstracts, 1927-1974. 6 vols. 2 supplements. Boston: G. K. Hall, 1966-1975.

Ferrer-Hombravella, José. "Report: The Psychological Doping Concept Must be Rejected." *Contemporary Psychology of Sport: Proceedings of the Second International Congress of Sport Psychology*. Edited by Gerald S. Kenyon and Tom M. Grogg. Chicago: The Athletic Institute, 1970.

Frankl, Viktor E. *The Unheard Cry for Meaning: Psychotherapy and Humanism*. New York: Simon and Schuster, 1978.

Fuller, Peter. *The Champions: The Secret Motives in Games and Sports*. New York: Urizan, 1977.

Gilbert, Bill. "Drugs in Sports." *Sports Illustrated*: "Problems in a Turned-on World," 23 June 1969, pp. 64-72; "Something Extra on the Ball," 30 June 1969, pp. 30-42; and "High Time to Make Some Rules," 7 July 1969, pp. 30-35.

Hughston, Jack C., and Kenneth S. Clarke. *A Bibliography of Sports Medicine*. Chicago: American Academy of Orthopaedic Surgeons, 1970.

Jokl, Ernst. *What is Sportsmedicine?* Springfield, Ill.: Charles C. Thomas, 1964.

Journal of Sport Psychology. Champaign, Ill.: Human Kinetics Publishers. 1979-.

Mandell, Arnold J. *Nightmare Season*. New York: Random House, 1976.

_____. "Pro Football Fumbles the Drug Scandal." *Psychology Today* 9 (June 1975), 39-47.

Morgan, William P. *Contemporary Readings in Sport Psychology*. Springfield, Ill.: Charles C. Thomas, 1970.

_____. "Sport Personology: The Credulous-Skeptical Argument in Perspective." In *Proceedings of the Third Symposium on Integrated Development: Psycho-*

Social Behavior of Sport and Play, edited by A. H. Ismail. Indianapolis: Indiana State Board of Health, 1978.

_____. "Sport Psychology." In *Psychomotor Domain: Movement Behaviors*, edited by Robert N. Singer. Philadelphia: Lea and Febiger, 1971.

Murphy, Michael, and Rhea White. *The Psychic Side of Sports*. Reading, Mass.: Addison-Wesley, 1978.

Ogilive, Bruce C., and Thomas A. Tutko. *Problem Athletes and How to Handle Them*. London: Pelham Books, 1966.

_____. "Sports: If You Want to Build Character, Try Something Else." *Psychology Today* 5 (October 1971), 61-63.

The Physician and Sportsmedicine. McGraw-Hill serial 1973-.

Psychological Abstracts. Washington, D.C.: American Psychological Association, 1927-.

Reese, Don with John Underwood. "I Ain't Worth a Damn." *Sports Illustrated*. June 14, 1982, front cover and pp. 66-82.

Ryan, Allan J. *Medical Care of the Athlete*. New York: McGraw-Hill, Blackiston Division, 1962.

Sacks, Michael, M.D. "Psychological Aspects of Sports." *Psychiatric Annals* 10 (March 1980).

Scott, Jack. *The Athletic Revolution*. New York: Free Press, 1971.

Sheehan, George. *Encyclopedia of Athletic Medicine*. Mountain View, Calif.: Runner's World Magazine, 1972.

_____. *On Running*. New York: Bantam, 1978.

Slovenko, Ralph, and James A. Knight, eds. *Motivation in Play, Games, and Sports*. Springfield, Ill.: Charles C. Thomas, 1967.

Tutko, Thomas, and William Bruns. *Winning Is Everything and Other American Myths*. New York: Macmillan Co., 1976.

Tutko, Thomas, and Umberto Tosi. *Sport Psyching: Playing Your Best Game All the Time*. Los Angeles: J. P. Tarcher, 1976.

Underwood, John. "Brutality: The Crisis in Football." *Sports Illustrated*: "An Unfolding Tragedy," 14 August 1978, pp. 68-72; "Punishment is a Crime," 21 August 1978, pp. 32-56; and "Speed is All the Rage," 28 August 1978, pp. 30-41.

CHAPTER 14

Philosophy and Religion

In the last two decades all the discussion of "psyching" and the inner life have resulted in part in the growth of not only sports psychology but also another new field, the philosophy of sport. Paul Weiss's *Sport: A Philosophic Inquiry* may be a pioneer work as Weiss claims, but Howard S. Slusher's *Man, Sport, and Existence: A Critical Analysis*, is more penetrating philosophically. Both books deal with myriad aspects of the mind/body problem, but Slusher, whose book was published two years earlier, begins in effect where Weiss leaves off in his last chapter, which is entitled "A Metaphysical Excursus." Weiss concentrates on "the athlete in his athletic role," the athlete's pursuit of excellence, sport and war, and women in sport; Slusher, instead of narrowing his subject, has broadened it to include the cosmos with the central focus on the sporting endeavor. Slusher is more of an explorer than a pioneer. His book is an ontological binge, a shot in deep space where wonders abound for those brave enough to look.

For the beginner in the philosophy of sport the best work is *Toward a Philosophy of Sport* by Harold J. Vanderzwaag. It is even a good introduction to philosophy but especially to the ways in which this ancient discipline may be used in the humanistic study of sport. Like history and psychology, this discipline also has an official publication entitled *Journal of the Philosophy of Sport*, which is published under the auspices of the Philosophic Society for the Study of Sport. The *Journal* is a basic work for anyone beginning to study the field. Another fundamental but challenging work is *Sport and Body: A Philosophic Symposium*, edited by Ellen Gerber. So too is the *Philosophy of Sport: A Collection of Original Essays*, which was edited by Robert G. Osterhoudt. The articles in both books come under the general philosophical categories of metaphysics, epistemology, ethics, and aesthetics, in which metaphysics and epistemology can be considered the search for truth and ethics and aesthetics, dealing with the search for good and the beautiful. Another term often encountered in the philosophy of sport is "ontology," a branch of metaphysics that constitutes a knowledge of being. Ontology, therefore, is concerned with first principles, categories, and definitions. (In the bibliography of this chapter, there are a number of works discussed in the introduction in the attempt to arrive at working definitions.) Since there is so much disagreement over what constitutes sport, play, games, and so on, sizeable portions of both Gerber's and Osterhoudt's books are taken up with ontological essays, which require a great deal of concentration.

Though it doesn't deal with sports per se, *The Human Condition* by Hannah Arendt is an essential book for the study of the philosophy of sport since it examines the broad human categories of play, work, and leisure and suggests that the most active life of all might not involve the motion of the body but the play of the mind, the contemplative life. For a listing of works relating directly to the philosophy of sport the reader should consult the *Philosopher's Index* under the heading "sport."

Reading in the philosophy of sport is not like reading the daily sports page, and philosophers of sport, although they may be fans, are not the ones to turn to for either easy affirmations or denunciations. The one thing that the philosophy of sport teaches, is that questions are difficult to pose, much less to answer, and categories and subjects are difficult to distinguish and impossible to isolate as some of us would like to do.

Zen is a good example of the problems that arise. Technically it is neither a philosophy, a religion, nor a psychology but simply a way, as votaries claim. Zen is actually a form of sports "psyching," but its implications go beyond sports and allow the adherent to shape a total response not just to games but life itself. For this reason, the Zen way will be considered here as a philosophy. No other philosophy has been so popular in the last several years, and probably none has been so abused. The Zen approach has been tried in everything with questionable claims of success. Concentration and development of the inner game no doubt enhance certain personality traits as well as skill and efficiency, but claims of its superiority have resulted in a fad that invariably results in skepticism as well as good humor. Adam Smith sums up the feeling of many in his chapter "Sport Is a Western Yoga" in *Powers of Mind:*

> Zen has gotten to be a good word now, the true thing, the thing itself. We have *Zen and the Art of Running,* and *Zen and the Art of Seeing,* and an autobiography, *Zen and the Art of Motorcycle Maintenance.* We still have to go through *Zen and Turning Your Spares into Strikes,* and *Zen Your Way to Higher Earnings*; the Zen books are getting shorter and more flowery, with any luck they will soon be mostly soupy photographs and we can be done with it.[1]

Though not strictly advocating Zen, other books of note that would come under the how-to-succeed-by-concentration-and-development-of-inner-harmony category are *The Inner Game of Tennis* by Timothy W. Gallwey,

The Inner Athlete: Mind Plus Muscle for Winning by Robert M. Nideffer, *On Running* by Dr. George Sheehan, and finally *Inner Running* by Donald Porter. *The Complete Book of Running* by James F. Fixx also deals with inner running as well as outer running. In fact, it deals with every imaginable aspect of running from what clothes to wear to where to buy them, from what to read to where to run. In addition, it has a sixteen-page bibliography on every subject Fixx has examined and possibly a few more. Apparently the *Complete Book* was not as complete as either Fixx or his publishers thought since three years later there appeared *James Fixx's Second Book of Running*. It is no surprise that a spoof should appear after all this instruction nor that the name of it should be *The Non-Runner's Book* by Vic Ziegel and Lewis Grossberger. It is fortunate that this book was written to compensate for the general absence of humor in others. Like Calvin Coolidge, the authors "do not choose to run." Certainly any program that calls for joy, or at least joy through pain, and finds little place for laughter is suspect to some degree.

This is not to imply that there are not splendid values in the inner approach to joy, goodness, and truth but only to suggest limitations, some of which are more serious than the absence of humor. Among these is the tendency to attribute all success to self. For example, as marvelous as Dr. Sheehan's book is, it ends on this very disconcerting note:

> Success rests with having the courage and endurance and, above all, the will to become the person you are, however peculiar that may be. Then you will be able to say, "I have found my hero and he is me."[2]

This is a debatable philosophy to say the least and one that has been the cause of a good deal of suffering in the world. If winning is not the only thing, then neither is running. It is a startling thing to discover the miracle of the body, a sort of epiphany, and to become engrossed in too many "shoulds" and "oughts" can be as depressing as Dr. Sheehan argues. There are, however, models that demand our respect and modes that we ought to study and adopt for ourselves and our posterity. Jefferson, Emerson, Thoreau, Whitman, and Lincoln, for instance, can tell us more about truth and goodness than the same number of outlaws or even runners. The determination of these higher representations is one goal of philosophy. While it is not objectionable that Dr. Sheehan finds a hero in himself, it is troublesome that the same conclusion might be drawn by less wise and gifted men after some new feat of running or other expenditure of energy.

Both the time involved and the repetitive method are two other dubious aspects of the becoming-the-person-you-are-philosophy. Arthur Koestler's *The Lotus and the Robot* is a devastating analysis of these problems and the little book that started all the other Zen books, Eugen Herrigel's *Zen in the Art of Archery*. Koestler asks what any Westerner of common sense would ask:

[w]as that six-years' detour into the metaphysical fog really necessary before shooting an arrow was revealed as the "ridiculously simple" act which it always had been? The answer is, of course, that every skilled performance appears hopelessly complicated until, through training, it becomes automatic and thereby "simple." The training has a technical and a psychological aspect. About the technical side we learn . . . that it consisted of "practice, repetition, and repetition of the repeated with ever increasing intensity." There is nothing new about that method; its aim is to enable the pupil to exercise his skill automatically, even "in his sleep." The psychological side of the training is designed to eliminate self-consciousness; its mystic verbiage and esoteric ceremonial are expected to facilitate this process by their irrational appeal to the unconscious. For a pupil brought up in traditional Japanese ways, this may be—or may have been—the proper antidote to mental cramp. On an occidental, the main effect of it is to befuddle him.[3]

Koestler is certainly not one to dampen the possibility of the diversity of human potentiality, as he clearly reveals in all his works, especially *The Roots of Coincidence.* He is attracted to the mystical, but he maintains an almost stubborn skepticism not so much about miraculous feats of mind and body but about their moral worth. Theoretically, Zen is, among other things, an antidote to the winning-is-the-only-thing syndrome, but the cure can be just as bad as the ill. Too much emphasis on being can be as bad as too much emphasis on doing, for as always the question is one of emphasis. After all these years, the words of the Stoic Epictetus, quoted by Matthew Arnold in *Culture and Anarchy,* still are haunting whether the scene is the football dorm of a modern university or a runner after a ten-mile jaunt sitting down with *Runner's World* as if there were still something that he didn't quite find out on the road. According to Epictetus:

It is a sign [of a nature not finely tempered] to give yourself up to things which relate to the body; to make for instance, a great fuss about exercise, a great fuss about eating, a great fuss about drinking, a great fuss about walking, a great fuss about riding. All these things ought to be done merely by the way: the formation of spirit and character must be our real concern.[4]

Too much becoming what one is may bring on indifference to the condition of others, which some would argue always has been the fundamental flaw of Eastern philosophy. Moreover, it would seem that one could develop a sense of self-worth and meaning through personal discipline and a balanced exercise program without invoking any Eastern masters, joining a cult, or becoming hopelessly one-sided. This is essentially the low-keyed message in two deep but sensible books by Eleanor Metheny entitled *Movement and Meaning* and *Moving and Knowing in Sport, Dance, Physical Education*. Both books reflect the profound influence that Wallace Stevens, a poet notably concerned with form and meaning, had on the author. Although there is no single definition for either meaning or knowing, there are more and more who, like Metheny, are convinced that the states of mind suggested by the terms are positively related to the health of the body. There may not be any truth that man can ever know, but he can experience degrees of goodness provided his mind and body are united in some relatively sane manner. Although they are not guides per se, Metheny's books are helpful in discovering happy connections.

Sports and religion is a topic that has attracted the attention of writers of fiction and nonfiction for well over a century. Sports, most historians now believe, had their origins in religious festivals and the two have influenced each other either antithetically or symbiotically ever since. The Olympics were banned in 351 in the name of Christianity, and Puritan hostility to sports both in England and America took the form of injunctions against them well into the nineteenth century. In Victorian England, however, sport and religion once again joined hands, and the marriage is still going strong. So too is the muscular Christian who, as Gerald Redmond has shown in his article, "The First Tom Brown's Schooldays: Origins and Evolution of 'Muscular Christianity' in Children's Literature," has been a familiar figure in literature since the eighteenth century. In fact, the phenomenon of muscular Christianity has become so widespread that *Sports Illustrated* devoted a three-part series to the subject. The author of the series, Frank Deford, coined the telling term "sportianity," to cover the "jocks-for-Jesus" movement that was spearheaded by the FCA (the Fellowship of Christian Athletes) and AIA (Athletes in Action). Something of the spirit of "sportianity" can be inferred from the following newspaper account by Lester Kinsolving, which appeared in January 1971:

"Your son is our quarterback and you are our coach," prayed Miami's Catholic Archbishop Coleman F. Carroll, while delivering the invocation for the Miami Dolphins-Atlanta Falcons football game.

"We sometimes get blitzed by heavy sorrows or red-dogged by Satan," continued the Archbishop. "Teach us to run the right patterns in our life so that we will truly make a touchdown one day through the heavenly gates, as the angels and saints cheer us on from the sidelines."

In reporting this notable invocation, the national Catholic reporter added: "And when that final gun goes off dear Lord, lead us out of the parking lot of life through the interchange of Purgatory, on the freeway into Heaven, with our fenders undented, our spirits undaunted and our metaphors untangled. Amen."⁵

Muscular Christianity is easy satire and has received its share in literature, as seen, for example, in *Elmer Gantry* by Sinclair Lewis, probably because it is the most popular form of muscular religion. There are, however, other forms. According to the entry for the Zionist leader Max Nordau in *The Universal Jewish Encyclopedia*, he encouraged young Jews to train their bodies to become "Muscle Jews," and the *Encyclopedia of Jews in Sports* by Bernard Postal and Jesse and Ray Silver, finds the success of American Jewish athletes to be a major influence in helping to dispel the myth of the ethnic superiority of any group. Anyone wishing to understand more about the history of Jewish athletics would certainly benefit from H. A. Harris's *Greek Athletics and the Jews*. From a reexamination of the works of Philo Judaeus and a rereading of Josephus, Harris produces evidence that the Jews, at least those of the Dispersion, may have had a greater involvement in Hellenic culture than previously believed. Other important works on the subject are *Physical Education and Sports in the Jewish History and Culture* (Proceedings of International Seminars in 1973 and 1977) and a doctoral dissertation by George Eisen, entitled *The Maccabiah Games: A History of the Jewish Olympics*. Other related works may be available through the Wingate Institute or the Maccabi World Union Archives and Museum (see Appendix 2).

There is also a type of "Muscular Muhammadism," although no one to my knowledge has used such a term. However, in "The Chinese Boxes of Muhammed Ali," an article that appeared in the *Saturday Review*, Budd Schulberg quotes Malcolm X as telling Ali, then Cassius Clay, before his fight with Sonny Liston in 1964 in Miami, "This fight is the truth. It's the cross and the crescent fighting in a prize ring—for the first time. It's a modern crusade—a Christian and a Moslem facing each other with television to beam it off Telstar for the whole world to see what happens."⁶ The correlation of a particular fight with a larger faith has not been confined to a single religion.

What lies behind this kinship? Thorstein Veblen has written extensively on the subject in *Theory of the Leisure Class* but as compelling as his arguments are, his view is perhaps too narrow, for he sees sports as a means of attracting converts to one or more of the anthropomorphic cults. Certainly this is a factor, but it doesn't tell the whole story, as Malcolm X well knew.

However puzzling the alliance of sport and religion may appear to the objective observer, to the athlete the association of what he does with something transcendental is very serious. In fact, the seriousness with which many regard both religion and sport may be part of the problem of discovering the good life. This idea is dealt with brilliantly in David Miller's *Gods and Games: Toward a Theology of Play*. Two chapters particularly, "Play is Religion" and "Religion is Play" reveal Miller's thesis, which is that we ought to regard "life as a children's game." Miller perhaps becomes too playful toward the end of the book, as he himself warns, but it is a charming book of great insight. His compelling arguments, which are so well supported by saints and sages, are refuted not by logic but by one's own experience and experiences of mankind. Play, that most essential of all paradises, is not enough; one must have meaning, which can only come from some type of heroic encounter. As Robert Pirsig does later in *Zen and the Art of Motorcycle Maintenance*, Miller knocks some of the shine off the halos of Plato and Aristotle and charges them with dividing the original unity of *spoudogeloios* (serious-mirth-provoking) by subordinating the virtue of play to the higher virtue of seriousness. Miller equates play with Eden; work with the building of the City of God, devotion to truth, beauty, law, and so on. Both are ways of seeking God, the one by going back, the other by going forward. Man cannot go back to the world of innocent childhood play, so he attempts to go forward to glory by restructuring his world through the agony of contests.

In Miller's view, another philosophical giant guilty of subordinating play to seriousness is Aquinas who endorsed *eutrapelia* as Aristotle had done and as Hugo Rahner does in *Man and Play*. Miller points out an interesting distinction between *eutrapelia* and *spoudogeloios*:

At first glance *eutrapelia* would seem to be the idea that we referred to earlier as *spoudogeloios*, the ideal of making play primary after all, because it, like games and the spirit of mirth, is a virtue directed to the intellectualistic higher principle of rationality. It is therefore not really a primary category or a metaphor of ultimacy. Thus, Aristotelian Puritanism is here given religious sanction in the theology of Western Christendom.[7]

As good scholars should, Miller refers the reader to other interpretations of *eutrapelia*, and his extensive bibliography encompasses works on the whole spectrum of approaches to a *theologia ludens*. In line with his argument, Miller's book is not "serious," but it is not exactly fun either. The same can be said of another book on this topic, in *Praise of Play: Toward a Psychology of Religion* by Robert E. Neale. These books by the play theologians are certainly mind-stretchers, but there seem to be no braking devices to prevent the mind from playfully spilling over into meaninglessness and utter absurdity. This is exactly what happens, for example, in the case of Robert Neale's conclusion in his chapter, "The Crucifixion as Play," which appears as a response in *Theology of Play* by Jürgen Moltmann. Neale disagrees with Moltmann's argument that the crucifixion is inconsistent with God's play. The crucifixion, according to Neale, is an extension of the spirit of adventure.

Other theologians who responded to Moltmann's book are David Miller and Sam Keene, and finally Moltmann responded to the responders. Not surprisingly they don't agree with each other or perhaps even understand each other. One reading in the theology of play should be prepared for strange encounters, for it is a game that most people have never before played. It is not clear what the rules are, and it will probably be a long time before any decision can be reached on the worth of the endeavor.

It is not implied that the theology of play belongs entirely to the academic realm. Although the study of the play element in society may be ignored except for a relative few, the practice of playful philosophy is widespread. Our whole era has been tabbed the "fun generation," and seriousness, to say nothing of high-seriousness, has become a virtual villain. Seriousness is seen as a Western phenomenon, and counterforces, as might be expected, have come from the East to a large degree. An advertisement for the Rajneesh Meditation Center in a recent issue of *Time* is revealing. Says the Bhagwan Shree Rajneesh:

> My whole effort is to help you to become sincere but not serious. Seriousness is a kind of disease: Playfulness should be the foundation of a true religion. So I teach be playful: the more playful you are the closer you are to existence, the more serious you are the more egoist you become, and the more serious you are the more closed. Then you are not open to the wind, to the sun, to the rain; you are not open to anything. You are no more vulnerable. One has to be vulnerable, keep all the windows open, allow existence to penetrate you and don't take things seriously.[8]

Bhagwan Shree Rajneesh may be attempting to integrate the whole person, but the emphasis on play would seem to take him as far in another direction as Aristotle and Aquinas have been charged with going into the realm of the serious. The middle way, a third alternative, seems to have been lost.

A book that is truly playful in spirit and quite humorous is Bernard Suits's funny volume called *The Grasshopper: Games, Life, and Utopia.* *The Grasshopper* is a thoroughly delightful treatise that achieves that truly rare distinction, the integration of wit and profundity. The central argument of the grasshopper, as one might expect, is that play is the *only* human activity that is "intrinsically valuable," all others being "instrumentally valuable," that is, a means to some other end, for example, work, art, or labor. Therefore, according to the grasshopper, instead of storing up items for material needs as the ant does we should, in anticipation of utopia, make other plans for the only truly intrinsic need man has, game playing. This is evident in the following dialogue with Skepticus:

GRASSHOPPER: What I envisage is a culture quite different from our own in terms of its *basis*. Whereas our own culture is based on various kinds of scarcity—economic, moral, scientific, erotic—the culture of Utopia will be based on plenitude. The notable institutions of Utopia, accordingly, will not be economic, moral, scientific, and erotic instruments—as they are today—but institutions which foster sport and other games. But sports and games unthought of today; sports and games that will require for their exploitation—that is, for their mastery and enjoyment—as much energy as is expended today in serving the institutions of scarcity. It behoves us, therefore, to begin the immense work of devising these wonderful games now, for if we solve all of our problems of scarcity very soon, we may very well find ourselves with nothing to do when Utopia arrives.

SKEPTICUS: You mean we should begin to store up games—very much like food for winter—against the possibility of an endless and endlessly boring summer. You seem to be a kind of ant after all, Grasshopper, though, I must admit, a distinctly odd kind of ant.

GRASSHOPPER: No, Skepticus, I am truly the Grasshopper; that is, an adumbration of the ideal of existence, just as the games we play in our non-Utopian lives are intimations of things to come. For even now it is games which give us something to do when there is nothing to do. We thus call games "pastimes," and regard them as trifling fillers of the interstices in our lives. But they are much more important than that. They are clues to the future. And their serious cultivation now is perhaps our own salvation. That, if you like, is the metaphysics of leisure time.[9]

The grasshopper finally realizes that even in paradise most people will not be happy with nothing to engage in but endless play. "Life," he says, "will not be worth living if they cannot believe that they are doing *something* useful, whether it is providing for their families or formulating a theory of relativity."

Just as others will be unable to change their natures so neither will the grasshopper. In Suits's book, though, the grasshopper does not take himself too seriously, which is probably the besetting sin of some of those who try to merge play and religion. Philosophers, the grasshopper excluded, are almost always glum even when declaring that winning is nothing, though never so deadly serious as the promoters of muscular forms of religion who believe that winning is essential for the conversion of others. In the view of Shirl J. Hoffman in "The *Athletae Dei*: Missing the Meaning of Sport" the athletes of God miss the point of both religion and play. Hoffman's article is a good introduction to sports and religion. It is a sound survey of the issues involved and contains a short but basic bibliography. Although he grounds his discussion in the works of theologians, his criticism of the adherents of muscular Christianity is little more than an appeal to common sense: "For what is more joyous than to be lost in the world of sport and yet what is more temporal, more transitory than the *ad interim* pronouncement of the winner of the game."[10] For a history of the rise of muscular Christianity in America, a short but solid piece to turn to is "The Muscular Christianity Movement" by Guy Lewis in the *Journal of Health, Physical Education and Recreation*. On the history of the beginnings of the movement in England, in addition to Bruce E. Haley's treatment of the subject in *The Healthy Body and Victorian Culture*, there is the *Quest* article by Gerald Redmond entitled "The First Tom Brown's Schooldays: Origins and Evolution of 'Muscular Christianity' in Children's Literature, 1762-1857."

A book that makes no attempt to justify such movements as muscular Christianity but that insists on the religious characteristics of sports is Michael Novak's *The Joy of Sports: End Zones, Bases, Baskets, Balls, and the Consecration of the American Spirit*. Novak claims that sports constitute the real world; labor and politics the illusory one. Sports, therefore, belong to the "Kingdom of Ends" and other activities to the "Kingdom of Means." These terms, incidentally, correspond to those used by Bernard Suits in *The Grasshopper: Games, Life, and Utopia*. The "Kingdom of Means" is equated with the "instrumentally valuable" and the "Kingdom of Ends" with the "intrinsically valuable." Sports form a natural religion and explain "regional religions," for example, the statewide religion of college football in states like Mississippi and Alabama. Sports partake of the divine because they foster glorious abstractions. According to Novak, "*Being, beauty, truth, excellence, transcendence*—these words, grown in the soil of play, wither in the sand of work. Art, prayer, worship, love, civilization: these thrive in the field of play."[11] Novak's thesis is powerful, and his book is the best book on the religion of sports for the general audience yet written. There are, however, problems with it that need to be recognized.

The most obvious flaw is the vagueness of frequently used terms. Religion, for example, is not explicitly defined until the end of the book, where the reader learns, in contrast to what has been said earlier, that it lives in worlds of politics and economics as well as sports. Like Whitman, Emerson, and the Catholic G. K. Chesterton, Novak does not appear to be bothered by contradictions or paradoxes. Whatever else religion is, it is that quality of being that binds (from *ligare*) and rebinds (from *religare*) man to God or the Good. In the list of such noble ideals as being, beauty, truth, excellence, and transcendence, the one ideal obviously missing is goodness. Sports in modern America may exhibit all the qualities that Novak mentions, but are they good? Sports obviously render joy, but what is the nature of that joy? Is it good? Arguing logically from Novak's list on relatively safe grounds, one could state that whatever Novak says about contemporary sports could also be said about sports under the Nazis, for example, Novak might answer that one group's glories is another's sins, but this doesn't excuse the absence of the crucial consideration of goodness, especially when the subject is religion. What is obvious here is Novak's romantic celebration of being and the praise of beauty at the expense, so to speak, of goodness. It is at this point the nineteenth-century romantics, the giants of the Renaissance and the pagan worthies all cross swords with traditional Christianity, which insists upon holding fast to that which is good. Novak is a brilliant describer, but he is a lenient judge, which may help to explain why his modest proposals are "Burkean reforms" as opposed to "Jacobean." The Puritans may have been too suspicious of beauty and the frivolity of sports and games, but something of their judgmental attitude is needed today as sports move more and more into questionable modes.

Another problem, although less serious, is Novak's treatment of sources. He states that Paul Weiss's *Sport: A Philosophic Inquiry* stands "virtually alone." This is essentially the same lament that Weiss himself made. Weiss obviously saw himself as a pioneer in the philosophy of sport, yet he echoed ideas that in American literature alone had been worn absolutely threadbare, and while proclaiming that the ancient philosophers had neglected sports, he did not mention even in his bibliography the classic work by Rachel S. Robinson, *Sources for the History of Greek Athletics*. For some reason, the more one defends sports or is involved in them, the more one tends, or so it seems, to denigrate works that have preceded him or her. Bill Russell, for example, makes the following statement near the beginning of his chapter on sports in *Second Wind: The Memoirs of an Opinionated Man*: "There is no philosophy of sports worth mentioning."[12] He then goes on to discuss at some length "rules" to which Weiss in *Sport: A Philosophic Inquiry* had given considerable attention. This is not to imply that Russell's book adds nothing new to the understanding of sport. Indeed it does as does Weiss's, but both could have been even better without the burden of the Moses complex.

So too with Novak. In saying that sports belong to the "Kingdom of Ends" he is speaking of competitive games, and not capricious games. There is a fundamental teleological difference here—the difference between becoming (competition) and being (games of togetherness). Is the goal of man to be in a state of endless competition or in some blissful condition in which the only effort required is enough to play "ring-around-a-rosie"? This is a fundamental question that Novak never really engages. Had he done so he certainly would have dealt in depth with Roger Caillois's *Man, Play, and Games*, which distinguishes between *ludus* (competition) and *paidia* (spontaneous play) and which is at least of the stature of Weiss's book. In a similar vein, one wishes Novak had dealt more with David Miller's *Gods and Games* which he dismisses too handily along with the work of other Protestant theologians. The "play" that Miller celebrates, whether in reaction to Puritan culture or not, is not the same as the sports that, according to Novak, belong to the "Kingdom of Ends." Both are opposed to the belief in the sacredness of work, but they are at opposite ends of the spectrum. Novak is Christian in his emphasis upon *agon* (the fifth seal), while Miller is adamic in his praise of the unfettered play that existed in Prelapsarian days. Novak's teleology points toward a city of God with a gymnasium on every corner and a Super Stadium in the middle; Miller's points back toward the green pastures and abundant orchards of Eden, where competition would be unthinkable. Novak's philosophy is more realistic and sensible, but he never demonstrates philosophically why his world view is preferable to that of Miller's.

Novak essentially bases his case for an agonic view of life upon the encounter with fate, the inherent need for transcendence in the individual, and most of all upon the presence of death in various forms. This idea runs throughout the work like a *leitmotif*, which is why one is astonished not to find anywhere any mention of Ernest Becker's *The Denial of Death*. Although Becker's book does not deal with sports, it is almost inconceivable that Novak could have been unaware of it since it won the Pulitzer Prize in 1974. Could have an acknowledgment of the thesis of this powerful book in any way invalidated Novak's implicit claim to originality? Possibly, but if this was the case, it was a needless concern. The strength of Novak's book lies in its style of language. It is a matter of simple fair play to acknowledge the efforts of precursors.

Novak appears to be guilty of an oversimplification in calling sports "real" and work and politics "illusory." While some sports philosophers have been laboring diligently merely to remove the "non-real" or "make-believe" tag from sports, Novak turns the tables completely and calls the other world unreal! One can admire his courage in so doing, while questioning his wisdom. Why does either world have to be regarded as unreal? Both are bounded in space and time, and both offer possibilities for heroism. It is simplistic, therefore, to think of either world as more or less illusory than the other. What is needed in all human endeavors, whether in labor or leisure, is as much beauty, truth, and goodness as possible.

Michael Novak and Paul Weiss have made great contributions to the study of sports, but their approach is analogous to what was once called the "new" criticism of literature. It is an examination of the thing itself without reference to moral or social consequences. Weiss makes no bones about the matter and concentrates only upon the athlete in his athletic role; while Novak does not go quite that far, for he does take time out to advocate reform, he is still in the camp of Weiss. There is ample justification for such studies, but it would be most unfortunate if these attitudes became dominant in the philosophical study of sport. The "new criticism" almost killed literature, and a similar approach could do the same for the study of sports. At the end of his book, Novak refers to Karl Barth who once said "that a systematic theologian *ought* to begin with ethics—that is, with life as it is lived."[13] Novak thinks that this is what he has done, but in fact he has dealt with practically every aspect of philosophy and religion *except* ethics. What Novak thinks he has done and what he has accomplished are two different things, but he is right in supporting Barth. The emphasis should be on ethics.

In the view of Christopher Lasch, the problem in Novak's book stems from the failure of the author to understand that while work and play may be different, "the degradation of play originates in the degradation of work, which creates both the need for and opportunity for commercialized 'recreation.' As Huizinga has shown, it is precisely when the element of play disappears from law, stagecraft, and other cultural forms that men turn to play not to witness a dramatic reenactment of their common life but to find diversion and sensation."[14]

S. K. Wertz also finds difficulty with Novak's now almost celebrated analogy between sports and religion in his review essay, "Novak's Analogies" in *Journal of the Philosophy of Sport* (Fall 1979). Wertz argues that Novak's analogies of sports as liturgies breaks down, especially for Protestants, whose services are less liturgical than those of Catholics.

Overall, Wertz's review essay is complimentary and rightly so. In spite of these reservations, *The Joy of Sports* remains the most articulate expression in modern times of the beauty and pleasure inherent in sports. Grace, intelligence, and the courage of conviction abound throughout. Although joy is the subject, it is a serious book, and in his seriousness Novak is probably closer to the truth of the nature of man than the supporters of the play approach. A compulsion exists in man to achieve some form of transcendence, and it is a compulsion found in all religions. The spirit of fun and play may and should moderate the intensity of the commitment, but it cannot in any way replace it. Zen, which is not a religion, may be an exception, but judging from the severity of some of its adherents, one must wonder if even it is immune. It too has seemingly senseless koans that supposedly represent some type of humor or an attitude of "hanging loose," which is how Miller defined *eutrapelia* and which he thought was too severe. In *The Lotus and the Robot* Koestler describes "a stink of Zen," which occurs in the view of those in Zen circles when questions of religion and metaphysics are brought into the cosmic picture. These questions obtrude even in Zen circles for a simple reason: There is a "stink" in the nature of things which in the West has been traditionally called sin. Whoever ignores it or rises indifferently above it runs the risk of becoming inhuman.

The body may be enjoyed and even indulged in, but somewhere it must be transcended. "Nature," as Henry David Thoreau said, "is hard to overcome, but she must be overcome."[15] This one statement by Thoreau gainsays in one sense his much professed love of nature. In this same chapter on higher laws, Thoreau says, "We may be well, yet not pure."[16] Thus, there is always the need for transcendence, and it is the effort at transcendence that explains the bowman shooting alone day after day, joggers for Jesus and roadside masses, and pregame prayers in the locker room. However political or bizarre the manifestation of this impulse, or "driveness" as Michael Novak calls it, it is inescapably human, common to East and West alike, and it is essentially noble, as Jean Marie Déchanet points out in his remarkable book *Christian Yoga* in which he quotes from *l'Athlète chrétien, Comment le former* by Max Marin.

> The key to the whole affair can be summed up in this precept: sanctify the body by exercising it, work for the health and spiritualization of all its activities. Then, instead of being an obstacle to sanctity, the body will become an instrument.[17]

In another impressive book, *Attitudes to the Body in Western Christendom*, Frank Bottomley argues in effect that the body is not just an instrument of sanctity but is itself sacred. "Enfleshment of God," according to Bottomley, is the cardinal belief of Christianity as expressed in the Incarnation and Eucharist. The ancient world, by contrast, posited a body-soul dualism, and the original Christian teaching on the comparison of the flesh and the spirit was later misunderstood and falsely used to support ascetic theories, according to the author. Bottomley may be too hard on the Puritans for their asceticism and possibly unfair to the ancients, especially the Greeks, in their own attempts at a synthesis of beauty and goodness as seen in some of their thought and art. Still his thesis is compelling. With its seventy plus pages of notes, extensive bibliography, and frequent references to athletics and physical appearances, *Attitudes to the Body in Western Christendom* must be regarded as a significant work of scholarship, reflecting as it does the traditional Catholic view of the flesh and the spirit which should be used to contrast theories that regard the body as either a mere machine or an instrument of sensuality as opposed to sensuousness.

Clearly, Bottomley has found treasures in his own house as precious as any imported from the supposedly more exotic Orient. It is a book that brings to mind the thought and work of Dr. Paul Tournier as reflected in another impressive book, *The Meaning of the Body* by Jacques Sarano who, though the does not deal with sports and play, presents a sacramental view of work that is dramatically opposite that of Novak. Both *The Meaning of the Body* and *Attitudes to the Body in Western Christendom* reflect personalistic philosophy which has shown amazing growth the past three decades.

In *The Eye of Shiva: Eastern Mysticism and Science*, Amaury de Riencourt underscores the role of the body in East and West alike in attaining what he calls the "theopathic state," a fusion with God rather than a vision of God. For mystics in both the East and West, the *agon* in the process is between will and body in reaching this "*mysterium ineffabile*." In Eastern mysticism the body remains essentially sedentary, especially when compared to such Western activities as boxing or wrestling where the *agon* is between individuals. In boxing or wrestling the prize is money or a medal; in spiritual exercises the prize is fusion with God. Thus, for both *yogis* of India and professional athletes of America, the body is important as a means rather than an end. In general the end (or goal) for athletes in the West is personal heroism; for practicing mystics of the East *samadhi* (Indian) or *satori* (Japanese).

While in both East and West the body is often an instrument, it is generally endowed with greater sanctity or perhaps potential for sanctity in the East, especially among mystics, than in the West. In *The Denial of Death* Ernest Becker reminds us again and again that no matter how sanctified the body may become in a moment of glory or beautitude, it still stinks at times, and more importantly it dies. Walt Whitman, Allen Ginsberg, and other Western romantics with Eastern ideals may proclaim that not an inch of the body is vile, but the stench, Becker claims, will not go away. Nature is at play, but she is also at war. Life feeds on life, and the result is spilled blood and human waste. Even de Riencourt, who clearly believes in the theopathic state, acknowledges that the "*mysterium ineffabile*" is extremely rare. Still it offers hope, and proof, some will say, that cosmic consciousness for the select few does exist. Becker's view of the world may be depressing, but it may possibly offer hope rather than despair. We must realize, Becker believes, the universal need for heroism (essentially a Western tradition), a "second" world, a "world of humanly created meaning," a world of quality illusions: " 'Illusion' means creative play at the highest level. Cultural illusion [therefore] is a necessary ideology of self-justification, a heroic dimension that is life itself to the symbolic animal. . . . To lose security of heroic cultural illusion is to die."[18]

The key word here is "illusion," which as Roger Caillois points out in *Man, Play, and Games* comes from "*in-lusio*," meaning "beginning a game." Another key word is "quality." What is it? It is "the third" event in the universe, according to Robert Pirsig in *Zen and the Art of Motorcycle Maintenance: An Inquiry into Values*, the coming together of the classical and romantic, energy and form. It is synonymous with the Greek concept of *aretê* or excellence and depends on caring. The athlete, as Paul Weiss shows in *Sport: A Philosophic Inquiry*, also strives for excellence, but we should never forget that this excellence cannot be viewed outside its context, or the society in which it is achieved. Neither should athletic excellence receive praise at the expense of equally deserving endeavors of the mind.

Perspective is important in the concept of quality and so too "compensation," which Emerson in his essay of the same name called "the law of laws." Effort, whether in labor or in sports, demands reward. While money is the usual compensation for the laborer, the athlete seeks something more. What is it he desires and why will he sacrifice so much, sometimes years of his life, for such vague and elusive goals? Why does the boxer in the fifteenth round, the tight end with cracked ribs, the center fielder with a bone spur on his heel, the long-distance runner, endure so much pain? Admittedly athletes are notorious complainers and will fuss about a sore toe or finger that a shoe salesman, as someone has said, will endure stoically all day. Yet the situation is paradoxical, for while the athlete's concern for minor pains enhances his image as a prima donna, few people endure willingly as much agony as the athlete does in a contest. There is no way for the vast majority of the human race to have any concept of what a boxer goes through either in training or in an actual bout. The word "agony" comes from the Greek *agon*, which means struggle, and by extension, pain. The essence of this feeling has been captured by R. Tait McKenzie in his sculpture entitled *Agony*, which depicts an athlete's expression at the limits of his endurance. What might drugs do to the concept of agony? Sports can always be appreciated as art, but unless something of the mystery of pain accompanies that aesthetic experience, something human will have died in sports and man as well. As George Sheehan says, "Pain and the fear of pain is our undoing."[19]

Perhaps the most disturbing invention of all times would be a "sufferometer," a little meter with a single dial that everyone would wear to reveal his or her agony at any one time. Such a device might revolutionize sports, or at least shock us into the recognition of mystery. If a player were to put on one stunning performance after another but never registered any pain on his "sufferometer," it seems likely that sooner or later the crowd would tire of his success and charge that "the guy ain't human." We deceive ourselves into thinking that what we really admire in sports is victory and/or art. The Greeks appreciated these too, but they knew that a much dearer prize lay in the mystery of pain, the paradox of "the delight in the agony." We are drawn to the spectacle at the beginning, but tin wreaths and wooden gods will not enthrall us forever. Eventually that which is cheap and mechanical will cease to attract. What we all finally admire in an athlete or team is what coaches, in the deepest sense of the word, call "character," or what Grantland Rice in an immortal metaphor termed the "uphill heart."

NOTES

1. Adam Smith, *Powers of Mind* (New York: Ballantine, 1975), p. 193.
2. George Sheehan, *On Running* (New York: Bantam, 1978), p. 205.
3. Arthur Koestler, *The Lotus and the Robot* (New York: Macmillan Co., 1961), p. 252.
4. Quoted in Matthew Arnold, *Culture and Anarchy* (Cambridge: Cambridge University Press, 1935), p. 53.
5. Lester Kinsolving, "Exploiting Athletes in Religion Questioned," Johnson City (Tenn.) *Press Chronicle*, 12 January 1971, p. 10.
6. Budd Schulberg, "The Chinese Boxes of Muhammad Ali," in *The Sporting Spirit: Athletes in Literature and Life*, ed. Robert J. Higgs and Neil D. Isaacs (New York: Harcourt, Brace, Jovanovich, 1977), p. 198. For a further discussion of the religious (and ethnic) implication of Ali's rise to fame, see Norman Mailer, *The Fight* (Boston: Little, Brown and Company, 1975). In the third part of his *Sports Illustrated* series on "Religion is Sports," Frank Deford points to the distinction made between "orthodox Muslims and the independent Black Muslim sect made famous first by Malcolm X and then by Muhammad Ali. In fact, Abdul-Jabbar refers to the heavyweight champion only as Cassius Clay, believing that the Black Muslim sect holds views contrary to Islam. Those Muslims who are black—as opposed to Black Muslims—are anxious to make it clear that theirs is not a racial religion." "Reaching for the Stars," *Sports Illustrated*, 3 May 1976, pp. 57-58.
7. David Miller, *Gods and Games: Toward a Theology of Play* (New York: World, 1970), p. 111.
8. Advertisement of Rajneesh Meditation Center in *Time*, 31 August 1981, p. 56.
9. Bernard Suits, *The Grasshopper: Games, Life, and Utopia* (Toronto: The University of Toronto Press, 1978), p. 176.
10. Shirl J. Hoffman, "The *Athletae Dei:* Missing the Meaning of Sport," *Journal of the Philosophy of Sport* 3 (September 1976), 50.
11. Michael Novak, *The Joy of Sports: End Zones, Bases, Baskets, Balls, and the Consecration of the American Spirit* (New York: Basic Books, 1976), p. xii.
12. Bill Russell and Taylor Branch, *Second Wind: The Memoirs of an Opinionated Man* (New York: Random House, 1979), p. 94.
13. Novak, p. 342.
14. Christopher Lasch, "The Corruption of Sports," *New York Review of Books*, 28 April 1978, p. 30.
15. Henry David Thoreau, *Walden and Other Writings*, ed. Joseph Wood Krutch (New York: Bantam, 1962), p. 269.
16. Ibid., p. 267.
17. Quoted in Jean Marie Déchanet, *Christian Yoga*, trans. Roland Hindmarsh (Westminster, Md.: Christian Classics, 1978), p. 136. In appendix I, "A Note on the Prayer of the Heart," Jean Gouillard discusses the evolution of prayer combined

with physical techniques of mental concentration as found in the *Philokalia*, a collection of writings from the fourth century to the fourteenth by fathers of the Eastern church. Gouillard shows the influence this synthesis of "breathing rhythm" in prayer had upon Ignatius, who according to Amoury de Riencourt, is the figure most responsible for synthesizing body and soul during periods of prayer and contemplation: "There is one noteworthy exception to the fact that, by and large, Western mysticism is a form of art rather than of science: Ignatius Loyola's *Spiritual Exercises*. Here for the first time in the West, mysticism is treated almost as science and technique rather than art. For the first time, it is handled in almost Yoga fashion, brought under control of human will, disciplined." *The Eye of Shiva: Eastern Mysticism and Science* (New York: William Morrow, 1981), pp. 114-115. Déchanet's book, advertised as "a major document of our times," provides "a competent handbook where Christians [can] find and set out a comprehensive discipline for living, including the bodily aspect." This quotation is from an address by the Reverend Fr. Régamey, O.P., that serves as the conclusion to Déchanet's book. Presumably the attitude of Fr. Régamey is indicative, at least to some extent, of the endorsement of the Catholic church. This obviously is a branch of Catholicism that differs from that of Vince Lombardi, for example, who held locker room prayers before "spiritual exercises" of another sort. Another work, in addition to Déchanet's, that draws upon the Jesuit tradition is the dissertation "Spiritual Direction: A Project Modelled on St. Ignatius' *Spiritual Exercises*" by Alexander B. Aronis, a former Navy Chaplain and star athlete at the Naval Academy. This work is especially helpful for those in counseling or the ministry wishing to instruct others in practical preliminaries to prayer or contemplation such as place, time of day, posture, relaxing, and centering.

  18. Ernest Becker, *The Denial of Death* (New York: Free Press, 1973), p. 189.

  19. Sheehan, p. 61.

BIBLIOGRAPHY

Arendt, Hannah. *The Human Condition*. Chicago: The University of Chicago Press, 1958.

Aronis, Alexander B. "Spiritual Direction: A Project Modelled on St. Ignatius' *Spiritual Exercises*. D. Min. Thesis. Fuller Theological Seminary, 1981.

Arnold, Matthew. *Culture and Anarchy*. Cambridge: Cambridge University Press, 1935.

Becker, Ernest. *The Denial of Death*. New York: Free Press, 1973.

Bottomley, Frank. *Attitudes to the Body in Western Christendom*. London: Lepus Books, 1979.

Caillois, Roger. *Man, Play, and Games*. Translated by Meyer Barash. New York: Free Press, 1961.

Déchanet, Jean Marie. *Christian Yoga*. Translated by Roland Hindmarsh. Westminster, Md.: Christian Classics, 1978.

Deford, Frank. "Religion in Sport." *Sports Illustrated*, 19 April 1976, pp. 88-102; "Endorsing Jesus," 26 April 1976, pp. 54-69; "Reaching for the Stars," 3 May 1976, pp. 42-60.

de Riencourt, Amaury. *The Eye of Shiva: Eastern Mysticism and Science*. New York: William Morrow, 1981.

Eisen, George. "The Maccabiah Games: A History of the Jewish Olympics." Ph.D. Dissertation, University of Maryland, 1979.

Fixx, James F. *The Complete Book of Running.* New York: Random House, 1977.

———. *James Fixx's Second Book of Running.* New York: Random House, 1980.

Gallwey, Timothy W. *The Inner Game of Tennis.* New York: Random House, 1974.

Gardiner, E. Norman. *Athletics of the Ancient World.* London: Oxford University Press, 1930.

Gerber, Ellen, ed. *Sport and Body: A Philosophic Symposium.* Philadelphia: Lea and Febiger, 1972.

———. "Arguments on the Reality of Sport." In *Sports and the Body: A Philosophical Symposium,* ed. Ellen Gerber. Philadelphia: Lea and Febiger, 1972.

Guttman, Allen. *From Ritual to Record: The Nature of Modern Sports.* New York: Columbia University Press, 1978.

Haley, Bruce E. *The Healthy Body and Victorian Culture.* Cambridge, Mass.: Harvard University Press, 1978.

Harris, H. A. *Greek Athletics and the Jews.* Cardiff, Wales: The University of Wales Press, 1976.

Herrigel, Eugen. *Zen in the Art of Archery.* Translated by R. F. C. Hull. 1953. Reprint. New York: Pantheon Books, 1971.

Hoffman, Shirl J. "The *Athletae Dei:* Missing the Meaning of Sport." *Journal of the Philosophy of Sport* 3 (September 1976), 42-51.

Huizinga, Johan. *Homo Ludens: A Study of the Play Element in Culture.* Translated by R. F. C. Hull. Boston: Beacon Press, 1960.

Journal of the Philosophy of Sport. Champaign, Ill.: Human Kinetics Publishers, 1974-.

Kenyon, Gerald S., ed. *Contemporary Psychology of Sport: Proceedings of the Second International Congress of Sport Psychology.* Chicago, Ill.: The Athletic Institute, 1968.

Kinsolving, Lester. "Exploiting Athletes in Religion Questioned." Johnson City (Tenn.) *Press Chronicle,* 12 January 1971, p. 10.

Koestler, Arthur. *The Lotus and the Robot.* New York: Dutton, 1961.

———. *The Roots of Coincidence.* New York: Random, 1972.

Lasch, Christopher, "The Corruption of Sports." *New York Review of Books* 24 (April 28, 1977), 24-30. Revised and reprinted as "The Degradation of Sport," in *The Culture of Narcissism.* New York: W. W. Norton, 1978.

Lewis, Guy. "The Muscular Christian Movement." *Journal of Health, Physical Education and Recreation* 37 (May 1966), 27-28, 42.

Lewis, Sinclair. *Elmer Gantry.* New York: Harcourt Brace, 1927.

Loy, John. "The Nature of Sport: A Definitional Effort." *Quest* (May 1968), 15.

Mailer, Norman. *The Fight.* Boston: Little, Brown and Company, 1975.

Methany, Eleanor. *Movement and Meaning.* New York: McGraw-Hill, 1968.

———. *Moving and Knowing in Sport, Dance, Physical Education.* Mountain View, Calif.: Peek Publications, 1975.

Miller, David. *Gods and Games: Toward a Theology of Play.* New York: World, 1970.

Moltmann, Jürgen. *Theology of Play.* Translated by Reinhard Ulrich. New York: Harper and Row, 1972.

Morgan, Williams J. "On the Path Towards an Ontology of Sport." *Journal of the Philosophy of Sport* 3 (September 1976), 25-34.

Murphy, Michael, and Rhea A. White. *The Psychic Side of Sport*. Reading, Mass.: Addison-Wesley Publishing Co., 1978.

Neale, Robert E. *In Praise of Play: Toward a Psychology of Religion*. New York: Harper and Row, 1973.

Nideffer, Robert M. *The Inner Athlete: Mind Plus Muscle for Winning*. New York: Thomas Crowell, 1976.

Novak, Michael. *The Joy of Sports: End Zones, Bases, Baskets, Balls, and the Consecration of the American Spirit*. New York: Basic Books, 1976.

Osterhoudt, Robert G., ed. *The Philosophy of Sport: A Collection of Original Essays*. Springfield, Ill.: Charles C. Thomas, 1973.

Philosopher's Index. Bowling Green, Ohio: Philosophy Documentation Center, 1967-.

Physical Education and Sports in the Jewish History and Culture (Proceedings of International Seminars in 1973 and 1977). Israel: Wingate Institute for Physical Education and Sport.

Pirsig, Robert. *Zen and the Art of Motorcycle Maintenance: An Inquiry into Values*. New York: Morrow, 1974.

Porter, Donald. *Inner Running*. New York: Grosset and Dunlap, 1978.

Postal, Bernard, Jesse Silver, and Ray Silver. *Encyclopedia of Jews in Sports*. Forward by Abraham Ribicoff. New York: Block Publishing Company, 1965.

Puhl, Louis J., ed. *The Spiritual Exercises of St. Ignatius*. Chicago: Loyola University Press, 1951.

Rahner, Hugo. *Man at Play*. New York: Herder and Herder, 1972.

Rank, Otto. "Self and Ideal." In *Myth of the Birth of the Hero and Other Writings*, ed. Philip Freund. New York: Vintage Books, 1964.

Redmond, Gerald. "The First Tom Brown's Schooldays: Origins and Evolution of 'Muscular Christianity' in Children's Literature, 1762-1857." *Quest* 30 (Summer 1978), 4-18.

Robinson, Rachel S. *Sources for the History of Greek Athletics*. 1955. Reprint. Chicago: Ares, 1980.

Russell, Bill, and Taylor Branch. *Second Wind: The Memoirs of an Opinionated Man*. New York: Random House, 1979.

Sarano, Jacques. *The Meaning of the Body*. Translated by James H. Farley. Philadelphia: The Westminster Press, 1966.

Schulberg, Budd. "The Chinese Boxes of Muhammad Ali." In *The Sporting Spirit: Athletes in Literature and Life*, ed. Robert J. Higgs and Neil D. Isaacs. New York: Harcourt, Brace, Jovanovich, 1977.

Sheehan, George A. *On Running*. New York: Bantam, 1978.

Slusher, Howard S. *Man, Sport, and Existence: A Critical Analysis*. Philadelphia: Lea and Febiger, 1967.

Smith, Adam. *Powers of Mind*. New York: Ballantine, 1975.

Suits, Bernard. *The Grasshopper: Games, Life, and Utopia*. Toronto: The University of Toronto Press, 1978.

Thoreau, Henry David. *Walden*, ed. by Joseph Wood Krutch. New York: Bantam, 1962.

The Universal Jewish Encyclopedia: An Authoritative and Popular Presentation of Jews and Judaism Since the Earliest Times. 10 vols. Edited by Isaac Landman, Louis Rittenberg, and others. New York Ktav Publishing House, 1969.

Vanderzwaag, Harold J. *Toward a Philosophy of Sport*. Reading, Mass.: Addison-Wesley, 1972.

Veblen, Thorstein. *Theory of the Leisure Class*. 1899. Reprint. New York: Macmillan Co., 1953.

Weiss, Paul. *Sport: A Philosophic Inquiry*. Carbondale, Ill.: Southern Illinois University Press, 1969.

Wertz, S. K. "Novak's Analogies" (Review Essay). *Journal of the Philosophy of Sport* 6 (Fall, 1979), 79-85.

Ziegland, Vic, and Lewis Grossberger, *The Non-Runner's Book*. New York: Collier, 1978.

Important Events in the History of American Sports: A Chronology

JACK W. BERRYMAN

The following compilation has been made possible by the efforts of many historians who have delved into the specifics of American sports history. It is intended only to be a chronological framework, or scaffold, from which to view the many facets of the rise of American sports. By utilizing such a list, one can survey the accomplishments in running, jumping, and throwing by man or in speed and endurance by animals and machines with some appreciation of what went before. These key events illuminate the larger themes of amateurism versus professionalism, the role of the media, the formation of sports clubs, the standardization of rules, the pursuit of records, and connections with education, race, and sex. Thus, the chronology should serve as an aid in organizing the story of the maturation of American sports.

The list should not be considered as definitive evidence for any particular event. If an exact date is necessary, one should seek such specific primary sources as newspapers, record books, or manuals. The selections in this chronology are emblematic of the major developments, changes, progressions, fads, and manias apparent in American sports from the colonial period to early 1980.

For a comprehensive listing of dates and events on approximately seventy-five Canadian sports see *Sport Canadiana* by Barbara Schrodt, Gerald Redmond, and Richard Baka.

1618	Governor Argall of Virginia forbids dancing, fiddling, card playing, hunting, and fishing on Sundays.
1619	Probably the first picture of the sports of the American colonists appears as an engraving in a section of Theodore DeBry's *America* to illustrate a passage in a Latin translation of Captain John Smith's *Description of New England*.
1621 Dec. 25	Governor Bradford of the Plymouth colony stops newcomers from playing games on Christmas Day. These games include "pitching the barr" and "stoole ball."
1629 Mar. 24	Virginia passes the first colonial game law, which prohibits the shipment of hides or skins outside Virginia.
1647	Massachusetts Bay passes a law against the playing of shuffleboard ("shoffleboard").

1650	A Massachusetts Bay law is passed against "bowling or any other play or game in or about houses of common entertainment."
1650	Notices appear describing fox hunting on shores of Chesapeake Bay.
1652	A vague form of miniature golf begins in New Netherland. It involves putting a small ball around a green by means of a crooked club.
1657	Horse racing within city limits of New Amsterdam is forbidden by the governor.
1664	America's first organized sport, horse racing, begins when New York's first governor establishes Newmarket Course at Hempstead Plains, Long Island.
1668 Mar. 25	America's first sports trophy, a silver porringer hand-wrought by Pieter van Inburg, is presented to the winner of a horse race at Newmarket Course at Hempstead Plains, Long Island.
1669	Governor Lovelace of New York encourages horse racing by actively participating himself.
1670	Salisbury Plains, New York, develops a regular race course for horses.
1705	Robert Beverly's *History of Virginia* is published, giving details of various methods of hunting in the South: stalking deer, hunting rabbits with mongrel dogs, hunting coons and opossums by the light of moon, and so on.
1706	A closed season on deer is established on Long Island, where continuous hunting has almost eliminated this popular game.
1708 Apr.1-July 31	A closed season is established on turkeys, heath hens, partridges, and quail in Kings, Queens, and Suffolk counties in New York.
1716	The yearly meeting of the Society of Friends in Philadelphia advises that disciplinary action should be taken against races, either on horseback or on foot, wagers, or "any garning on needless and vain sports and pastimes, for our time passeth swiftly away and our pleasure and delight ought to be in the law of the Lord."
1722 Apr. 30	A public house in Charlestown, Massachusetts is established for billiards.
1732	Schuylkill Fishing Club in Philadelphia, Pennsylvania, is established. It is the first fishing club and oldest sporting organization in the United States.
1734 May 28	The first American fish protection legislation, limiting the ways in which fish can be caught, is enacted by New York City.

1735	The first jockey club in the United States is formed as the South Carolina Jockey Club.
1743 Aug. 10	Jack Broughton formulates the earliest prize-ring code of rules.
1745 May 17	The first notice of a horse race in Maryland appears in the *Maryland Gazette*.
1745	Whist, brought over from England where it has been the rage among men and women, becomes very popular in colonies.
1750	A big horse race at Newmarket Course in Hempstead Plains, Long Island, brings heavy business to the Brooklyn ferry.
1750	Colonel Tasker of Belair, Maryland, imports Selima, daughter of Godolphin Arabian. She becomes the dam of several good American racers.
1751 May 1	The first cricket tournament in America is held in New York.
1766	Gloucester Fox Hunting Club begins in Philadelphia, Pennsylvania.
1766	James Rivington advertises the importation of battledores, shuttlecocks, cricket balls, pellets, raquets for tennis and fives, and backgammon tables.
1774	The Continental Congress recommends a ban on horse racing, cockfighting, gambling, and theatrical exhibitions.
1774	According to early advertisement, bullbaiting is scheduled for every Thursday afternoon at 3 P.M. on Tower Hill in New York.
1774	The first known hunting scene is actually engraved and published in the colonies as the head to a piece of music in the *Royal American Magazine* of Boston.
1779	Sprint races, or quarter racing, become the popular diversions of lower and middle classes around Charlottesville, Virginia.
1780 Nov.	Three days of racing at Hempstead Plains, Long Island, include a Gentlemen's Purse, a Ladies' Subscription, and a race run by women riders.
1783	*The Sportsman's Companion, or An Essay on Shooting* is published in New York.
1784	Nocturnal deer hunting bcomes a misdemeanor in Carolinas because of the accidental slaughter of many domestic cows and horses.
1785	George Washington retires from active hunting and gives away his valuable kennel of hounds.
1788 May	Messenger, a famous gray stallion, believed to be original sire of fine breed of trotting horses, the first in America, arrives from England.

1788 Dec. 9	George Washington's diary notes the sale of his race horse, Magnolia, to Colonel Henry Lee for 5,000 acres of Kentucky land.
1790	Followers of horse racing begin to take interest in blood and breed of horses.
1793 Jan. 9	The first balloon ascent in America is made by Jean Pierre Blanchard.
1796 May 19	The first national game law is approved and provides penalties for hunting or destroying game within Indian territory.
1798 —	Diomed, a great English champion who won the Epsom Derby in 1780, is brought to United States by Colonel John Hoomes of Virginia.
1802	New York state passes a law forbidding public horse races. The only races in state are those held by jockey clubs.
1805 July 8	Bill Richmond becomes the first American to win distinction in the prize by defeating Jack Holmes, alias Tom Tough, in twenty-six rounds at Cricklewood Green, Kulburn Wells, England.
1806 June 10	Harness race horses and harness racing are first recorded in the United States with a report of a trotting race at the Harlem race course in New York. According to the New York *Commercial Advertiser*, the race is won by a horse named Yankee, who trots the mile in 2 minutes 59 seconds.
1806	The first picture of a football game on American soil shows Yale students kicking a ball under the stern eye of Timothy Dwight, the president of Yale.
1808	There is widespread mourning in Virginia for the death of the race horse Diomed. His funeral includes full military honors.
1810 Dec. 10	Tom Molineaux, an American Negro, fights Tom Cribb for the world heavyweight title. He loses on a fluke in forty rounds at Copthall Common, England. This is the first interracial title bout in world history.
1811	A rowing race is held between the shells Knickerbocker of New York and Invincible of Long Island.
1816	New mile record in horse racing is set by Timoleon. His time is 1 minute 47 seconds.
1816	In the first "pugilistic encounter" in America, Jacob Hyer beats Tom Bensley in grudge fight and calls himself America's first champion.
1820	The first football games appear in American colleges as a form of hazing.
1821	New York state relaxes its laws against public horse racing and permits tracks to open up in Queens County.

1822	Football at Yale is prohibited by President Timothy Dwight.
1823 May 27	The most famous horse race of a series of races held in the nineteenth century is run at the Union Race Course in New York. Sixty thousand spectators attend the first great North-South horse race to see American Eclipse, representing the North, win the race from Sir Henry, representing the South, by winning two of the three heats.
1823 Oct. 1	The first American gymnasium to offer systematic instruction is opened by the Round Hill School in Northampton, Massachusetts.
1824	An estimated crowd of 50,000 witness a boat race in New York Harbor for a purse of $1,000.
1825 Jan. 21	John Stuart Skinner, editor and founder of the weekly *American Farmer* in Baltimore, Maryland, starts the "Sporting Olio," as a section of the magazine devoted to sports. This is the first time American sports are covered in a regular and systematic way in a major magazine.
1825 May 16	The first American trotting course is opened at Jamaica, Long Island, by the New York Trotting Club.
1827 July 23	The first swimming school in America is opened in Boston, Massachusetts.
1827	The second handbook for American sportsmen, *American Shooter's Manual*, is published in Philadelphia, Pennsylvania.
1828	The United Bowmen of Philadelphia, Pennsylvania, form a club, the first of its kind in the United States.
1829 Apr. 25	Rattler, an American horse, and Miss Turner, a Welsh mare, meet in the first international horse race. The course is ten miles long, between Cambridge and Godmanchester in England, and Rattler wins by sixty yards.
1829 Sept.	*American Turf Register and Sporting Magazine*, a monthly magazine, the first American publication of its kind, is founded by John Stuart Skinner in Baltimore, Maryland.
1830 Feb. 11	Interest in cockfighting continues. A large main is held in Harrisburg, Pennsylvania, in which one dollar is put up for each fight.
1830	Exceptional endurance is shown in a walking feat. Joshua Newman of Philadelphia, Pennsylvania, covers 100 miles in eighteen days.
1831 Dec. 10	*Spirit of the Times*, a popular weekly sporting paper, is founded by William Trotter Porter in New York City.
1833	Patrick Nisbett Edgar's *The American Race-Turf Register, Sportsman's Herald, and General Stud Book* is published in New York.

1833	A rudimentary form of baseball is played in Philadelphia by the Olympic Ball Club.
1834	Possibly the first hurdle race ever run in America is held at the Washington, D.C., Jockey Club.
1834	The first printed rules for rudimentary baseball appear in Robin Carver's *The Book of Sports.*
1835	Nearly 30,000 spectators see the famous ten mile foot race at Union Course, Long Island. The offer of $1000 to any man who can run ten miles in less than an hour draws nine contestants. Henry Stannard completes the distance in a time of 59 minutes 44 seconds.
1836	A southern horse, John Bascombe, defeats Post Boy, a northern horse, at the Union Course, Long Island.
1838	Rolling hoops becomes a new craze in New York City.
1840 Jan. 1	The first American bowling tournament match ever recorded is held in New York at the Knickerbocker Alleys.
1840	Saint George Cricket Club is formed in New York City.
1840	The first international cricket match in which an American team has participated is won by the United States over a Toronto team.
1841	*Schreiner's Sporting Manual: A Complete Treatise on Fishing, Fowling, and Hunting, as Applicable to this Country* is published in Philadelphia, Pennsylvania.
1842 May 20	Northern Horse Fashion defeats southern horse Boston for a purse of $20,000 at the Union Course on Long Island. Among the 70,000 spectators are forty United States senators and congressmen.
1843 Oct. 10	The first American futurity race, the Peyton Stakes, is held in Nashville, Tennessee. The winner is later named Peytona.
1843	Rowing is introduced at Harvard by William Weeks, a student.
1844 May 20	The New York Sportsmen's Club, a club devoted to wildlife protection, is formed in New York.
1844 July 30	The New York Yacht Club is founded in New York.
1844 Oct. 16	At an international track meet at Beacon Race Course, near New York, John Gildersleeve of New York outruns British racers in a ten-mile race for a purse of $1,000 before a crowd of about 35,000.
1845 July 16	The first American regatta of importance is held by the New York Yacht Club in New York.
1845 Oct. 18	Lady Suffolk, at the Beacon Course in Hoboken, New Jersey,

	trots a mile under saddle in 2 minutes 29½ seconds. It is the first time the mark of 2 minutes 30 seconds is lowered.
1845	Alexander J. Cartwright, a member of the Knickerbocker Club, devises the first formal rules for playing baseball.
1846 June 19	First recorded baseball game in history is played at Elysian Field, Hoboken, New Jersey, between the New York Nine and the Knickerbockers. The Nines win 23-1.
1848 Nov. 21	The Cincinnati Turngeneide, the oldest of the Turnverein societies, is founded.
1849 Feb. 7	Tom Hyer, unofficial American heavyweight champion, knocks out Yankee Sullivan, an English challenger.
1849 Dec. 21	The first American ice-skating club, the Skaters' Club of the City and County of Philadelphia, is formed in Philadelphia, Pennsylvania.
1851 June 3	The Knickerbockers of New York become the first baseball team to wear uniforms. They appear on the field in blue trousers, white shirts, and straw hats.
1851 Aug. 22	The first international yacht race is won by the American yacht *America* over boats of the Royal Yacht Club at the Isle of Wight off the coast of England.
1852 Aug. 3	Yale and Harvard hold the first American intercollegiate rowing race in eight-oared boats on a two mile course at Lake Winnipesaukee, Centre Harbor, New Hampshire.
1853 Oct. 12	John C. Morrissey, who claims the heavyweight boxing championship, is challenged by Yankee Sullivan. Sullivan leads for thirty-six rounds but loses the decision for failure to get back in the ring on time after taking on a few of Morrissey's supporters.
1854 May 13	The first American billiard match of importance is held by Joseph White and George Smith in Syracuse, New York. White wins.
1854	Baseball rules stipulate the exact weight and size of a baseball for the first time.
1854	Numerous baseball clubs are established, including the Eagle and the Empire of New York and the Excelsior of Brooklyn.
1854	Superb trotting horse, Flora Temple, becomes the first horse to run mile under 2 minutes 20 seconds. The news is flashed via telegram throughout nation, making her a national legend.
1855 Apr. 30	The first American three-ball billiard match on a six-by-twelve carom table is held in San Francisco, California, between Michael Phelan and M. Damon of Paris, France.
1855 Oct. 2	Jem Mace, later known as the Father of Scientific Boxing, defeats Slasher Stack in his first professional fight.

1856 June	The Fashion Race Course in Newton, Long Island, opens.
1857 Oct. 6	The first important American chess tournament is held in New York under the auspices of the New York Chess Club.
1857 Oct. 6	The American Chess Association is organized at the first American Chess Congress in New York City. Paul C. Morphy becomes the first American international chess master.
1857	The America's Cup is presented to the New York Yacht Club as a perpetual challenge cup by its owners.
1857	New baseball rules fix the length of a game at nine innings and provide that an interrupted game is legal after five innings.
1858 Mar.	The first baseball association is formed. Twenty-five amateur baseball clubs become the National Association of Baseball Players.
1858 May 2	A craze for marathon riding develops in California, and John Powers rides 150 miles over the San Francisco Pioneer Course race track in 6 hours 43 minutes 31 seconds, using twenty-five mustangs to accomplish this feat which wins him a $5,000 bet.
1859 Apr. 12	The first American billiard match to attain international prominence is held in Detroit, Michigan, between Michael Phelan of New York and John Seeriter of Detroit for the billiard championship of the world. Phelan wins.
1859 May 31	The Philadelphia Athletics are organized to play "town ball," one of several base ball games popular at the time.
1859 July 1	The first intercollegiate baseball game is played in Pittsfield, Massachusetts, between Amherst and Williams colleges with Amherst winning 66-32.
1859 July 20	For the first time in a baseball game, a fifty cent admission fee is charged at the Fashion Race Course, Long Island, New York, in a game between teams representing Brooklyn and New York.
1859 July 26	Harvard wins the first intercollegiate regatta over Yale and Brown.
1859 Oct. 3	The first American international cricket tournament begins at Hoboken, New Jersey, between an All-England team and the Saint George's Cricket Club of New York. The English team wins.
1859	Flora Temple trots a mile in 2 minutes 19¾ seconds in Kalamazoo, Michigan.
1860 Feb. 22	The first organized baseball game in San Francisco is played.
1860 Apr. 17	The first international title match between the British champion Tom Sayers and the American champion Tom Heenan is held in London, England.
1860 May 6	The Olympic Club of San Francisco, the oldest club in the United States dedicated to athletics, is founded.

1860 June 30	The Brooklyn Excelsiors, the first baseball team to tour, leave for Albany, New York, the West, and the South.
1860 July 25	The first American intercollegiate billiard match is held in Worcester, Massachusetts, by Harvard and Yale freshmen.
1860 Aug. 3	The American Canoe Association is formed at Lake George, New York.
1860 Oct. 4	The Prince of Wales, bored by a reception at the White House, slips off with the niece of President Buchanan to the gym of Mrs. Smith's Institute for Young Ladies, where the prince and his partner play tenpins.
1860	Croquet, which is considered well adapted to female participation, enjoys wide popularity.
1861 June 18	The first American fly casting tournament is held in Utica, New York.
1861	New York *Clipper*, a newspaper, offers the first baseball trophy.
1861	The Seneca Indian foot racer Deerfoot, running in breechcloth and moccasins, outraces every available English runner.
1862 May 14	Adolphe Nicole of Switzerland patents the first chronograph, and accurate timing of athletic events becomes possible.
1862 May 15	The first enclosed baseball field is opened at Union Grounds in Brooklyn, New York.
1863	Roller skating is introduced by James L. Plimpton.
1864 Apr. 30	The first American state hunting license fee is enacted by New York state.
1864 June 7	America's first Derby race, the Jersey Derby, is won by Norfolk.
1864	The first American croquet club is founded as Park Place Croquet Club of Brooklyn, New York.
1864	John Morrissey, ex-prize fighter, builds a race track at Saratoga, New York, and organizes the first race meets there.
1865 Oct. 10	John Hyatt patents a billiard ball of a composition material resembling ivory.
1865	There is a tremendous upsurge in the popularity of baseball after the Civil War. This year sees ninety-one clubs included in the National Association of Baseball Players.
1865	Dexter trots a mile under saddle in 2 minutes 17¼ seconds at the Driving Park in Buffalo, New York.
1866	James Gordon Bennett's 107 foot schooner, *The Henrietta*, wins the first transoceanic yacht race.
1866	The Brooklyn Atlantics play the Philadelphia Athletics for the unofficial baseball championship of the United States.
1867	The record for long-distance walking is set by Edward P.

Weston, who does the distance from Portland, Maine, to Chicago, Illinois, in twenty-six days, and wins $10,000.

1867   Ruthless wins the first annual Belmont Stakes at Jerome Park, Westchester County, New York.

1868 Sept. 8   The New York Athletic Club is organized in New York City.

1868 Nov. 11   The first American amateur indoor track and field meet is held in New York by the New York Athletic Club.

1868 Dec. 5   The first American bicycle school for velocipede riding opens in New York.

1868   The great vogue for ice skating leads to the meeting of the American Skating Congress in Pittsburgh, Pennsylvania, to formulate regulations for the sport and to encourage its spread.

1869 Mar. 15   The Cincinnati Red Stockings become the first professional baseball team and announce that they are making regular payments to players and are beginning an eight-month tour of the East and Midwest.

1869 June 15   The first American international fight with bare knuckles is held in Saint Louis, Missouri, between Mike McCoole of the United States and Tom Allen of England. McCoole wins.

1869 Aug. 17   The first international boat race is held in London, England, on the Thames River between an Oxford and a Harvard crew. The Oxford crew wins.

1869 Oct. 26   The first American steeplechase horse race is held at Jerome Park, Westchester County, New York.

1869 Nov. 6   The first intercollegiate football game in America takes place between Rutgers and Princeton in New Brunswick, New Jersey. The game is played with twenty-five players on each side, and Rutgers wins 6-4.

1869   The first Ice Yacht Club is formed in Poughkeepsie, New York.

1870 Aug. 8   *Magic* defeats *Cambria* for the first America's Cup race and begins the undefeated streak of the United States.

1870 Oct. 25   Pimlico Race Course is opened in Baltimore, Maryland, with Preakness winning the featured race, known as the Dinner Party Stake.

1870   The craze for roller skating spreads throughout America.

1870   Walking becomes one of most popular spectator sports. Gilmore's Gardens in New York City usually is sold out for heel-and-toe races.

1871 Mar. 17   The first baseball league of importance, the National Association of Professional Base Ball Players, is organized in New York.

1871 Oct. 12	The first American amateur outdoor athletic games are held in New York by the New York Athletic Club.
1871 Nov. 24	The National Rifle Association is incorporated.
1871	The creation of the United States Commission of Fish and Fisheries leads to the formation of similar agencies at the state level to promote and support sport fishing.
1872 June	The National Association of Amateur Oarsmen holds its first regatta.
1873 Apr. 25	The first National Rifle Association shooting meet is held in Creedmoor, Long Island.
1873 May 14	The first running of the California Derby occurs at Darland Trotting Park in Oakland, California.
1873 May 27	The first Preakness Stakes is run at Pimlico Race Track in Baltimore, Maryland. The race is won by Survivor.
1873 Aug. 14	*Forest and Stream*, a weekly sporting magazine that played an important part in the conservation of fish and game in America, is first issued.
1873 Oct. 18	Football rules are formulated in New York City at a meeting attended by delegates from Columbia, Princeton, Rutgers, and Yale. The delegates adopt the London Football Association code prohibiting carrying the ball in play.
1874 May 14	The football goal post is used for the first time, in a game between McGill University and Harvard, held in Cambridge, Massachusetts. In this same game an admission fee is charged for the first time to a collegiate sporting event.
1874 Sept. 16	The first American international rifle tournament of consequence is held in Creedmoor, New York, between American and Irish teams.
1874	Goldsmith Maid trots a mile in 2 minutes 14 seconds at Mystic Park in Boston, Massachusetts.
1875 Feb. 5	The first issue of the *Kentucky Live Stock Record*, covering all breeds of livestock, is published. Its name is changed in 1891 to *The Thoroughbred Record*, and it devotes itself strictly to thoroughbred race horses.
1875 May 17	The first running of the Kentucky Derby is held at Louisville's Churchill Downs.
1875 Nov. 13	Bowling rule standardization begins in New York City with the organization of the National Bowling Association.
1875 Dec. 4	The Intercollegiate Association of Amateur Athletes of America holds its organizational meeting in Saratoga, New York.
1876 Feb. 2	Eight baseball teams band together to form the National League.

1876 Apr. 22   The first official National League baseball game is held in Philadelphia between Philadelphia and Boston. Boston wins 6-5.

1876 May 23   Joe Borden of Boston pitches the first no-hitter in National League baseball history.

1876 July 20   The first intercollegiate track meet under the auspices of the Intercollegiate Association of Amateur Athletes of America opens in Saratoga, New York.

1876 Nov. 23   The Intercollegiate Football Association is formed in Springfield, Massachusetts. Columbia, Harvard, and Princeton become chartered members.

1876   Because of James Gordon Bennett, Jr., and his sponsorship, the first polo game in the United States is played inside the Dickel Riding Academy in New York City.

1877 Feb. 20   Baseball's International Association is formed.

1877 May 8   The first American dog show of importance is held in New York under the auspices of the Westminster Kennel Bench Show of Dogs.

1877 Sept. 30   The first amateur swimming championship in the United States is held under the auspices of the New York Athletic Club at Mott Haven Boat House on the Harlem River in New York.

1877 Dec. 22   *The American Bicycling Journal* begins publication in Boston, Massachusetts.

1878 Feb. 11   The Boston Bicycle Club, the first American bicycle club, is formed in Boston, Massachusetts.

1878 July 4   Ten Broeck defeats Mollie McCarthy in a match race at Churchill Downs in Lexington, Kentucky. The race was the nineteenth-century equivalent to the later match races between Man O'War and Sir Barton, Seabiscuit and War Admiral, and Swaps and Nashua.

1878   Sir John Astley, a member of Parliament and a prominent British sportsman, offers a £500 purse and a championship belt to the winner of a six days' test, go-as-you-please race. The belt becomes symbolic of pedestrian proficiency on both sides of the Atlantic.

1878   Westchester, New York, Hare and Hounds sponsors its first "chase over hill and dale." It is the early beginnings of cross-country running in the United States.

1879 Jan. 23   The National Archery Association is formed at Crawfordsville, Indiana.

1879 June 24   The first Childs Cup, now the oldest trophy in sprint crew racing, is won by the University of Pennsylvania.

1879 Aug. 12	The first National Archery Association tournament opens at White Stocking Park in Chicago, Illinois.
1879 Nov. 19	The National Association of Trotting Horse Breeders agrees upon the qualities that constitute a trotting horse.
1879	The Intercollegiate Cricket Association is formed.
1880 Jan. 19	William Muldoon, the most famous nineteenth-century wrestler in America, wins the Greco-Roman wrestling championship of America.
1880 Feb. 12	The National Croquet League is organized in Philadelphia, Pennsylvania.
1880 Mar. 13	Recognizing the growth of new sports, *American Cricketer*, a journal founded in 1877 especially for cricket, states it will embrace boating, tennis, bicycling, and other outdoor sports.
1880 May 31	The first American national bicycle society, the League of American Wheelmen, is formed in Newport, Rhode Island.
1881 May 21	The United States Lawn Tennis Association is formed in New York.
1881 Aug. 31	The first American lawn tennis national championship matches are held in Newport, Rhode Island, with Richard Sears winning the singles title.
1881 Oct. 15	The first American fishing magazine, the *American Angler*, is published in Philadelphia, Pennsylvania.
1882 Jan. 14	The first United States country club, the Myopia Hunt Club of Winchester, Massachusetts, is formed.
1882 Mar. 11	The Intercollegiate Lacrosse Association is organized in Princeton, New Jersey.
1882 Sept. 25	The first major league baseball double header is held between teams from Providence, Rhode Island, and Worcester, Massachusetts.
1882	The National Croquet Association is founded and holds its first national tournament in Norwich, Connecticut.
1883 May 1	The first American professional sports trainer, Bob Rogers, is hired by the New York Athletic Club.
1883 June 2	In Fort Wayne, Indiana, the first baseball game under electric lights is played.
1883 June 7	The first American intercollegiate lawn tennis match is held in Hartford, Connecticut, on the grounds of Trinity College.
1883 June 16	The first "Ladies Day" baseball game is staged by the New York Giants. Escorted and unescorted ladies are admitted free of charge to the ball park.
1883 Oct. 17	Football adopts numerical scoring systems (five points for a

field goal, two for a touchdown, one for a safety, and four for a goal after touchdown.)

1883 Nov. 6	The first American cross-country championships are run under the auspices of the New York Athletic Club.
1883	The Intercollegiate Rowing Association is formed with seven charter member institutions.
1884 June 28	The first American Derby, one of the great races for three-year-old race horses, is run in Chicago, Illinois at Washington Park Club.
1884 Dec. 9	Levant Richardson patents the ball-bearing skate.
1884	Greyhound racing is introduced in Philadelphia, Pennsylvania.
1884	The first Negro to play baseball in a major league is Moses Fleetwood Walker of Toledo of the American Association.
1885	The first exhibition of the National Horse Show Association is held in Gilmore's Garden, New York. Rather than emphasizing speed, horses are judged on form and conformity to type.
1885	The National Brotherhood of Baseball Players is organized under the leadership of John Montgomery Ward.
1886 Aug. 25	The first international polo series between teams representing England and the United States is held in Newport, Rhode Island.
1886	The first national trap shooting tournament is held in New Orleans, Louisiana, under the regulations of the National Gun Club.
1887 Feb. 8	The Aurora Ski Club, the first active American local ski club, holds its first skiing competition in Red Wing, Minnesota.
1887 Mar. 2	The American Trotting Association is organized in Detroit, Michigan.
1887 Mar. 8	Everett Horton patents a fishing rod of telescoping steel tubes.
1887 Mar. 15	William Alden Smith becomes the first salaried fish and game warden under the provisions of the state laws of Michigan.
1887 Mar. 26	Legal betting takes place at tracks in New York state.
1887 Dec.	Hunting's prestigious Boone and Crockett Club is established in New York City.
1887	The National Cross-Country Association is formed to promote long distance running in the United States.
1888 Jan. 21	The Amateur Athletic Union of the United States is formed.
1888 May 12	The crouching start to get a quick break in a foot race is first used by Charles Sherrill, captain of the Yale team, at the Rockaway Hunt Club games in Cedarhurst, Long Island.

1889 Feb. 2	The United States National Lawn Tennis Association issues a statement extending its protective wing to "lady lawn tennis" players.
1889 July 8	John L. Sullivan and Jake Kilrain meet in the last bare-knuckle championship fight. Sullivan wins after seventy-five rounds.
1889 Aug. 29	The first American international professional lawn tennis contest begins in Newport, Rhode Island, at Newport Casino.
1889	The first All-American football team is selected by Walter Camp in *Collier's Weekly*.
1890 Jan. 1	The first Tournament of Roses, which also featured amateur sports, is held in Pasadena, California.
1890 June 6	The United States Polo Association is formed in New York.
1890 Oct. 11	John Owens runs the first 100 yard event under championship conditions in less than 10 seconds.
1890 Nov. 29	The first Army-Navy football game is played at West Point. Navy is victorious by 24-0.
1891 Jan. 16	The first American ski club association, the Central Organization, holds its first meeting and tournament at Ishpeming, Michigan.
1891 Feb. 16	A system of control for horse racing is established by the American Jockey Club.
1891 May 6	The Amateur Fencers League of America is organized in New York.
1891 May 21	Peter Jackson and Jim Corbett fight to a sixty-one round draw at the California Athletic Club in San Francisco.
1891 Oct. 18	The first international six-day bicycle race is run in the old Madison Square Garden in New York City.
1891	Basketball is invented by Dr. James Naismith in Springfield, Massachusetts, as an indoor substitute for football and baseball.
1891	W. Byrd Page of the University of Pennsylvania sets the world's high jump record with a leap of 6 feet 4 inches.
1892 Jan. 15	Basketball rules are published for the first time in the *Triangle Magazine* in Springfield, Massachusetts.
1892 Jan. 20	Students at the International YMCA Training School in Springfield, Massachusetts, play the first official basketball game.
1892 Mar. 18	Jockeys are prohibited from using anything but a whip and a spur on a horse after a jockey is discovered using an electric spur while riding Gyda in Gutterburg, New Jersey.
1892 Mar. 19	The first big game between Stanford and California takes

	place in San Francisco. Stanford wins 14-10. The game initiated interest in football on the West coast.
1892 June 8	The first reference to the low-wheel bike sulky being used in a harness race at the old Agricultural Park race track in Worcester, Massachusetts, is made.
1892 Sept. 7	The first world heavyweight title fight of importance under Marquis of Queensberry rules with gloves and three minutes rounds is held in New Orleans, Louisiana, between John L. Sullivan and James Corbett. Corbett wins by knocking out Sullivan in the twenty-first round.
1892	Basketball is first played by women at Smith College in Northampton, Massachusetts.
1892	Edward Geers uses the ball-bearing axle and pneumatic tires introduced with the bicycle for the sulky to improve trotting race speeds.
1893 July 1	The first American bicycle race track of wood is opened in San Francisco, California by the Bay City Club.
1893	Ice hockey is introduced to United States at Yale and Johns Hopkins Universities.
1893	The first relay race, America's contribution to track and field, is held by the University of Pennsylvania.
1894 Jan. 27	The University of Chicago, the first college to play a full basketball schedule, plays its first basketball game. It defeats the Chicago YMCA Training School 19-11 and winds up the season with a six wins and one loss record.
1894 Dec. 22	The Amateur Golf Association of the United States is formed in New York.
1894 Dec. 25	The University of Chicago becomes the first midwestern football team to play on the Pacific coast. Chicago plays against Stanford in San Francisco.
1895 May 5	A group of New York golfers ask the New York park commissioners to build links in Van Cortlandt Park. The links become the first public links in the country.
1895 May 5	The first American intercollegiate fencing championship competition is held in New York by Harvard and Columbia universities.
1895 May 25	The first American golf book, *Golf in America, A Practical Manual* by James P. Lee is published in New York.
1895 Sept. 3	The first professional football game is played at Latrobe, Pennsylvania, between the Latrobe Young Men's Christian Association and the Jeannett Athletic Club of Jeannett, Pennsylvania. Latrobe wins 12-0.
1895 Sept. 9	The American Bowling Congress is organized in New York to standardize bowling rules.

1895 Sept. 21	The first amateur international track and field meet in the United States is held at New York between the New York Athletic Club and the London Athletic Club.
1895 Oct. 12	The first American official amateur golf tournament under the rules of the United States Golf Association is held in Newport, Rhode Island, at the Newport Country Club. It is won by Charles Blair Macdonald.
1895 Nov. 9	The first women's amateur tournament of the United States Golf Association is held at the Meadow Brook Club in Westbury, New York. It is won by Mrs. C. S. Brown.
1895 Nov. 28	The speed and stamina of American-made cars are tested in a 54:36 measured mile race from the heart of Chicago to the suburbs and return. The race is won by J. Frank Duryea with an average speed of 7.5 miles per hour in a Duryea car.
1895	The "Penn Relays" begin at the University of Pennsylvania in Philadelphia. They become a mainstay for track competition in the United States.
1895	The Intercollegiate Ice Hockey League is formed.
1895	William G. Morgan, physical director of the YMCA in Holyoke, Massachusetts, invents the sport of volley ball.
1896 Jan. 6	The first American women's six-day bicycle race begins at Madison Square Garden in New York.
1896 Feb. 8	Faculty representatives from Midwestern universities meet and form the Western (Big Ten) Conference.
1896 Apr. 4	One of the first intercollegiate women's basketball games is played between the University of California and Stanford at the San Francisco Armory in San Francisco, California. Stanford wins 2-1 before an audience of 700 women. At California's insistence, no men were admitted.
1896 Apr. 6	The first modern Olympic Games in Athens, Greece, are dominated by a small group of Americans who arrive just as the roll of athletes for the first time events is being called. The United States wins nine of twelve events after a long ocean trip.
1896 Apr. 24	A YMCA tournament for basketball, called the "Championship of America," is staged in Brooklyn, New York. The East Division team defeats the Brooklyn Central team 4-0.
1896 May 27	The first American intercollegiate bicycle race is held in New York at the Manhattan Beach Track.
1896 Sept. 7	The first American automobile race on a track is held in Cranston, Rhode Island, at Narragansett Park.
1896 Nov. 26	The first large indoor football game is played in the Chicago Coliseum in Chicago, Illinois, between the University of Chicago and the University of Michigan. Chicago wins 7-6.

1896 Nov.	The first United States hockey league, the American Amateur Hockey League, is organized in New York City.
1896 Dec. 10	The first intercollegiate basketball game is played in New Haven, Connecticut, between Yale and Wesleyan University. Wesleyan wins 4-3.
1897 Jan. 1	The first football game between Negro colleges is held in Atlanta, Georgia, between Atlanta University and Tuskeegee Normal and Industrial Institute. Atlanta wins 10-0.
1897 Jan. 7	The first national handball championship match for amateurs begins in Jersey City, New Jersey. The first winner is Michael Eagen.
1897 Mar. 15	The first indoor fly casting tournament begins in New York at Madison Square Garden under the auspices of the Sportsmen's Association.
1897 Mar. 17	The first fight at which motion pictures are taken is Robert Fitzsimmons of England against James Corbett. Fitzsimmons knocks out Corbett in fourteen rounds in Carson City, Nevada.
1897 Apr. 19	The first American annual marathon race, a 26 mile 385 feet distance event, is held from Hopkinton, Massachusetts, to Boston, Massachusetts.
1897 Aug. 28	Star Pointer becomes the first horse to pace better than 2 minutes for the mile in a race in Readville, Massachusetts. Star Pointer goes the distance in 1 minute 59¼ seconds.
1898 Mar. 25	The Intercollegiate Trapshooting Association is formed in New York.
1898	Alvin C. Kraenzlein of the University of Pennsylvania sets a record of 15 1/5 seconds in the high hurdles race.
1899 Mar. 22	The first meeting of college gymnasts in formal competition is staged at the gymnasium of New York University in New York. Of the eighteen eastern and southern schools represented, eight join in the formation of the Intercollegiate Gymnastics Union.
1899 July 29	The Southern California Golf Association is formed.
1899	The Intercollegiate Cross-Country Association is founded.
1900 Jan. 29	A new baseball league, the American League, is organized in Chicago, Illinois.
1900 June 12	The first American trapshooting tournament with clay targets is held at Interstate Park in New York.
1900 June 16	The first American international revolver shooting tournament is held in Greenville, New Jersey, between teams representing the United States and France.
1900	A conference of representatives from Columbia, Cornell, Harvard, Princeton, and Yale forms a basketball league.

1900	Alvin C. Kraenzlein of the University of Pennsylvania sets a world's record in the broad jump with a leap of 24 feet 4½ inches. Later this year, Meyer Prinstein of Syracuse increases the record to 24 feet 7¾ inches.
1900	International tennis competition with England is stimulated by a permanent silver trophy given by Dwight F. Davis. Davis was the doubles champion with H. F. Ward and later Secretary of war under President Calvin Coolidge.
1901 Jan. 8	The first bowling tournament sponsored by the American Bowling Congress convenes in Chicago, Illinois.
1901 June 14	The first professional open championship played under the rules of the United States Golf Association opens in Hamilton, Massachusetts, at the Myopia Hunt Club.
1902 Dec. 28	The first indoor professional football game takes place in Madison Square Garden in New York. Syracuse defeats the Philadelphia Nationals 6-0.
1903 May 30	The first American motorcycle hill-climbing contest is held in Riverdale, New York.
1903 Oct. 1	The first World Series of Baseball begins in Boston between Boston of the American League and Pittsburgh of the National League in a best of nine series.
1903 Oct. 24	Lou Dillion, driven by his owner, C. K. G. Billings, achieved the first under two minute mile for trotters in Memphis, Tennessee in 1 minute 58½ seconds.
1903	Luther H. Gulick begins the New York Public School Athletic League, the first of its kind in the United States.
1904 Feb. 21	The National Ski Association is formed in Ishpeming, Michigan.
1904 Mar. 2	The official playing rules for professional baseball clubs are adopted in New York City.
1904 May 14	The Olympic Games begin in Saint Louis, Missouri. It is first time the Olympics are held in the United States.
1904 June 3	Walter Travis becomes the first American and the first foreigner to win the British amateur golf title.
1904 June 23	The first American motor boat race to be held under the rules of the American Power Boat Association begins in New York on the Hudson River under the jurisdiction of the Columbia Yacht Club.
1904 Oct. 8	Formalized automobile racing begins in America with the first Vanderbilt Cup automobile race. The race starts in Hicksville, New York on a ten-lap course over a thirty-mile circuit. The winner is George Heath.
1904 Dec. 31	The Public Schools Athletic League of New York presents its first track meet at Madison Square Garden in New York.

1905 Apr. 7	The Intercollegiate Wrestling Association is formed in Philadelphia, Pennsylvania.
1905 Dec. 28	A conference of sixty-two colleges is called because of threats from President Theodore Roosevelt to ban football if the brutality of the game is not stopped. The Intercollegiate Athletics Association of the United States, a predecessor of the National Collegiate Athletic Association, is formed.
1906 Jan. 12	The American Inter-Collegiate Football Rules Committee legalizes the forward pass to make games safe.
1906 May 30	The Inter-Scholastic Athletic Association of the Middle Atlantic States, the first athletic association among Negro schools, holds its first event, a track and field meet at Howard University in Washington, D.C.
1906 Sept. 5	The first legal forward pass in football is thrown by Brandbury Robinson, a Saint Louis University halfback who tosses the ball to Jack Schneider in a game with Carroll College in Waukesha, Wisconsin.
1906 Sept. 8	Dan Patch trots the mile in 1 minute 55 seconds in Saint Paul, Minnesota.
1906	Haverford College in Pennsylvania in conjunction with Harvard, Pennsylvania, Columbia, and Cornell form the Intercollegiate Association Football League for soccer.
1907 Feb. 14	The Masters of the Fox Hounds Association, the first American fox hound association, is formed in New York.
1909 Jan. 30	The Rocky Mountain Conference is organized under the name Colorado Faculty Athletic Conference.
1909 June 1	The first American transcontinental automobile race from New York to Seattle, Washington, is begun.
1909 June 22	The first American transcontinental automobile race is completed in Seattle, Washington.
1909 Aug. 19	The first race meet is held at the Indianapolis Speedway in Indianapolis, Indiana, over a brick-paved track.
1910 June 10	The first American school stadium is dedicated in Tacoma, Washington.
1910 Aug. 8	The first Davis Cup international lawn tennis challenge matches begin at Longwood Cricket Club in Brookline, Massachusetts.
1910 Dec. 29	The Intercollegiate Athletic Association changes its name to the National Collegiate Athletic Association.
1911 Mar. 20	The National Squash Tennis Association is formed in New York.
1911 Apr. 8	The first United States squash tennis tournament to be spon-

sored by the National Squash Tennis Association is held in New York.

1911 May 30   Ray Harroun wins the first 500 mile race at the Indianapolis Speedway in Indianapolis, Indiana.

1912 Aug. 24   Jim Thorpe, leading the victorious Olympic athletes, marches through the streets of New York with hundreds of thousands lining the parade route.

1913 Jan. 26   Jim Thorpe confesses in a letter to James E. Sullivan, chairman of the Amateur Athletic Union, that he had played professional baseball in 1909 and 1910. He thereby disqualifies himself from amateur competition and is forced to return the prizes he won in the 1912 Olympic Games in Stockholm, Sweden.

1913 Mar. 10   William Knox becomes the first bowler to make a perfect score of 300 in an American Bowling Congress tournament held in Toledo, Ohio.

1913 Apr. 5   The United States Football Association, now known as the United States Soccer Football Association, is formed in New York.

1913 Sept. 20   Francis Ouimet becomes the first amateur and the first native American to win the United States Open golf championship. By winning this tournament he helps to popularize golf as a sport for everyone.

1913 Nov. 1   The possibilities of the forward pass are shown as Notre Dame beats highly favored Army in the first Notre Dame-Army football game. Notre Dame wins 35-7.

1914 May 16   The American Horseshoe Pitchers Association is formed in Kansas City, Kansas.

1914 July 4   The first motorcycle race in America is a three-hundred-mile race held in Dodge City, Kansas.

1915 Apr. 5   Jess Willard wins the heavyweight championship by knocking out Jack Johnson in the twenty-sixth round of a fight in Havana, Cuba.

1915 Sept. 18   The first American asphalt-covered automobile race track is opened in Cranston, Rhode Island, at the Narragansett Speedway.

1915 Oct. 23   The first national horseshoe championship tournament is held in Kellerton, Iowa, under auspices of the Grand League of the American Horseshoe Pitchers Association.

1915 Dec. 2   The Pacific Coast Intercollegiate Athletic Conference is founded in Portland, Oregon.

1916 Jan. 17   The Professional Golfers' Association of America is formed in New York.

1916 Mar. 25	Jess Willard and Frank Moran meet in a ten-round, no-decision heavyweight fight in New York at Madison Square Garden. It is the first fight that women attend in any numbers. The promoter, Tex Rickard, gets 300 women, mostly of the fashionable set, to attend.
1916 Oct. 14	The first Professional Golfers' Association tournament ends in Mount Vernon, New York. James Barnes of Philadelphia, Pennsylvania, is the winner.
1916 Nov. 29	The organizational meeting of the Women's Bowling Association, later known as the Women's International Bowling Congress, is held at the Washington Recreation Parlor in Saint Louis, Missouri.
1917 Mar. 17	The first bowling tournament for women under the auspices of the Women's International Bowling Congress is held in Saint Louis, Missouri.
1917 Mar. 27	The Seattle Metropolitans of the Pacific Coast League of Canada becomes the first United States hockey team to win the Stanley Cup.
1918	The Interstate Trapshooting Association is formed with more than five thousand affiliated gun clubs.
1919 June 11	Sir Barton wins the Belmont Stakes to become the first of the Triple Crown winners in American thoroughbred racing history.
1919 Oct. 11	The first transcontinental air race is completed in San Francisco, California, on a flight from Mineola, New York. The race began October 8, and Lieutenant Belvin Maynard is the elapsed time winner.
1919	One of the most successful of all national basketball tournaments for high school and academy students is begun by Amos A. Stagg at the University of Chicago's Bartlett Gymnasium.
1920 Feb. 22	The first United States dog race track to use imitation rabbits is opened in Emeryville, California, by Owen Smith.
1920 Sept. 17	Eleven league franchises are sold for $100 each when the American Professional Football Association is formed.
1920 Sept. 28	A Chicago grand jury indicts eight players of the Chicago White Sox for throwing the 1919 World Series.
1920 Nov. 12	Kenesaw Landis is elected the first baseball commissioner.
1920 Nov. 25	The first play-by-play description of a football game in radio history takes place as Station WTAW of College Station, Texas, reports the Texas University-Texas Aggies game.
1920 Dec. 19	The first American indoor curling rink opens in the Brookline Country Club in Brookline, Massachusetts.
1921 June 17	At Stagg Field at the University of Chicago in Chicago, Illi-

nois, the first NCAA National Collegiate Track and Field Championships are held.

1921 July 2 — Jack Dempsey wins over Georges Carpentier by a knockout in the first prize fight with a $1 million gate. The fight is held in Jersey City, New Jersey.

1921 Nov. 18 — The first American international fencing championship competition begins at the Racquet Club in Washington, D.C., with teams representing the United States and Great Britain.

1921 — The biennial international competition of golf begins with England for possession of the Walker Cup.

1922 Jan. 30 — Professional football gets its first eight-column newspaper headline, "Stagg says conference will break professional football menace," in the Chicago *Herald and Examiner*.

1922 Jan. — The United States Field Hockey Association is formed.

1922 Feb. 18 — Kenesaw Landis resigns as a United States District Court judge in Illinois to devote all his time to baseball.

1922 May 14 — The Midwest Federation of State High School Athletic Associations, the forerunner of the National Federation of State High School Athletic Associations, is formed in Chicago, Illinois.

1922 June 24 — The American Professional Football Association changes its name to the National Football League.

1923 Apr. 11 — The National Committee on Women's Athletics of the American Physical Education Association approves resolutions stating that every school or institution should provide an opportunity for every girl to have a full season's program of all-around athletic activities.

1923 Apr. 18 — Yankee Stadium in New York is opened officially with a game between the New York Yankees and the Boston Red Sox before a crowd of 74,000, the largest crowd in baseball history and a record that stood for thirty-one years.

1924 Apr. 24 — The first meeting of the Women's Division of the National Amateur Athletic Federation is held in Chicago, Illinois.

1924 Nov. 1 — A franchise is granted to the Boston Bruins, the first United States team to enter the National Hockey League.

1925 Dec. 26 — The first Shrine East-West game, the nation's first real all-star football game, is played in San Francisco, California. The West wins 7-0.

1925 — DeHart Hubbard of the University of Michigan jumps 25 feet, 10 7/8 inches in Chicago, Illinois, to set a new world record for the broadjump.

1926 Feb. 6 — A rule is adopted that makes all college players ineligible for the National Football League competition until after their college classes have graduated.

1926 Feb. 16	Suzanne Lenglen remains the undisputed woman's tennis champion of the world by defeating Helen Wills in Cannes, France, in the only meeting between the two champions.
1926 Mar. 3	The International Greyhound Racing Association is formed in Miami, Florida.
1926 Aug. 6	Gertrude Ederle becomes the first American woman to swim the English Channel.
1927 Mar. 2	Babe Ruth becomes the highest paid baseball player among the players by signing a three-year contract with the New York Yankees, guaranteeing him $70,000 a year.
1927 Apr. 7	A two-day national meeting, called in Washington, D.C., by Mrs. Herbert Hoover to discuss sports and athletics for girls and women, concludes.
1927 Sept. 22	The greatest purse to that time in boxing history, $990,446, is received by Gene Tunney for his fight against Jack Dempsey at Soldier Field in Chicago, Illinois, in the famous "Long Count" match.
1927	Sabin Carr of Yale establishes the pole vault record at 14 feet.
1928 Jan. 19	The first United States women's squash racquets singles championship is won by Eleanora Sears at the Round Hill Club in Greenwich, Connecticut.
1928	The United States Volley Ball Association is formed, and the Herbert Lee Pratt Trophy is offered to the best amateur team.
1930 Feb. 13	Stella Walsh, a seventeen-year-old girl from Cleveland, Ohio, sets her second world's record in a week by winning the 220-yard dash in the international girls sprint competition at the Meadowbrook Games in Philadelphia in a time of 26 4/5 seconds.
1930 Mar. 4	Emma Fahning of Buffalo, New York, becomes the first woman bowler to make a perfect score in a sanctioned competition of the Women's International Bowling Congress in Buffalo, New York.
1930 Apr. 3	The University of Southern California polo team, scheduled to play a polo team from UCLA, announces it will not play them unless Barbara Rand, a member of the UCLA team, is replaced by a man.
1931 Mar. 30	Jackie Mitchell begins training for her initial appearance as the first woman to sign a contract as a pitcher for an organized baseball team. Newspaper headlines note "Uniform for Girl Pitcher Stumps Pilot" as a suitable uniform is rushed to completion in time for her use in an exhibition game against the New York Yankees.
1931 Apr. 28	A program of events calling for women athletes to participate in certain track and field events in the 1932 Olympic Games is

approved, but the 800 meter race is not approved because it is considered too strenuous for women.

1931 June 23 Lili de Alvarez appears on the center court at Wimbledon in England in a tennis outfit of her own creation featuring short trousers. Spectators say the innovation will be short lived despite the freedom of movement the costume provides because it is not becoming.

1931 July 2 For the first time in the history of heavyweight championship bouts, the weigh-in takes place the day before the fight in Cleveland, Ohio, at the studio of WTAM, which airs the weighing-in ceremonies between Max Schmeling and Young Stribing.

1931 July 21 A new system of wagering on horse races, the daily double, which is in vogue in Canada, begins at the Reno race track in Reno, Nevada. The system permits the bettor to wage on two horses instead of one by picking the winners of two races at a time.

1932 Feb. 4 The first American Winter Olympic Games begin at Lake Placid, New York.

1932 Feb. 9 The first American two-man bobsled competition begins at Lake Placid, New York, as a part of the Olympic Winter Games.

1932 Feb. 18 Sonja Henie retains the world women's figure skating championship. It is the sixth time she has won the title in a contest conducted in Montreal, Canada.

1933 Jan. 13 Mildred (Babe) Didrikson makes her first professional basketball appearance and scores nine points as her team, the Brooklyn Yankees, defeats the Long Island Ducklings 19-16 in a game played in New York.

1933 Jan. 28 Helen Wills Moody, the world's greatest woman tennis player, defeats Phil Neer, a man, in a tennis match before 3,000 fans at the Palace of Fine Arts in San Francisco, California. Sportswriters claim Moody is not tested by a good male tennis player.

1933 June 2 The first swimming pool in the White House is formally accepted by President Franklin Roosevelt.

1933 July 2 The first professional midget auto race in the world takes place in Sacramento, California.

1933 July 6 The first of the annual all-star baseball games is played in Chicago, Illinois, at Comiskey Park with the American League winning over the National League 4-2.

1933 Nov. 7 In elections throughout Pennsylvania, Sunday sports are approved. Such cities as Philadelphia, Pittsburgh, Wilkes-Barre, Harrisburg, and Allentown vote to eliminate the blue laws against playing on Sunday.

1933 Dec. 17   The first world championship game between National Football League divisional winners is played in Chicago, Illinois, with the Chicago Bears defeating the New York Giants 23-21.

1934 Jan. 5   The National and American leagues select a uniform ball to be used by both leagues. It is the first time in thirty-three years that both leagues will use the same type of baseball.

1934 Mar. 22   The first Masters Golf Tournament begins in Augusta, Georgia, and is won three days later by Horton Smith.

1934 Dec. 29   Big-time basketball is introduced at Madison Square Garden when Notre Dame meets New York University and Saint John's opposes Westminster before an audience of 16,188.

1935 Feb. 21   As guests of the Japanese government, thirty Pacific coast football players sail from San Francisco, California, for an exhibition tour of Japan designed to stimulate interest in the game in the Far East.

1935 Apr. 1   Before a crowd of 60,000 that includes Babe Ruth, other touring American baseball stars, and members of the Japanese royal family, an American football team defeats an all-star Japanese team 46-0.

1935 May 24   The first baseball game at night played by major league teams takes place in Cincinnati, Ohio, when the Cincinnati Reds defeat the Philadelphia Phillies 2-1.

1935 May 25   Jesse Owens sets or equals four world records in less than an hour in a Big Ten Conference track meet at Ann Arbor, Michigan. He wins the 100 and 200 yard dashes, the broad jump, and the 220 yard low hurdles.

1935 Aug. 13   The Transcontinental Roller Derby, the first roller derby, opens at the Coliseum in Chicago, Illinois.

1935 Aug. 31   The first national skeet tournament sponsored by the National Skeet Association is held in Indianapolis, Indiana.

1936 Jan. 1   The first Sun Bowl is played with Hardin Simmons University tying New Mexico State 14-14 in El Paso, Texas.

1936 Jan. 16   The first electric eye photo-finish camera for a race track is placed in operation at the Hialeah Race Track in Hialeah, Florida.

1936 Jan. 29   The first five members of the Baseball Hall of Fame are elected. They are Ty Cobb, Walter Johnson, Christy Mathewson, Babe Ruth, and Honus Wagner.

1936 Aug. 9   Jesse Owens becomes the first American athlete to win four medals in one Olympic Games in Berlin, Germany.

1936 Nov. 1   The Rodeo Cowboy's Association is organized under the name of the Cowboy's Turtle Association.

1937 Jan. 1   The first Cotton Bowl is played in Dallas, Texas, with Texas Christian University defeating Marquette 16-6.

1937 Sept. 4	Doris Kopsky becomes the first woman bicycle champion of the National Amateur Bicycle Association. She covers a mile in Buffalo, New York, in 4 minutes 22.4 seconds.
1937 Nov. 2	In a ruling by California State Attorney General Webb, the newest gambling innovation, direct wire betting in which a wire betting agency accepts bets and then wires the money to a representative at the race track where it is bet, is ruled legal in California as long as its activities are confined to racing establishments within the state.
1938 Jan. 1	The Eastern College Athletic Conference, the largest collegiate athletic conference in the nation, begins operations as the Central Offices for Eastern Intercollegiate Athletics.
1938 Jan. 13	The All-American Redheads, a women's basketball team from Missouri which has four girls on its team over six feet tall, meets a team of men from Warner Brothers Studios in Los Angeles at the Pan Pacific Auditorium. The team refuses any modification of the rules because they are women.
1938 Mar. 3	A record field of 24,765 begin competition in the Coliseum in Chicago, Illinois, in the largest American Bowling Congress tournament ever staged.
1938 Apr. 16	The National Collegiate Gymnastics Championships are held for the first time at the University of Chicago in Chicago, Illinois.
1939 Jan. 18	The Edward J. Neil Memorial Trophy, which is awarded to the person who has done the most for boxing in the preceding year, is awarded for the first time. The award goes to Jack Dempsey.
1939 Mar. 13	The Oakland Speedway, borrowing from the horse races, orders furlongs as the official standard of measurement for automobile races in Oakland, California.
1939 Mar. 27	The first National Collegiate Athletic Association university division basketball championship finals are held at Northwestern University. Oregon defeats Ohio State 46-33.
1939 Apr. 15	An underwater photo finish is taken for the first time in the history of the national AAU swimming meets in two events at the Detroit Athletics Club. Slow motion cameras enable the judges to watch underwater touching in the 100 yard freestyle and the 300 yard individual medley events.
1939 May 8	An electric starting gate is used for the first time at the Hollywood Park Race Track in Inglewood, California, when a two-stall working model invented by Clay Puett is installed.
1939 May 16	The American League's first night baseball game takes place at Shibe Park in Philadelphia, Pennsylvania, between the Philadelphia Athletics and the Cleveland Indians.
1939 May 17	Television offers its first collegiate sports event, a baseball

	game between Columbia and Princeton at Baker Field in New York. It is broadcast by NBC over W2XBS with a comment made by the publicity director of NBC that televised World Series games are ten years away.
1939 June 1	The heavyweight boxing fight between Lou Nova and Max Baer, which Nova wins, is telecast in New York. It is the first regularly scheduled fight ever televised and the fourth sporting event on television since NBC began its month-old television service.
1939 June 22	The first national water ski tournament is held at Jones Beach State Park on Long Island.
1939 June 26	The first NCAA sponsored golf championship begins at the Wakonda Country Club in Des Moines, Iowa.
1939 Aug. 20	The National Bowling Association, the first major Negro bowling association, is founded in Detroit, Michigan.
1940 Feb. 25	The first American hockey game to be televised is played at Madison Square Garden in New York between the New York Rangers and the Montreal Canadians. It is televised by W2XBS in New York.
1940 Mar. 29	A bill authorizing the installation of pari-mutuel betting machines at New York's five race tracks is passed by the New York legislature. It is designed to bring New York $5 million in revenue by July 1, 1941.
1940 Apr. 30	The first licensed American woman prize-fight referee, Belle Martell, is licensed by the California State Athletic Commission.
1941 Jan. 15	Jack Burke, Sr., wins the first Professional Golfers' Association Senior Championship, which is held in Sarasota, Florida.
1941 Feb. 26	The Cowboy's Amateur Association of America is organized in Hanford, California.
1941 Mar. 10	Larry MacPhail, general manager of the Brooklyn Dodgers, confirms that the Brooklyn players wear batting helmets invented by two Johns Hopkins Hospital surgeons, Dr. George Barnett and Dr. Walter Dandy. He predicts that every major league player will be wearing them before long.
1941 Mar. 29	The first National Collegiate Fencing Championship is held at Ohio State University with nineteen colleges and seventy-six individual contestants entered.
1941 Apr. 9	The Golf Hall of Fame is organized with Bobby Jones, Francis Ouimet, Walter Hagen, and Gene Sarazen as its first members.
1941 July 3	In Columbus, Ohio, at Ohio State University, Eleanor Dudley wins the women's national intercollegiate golf championship. It is the first time this competition is held.

1942 Jan. 20   The Amateur Athletic Union announces plans for broadening its competitive program to provide instruction and competition at various camps, forts, and naval stations to both train and entertain members of the armed forces and to bring non-military citizens into the sports fields to better fit them for future call to service.

1942 Feb. 14   Cornelius Warmerdan sets a new world record for the pole vault of 15 feet 7¼ inches. It is the fifteenth time he has vaulted 15 feet or better.

1942 Feb. 24   In order to make the weapons available for war plant protection and guard duties, the federal government stops all deliveries of twelve gauge shotguns for sporting use.

1942 Mar. 1   Torger Tokle sets an American ski jump record of 289 feet at Iron Mountain, Michigan.

1942 Mar. 19   The Thoroughbred Racing Association of the United States, an association of race track operators, is formed in Chicago, Illinois.

1942 July 8   As a rubber conservation measure, automobile and motorcycle racers are prohibited from racing after July 31, for the duration of the war by order of the Office of Defense Transportation.

1944 May 23   University of Chicago notifies the Big Ten Conference that it is withdrawing from all athletic competition.

1945 Jan. 4   Ann Curtis, holder of eight national AAU swimming titles, is announced as the first woman to receive the James E. Sullivan Memorial Trophy.

1945 Jan. 31   Five Brooklyn College basketball players admit they accepted a $1,000 bribe to throw a game with Akron University.

1945 May 7   Branch Rickey announces in Brooklyn the formation of the United States Negro Baseball League, which is composed of six teams.

1945 July 11   The Interstate Commerce Commission forbids railroads and commercial motor carriers to transport race horse and show animals as a wartime conservation measure.

1946 Jan. 1   The first Gator Bowl is played in Jacksonville, Florida. Wake Forest defeats South Carolina 26-14.

1946 May 6   The New York Yankees become the first baseball club to travel by air for a full season when they sign with United Airlines for the 1946 season.

1946 June 6   The Basketball Association of America is formed in New York.

1946 June 19   The Joe Louis-Billy Conn fight to be held in New York at Yankee Stadium becomes the first boxing match at which tickets sell for $100.

1946 June 19	The first heavyweight boxing championship fight to be televised outside of the local fight area is the Joe Louis-Billy Conn fight held in New York. It is transmitted to Washington, D.C., by coaxial cable.
1947 Mar. 11	The American Bowling Congress convention refuses to revoke a rule limiting participation in the annual tournament to "the white male race."
1947 Apr. 11	Jackie Robinson plays in an exhibition game for the Brooklyn Dodgers against the New York Yankees to become the first Negro major league baseball player in modern times.
1947 Apr. 15	Jackie Robinson plays his first major league game for the Brooklyn Dodgers, a game against the Boston Braves in Brooklyn.
1947 June 12	Mildred (Babe) Didrikson Zaharias becomes the first American-born woman golfer to win the British women's amateur golf tournament.
1947 June 27	The first collegiate world series baseball games begin at Western Michigan College in Kalamazoo, Michigan. California wins the baseball series 8-7 over Yale.
1947 July 5	Larry Doby joins the Cleveland Indians lineup in a game against the Chicago White Sox in Chicago, Illinois, becoming the first Negro in baseball's American League.
1947 July 16	Rocky Graziano wins the world middleweight title from Tony Zale in a Chicago, Illinois, fight that grosses $422,918, a record for an indoor fight.
1947 Nov. 23	In the South's first interracial football game, the black Willow Tree Athletic Club of Washington and the white Vulpine Athletic Club of Philadelphia play to a 6-6 tie in the Piedmont Tobacco Bowl before a nonsegregated crowd in Durham, North Carolina.
1948 Feb. 5	Gretchen Fraser becomes the first American woman slalom Olympic champion, winning the silver medal in the Alpine combination in Saint Moritz, Switzerland.
1948 Feb. 5	Richard Button becomes the first American Olympic figure skating champion.
1948 Mar. 11	Reginald Weir becomes the first Negro tennis player to participate in the United States Indoor Lawn Association Championship tournament by competing in the tournaments held in New York.
1948 Apr. 6	Mildred (Babe) Didrikson Zaharias is barred from the National Golf Tournament in Los Angeles, California, when the United States Golf Association rules the tournament is restricted to men only.
1948 Aug. 6	Bob Mathias wins the decathlon at the Olympic Games in London, England.

1948 Aug. 14   The first Junior Amateur Golf Championship, held at the University of Michigan Golf Course, is won by Dean Lind. He defeats Ken Venturi in match play.

1949 Aug. 3   The Basketball Association of America and the National Basketball League merge into the National Basketball Association.

1949 Sept. 13   The Ladies Professional Golf Association of America is formed in New York.

1950 Jan. 7   The first Senior Bowl football game for North and South all-star teams of college seniors is held in Jacksonville, Florida. The South defeats the North 22-13.

1950 Apr. 22   The American Bowling Congress is fined by Superior Court Judge John Sbarbaro in Chicago, Illinois, for limiting its membership to white males.

1950 Apr. 30   Fred Wilt runs the fastest outdoor mile ever run by an American, 4 minutes 5.5 seconds, in the Boardwalk Mile in Atlantic City, New Jersey.

1950 May 12   A thirty-four-year-old rule limiting the American Bowling Congress membership to white males only is abolished.

1950 May 24   Nat (Sweetwater) Clifton becomes the National Basketball Association's first Negro player when he is sold by the Harlem Globetrotters to the New York Knickerbockers.

1950 June 5   The Women's International Bowling Congress ends its membership restrictions against nonwhites.

1950 Aug. 8   Florence Chadwick swims the English Channel in 13 hours 28 minutes from France to England. It is a new speed record for women, beating Gertrude Ederle's 1926 record of 14 hours 31 minutes.

1950 Nov. 15   Arthur Dorrington becomes the first Negro player to be signed by organized hockey when he signs with Atlantic City of the Eastern Amateur League.

1951 Jan. 14   The first National Football League Pro Bowl All-Star Game is held in Los Angeles, California. The American Conference defeats the National Conference 28-17.

1951 Jan. 21   Mildred (Babe) Didrikson Zaharias wins the Tampa Women's Open Golf Tournament. Her total score of 288 sets a new women's golfing record for seventy-two hole medal play.

1951 Jan. 22   Phil Rizzuto, New York Yankee shortstop, wins the first annual Ray Hickok professional athlete of the year award with the prize of a $10,000 belt.

1951 Feb. 17   In an effort to discourage off-track gambling, the Florida State Racing Commission rules that race results cannot be transmitted by news services from Florida until twenty minutes after they are posted.

1951 Apr. 24   The Soviet Union, which has never competed in the Olympics, announces the formation of a National Olympic Committee and applies for Olympic competition in the 1952 games.

1951 July 14   Citation wins the Hollywood Gold Cup at Hollywood Park in Inglewood, California. The win pushes his career earnings to $1,085,760, and he becomes the first horse to top $1 million in winnings.

1951 July 14   The first sports event to be televised in color is the Molly Pitcher Handicap at the Monmouth Park Race Track in Oceanport, New Jersey. It is televised by the Columbia Broadcasting System.

1951 Aug. 11   The first baseball games televised in color are a doubleheader in New York between the Brooklyn Dodgers and the Boston Braves. They are televised by WCBS-TV.

1951 Sept. 29   The first network televised football game in color is the University of California versus the University of Pennsylvania, which California wins 35-0. It is televised over CBS from Franklin Field in Philadelphia, Pennsylvania.

1951 Oct. 3   The first coast-to-coast televised prize fight is a middleweight fight between Dave Sands and Bobo Olson, which Sands wins. The fight is televised by CBS from Chicago, Illinois.

1952 Jan. 19   The Professional Golfers' Association Tournament committee votes to modify a rule against Negro entries in golf tournaments that had been sanctioned previously by the PGA by deciding blacks could play if they were invited by local tournament sponsors.

1952 Jan. 20   Patricia McCormick, the first American woman bullfighter, makes her professional debut in Ciudad Juarez, Mexico.

1952 Feb. 4   Jackie Robinson of the Brooklyn Dodgers becomes the first Negro executive of a major radio or television network when he is named director of communication activities for NBC's New York stations.

1952 Feb. 16   A report adopted by the executive committee of the American Council on Education urges the deemphasis of football and other intercollegiate sports, including the banning of post-season games and the abolition of spring practice and outright athletic scholarships.

1952 Feb. 20   Emmet Ashford becomes the first Negro umpire in organized baseball when he is authorized as a substitute umpire in the Class C Southwestern International League.

1952 Apr. 26   Patty Berg shoots a 64 for eighteen holes, a women's record for major golfing competition, in a tournament at Richmond, California.

1953 Feb. 13   Senator Edward Johnson warns baseball's major leagues that

Congress will not stand for them destroying minor league baseball by nationwide telecasts such as a proposed baseball game-of-the-week program.

1953 Feb. 15 Tenley Albright becomes the first American woman world figure skating champion by winning the title at Devos, Switzerland.

1953 Feb. 20 United States Court of Appeals Judge Thomas McAllister of Cincinnati rules that organized baseball is a sport and not a business, and thus does not violate antitrust laws.

1953 May 2 The International Committee for Professional Boxing is formed in Paris, France, to standardize rules and regulate the recognition of world boxing titles.

1953 June 14 The Atlantic Coast Conference is established by Duke, South Carolina, North Carolina, Clemson, Maryland, Wake Forest, and North Carolina State, all former members of the Southern Conference.

1954 Mar. 4 The first National Collegiate Athletic Association Skiing Championship is held at Reno, Nevada, with the University of Reno as host.

1954 Mar. 19 The first United States prize fight televised in color, between Joe Giardello and Willie Troy, is shown from Madison Square Garden in New York.

1954 May 4 The first intercollegiate court tennis match in America is held in New York at the Racquet and Tennis Club between Princeton and Yale.

1954 May 6 Roger Bannister becomes the first man to run the mile in less than 4 minutes running the distance in 3 minutes 59.4 seconds at Oxford, England.

1954 Aug. 16 *Sports Illustrated* publishes its first issue.

1955 Jan. 24 For the 1955 season baseball's rule committee, in an attempt to speed up games, announces strict enforcement of the twenty second rule, which requires a pitcher to deliver the ball within twenty seconds after he takes his pitching position, providing the bases are unoccupied.

1955 Feb. 6 President Dwight D. Eisenhower is cited by the Golf Writers Association of America as the person making an outstanding contribution to golf in 1954.

1955 Aug. 26 The Davis Cup matches at Forest Hill in New York between Australia and the United States televised by the National Broadcasting Company become the first tennis tournament to be televised in color.

1956 May 5 The first runner to run a mile in less than four minutes in the United States is Jim Bailey, who runs it in 3 minutes 58.6 seconds in Los Angeles, California.

1956 June 23   Swaps sets a world record of 1 minute 39 seconds for thoroughbred racing for the one mile and a sixteenth distance at Hollywood Park Race Track in Inglewood, California.

1957 Jan. 28   Emmett Kelly, formerly the star clown of the Ringling Brothers, Barnum and Bailey Circus is signed by the Brooklyn Dodgers to entertain at ball games.

1957 Feb. 11   The National Hockey League Players Association is formed in New York.

1957 Feb. 23   The United States Supreme Court rules that the National Football League's operations are within the coverage of the antitrust laws.

1957 Apr. 15   President Eisenhower opens the baseball season by pitching two balls in Washington's Griffith Stadium. The first ball is sent to the Baseball Hall of Fame as the ten millionth A. G. Spalding and Brothers ball made for the major leagues since 1876.

1957 June 15   Gallant Man wins the Belmont Stakes in an American record time of 2 minutes 26.6 seconds for the one mile and a half distance.

1957 July 6   Althea Gibson becomes the first Negro to win a Wimbledon singles title when she wins the women's singles tennis title.

1957 July 21   Althea Gibson wins the women's national clay court singles title, the first Negro to win a major United States tennis title.

1960 Feb. 9   A no-tampering verbal pact concerning player contracts is announced between the American Football League and the National Football League.

1960 May 21   John Thomas makes a world outdoor high jump record of 7 feet 1¾ inches at a track meet in Cambridge, Massachusetts.

1961   Congress enacts the sports broadcast act, which allows teams to bargain for television money as a group.

1961 Jan. 16   Mickey Mantle signs a $75,000 contract to become the highest paid baseball player in the American League.

1961 Jan. 22   Wilma Rudolph sets a women's sixty yard dash world indoor record of 6.9 seconds; Ralph Boston sets a world indoor broad jump record of 25 feet 10 inches; and Parry O'Brien sets a world indoor shot-put record of 63 feet 1½ inches at a Los Angeles, California track meet.

1961 Jan. 28   Valeri Brumel of the Soviet Union breaks the world indoor high jump record by jumping 7 feet 4½ inches at a meet in Leningrad, Russia.

1961 Apr. 27   Canton, Ohio is selected as the site for the Professional Football Hall of Fame.

1962 Jan. 22   Jackie Robinson and Bob Feller are elected to the Baseball

Hall of Fame. With his election, Robinson becomes the first Negro to receive this honor.

1962 Feb. 2   John Uelses becomes the first man to pole vault 16 feet by clearing 16 feet ¼ inch at the Millrose Games in New York.

1962 Feb. 10   Jim Beatty becomes the first American to run the indoor mile in less than four minutes, accomplishing the feat in 3 minutes 58.9 seconds in Los Angeles, California.

1962 Feb. 15   CBS is contracted in New York to pay the National Collegiate Athletic Association $10,200,000 during the next two years for exclusive rights to televise NCAA football games. It is the highest fee paid so far for a sports package on a per year basis.

1962 Mar. 2   Wilt Chamberlain sets a record for the most free throws made by an individual in one professional basketball game with twenty-eight free throws and also sets a record of 100 points for the most points scored by an individual in one game in a game between Philadelphia and New York in Hershey, Pennsylvania.

1963 Jan. 29   Seventeen men are named as charter members of the Professional Football Hall of Fame in Canton, Ohio.

1963 Feb. 16   Mary Revell of Detroit, Michigan, makes the first recorded round trip swim across the strait of Messina between Sicily and the Italian mainland.

1963 Feb. 20   Willie Mays of the San Francisco Giants signs his 1963 contract for an estimated $100,000 and becomes baseball's highest salaried player.

1963 Aug. 24   Don Schollander becomes the first man to break the two minute mark for swimming the 200 meter freestyle in Osaka, Japan, with a winning time of 1 minute 58.4 seconds.

1963 Aug. 24   John Pennel becomes the first man to pole vault seventeen feet when he clears 17 feet ¾ inches with a fiberglass pole at the Gold Coast track and field meet in Miami, Florida.

1963 Dec. 7   The instant replay is used for the first time by CBS, while televising Army-Navy football game.

1964 Jan. 24   The Columbia Broadcasting Company wins the television rights to the American Football League games for 1965-1969 with its bid of $36,000,000.

1964 Feb. 25   Muhummad Ali (Cassius Clay) wins the world heavyweight boxing championship from Sonny Liston.

1965 Jan. 2   Joe Namath signs a $400,000 contract with the New York Jets to become the richest rookie in professional football history.

1965 Feb. 13   Sixteen-year-old Peggy Fleming wins the United States ladies senior figure-skating title at Lake Placid, New York.

1965 Apr. 9   President Lyndon Johnson attends the opening of the Astrodome in Houston, Texas, for the first major league baseball game ever played indoors.

1966 Feb. 14   Wilt Chamberlain of the Philadelphia 76ers sets a National Basketball Association career scoring record of 20,884 points in seven seasons of play in a game in Charleston, West Virginia.

1966 Apr. 18   Bill Russell is named the Boston Celtics player-coach becoming the first Negro to coach a major professional sports team.

1966 June 20   The United States Open golf championship begins in San Francisco, California. It is the first time a golf tournament is held with major television color broadcasting.

1966 July 17   Jim Ryun runs the mile in 3 minutes 51.3 seconds, trimming 2.3 seconds from the world record.

1967 Jan. 1   The Green Bay Packers defeat the Dallas Cowboys 34-27 for the National Football League Championship and the right to represent the National Football League in the first Super Bowl.

1967 Jan. 15   The first Super Bowl game is held in Los Angeles, California at the Coliseum. The Green Bay Packers defeat the Kansas City Chiefs 35-10.

1967 Jan. 31   Thirty-eight members of the Harness Tracks of America establish a protective force similar to the Thoroughbred Racing Protective Bureau to control unlawful practices in their sport.

1967 Feb. 2   The formation of the second professional basketball league, the American Basketball Association, is announced.

1967 Feb. 18   Bob Seagren sets a world indoor pole vault record of 17 feet 3 inches at the Knights of Columbus meet in Cleveland, Ohio.

1967 Feb. 23   Jim Ryun sets an indoor half mile record of 1 minute 48.3 seconds at a meet in Lawrence, Kansas.

1967 Mar. 18   Doris Brown of Seattle, Washington, wins the first international cross-country race for women in Barry, Wales.

1967 June 20   Muhummad Ali is given five-year sentence and a $10,000 fine for draft avoidance.

1968 Jan. 4   The United Soccer Association and the National Professional Soccer League announce their merger into a new two-division Professional Soccer League.

1968 Jan. 25   Bob Seagren clears 17 feet 4¼ inches for a new world record mark for the indoor pole vault at the Millrose Games, in Madison Square Garden, New York.

1968 Feb. 17   The Naismith Memorial Basketball Hall of Fame at Springfield College in Springfield, Massachusetts, is opened.

1968 Feb. 21	An agreement between the Major League Baseball Players Association and club owners is ratified and increases the minimum annual salary for major league players to $10,000.
1968 May 27	The National League votes to expand its league to twelve teams by awarding new baseball franchises to San Diego and Montreal.
1969 Jan. 12	The New York Jets score a 16-7 upset over the Baltimore Colts giving the American Football League its first major triumph over the National Football League and its first Super Bowl victory.
1969 Feb. 7	At Hialeah Race Track in Miami, Florida, Diane Crump becomes the first woman jockey to ride at a United States pari-mutuel track, but she finishes tenth in a field of twelve horses.
1969 Feb. 22	Barbara Jo Rubin becomes the first winning woman jockey at a United States thoroughbred race track with pari-mutuel betting. She rides Cohesion to victory in Charleston, West Virginia.
1969 Mar. 22	UCLA becomes the first collegiate team to capture three consecutive National Collegiate Athletic Association basketball championships by defeating Purdue 92-72. John Wooden, the UCLA coach, becomes the first coach to win five NCAA titles, and Lew Alcindor becomes the first to win the tournaments' most valuable player award three years in a row.
1969 Apr. 8	The first international baseball game of the major leagues is played by the Montreal Expos and the New York Mets in New York's Shea Stadium.
1969 May 10	The American Football League and the National League agree on plans to merge the two leagues for the 1970-1971 season into two conferences of thirteen teams each.
1969 Aug. 23	Audrey McElmory of La Jolla, California, wins the road race title at the world cycling championships in Brno, Czechoslovakia. She gives the United States its first bicycle racing title since 1912.
1970 Jan. 26	National Football League Commissioner Pete Rozelle announces a $124,000,000 four-year television pack with the three major television networks for the rights to televise National Football League league games, preseason games, playoff games and the Super Bowl.
1970 Jan. 28	Arthur Ashe, American Negro tennis star, is refused a visa by the South African government, which he was trying to obtain in order to compete in the South African Open Tennis Championships.
1970 Feb. 2	Pete Maravich of Louisiana State University becomes the first collegiate basketball player in history to shatter 3,000 points when he tallies 49 points in a game against Mississippi State.

1970 Feb. 15   Billy Kidd of Vermont wins the men's combined title in the
                      Alpine World Ski Championship in Val Gardena, Italy. It is
                      the first United States world title in the Alpine combination.

1970 Aug. 15   Mrs. Pat Palinkas becomes the first woman on record to play
                      in a professional football game when she holds in a game for
                      the Orlando, Florida, Panthers of the Atlantic Coast Con-
                      ference.

1971 Feb. 4   Bowie Kuhn, baseball commissioner, announces a separate
                      section of the Baseball Hall of Fame to honor black players of
                      the preintegration era before 1947.

1971 Feb. 21   Ruth Jensen wins the $60,000 Sears Women's World Classic,
                      the richest event on the women's professional golf tour.

1971 Mar. 8   Joe Frazier defeats Muhummad Ali in Madison Square
                      Garden, New York, in a fight that grosses $1,250,000, a record
                      for an indoor fight.

1971 Apr. 7   New York City opens the country's first legalized off-track
                      betting system.

1971 Oct. 3   Billie Jean King becomes the first female athlete to earn
                      $100,000 in a single year by winning a tennis tournament in
                      Phoenix, Arizona.

1972 Jan. 8   The National Collegiate Athletic Association votes to give
                      major colleges permission to let freshmen play varsity football
                      and basketball thereby expanding the previous 1969 ruling that
                      allowed varsity status in other sports at major colleges and
                      allowing major schools the same basketball-football programs
                      as small schools.

1972 Feb. 16   Wilt Chamberlain of the Los Angeles Lakers becomes the first
                      player in the National Basketball Association to score 30,000
                      points when he finishes a game against the Phoenix Suns with
                      30,003 points. His total is achieved in 940 regular season
                      games.

1972 Mar. 2   Bill Shoemaker sets a new career stakes winning mark by
                      winning the San Jacinto Stakes at Santa Anita Race Track,
                      Arcadia, California, aboard Royal Owl for his 555th lifetime
                      stakes win, one more than retired jockey Eddie Arcaro.

1972 Mar. 6   Jack Nicklaus becomes golf's all-time money winner with his
                      first-place purse of the Doral Eastern Open Tournament. His
                      career earnings reach $1,477,200, which surpass Arnold
                      Palmer's earnings.

1972 Apr. 17   The first women run in the Boston Marathon. Nina Kuscsik,
                      the first of the nine women to cross the tape, finishes ahead of
                      eight hundred male runners.

1972 Sept. 4   Mark Spitz wins his seventh Olympic gold medal competing in
                      the 400 meter swimming medley relay. It is the most ever won

in modern Olympic Games history by one competitor in one series of games.

1973 Jan. 16   Philadelphia Phillies pitcher Steve Carlton signs a one-year contract for a reported $167,000 making him the highest paid pitcher in baseball.

1973 Feb. 20   "The Superstars" in which each performer competes in seven of ten events, although not in his specialty, takes place in Rotonda, Florida. Bob Seagren wins four of seven events and $39,700 in prize money.

1973 Feb. 23   George Woods sets an indoor shot-put record of 69 feet 9½ inches in the National Athletic Amateur Union Indoor Track and Field Championships in New York.

1973 Feb. 25   Negotiators for baseball club owners and players' representatives conclude an agreement calling for the arbitration of individual player salaries, the first time such an agreement has been reached in baseball history.

1973 Feb. 26   Secretariat is syndicated for $5,700,000, which is believed to be the highest price ever paid for a thoroughbred race horse.

1973 Mar. 1   North Sea ridden by Robyn Smith wins the Paumonok Handicap at Aqueduct Race Track in New York and becomes the first major stakes winner ridden by a female jockey.

1973 Apr. 15   Mickey Wright wins $25,000 for winning the Colgate-Dinah Shore Winners Circle Tournament, the richest golf tournament ever held for women.

1973 Apr. 9   Major Jones Wigger of the United States Army shoots a world record 600 for 600 to take a gold medal and lead the United States to a team gold medal for English match shooting in the Benito Juarez International Shooting Meet in Mexico City, Mexico.

1973 May 5   Rosemary Casals earns the largest purse, $30,000, in professional women's tennis history by winning the NBC Family Circle Cup Tournament at Hilton Head Island, South Carolina.

1973 May 26   Kathy Schmidt sets an American women's javelin record of 207 feet 10 inches in the California Relays in Modesto, California.

1973 June 11   The Pennsylvania Justice Department rules that women may be licensed to box or wrestle in Pennsylvania.

1973 July 11   Dwight Stones sets a world record in the high jump with a leap of 7 feet 6½ inches at a track meet in Munich, Germany.

1973 Aug. 10   Lynne Cox, a sixteen-year-old California girl, sets a world record for swimming the English Channel from England to France in 9 hours 36 minutes, just one minute slower than the men's record set in 1964 by Barry Warson.

1973 Oct. 3   A new organization to represent the interest of the fans against professional team owners and players, known as Fans, Inc., a nonprofit corporation, is established in Wilmington, Delaware, with Charles Reilly, Jr., as president.

1973 Nov. 7   New Jersey becomes the first state in the nation to permit girls to play on little league baseball teams by order of a state civil rights division hearing examiner who says girls should be treated no differently than boys.

1974   By knocking out George Foreman in the eighth round in Zaire, Muhummad Ali becomes the second ex-heavyweight to regain the title.

1974 Sept.   Colonial Charm sets a world record for trotting mares of 1 minute 56.2 seconds when she wins the Transylvania Stakes at Red Mile Race Track in Lexington, Kentucky.

1974   Lou Brock steals 118 bases, shattering Maury Wills's mark of 104 set in 1962.

1975 Apr. 8   Frank Robinson makes his debut as the first black manager in major league baseball. As designated hitter for the Indians, he hit a home run in his first at-bat as Cleveland defeats the New York Yankees 5-3.

1975   Pelé comes out of retirement to play for the New York Cosmos and gives a great boost to soccer in the United States.

1976   The Philadelphia Phillies professional baseball team is paid $3,497,900 in player salaries.

1976 Feb. 4   U.S. District Judge John W. Oliver upholds arbitrators' 1975 ruling that pitchers Dave McNally and Andy Messersmith were no longer bound by their contracts. The decision, upheld on March 9 by a three-judge panel in U.S. Court of Appeals, Eighth Circuit, in St. Louis, struck at the reserve clause and cleared the way for free agent status of players qualifying.

1976 June 18   The National Basketball Association and the American Basketball Association agree to merge for the upcoming season.

1976   Janet Guthrie becomes the first woman driver to enter the Indianapolis 500.

1976   The North American Soccer League expands to twenty teams.

1977   A. J. Foyt becomes the first driver to win the Indianapolis 500 four times.

1977 Jan. 4   The Chicago White Sox hire Mary Shane as a television play-by-play announcer. She is the first woman announcer in major league baseball.

1977   Average annual salary for a professional basketball player is $143,000.

1977	Twenty-eight professional football teams gross $250 million, which includes $60 million from national television.
1977	Seattle Slew wins the Triple Crown, the first since Secretariat in 1973.
1977	Muhummad Ali earns $5.75 million boxing; Jimmy Connors $922,657 playing tennis; and O. J. Simpson $733,358 playing football.
1978	Affirmed, the Trip Crown winner, becomes the first thoroughbred to win over $2 million in purses.
1979 June 26	Muhummad Ali retires from boxing after regaining the world heavyweight boxing championship for the third time.
1979	Sebastian Coe of England sets the world mile running record at 3 minutes 49 seconds.
1979	AFL-CIO grants a charter to the 1,900 member Federation of Professional Athletes. The group becomes the 105th affiliate and the first card-carrying athletes.
1980 July 19-Aug. 13	The XXII Olympic Games are held in Moscow, the first ever staged in a Communist country. The U.S.-led boycott reduces the number of participating athletes from an estimated 10,000 to 6,000.
1981 June 12	First midseason baseball strike is caused by disagreement between players and owners over free-agent compensation. All 650 active major-league players take part in the strike. The average income of a major leaguer is $173,000 a year.

Important Research Centers, Collections, and Directories

This appendix presents information on important research centers and collections; these are divided into two general categories: (1) art centers, halls of fame, and museums and (2) libraries, archives, and institutes. Material in the first category is divided alphabetically by sport and followed by information on general, regional, and special sports art collections; libraries and institutes also are listed alphabetically. There is finally a bibliography of books that are helpful in locating important centers. With few exceptions, the information on centers and collections is based upon responses received directly from librarians, curators, and directors. Still, directories were helpful in many ways. In some volumes, some of the information is outdated, but this is only to be expected, for the accuracy of any directory or encyclopedia cannot be guaranteed indefinitely, especially in the cases of museums and libraries. While one museum opens, another may close; a library may cease collecting in one area and begin again in an entirely different field. Even with these limitations in mind, these directories and guides are of great value in locating sporting material in the United States and Canada.

ART CENTERS, HALLS OF FAME, AND MUSEUMS

ARMS AND RIFLERY

The National Rifle Association of America. 1600 Rhode Island Avenue N.W., Washington, D.C. 20036. The NRA Firearms Museum is one of the largest concentrated displays of guns in the United States. It contains more than 1,500 rifles, carbines, shotguns, air guns and pistols, including basic models and many rare variations. Also exhibited are sporting arms, military weapons, and police handguns. The NRA publishes *The American Rifleman*.

The Remington Arms Museum. Ilion, N.Y. 13357. This collection of firearms includes examples of every type of sporting and military gun made by the Remington Arms Company from its founding in 1816. Consisting of over 300 different models, including rifles, shotguns, and handguns, the collection spans the development of firearms in America from the earliest flintlock to the latest autoloader.

AUTO RACING

The Indianapolis Motor Speedway and Museum. Indianapolis, Ind. 46224. One of the most fascinating tourist attractions in America, the museum exhibits sixty famous cars simultaneously, including those that won twenty-two of the annual Indianapolis 500 events. Among the winning cars are Ray Harroun's 1911 Marmon Wasp and Bobby Unser's 1968 Rislone Special.

BASEBALL

The National Baseball Hall of Fame and Museum. Cooperstown, N.Y. 13326. The collection of memorabilia in America's most famous sports hall of fame consists of uniforms, gloves, autographed baseballs, hats, trophies, and medals. A vast library houses 1,200 volumes of scrapbooks as well as numerous films, records, and tapes. A $2 million addition was begun in 1980. See the annual brochure *National Baseball Hall of Fame and Museum.*

BASKETBALL

Naismith Memorial Basketball Hall of Fame. 460 Alden Street, Springfield, Mass. 01109. Like the Baseball Hall of Fame, this is a staggering collection of historical items, including trophies, uniforms, photographs, and audio-visual displays. Movies are shown hourly. A large basketball library is available for research by appointment. For a comprehensive description, see Sandy Padwe, *Basketball's Hall of Fame* (Englewood Cliffs, N.J.: Prentice-Hall, 1970).

FIGURE SKATING

The United States Figure Skating Association. 21 Weybosset Street, North Weymouth, Mass. 02191. The association, housing trophies and medals, offers a retrospective look at competitive figure skating, works of art depicting skating scenes, and exhibits illustrating the history of the figure skate, as well as relevant pamphlets, rule books, and other publications.

FISHING

American Fishing Tackle Manufacturers Association. 2625 Clearhook Drive, Arlington Heights, Ill. 60005. The association has recently opened a library and museum.

Gladding International Sport Fishing Museum, Inc. Octagon House, South Otselic, N.Y. 13155. Dedicated to the preservation of sport fishing and committed to the promotion of sensible conservation measures, the nonprofit Gladding International Sport Fishing Museum is supported by America's oldest fishing tackle manufacturer, the Gladding Corporation, which was founded in 1816. Their collection, donated by people who love sport fishing, features valuable, handmade, antique fishing rods, rare reels and lures, historic fishing tackle catalogs, famous paintings and original prints of fishing scenes, and a significant library of old and new books on angling and related subjects.

The International Game Fish Association. Fort Lauderdale, Fla. 33300. They have an excellent library and collection of material on fly fishing.

Museum of American Fly Fishing. Manchester, Vt. 05254. The museum is a major repository of material, consisting of over 600 rods, 400 reels, 1,000 hooks, and countless other items. The collection is uncatalogued, but the museum publishes a quarterly journal, *The American Fly Fisher.*

FOOTBALL

Canadian Football Hall of Fame. 58 Jackson Street West, Hamilton, Ontario, Canada L8P 1L4. One of the most impressive of the halls of fame in its visual displays, the Canadian Football Hall of Fame is a national shrine to professional football in Canada. It traces the history of the game for 100 years. Among intriguing features of the center are a pigskin wall, a stained-glass wall, and a computer that answers questions put to it by fans.

The National Football Foundation and Hall of Fame, Inc. 201 East 42d Street, Suite 1506, New York, N.Y. 10017. The foundation recognizes distinguished coaches and players and grants graduate scholarships and awards, one of which is the MacArthur Bowl. Executive offices are maintained in New York, but the memorabilia have been moved to the College Football Hall of Fame, P.O. Box 300, Kings Mills, Ohio 45034.

Pro Football Hall of Fame. 2121 Harrison Avenue, N.W., Canton, Ohio 44708. In addition to the museum, which surveys the entire history of pro football by means of graphics, films, mementoes, and audio aids, there is a research library containing files on thousands of players, defunct teams, current teams, and items of general interest, game programs dating back to 1920, complete sets of major sports periodicals, and a comprehensive football book collection. Research help is offered via the postal service.

GOLF

The Canadian Golf Museum and Historical Institute. Kingsway Park, Mountain Road, Alymer East, Quebec, Canada JH9 5C9. The museum contains the private collection of William Lyn Stewart, which consists of equipment, books, and prints gathered over a lifetime. Among the items are excellent examples of nineteenth-century clubs. The evolution of the golf ball is depicted from the 1830s to today's high compression ball. Old golf prints as well as several autographed pictures of champions are on exhibit. The library contains numerous volumes, including rare editions.

Golf House. Route 512, P.O. Box Golf, Far Hills, N.J. 07936. This is a permanent exhibit of clubs, halls, medals, pictures, portraits, and documents that trace the history of golf. It is believed to be the most extensive golf collection on display. An excellent golf library of some 6,000 volumes is available for reference or browsing. Among notable items is the Moon Club used by Admiral Alan B. Shepard, Jr., to play a shot on the surface of the moon on February 6, 1971. Also on display are the golf balls and clubs used by several U.S. presidents. The medals won by Bobby Jones also are housed in the museum, as well as portraits of a number of prominent golfers, men and women, a head sculpture of Arnold Palmer by Eleanor Mellon, and a statue of Ben Hogan by Henry Van Wolfe.

James River Golf Museum. James River Country Club, U.S. Highway 60, Newport News, Va. 23601. Depicting the history of golf in the United States and abroad, the museum claims to house the finest collection of antique golfing implements in this country, perhaps the world. The library has a collection of over 750 volumes.

The World Golf Hall of Fame. P.O. Box 1908, Pinehurst, N.C. 28374. Housed in a beautiful building on a famous course, the World Golf Hall of Fame attracts thousands of visitors annually. Induction into the hall is based on the simple criterion of achievement. As of 1979 a total of thirty-seven golfers had been inducted in three categories; Modern Era, Distinguished Service, and Pre-modern Era. Among the Moderns are such familiar names as Palmer, Nicklaus, Snead, Hogan, Berg, and Zaharias. Among the exhibits collected by Don Collett is the memorabilia previously belonging to Laurie Auchterlonie, the Saint Andrews professional, and containing the two oldest known clubs in the world, made in 1690. Works of art include montage paintings of the enshrinees for each year and a Bobby Jones display. Golf films are shown daily in the theater, and the library owns volumes dating back to 1800. An interesting and perhaps unique feature of the hall is the "Golf History Wall," which depicts the evolutionary aspects of the game for the past 500 years.

GREYHOUND RACING

Greyhound Hall of Fame. 407 South Buckeye, Abilene, Kan. 67410. The exhibits deal briefly with the history of the Greyhound animal from ancient Greece through eighteenth-century England to the modern racing Greyhound. The collection includes photos from *Harpers Weekly* and prints of the first organized coursing meet near Great Bend, Kansas, in 1886. The research area has several hundred photos, programs, and magazines dating from 1900 to the present.

HOCKEY

Hockey Hall of Fame. Exhibition Place, Toronto, Ontario, Canada M6K 3C3. The picture and photo library is composed of approximately 37,000 pieces. Almost 3000 items are on tangible display, and there are collections of scrapbooks, cards, and miscellaneous items. A book collection of some 500 to 600 works is not open to the public.

International Hockey Hall of Fame and Museum. P.O. Box 82, York and Alfred Streets, Kingston, Ontario, Canada K7L 1X4. No detailed listing of its holdings is available at present. However, among its significant items are photographs of all players, referees, and builders inducted into the hall, several scrapbooks that date from the early 1900s but concentrate primarily on the NHL in 1930s, 1940s, and 1950s, and assorted hockey guides and programs from the 1930s, as well as assorted copies of *The Hockey News* and hockey magazines from the 1940s and 1950s. Its president and historian, J. W. (Bill) Fitsell, has a personal collection of approximately 200 hockey books dating from 1899.

United States Hockey Hall of Fame. P.O. Box 657, Eveleth, Minn. 55734. The center employs the unique concept of honoring inductees by pylons instead of paintings or busts. Each pylon contains a photograph and biography. Another special feature is the Hockey Time Tunnel, which relates by sight and sound the evolution of hockey.

HORSE RACING

Hall of Fame of the Trotter. Goshen, N.Y. 10924. As a national registered historic landmark, the museum seeks to preserve the history and appreciation of harness racing. It circulates its exhibits to other galleries, universities, and civic institutions.

Kentucky Derby Museum. Central Avenue, Louisville, Ky. 40208. Founded in 1962 and located on the grounds of Churchill Downs, the museum contains murals, racing memorabilia, saddles, bridles, and trophies. A field research station is listed among its facilities in the *Official Museum Directory*. A valuable compendium for racing historians is *The Kentucky Derby Churchill Downs 1875-1979*, which was published by Churchill Downs, Inc., in 1979. It contains information on Derby winners, owners, trainers, jockeys, breeders, record times, post positions, and even Derby-day weather. It is a racing buff's delight.

The National Museum of Racing, Inc. Saratoga Springs, N.Y. 12866. Located on Union Avenue directly across from the Saratoga Racetrack, the museum was founded in 1950 for the purpose of collecting and preserving material and articles associated with the origin, history, and development of horse racing and the breeding of the thoroughbred horse. The museum has approximately 250 oil paintings on exhibition, including those of Man O' War, Citation, War Admiral, Cavalcade, Sword Dancer, Domino, Lexington, American Eclipse, and Kelso. Among the artists represented are Ben Marshall, Edward Troye, Franklin B. Vors, Richard Stone Reeves, Henry Stull, Sir Alfred J. Munnings, and Rembrandt Peale. Also found in the collection are 200 sets of famous racing colors, bronze statuary, and gold and silver trophies won by famous horses. The museum serves as a hall of fame for trainers, jockeys, and horses.

LACROSSE

The Canadian Lacrosse Hall of Fame. Box 308, New Westminister, British Columbia, Canada V3L 4Y6. This exhibits a great number of photographs and a sizeable collection of memorabilia relating to the history of the game in Canada. There is a small book collection as well. An expansion program was underway in 1980.

The Lacrosse Foundation, Inc. Hall of Fame and Museum, Newton H. White, Jr., Athletic Center, Homewood, Baltimore, Md. 21218. This is a vast collection of books and memorabilia. The foundation publishes *Lacrosse Magazine* five times per year and distributes *The Official Lacrosse Guide* and other books on history and fundamentals.

RODEO

National Cowboy Hall of Fame and Western Heritage Center. 1700 Northeast 63d Street, Oklahoma City, Okla. 73111. The center has various sporting material representing the rodeo cowboy. The Rodeo Hall of Fame section features the saddles and trophies of the all-round champion cowboys since 1929.

SKIING

The Canadian Ski Museum. 457A Sussex Drive, Ottawa, Ontario, Canada K1N 6Z4. The purpose of the museum is to preserve the skiing way of life by focusing upon "its meaningful context in the development of man."

The Society of the National Ski Hall of Fame. United States Ski Educational Foundation, Inc., National Headquarters Division, P.O. Box 191, Ishpeming, Mich. 49849. The society has a sizeable collection of skis and poles, mostly handmade and varying greatly in design and workmanship. The library contains an estimated 500 books, as well as several hundred yearbooks, both domestic and foreign, and hundreds of periodicals and ski newspapers.

SOARING AND HANG-GLIDING

Frankfort-Elberta National Soaring Hall of Fame and Museum. 403 Main Street, Frankfort, Mich. 49635. This hall of fame claims to be the only one staging an annual festival. Upwards of 60,000 people attend a week-long competition in soaring and hang-gliding. Mementoes in the museum highlight the history of sport for half a century.

SOFTBALL

National Softball Hall of Fame and Museum. P.O. Box 11437, 2801 N.E. 50th Street, Oklahoma city, Okla., 73136. This center honors the outstanding players of America's largest team participant sport. The center recognizes stars of the game, displays memorabilia and equipment of the past and present, and maintains a library and research center.

SWIMMING

Aquatic Hall of Fame and Museum of Canada, Inc. 436 Main Street, Winnipeg, Manitoba, Canada R3B 1B2. The hall possesses a large collection of aquatic memorabilia, works of art, and an extensive library. The natatorium complex covers an area of more than thirteen acres on Poseidon Bay. The center boasts an impressive exhibition of aquatic art and one of the finest sports stamp collections in the world.

International Swimming Hall of Fame, Inc. 1 Hall of Fame Drive, Fort Lauderdale, Fla. 33316. The general collection on the first floor consists of trophies and medals, sculpture, paintings, stamp collections, old swim suits, various displays on swimming, including marathon swimming, diving, water polo, and Olympic games, and various scrapbooks and publications. The second floor is devoted to exhibits of honorees.

TENNIS

International Tennis Hall of Fame. 194 Bellevue Avenue, Newport, R.I. 02840. The library of the hall contains approximately 500 volumes, a large collection of tennis magazines, United States Tennis Association handbooks, and many old photographs. The scores of tennis matches dating from the first men's national championships held in Newport in 1881 are also available.

TRACK AND FIELD

The National Track and Field Hall of Fame of the U.S.A. 1524 Kanawha Boulevard East, Charleston, W. Va. 25311. This is a national shrine honoring those heroes and heroines of the past and present and dedicated to the youth of the future. A library and films are available.

The United States Track and Field Hall of Fame. P.O. Box 297, Angola, Ind. 46703. This is still a young organization and its memorabilia have been obtained from inductees. The first induction ceremonies were held in August 1974. The overall goals are to search out, record, preserve, honor, and perpetuate through research and education, the records and histories and evaluation of events of those American men and women who have performed so well in track and field. The permanent facility will house research and development laboratories, complete indoor and outdoor track facilities, exhibition areas, a seminar auditorium, and a fieldhouse.

WRESTLING

National Wrestling Hall of Fame. 405 West Hall of Fame Avenue, Stillwater, Okla. 74074. Displays, library, and films are built around the history of collegiate and amateur wrestling, including Olympic competition, from the late 1890s to the present. The collection includes medals, wrestling uniforms, items on the evolution of protective headgear, and over a hundred titles of nonfiction works on wrestling, sports medicine, the history of Olympic Games, and biographies, as well as some fiction on wrestling. The focal point of the museum is the life-size copy of the *The Wrestlers* by Cephisodotus, which is the largest known sculpture in the world created from a single block of green marble. The museum also contains Honors Court, an area that recognizes outstanding wrestlers, coaches and contributors.

GENERAL COLLECTIONS

Buffalo Bill Historical Center. Box 1020, Cody, Wy. 82414. One of the great attractions of the American West, the Buffalo Bill Museum could be a valuable source for anyone doing research into the history of American sporting life or even show business. It contains not only a fabulous collection of Winchester guns and memorabilia relating to the wild west show but also the impressive Whitney Gallery of Western Art, which has numerous scenes of hunting and outdoor life, as well as the Plains Indian Museum.

Citizens Savings Athletic Foundation Sports Museum, Sport Libraries. 9800 South Sepulveda, Los Angeles, Cal. 90045. The museum maintains a comprehensive collection of sporting memorabilia, consisting of uniforms and equipment worn by champions, hundreds of photographs of noted athletes, and countless awards, trophies, and medallions entrusted to it by athletes, coaches, and sportsmen. The sports library, which is open to members of the press, scholars, and students, is especially strong on the Olympic Games. The foundation also maintains an extensive sports film library.

The Smithsonian Institution, The National Museum of History and Technology. Washington, D.C. 20506. Numerous artifacts related to the history of American sports and recreation are currently on display in the "A Nation of Nations" exhibit in the National Museum of History and Technology. Among representative examples of this category are Hank Aaron's baseball uniform, over 1,500 baseball cards from cigarette and gum packets from 1900 to 1975, the boxing gloves of Muhummad Ali, the professional uniform of Pelé and 103 scrapbooks and memorabilia pertaining to the career of Joe Louis. On exhibit from the Division of Community Life are "Ride On," a display on the history of bicycling and "The American Skating Mania," featuring nineteenth-century skates and equipment. The sports and recreation collection in the Division of Community Life is relatively new, but a period of growth is anticipated during the next five to ten years.

REGIONAL CENTERS

British Columbia Sports Hall of Fame. British Columbia Pavilion, Vancouver, British Columbia, Canada VSK 4A9. The hall traces the story of sport in British Columbia. The collection of medals from Olympic, Pan-American, and Commonwealth games is impressive. There is a theatre and a sports film library for use in education and research.

Canada Sports Hall of Fame. Place Exhibition Place, Toronto, Canada, M6K 3C3. Those Canadians who have achieved excellence nationally and internationally in sport are honored here. The library is small but contains the personal collection of John W. Davies, a mainstay of the Commonwealth Games in Canada.

Greater Cleveland Sports Hall of Fame Foundation, Inc. 1375 Euclid Avenue, Suite 412, Cleveland, Ohio 44115. Established in 1976, the Greater Cleveland Sports Hall of Fame honors men and women from the Cleveland area who have distinguished themselves in athletics. Thirteen sports are represented in both the amateur and professional categories. There are no memorabilia other than the plaques that hang on the walls of the Grand Lobby of the Cleveland Public Auditorium. Among the athletes honored are Bob Feller, Lou Groza, Jesse Owens, and Harrison Dillard.

The Michigan Sports Hall of Fame. 1010 Joanne Court, Bloomfield Hills, Mich. 48013. The year 1979 marked the silver anniversary of the Michigan Sports Hall of Fame. The chief activity of the organization is the induction of athletes whose likenesses are inscribed on honorary plaques along with their records of achievement. Inductees include some of the most famous names in the world of sport, such as Ty Cobb, Tom Harmon, Gordie Howe, Joe Louis, and Branch Rickey. Among the inductees for 1979 is Graham Steenhoven, the president of the United States Table Tennis Association, who in 1971 led a party of fifteen American table tennis players to Mainland China and thus helped to open up a new era of relations between the two countries. The induction program for 1979 contained an itinerary of Steenhoven's historical trip.

New Brunswick Sports Hall of Fame. Queen Street, P.O. Box 6000, Fredericton, New Brunswick, Canada ESB 5H1. Permanently located on the second floor of the John Thurston Clark Memorial Building, the hall has honored athletes in all the familiar American sports and in curling and rugby as well. Among those honored is the jockey Ron Turcotte, winner of the Triple Crown of thoroughbred racing aboard Secretariat.

The Newfoundland Sports Hall of Fame. Colonial Building, Room 18, Saint John's, Newfoundland, Canada A1C 2C9. The Newfoundland Sports Hall of Fame and the Newfoundland Archives are related operations that are controlled by the Newfoundland Sports Federation. Although the facilities at present are modest, an amazing number of sports artifacts have been collected, including collections of newspaper clippings and sports photographs and memorabilia dealing with the local scene from the mid-nineteenth century to the present. The oldest continuous sporting event on the North American continent takes place in the province. This is the Saint John's Annual Regatta rowed on Quidi Vidi Lake near the capital.

Saint Louis Hall of Fame. 100 Stadium Plaza, Busch Stadium, Saint Louis, Mo. 63102. The hall features Saint Louis sports with its emphasis on baseball, as its Stan Musial Area and World Series movies of the Cardinals from 1926 to 1967 indicate.

San Diego Hall of Champions, Balboa Park, San Diego, Cal. 92101. This is a public exhibition hall honoring the San Diego area athletes of national fame. The film library contains over 350 films on various sports.

Saskatchewan Sports Hall of Fame. 2205 Victoria Avenue, Regina, Saskatchewan, Canada S4P OS4. The Saskatchewan Sports Hall of Fame has recently undertaken the operation of a museum. It collects artifacts and materials related to the history of sports in the province. The book collection is devoted to general sports histories, biographies of Saskatchewan sportsmen, and archival material.

Sport Nova Scotia. P.O. Box 30105, Halifax, Nova Scotia, Canada B3J 3G6. Although the Nova Scotia Sport Heritage Center exists largely on paper at present, over 1,000 artifacts relating to sports in the area have been collected. The library of approximately 1,000 items consists of general texts and technical materials. An expanded role in the sports history of Nova Scotia is anticipated.

Texas Sports Hall of Fame Foundation. 601 Fidelity Union Life Building, Dallas, Tex. 75201. Founded in 1951 by the Texas Sports Writers Association, the Hall is designed to honor those "whose achievements have brought lasting fame and honor to Texas." Although not yet completed, the main building for Texas Sports Hall of Fame will be located in Grand Prairie between Dallas and Forth Worth on 8.2 acres of land. Among the many legendary heroes of Texas already enshrined are Tris Speaker, Ben Hogan, Sammy Baugh, A. J. Foyt, and Jack Johnson, who was inducted in 1971.

SPORTS ART COLLECTIONS

The Joseph B. Wolfe Collection of the Sculpture of R. Tait McKenzie. Physical Education Building, 1914 Andy Holt Avenue. University of Tennessee, Knoxville, Tenn. 37916. This impressive collection consists of over 100 bronze statuettes, sketches, bas reliefs, medals, portraits, medallions, and plaques. The Wolfe collection is a good representation of the nearly 400 sculptured works of McKenzie, who is generally recognized as the greatest sculptor of athletes of modern times.

Museum of Fine Art. Department of Classical Art, Boston, Mass. 02115. The museum has many pieces of athletic art and objects relating to sports. These include the stone discus, strygils, and weights used in jumping. There are also vases that picture athletes in a variety of activities such as boxing, running, and preparing to jump or to throw the discus, as well as athletes crowned and beribboned. See the following publication of the Department of Classical Art, *Greek, Etruscan and Roman Art: The Classical Collections of the Museum of Fine Arts, Boston* by George Chase and revised by Cornelius Vermeule.

The Smithsonian Institution, National Collection of Fine Arts. Eighth and G Streets, N.W., Washington, D.C. 20560. One group of works in the collection depicts various Indian games by George Catlin.

Spectrum Fine Art Ltd. 30 West Street, N.Y. 10019. Directed by Bill Goff, a sports fan and art dealer, Spectrum is devoted exclusively to the exhibition of art using sports subjects. Thus far Spectrum has featured tennis, baseball, football, hockey, basketball, and boxing. The media include sculptures, paintings, drawings, prints, photographs, and lithographs. Among the artists represented are Thomas Hart Benton, George Bellows, Joe Brown, Ernie Barnes, Curt Flood, and Tug McGraw. Other shows are planned since in Goff's view there is no "shortage of sports art."

Sports Art Center. State University of New York, College at Cortland, N.Y. 13045. Established and directed by Dr. Merle Rousey, the Sports Art Center could and indeed should pave the way for similar approaches at other universities. Housed in the same building as the athletic facilities, the Sports Art Center contains approximately 800 reproductions. Among the artists represented are Winslow Homer, Andrew Wyeth, Salvador Dali, Eastman Johnson, Toulouse-Lautrec, Raoul Dufy, Paul Gauguin, A. F. Tait, Paul Cézanne, Auguste Renoir and Norman Rockwell. One of the corridors of the center is devoted to Olympic art, including an entire series of Russian postage stamps issued in honor of the Olympics.

The Whitney Collection of Sporting Art. Yale University, New Haven, Conn. 06520. The collection contains over 2,000 items, primarily lithographs, which decorate the walls of Payne-Whitney Gymnasium.

Whitney Museum of American Art. 945 Madison Avenue at 75th Street, New York, N.Y. 10021. Sixteen pieces in the permanent collection deal with sports. Among these are *Dempsey and Firpo*, 1924 (oil on canvas) by George Bellows, *Wrestlers*, 1933 (oil on canvas) by Gus Mager, *Ice Skates, Central Park*, 1934 (watercolor on paper) by Cecil C. Bell, and *Four Football Players*, n.d. (gouache) by Carl Sprinchorn.

LIBRARIES, ARCHIVES, AND INSTITUTES

COLLEGES AND UNIVERSITIES

The Bancroft Library. University of California, Berkeley 94720. The quality and quantity vary with each sport. The archives have minute books for crew dating from the late nineteenth century, as well as programs for the Olympic Games. The financial records for the first eastern trip made by the track team in 1895 also are available. Memorabilia include balls used in the Rose Bowl and other games. On file is a history of basketball at the university as well as student papers, dating back several years, on the histories of various sports. The archives contain a large photograph collection that includes many relating to sport. It has been heavily used not only for temporary displays but also for book and periodical illustration.

Beloit College Library. Beloit College, Beloit, Wisconsin 53511. The library possesses the collection of Bob Becker, a sports feature writer for the *Chicago Tribune*. It consists of 320 titles on hunting and fishing.

Bentley Historical Library. University of Michigan. 1150 Beal Avenue, Ann Arbor, Mich. 48109. The Michigan Historical Collections have substantial holdings of manuscript materials, photographs, and memorabilia relating to the history of athletes at the University of Michigan. The library also holds ninety-three volumes of scrapbooks on Joe Louis. A bibliography of materials relating to sports is soon to be published. The materials on hand are briefly described in Thomas E. Powers and William H. McNitt, *Guide to Manuscripts in the Bentley Historical Library* (Ann Arbor, Mich., 1976).

Butler Library. Columbia University, New York, N.Y. 10027. The Butler Library possesses three collections dealing with sports. The Elliot V. Bill Collection consists of over 500 books, covering all aspects of the art and technique of fishing from the seventeenth through the twentieth centuries and twenty-two editions of *The Compleat Angler*. The earliest work in the gift is the London 1615 edition of *The Pleasures of Princes* by Gervase Markham, a scholar and military man who later became a writer of country pursuits, principally fishing and the breeding of horses. The Paul Magriel Boxing Collection contains correspondence, photographs, photographic plates, photostats, clippings, periodicals, and books relating to the history and literature of boxing and the prize ring from Homer to the twentieth century. There is also an unpublished typescript by Magriel on the history of pugilism. The L. S. Alexander Gumby Collection is concerned with various phases of Negro life in America. The material consists of clippings, pamphlets, photographs, extracts from periodicals, letters, signatures, manuscripts, and documents. Most of the material is mounted in 161 scrapbooks of folio leaves. Among the sporting figures represented are Jack Johnson, Joe Louis (9 volumes), Paul Robeson, Jackie Robinson (two volumes), and Sugar Ray Robinson. Other subjects include basketball, football, Negro sports, Olympic Games, and white fighters.

C.W. Post Library. Long Island University, Greenvale, Long Island, N.Y. 11548. The Franklin B. Lord collection consists of nearly 600 books on fishing and hunting. Many of the books date back to the nineteenth century.

The Charles Patterson Van Pelt Library. University of Pennsylvania, Philadelphia, Pa. 19104. The archives and records center contains the personal papers of R. Tait McKenzie and the J. William White Collection, a noncirculating collection of approximately 1,500 books on physiology, medicine, and sports skills. The collection contains McKenzie's glass slides (approximately 100 to 120) on sports, athletic injuries, and war injuries and his photographs of anatomical studies (approximately 50 to 100).

The D.B. Weldon Library (Special Collections). University of Western Ontario, London, Ontario, Canada N6A 3K7. This is an important collection concerning rules, regulations, and pre-Olympic Games organizations. Valuable sources are available on Canadian participation in the British Empire and Commonwealth games, Inter-Allied Games and Pan-American Games. Among a wide range of materials are the minutes of the annual meeting of the Athletic Union of Canada, 1884-1898 and 1908-1954. The collection was useful in the compilation of *Olympic Gold: Canada's Winners in the Summer Games* (Toronto, 1975) by Frank Cosentino and Glynn Leyshon.

The General Libraries, University of Texas at Austin. Austin, Tex. 78712. The Barker Texas History Center houses materials on athletics at the University of Texas in Austin that includes clippings, photographs, and other memorabilia, as well as official archives. The photography collection of the Humanities Research Center includes photographs of sporting figures and teams, not necessarily American.

Goldfarb Library. Brandeis University, 415 South Street, Waltham, Mass. 02154. *Subject Collections* lists a remarkable collection of Dime Novel Judaica and two complete sets of the Merriwell library (245 volumes).

Hallis Burke Frissel Library. Tuskegee Institute, Tuskegee, Ala. 36088. The Robert Stewart Darnaby Collection contains papers on the Negro in American sports, historical materials on the Southern Intercollegiate Athletic Conference, and photographs, programs, and schedules dealing with athletics at Tuskegee.

Haverford College Library. Haverford College, Haverford, Pa. 19041. The C. C. Morris Cricket Library Association collection of books, periodicals, pictures, blazers, trophies, and other cricket memorabilia is the largest in the western hemisphere. Much of the material has to do with cricket in the Philadelphia area, but many of the pictures and most of the books are English. The library has two complete sets of *The American Cricketer* and a complete set of Wisden's *Cricketer's Almanack* (English) from its beginning in 1864. The association distributes newsletters announcing events and other items of interest.

The University of Pittsburgh, Special Collections Department, Hillman Library, Pittsburgh, Pa. 15260. The library is notable for the Bernard S. Horne Memorial Collection, which consists of over 230 editions of *The Compleat Angler*. The library also has a good number of papers collected as *Jorrocks' Jaunts and Jollities* (1838) by the English novelist Robert Smith Surtees, most of which are first editions.

The Karl Auty Memorial Cricket Library. Ridley College, P.O. Box 3013, Saint Catherines, Ontario, Canada L2R 7C3. This remarkable collection of cricket books and artifacts was established in memory of Karl André Auty, who achieved distinction in the field of electrical engineering. There are some 3,000 books in the collection, which is kept up to date by means of endowments. Among the holdings are the scrapbooks of Sir C. Aubrey Smith whose career in cricket dates back to the nineteenth century.

The Leddy Library. University of Windsor, Ontario, Canada N9B 3P4. In addition to maintaining a collection of monographs and serials to support a program to the masters level in human kinetics, emphasizing the philosophy, psychology, sociology, and history of sport, sport administration and organization, and motor learning, the Leddy Library houses the sports archives of the University of Windsor. The sports archives hold materials on the history of Canadian intercollegiate athletics. As the designated depository of the Canadian Intercollegiate Athletic Union (CIAU), the sports archives contain many materials of the CIAU, including its minutes from the founding meeting in 1906, statistics, and playing rules. Also held are the minutes of the Ontario-Quebec Athletic Association for 1956 to 1971 and the minutes of the Ontario Universities Athletic Association from 1972 to date. Along with these materials, the archives contain material on local sports. Included in the collection are transcripts of interviews with a number of local individuals active in sports beginning in the 1920s, as well as scrapbooks and memorabilia compiled by local athletes, coaches, and administrators.

Low Memorial Library. Columbia University, New York, N.Y. 10027. The Columbiana Collection has extensive biographical material and subject files on all sports figures and activities held at Columbia University through the years. These include subject clipping files on such figures as Lou Gehrig and Lou Little. In addition, there are files on all major sports, statistics on various sports, books and memoirs on sports, photographs, and memorabilia such as medals and cups.

McKelding Library. University of Maryland, College Park, Md. 20742. In its book collection, heavy emphasis is placed on sports medicine, that is the physiological, psychological, and social aspects of sports. The library is noted for its coverage on the history and philosophy of sports and the general topic of sports in the United States. McKelding Library concentrates on the research needs of upper division and graduate students and contains an extensive collection of master's theses and doctoral dissertations in microform.

Media Center. Depaul University, 2323 North Seminary Avenue, Chicago, Ill. 60614. The Stuyvesant Peabody Sports Collection contains approximately 900 volumes primarily on British field sports. The collection contains only monographs and periodicals except for one set of twenty hand-colored prints after the original paintings of famous American thoroughbreds by Edward Troye (1808-1874). These prints were published in 1832 at the sign of Gosden Head, New York. The holdings include several texts by Nimrod and Robert Surtees as well as a complete run of *The Sporting Magazine* from 1792 to 1870. Cataloging of the holdings is in process.

Memorial Library. University of Wisconsin, 728 State Street, Madison, Wis. 53706. This is a strong collection of books and serials on sports consisting of over 18,700 volumes.

Montclair State College Library. Montclair State College, Upper Montclair, N.J. 07043. The college library has a unique collection of 150 physical education textbooks from the nineteenth and early twentieth centuries.

Pennsylvania State University. University Park, Pennsylvania 16802. A leading institution in the study of various aspects of sports, it has a number of leading scholars in various fields. Among a wide range of organizations and programs sponsored by the university is the Center for Women and Sport, which is part of the Sports Research Institute of the University. The purpose of the center is to expand research interest in all areas relating to female involvement in physical activity. Specifically the center hopes to identify and describe the female's response to exercise and sport at all levels of involvement throughout her life span. Physiological, endocrinological, psychological, sociological, and biochemical aspects are included. Under the direction of Dr. Dorothy V. Harris, professor of Physical Education, the center also hopes to reduce the ignorance surrounding female involvement in vigorous physical activity and sports by conducting, synthesizing, and disseminating research.

Princeton University Library. Princeton University, Princeton, N.J. 08540. The library lists approximately 1,000 cards under sports in the public catalogue. In addition there are special collections on angling and mountaineering.

Syracuse University Library. Syracuse University, Syracuse, N.Y. 13210. Consisting of approximately thirty-five rare books, the George Arents Collection is not a large one, but it is a quality one as far as it goes. The holdings are primarily in the areas of gymnastics, fencing, hunting, boxing, and wrestling.

Trinity College Library. Trinity College, Hartford, Conn. 06106. The Sherman Parker Walton Collection consists of 250 editions of Izaak Walton's *The Compleat Angler* and over 300 other books on horses, hunting, fishing, and so forth.

University Libraries. University of Notre Dame, Notre Dame, Ind. 46556. The International Sports and Games Research Collection is perhaps the largest collection of sporting documents in the world. There are an estimated 500,000 items covering some 500 sports and games in the collection. Responding to the unprecedented surge of intellectual sensitivity to sports and games, the university established the center in 1966 with a basic commitment to provide serious and scholarly sports research. Recent acquisitions include fifty-six tons of sporting books and publications from around the world. Many of them are rare and irreplacable. The collection includes books, serials, journals, dissertations and theses, clippings, letters, diaries, manuscripts, encyclopedias, statistical records, annuals, programs, press, radio and television guides, photographs, drawings, recordings, motion-picture films, microtexts, and tapes. These holdings constitute a library and not a museum. The library which is unlimited in scope either geographically or categorically, hopes to promote historical and statistical research. The collection is also a repository of films and documents relating to Notre Dame athletics. *The Insport Newsletter*, marking developments and activities surrounding the International Sports and Games Research Collection, is published twice each year.

University of British Columbia Library. University of British Columbia, 2075 Westbrook Place, Vancouver, British Columbia, Canada V6T 1W5. The university collects materials relating to the history of sport in the province. There are a large number of books on angling and a collection of photographs reflecting the activities of the British Columbia Mountaineering Club for some years.

The University of Illinois, Urbana, Ill. 61801. The university is noted as one of the leading centers on many studies of sports and physical education. The Applied Life Studies Libraries is one of the strongest in North America. The four volumes of the *Dictionary Catalog of the Applied Life Studies Library* (Boston, 1976) contains approximately 51,600 cards. The university library is also the repository of the Avery

Brundage Collection compiled by Maynard Brichford, a university archivist. See Maynard Brichford, *Avery Brundage Collection, 1908-1975* (Schorndorf, 1977).

The University of Kentucky Library. University of Kentucky, Lexington, Ky. The university collection is good in boxing, hunting, and fishing. The library has issues of *The Spirit of the Times*, both Porter's *Spirit of the Times* and Wilkes' *Spirit of the Times*. It has a complete run of *The Sporting Magazine* (England) from 1792-1870. The Keeneland and University collections make Lexington a good location for research on history of nineteenth-century sport.

The University of Massachusetts. Amherst, Mass. 01002. The university has a strong faculty and a library capable of supporting a broad range of offerings in physical education, sports studies, exercise science, and leisure/recreation studies. One of the leading programs in the nation is located at the university, that is, the Department of Sports Studies in Curry Hicks Building. For more information see *Sport Management Handbook* (1979), University of Massachusetts, Amherst.

The University of Minnesota. 109 Walter Library, Minneapolis, Minn. 55455. The Kerlan Collection in the Children's Literature Research Collections has manuscripts and books by a number of authors who have written about sports. The Hess Collection has some 70,000 dime novels, many of which are indexed in Johannsen's *The House of Beadle and Adams* (Norman, Okla., 1950).

The Widener Library. Harvard University, Cambridge, Mass. 02138. The library contains approximately 600 cards under "sport" and "sports." The Fearing Collection on angling and fishing contains over 15,000 volumes, manuscripts, photographs, and so on. There is also a great deal of material dealing with collegiate sports in the Harvard University Archives and the Radcliffe Archives.

William L. Clements Library, University of Michigan, Ann Arbor, Mich. 48109. The William L. Clements Library of Early Americana has good holdings in early American sports. The library owns about 180 of the items listed in the third edition of R. W. Henderson's *Early American Sport* (1977). Among the periodicals are the *American Turf Register and Sporting Magazine* (1829-1844) and Porter's *The Spirit of the Times* (1831-1861).

Yale University Library. Yale University, Box 1603A Yale Station, New Haven Conn. 06520. The card catalog contains nearly one full drawer of cards under "sports," "sporting," and "sportsman." The Beinecke Rare Book and Manuscript Library has extensive collections on almost all aspects of sports with manuscripts from the fifteenth century onward, incunabula, and files of rare periodicals. In addition, *Subject Collections* lists holdings in the Merriwell series.

OTHER DEPOSITORIES AND INSTITUTES

The Cleveland Public Library. Fine Arts Department, 325 Superior Avenue, Cleveland, Ohio 44114. The Cleveland Public Library has extensive holdings on all sports, including summer, winter, and water sports. There are 12,000 catalogued items, which includes microforms and pictures. The holdings are especially strong in baseball.

Cumberland County Historical Society and the Hamilton Library Association. P.O. Box 626, 21 N. Pitt Street, Carlisle, Pa. 17013. The society possesses a unique collection of athletic records of the Carlisle Indian Industrial School, which operated from 1879-1918. The library has sports banquet programs, athletic celebration programs, a scrapbook on Jim Thorpe, and many of the Indian school periodicals, including *The Indian Helper* (1885-1900), *The Red Man* (1909-1917) and *The Red Man and Helper* (1880-1904), some of which report the athletic accomplishments of the school. Another special feature of the library is the collection of the Indian School photographer Choate, which includes team and individual photographs. The library offers for sale a publication by W. J. Gobrecht, *Jim Thorpe, Carlisle Indian, 2d ed.* (Carlisle, Pa., 1972).

Detroit Public Library. 5201 Woodward Ave., Detroit, Mich. 48202. The Burton Historical Collection contains the extensive sports collection of Ernie Harwell, a sports announcer for the Detroit Tigers. The collection consists of pictures, clippings, scrapbooks, brochures, baseball cards, leaflets, yearbooks, periodicals, letterbooks, and other forms as well as books. Some items are rare, some in series.

Esalen Sport Center. Esalen Institute, Big Sur, Calif. 93920. A part of the Esalen Institute, the Esalen Sport Center has as its primary purpose the development of new approaches to physical education, health, sports, and recreation and their application to programs in schools, industry, professional and amateur athletics, medicine, and other fields. The integration of mind, emotion, body and spirit in athletic activity is emphasized rather than competition and achievement per se. The center sponsors conferences, workshops, and special programs. For more information, see the *Esalen Catalog* published by the Esalen Institute, Big Sur, Calif. 93920.

Huntington Library. San Marino, Calif. 91108. The Huntington Collection of sports books is impressive. At present there are approximately 1400 rare books in the collection on a variety of English and American sports, dating from the Renaissance to modern times. Lyle H. Wright's *Sporting Books in the Huntington Library* (San Merino, 1937) lists the holdings as of that date. Approximately thirty-five items have been added since the publication of Wright's bibliography, including such works as *Experienced Jockey, Compleat Horseman . . .* (1684) and *Baseball Players Pocket Companion* (1859). The library also has a large collection of English sporting prints and some American sporting prints not listed in the bibliography.

Keeneland Library. Keeneland Race Course, Box 1690, Lexington, Ky. 40501. The Keeneland Library is a comprehensive turf reference and research library. Consequently, books there are not loaned. There are copies of the *Spirit of the Times* from the late 1830s to the early 1890s. There is a complete run of *The Sporting Magazine* (England) 1792-1870. Keeneland also has copies of racing calendars and British and American stud books from the beginning of thoroughbred racing. *The Keeneland Association Library* by Amelia King Buckley (Lexington, 1958) lists the holdings of the library at that time. A copy of the book may be ordered from University Microfilms International, 300 North Zeeb Road, Ann Arbor, Mich. 48106.

Los Angeles Public Library. 630 West Fifth Street, Los Angeles, Calif. 90071. The sports collection contains approximately 20,000 books, 140 periodicals, and 12,000 clippings with an additional 5,000 located in other departments, for example sports as a business in business and economics. There are special collections on boxing, bullfighting, chess, and Olympic Games. A special feature of the library is a sports file consisting of 15,000 entries on 3 by 5 inch cards. Sources are books, magazines, newspaper clippings, *Current Biography*, and so forth. It is an index designed to aid the staff in answering sports questions on a wide range of topics, such as sports records, equipment, rules, personalities, and definitions.

Maccabi World Union Archives and Museum. Kfar Hamaccabiah, Ramat Gan, Israel. The field of material covered by the archives and museum is as follows: (1) The history and development of Jewish gymnastics and sports from the early beginnings in 1895 until 1921. This period is known under the name "The History of the Organisation of Jewish Gymnasts." (2) The history of Jewish sports within the framework of the Maccabi World Union, which is the lead organization of the Maccabi affiliated territorial organizations and clubs. The Organisation of Jewish Gymnasts was the predecessor of MWU. (3) General organization of archives, according to the activities of the central organization. It contains such material as minutes of meetings, congresses, and congress reports, as well as special files on a great number of activities carried out by both organizations. There are also special archives on the Maccabiah Games.

Metropolitan Toronto Library Board. 789 Yonge Street, Toronto, Ontario, Canada M4W 2G8. The Science and Technology Department is responsible for the sports and recreation collection which covers a wide range of sports. Particular strengths include chess, golf, ice hockey, games, sports statistics, and biographical material on Canadian sports figures.

Milwaukee Public Library. 814 W. Wisconsin Avenue, Milwaukee, Wis. 53233. The library attempts to collect all materials published by local sports teams and organizations, including in some instances archival material. It also maintains an extensive collection on the modern Olympics, which includes everything published in the host country for each Olympic period. The boxing collection is excellent and includes many of the important reference works on the subject since the turn of the century. The library is a good source for the record books and yearbooks of all the major sports organizations, many of which go back twenty to seventy years. These consist primarily of the volumes in the *Spaulding Athletic Library* series and the NCAA yearbook series.

National Agriculture Library Building. United States Department of Agriculture, Beltsville, Md. 20705. Although the library has a limited amount of material that deals specifically with sports, some of the farm and agriculture journals contain sports sections as regular features. For an indivation of sports coverage in farm journals, see Jack W. Berryman, "John Stuart Skinner and the American Farmer, 1819-1829: An Early Proponent of Rural Sports," *Associates NAL [National Agriculture Library] Today*, n. s. Vol. 1, no. 3 (October, 1976) 11-32. See also *National Agriculture Library Catalog, 1966-1970* (Boston: G. K. Hall, 1973) under such topics as "Race Horses," "Fishing," "Hunting," and "Sports Periodicals." More recent holdings may by identified through online search of AGRICOLA which lists acquisitions since 1974.

National Archives and Record Service. Washington, D.C. 20408. The National Archives are the repository for the permanently valuable records of the U.S. federal government. Though the records are arranged by agency rather than by topic there is a great deal of valuable information on sports. The records of the Department of State include films of the Brussels World's Fair in 1957, which contain travel-logs of the United States showing industry, education, religion, and sports. The textual records of the Department of State, which extend through 1949, contain documents relating to the various Olympic Games and perhaps other international sporting events. The records of the chief signal officer also contain films of Olympic Games.

The Ford Collection in the National Archives Gift Collection has films of sports and recreation. Finally in the records of the United States Information Service, photographs of the *New York Times* (Paris Bureau) include photographs of sports coverage between 1900 and 1961. This is only a sample of the records in the custody of the National Archives. Depending on the topic, the enterprising researcher may also want to check the files of military agencies concerning recreation; the records of the National Youth Administration relating to sports activities; records of the Federal Trade Commission concerning sports monopolies; records of the United States House of Representatives or Senate concerning any sports legislation. For other possibilities see *Guide to the National Archives of the United States* (Washington, D.C., 1974).

National Council of the Young Men's Christian Associations of the United States of America. 291 Broadway, New York, N.Y. 10007. The historical library has a large collection of material on basketball, volleyball, wrestling, track and field, swimming, diving, and scuba. The collection includes photographs of the first basketball team. The library is repository for the U.S. Volleyball Association. The library is open to the public by appointment.

The National Sporting Library: A Research Center for Turf and Field Sports, Their History and Social Significance. Middleburg, Va. 22117. This is reputedly the only public library in the country devoted solely to turf and field sports. The library has, either in original issues or on microfilm, most of the North American periodicals devoted to turf and field sports published during the past two centuries. It hopes to complete this collection within the next few years. It is now in the process of indexing these periodicals in accordance with the standards adopted by the America Society of Indexers. Already completed are indexes of *The New York Sporting Magazine* (March 1833-December 1834), and its successor, *The United States Sporting Magazine* (November 1835-August 1836), and the first five years of available issues of *The Spirit of the Times* (1831-1835). Nearing completion is the index of the *American Turf Register* (1829-1844). The library publishes *The National Sporting Library Newsletter* twice yearly.

The New York Public Library. Fifth Avenue and 42d Street, New York, N.Y. 10018. The Research Libraries of the NYPL are among the world's leading repositories of sporting materials. The collection of 45,800 volumes and numerous manuscripts covers all sports and amusements with the exception of theatre, dance, and music. Among the strong features are the holdings on fishing, which include a fine collection of Izaak Walton's *Compleat Angler*; the chess materials center on the Pfeiffer chess collection; and the baseball resources include the Spalding, Swales, and Goulston collections. See section 41 and footnotes in *Guide to the Research Collections of the New York Public Library* (Chicago, 1975), compiled by Sam P. Williams.

The North American Youth Sport Institute. 4985 Oak Garden Drive, Kernersville, N.C. 27284. NAYSI offers a full range of services and products, including clinics, counseling, and research, to those dealing with youngsters in sports programs. A wide range of books and films is available through the institute, including the quarterly publication *Sport Scene Magazine*, which updates information of all kinds on youth in sport.

The Public Library of Cincinnati and Hamilton County. 800 Vine Street, Cincinnati, Ohio 45202. The main general collection consists of approximately 10,000 items, covering all major sports but emphasizing baseball. There are 620 books in the Rare Book Department, which is primarily made up of books on hunting and fishing that were published prior to 1900. There is also a nearly complete run of the Derrydale Press books. Among highlights of the sports collection are *The Proceedings of the Cincinnati Angling Club*, 1831; a scrapbook of James A. Henshall, author of *Book of the Black Bass* (1881); Dwight W. Huntington's *In Brush, Sedge and Stubble*, 1898, and William Milnor's *Memoir of the Schuyhill Fishing Company*, 1830.

Racquet and Tennis Club. 370 Park Avenue, New York, N.Y. 10022. The library of the Racquet and Tennis Club, which consists of over 15,500 volumes, is recognized by scholars to be the finest collection on the history of sports in the United States if not the world. It is a general collection on the history of sports but specializes in games played with bat and ball. It has a special interest in early American sports and a unique collection of American sporting songs before 1860. See *Dictionary Catalog of the Library of Sport*, published by G. K. Hall in 1970 and the third edition of Robert W. Henderson's *Early American Sport: A Checklist of Books by American and Foreign Authors Published in America Prior to 1860 including Sporting Songs* (Cranbury, N.J., Associated University Presses, 1977) which is based largely on Racquet and Tennis Club Collections.

SIRC (Sport Information Resource Center). 333 River Road, Ottawa, Ontario, Canada KLA 8B9. The material here has been added as a data base called SPORT, developed by Systems Development Corporation, to which many libraries have computer access. Coverage includes individual sports, recreation, sport medicine, physical education, sport facilities, and international sport history. The size of the file as of July 1979 was 45,000 citations with quarterly updatings of approximately 2,500 citations. It includes citations of monographs going back to 1949 and citations of journals back to 1975.

SIRLS (An Information Retrieval System for the Sociology of Leisure and Sport). Faculty of Human Kinetics and Leisure Studies, University of Waterloo, Waterloo, Ontario, Canada N2L 3G1. SIRLS is an information retrieval system for the sociology of leisure and sport and does not collect material strictly on the sport. About 7,000 citations are in SIRLS data bank. They consist primarily of journal articles, conference proceedings, and unpublished papers. Standard files list over fifty subareas of sports and leisure that reflect common areas of research, for example, "Politics, Leisure, and Sport," "Women, Sport, and Leisure," and "Sociology of Play and Games." The library on campus supports the courses offered by the faculty of Human Kinetics and Leisure Studies.

Society for the North American Cultural Survey. Department of Geography, Oklahoma State University, Stillwater, Okla. 74074. The purpose of this nonprofit research corporation is to engage in, finance, assist, and maintain the study of North American culture. Its primary goal is to produce a full-blown atlas of North American culture, including sports and games. The project is now underway. The Department of Geography at Oklahoma State University has produced approximately fifteen theses on the geography of sport. Recent research has focused on soccer, lacrosse, women's sport, and baseball. The *SNAC Newsletter* is published by the Department of Geography.

United States Olympic Committee. Olympic House. 1750 East Boulder Street, Colorado Springs, Colorado. 80909. The United States Olympic Committee does not have either a library or a museum of memorabilia, as such. However, the committee does have copies of the Official Reports of the Olympic Organizing Committees for all the Olympic Games, summer and winter, since 1896.

Wingate Institute for Physical Education and Sport. Wingate Post Office, Israel 42902. The Zvi Nishri Archives deal with sport and physical education in Israel as their primary topic and with sports in the Jewish diaspora as their secondary topic. A Jewish sport hall of fame was established at the institute in the summer of 1981. A number of publications on the proceedings of seminars are available through the institute.

DIRECTORIES AND GUIDES

The American Library Directory. 31st ed. Edited by Jaques Cattell Press. New York: R. R. Bowker, 1978. This volume provides some information on special collections and general information on libraries.

Directory of Afro-American Resources. Edited by Walter Schatz. New York: R. R. Bowker, 1967. This volume contains information on a number of collections. Entries are listed under the heading "Sports" and also by name. The directory is a good place to start for what is available at least through 1967.

Directory of Archives and Manuscript Repositories in the United States. Washington, D.C. National Historical Publications and Records Commission, 1978. There are a limited number of entries under the headings "Sports" and "Athletics," but certain of the collections listed there are extensive.

Directory of Special Libraries and Information Centers in the United States and Canada, 5th ed. Edited by Margaret L. Young and Harold C. Young. Detroit: Gale Research Co., 1979. This directory is useful to those working on special topics and local sports history.

Encyclopedia of Associations, 13th ed. 2 vols. Edited by Nancy Yake and Denise Yahey. Detroit: Gale Research Co., 1979. See Section 14, "Athletic and Sports Organizations." This volume describes 475 athletic and sporting organizations. It mentions the publications of the organizations and in some instances lists the type of research sponsored by them.

Guide to Reference Books, 9th ed. Compiled by Eugene P. Sheehy. Chicago: American Library Association, 1976. This guide should be consulted early in any extensive research. Entries are listed under "Recreation and Sports" and consist of bibliographies, dictionaries, and encyclopedias. There are some listings for individual sports. See also supplement to the 9th ed. Chicago, 1980.

Kyriazi, Gary. *The Great American Amusement Parks: A Pictorial History.* Secaucus, N.J.: Citadel Press, 1976. This is a delightful book of value to the cultural historian. It lists 100 of the best amusement parks in America.

Lewis, Guy, and Gerald Redmond. *Sporting Heritage: A Guide to Halls of Fame, Special Collections, and Museums in the United States and Canada.* South Brunswick: A.S. Barnes, 1974. This is an excellent book on museums and halls of fame. Organized by sections of the country, it contains thorough descriptions of the fifty centers in the United States and Canada as well as photographs of some of the halls. It is not quite as strong on library special collections, but it is a valuable reference nevertheless.

Libraries, Museums and Art Galleries Yearbook. Cambridge: James Clark and Co., 1976. This volume lists ten British institutions containing material on sports and recreation.

The Microbook Library of American Civilization: Subject Catalogue. Chicago: Library Resources, Inc., 1972. Under "Sports" there are listed five encyclopedias of sports or guides to American sports, all published prior to 1902.

Museums of the World. Compiled by Eleanor Braun. New York: R. R. Bowker, 1973. The listing of American sports museums is out-of-date, but the information on sports museums abroad is valuable.

National Recreational Sporting and Hobby Organizations of the U.S. Washington, D.C.: Columbia Books, Inc., 1981. This is a guide to 2,500 national organizations serving the recreational and avocational interests of Americans. Included is information on sport and hobby clubs and selected professional organizations of sporting goods manufacturers and professional athletes and coaches.

National Union Catalog of Manuscripts Collections. Washington, D.C.: The Library of Congress, 1959-. Known by the acronym NUCMAC, this yearly publication lists manuscript collections in the United States on an endless range of subjects, including sports. An index is published yearly.

The Official Museum Directory. Washington, D.C.: The American Association of Museums, 1982. This directory provides information on twenty-one museums and halls of fame. Institutions are listed by category (under "Sports") in the index and then by state and city in the text.

Redmund, Gerald. "Sport in the Museum and Hall of Fame." *Quest*, no. 19 (January 1973), 41-48. This is a humorous but insightful and informative survey of the phenomenon of the recent rise of numerous sports museums and halls of fame.

Research Centers Directory. 6th Edition. Edited by Archie M. Palmer Assisted by Laura E. Bryant. Detroit: Gale Research Co.: 1979. This directory has a limited number of entries under sports but contains information on centers in related fields, for example, tourism and recreation, physical education, and health.

Rowland, Howard S., and Beatrice L. Rowland. *The New York Times Guide to Student Adventures and Studies Abroad.* New York: Quadrangle, The New York Times Book Co., 1974. Although primarily a vocational guide, this book also contains information that might be of value to the researcher, especially in locating areas abroad for such sports as summer skiing, tennis, golf, hockey, horseback riding, sailing, underwater diving, and water skiing.

Subject Collections. 5th ed. Compiled by Lee Ash. New York: R. R. Bowker, 1978. This is a guide to special book collections and subject emphases as reported by university, college, public, and special libraries and museums in the United States and Canada. The researcher should remember to look not only under "Sports" but also under related topics, such as "Fishing" and "Hunting."

Index

About the Author

ROBERT J. HIGGS is Professor of English at Eastern Tennessee State University in Johnson City. His earlier books include *The Sporting Spirit: The Athlete in Literature and Life* (with Neil Isaacs) and *Laurel and Thorn: The Athlete in American Literature.*